Utah Studies
in Literature and Linguistics

edited by

**Gerhard P. Knapp – Luis Lorenzo-Rivero
Wolff A. von Schmidt**

Vol. 18

Special Editor
Gerhard P. Knapp

Peter Lang
Berne · Francfort/M. · Las Vegas

Boethius and the Liberal Arts

A Collection of Essays

Edited by Michael Masi

Peter Lang
Berne · Francfort/M. · Las Vegas

CIP-Kurztitelaufnahme der Deutschen Bibliothek

Masi, Michael:
Boethius and the liberal arts / Michael Masi.
– Berne, Francfort/M. [Frankfurt/M.], Las Vegas :
Lang, 1981.
  (Utah studies in literature and linguistics ; Vol. 18)
  ISBN 3-261-04722-4

© Peter Lang Publishers Ltd., Berne (Switzerland) 1981
Successors of Herbert Lang & Co. Ltd., Berne

PREFACE

More than a dozen scholars on two continents have contributed generously of their time and expertise to make possible this collection of essays on Boethius and the Liberal Arts. The concept behind the work was first given a public airing a decade ago at the International Conference on Medieval Studies at Kalamazoo, Michigan. Although none of the papers presented there found a place in this book, Professors Otto Bird and David Chamberlain played an important part in the work's genesis. More important still was the Conference on Boethius at the Newberry Library, Oct. 5-6, 1973, where some of the printed essays were first presented. The exchange of ideas by the participants was a notable experience for all of us and the staff of the Newberry Library deserve special consideration for their generosity at that event. The Director, Lawrence Towner, welcomed the speakers to his own home for dinner and John Tedeschi was especially encouraging in the publication of the papers. Professors Richard McKeon and Jerome Taylor contributed significantly to the discussions on Boethius during those two days and to them I owe my gratitude. Nor can I forget the special experience of several visits to Perugia, Italy, during my year in Rome, to discuss the English rendering of Professor Pizzani's essay with the author and his translator.

Michael Masi

Chicago, April 2, 1981

TABLE OF CONTENTS

INTRODUCTION

BOETHIUS AND THE LIBERAL ARTS

The essays in this volume represent an interdisciplinary effort to bring to bear on a central figure in the development of medieval thought a diversity of specialized research. They have grown out of a conviction that the various areas of medieval thought that could be represented in such a collection were deeply penetrated by one or more aspects of Boethius' multi-facted interests. It is, accordingly, the hope of each contributor that he may shed some light from his direction and that each beam, originating from a different specialization, may be focused on one major objective—the singular mind of Boethius. Collectively, it is hoped that these papers will provide new insight into a neglected body of writings which emerged in a time generally considered a very dark period in the history of Europe.

Boethius' name is certainly well known, but his reputation rests almost entirely on the *Consolation of Philosophy* and, to a lesser extent, on his logical works which are now seldom read and which have yet to be translated in their entirety. Yet if one were to have mentioned the name of Boethius to a learned man of the Middle Ages, he would probably have evoked memories of texts on music and mathematics. So well known was Boethius for his work on the *quadrivium* that Chaucer, for example, has the fox in the tale of Chauntecleer cite Boethius' name as a by-word for musical sensitivity:

Therewith ye han in musyk more feelyng

Than hadde Boece, or any that kan synge. (*Tales* VII, 4483-84)

The contributors to this volume have undertaken their writing with an assumption that the texts for the study of the seven Liberal Arts played a central role in the development of the way an educated man in the Middle Ages explained the world in which he lived. The implications of this assumption are manifold and enticing when one considers the applications of Boethian ideas possible in architecture, poetry, music, sculpture, and other arts. The possibilities become even more absorbing when one considers that the texts for the study of these disciplines were often taken directly from the writings of Boethius[1] and, as Professor Kibre demonstrates, the Boethian texts became standardized at many schools and universities. If we are to maintain that there is a central governing concept in these writings on the Liberal Arts-certainly in the texts which make up the *quadrivium* or the second half on the Liberal Arts curriculum—the other works of Boethius take on a new meaning. Boethius' *Consolation of Philosophy* extends to a broader intellectual context and is understood, then, as the culmination of the ideal of a Liberal Arts education. The ethical commitments demanded by the *Consolation* almost require the kind of intellectual training programmed in the Liberal Arts curriculum. As he entered his twenties, Boethius wrote the *De Institutione Arithmetica*, conscious that he was launching what he planned to be an ambitious intellectual enterprise. In the prefatory dedication addressed to his father-in-law, Symmachus, he asks him to examine and, if

---

1   This may be seen in such anthologies as the *Heptateuchon* of Thierry of Chartres (12th century) which draws from several of Boethius' works. Cf. A. Clerval, *Les Écoles de Chartres au Moyen-âge* (Chartres, 1855), pp. 222-223.

necessary, correct the following adaptation of Nicomachus' treatise on number theory. Although the young scholar's vision of his final intellectual goals was not yet clearly evident, he already exhibited his conception of how the arts and other intellectual disciplines grew and developed from the matrix of the mathematical concepts of the *Arithmetica:*

„So thus the reason of my work will be clear even to me if the things which I have labo-riously chosen from the teachings of wisdom will be approved by the judgment of a very wise man. You see therefore that the result of such labor awaits only your examination. Nor will it go to the public ear unless it rests on the support of a learned opinion. Nothing amazing should be seen in that this work, which attends to the discoveries of wisdom, relies in the final judg-ment of another, not of its author. This work of reason is in fact put forth by the author's abi-lities since it is constrained to undergo the judgment of a prudent man. But for this little gift I do not set up the same defenses which hang over the other arts, nor in fact is any science free from all of its parts, having need of nothing, and based only upon its own supports so that it might not lack the helps which come from the other arts. Indeed, in shaping statues out of marble, there is one labor in cutting away the stone, and there is another notion in forming the image: the beauty of the completed work cannot attend on the hands of the same artist. But the tablet of the picture has been trusted to the hands of various workers; the wax gathered to-gether into a rustic scene, the red ochre of the color examined with the expertness of mer-chants, the linen elaborated by the industrious weavers—these represent a multiplicity of artis-tic materials....From so many arts is one art made up. The completion of our labor traverses a long distance to a very simple end."[2]

In the first chapter of the *Arithmetica*, Boethius drew attention to an idea which became central to his entire philosophy of education—that the final goal of the Liberal Arts is a moral and ethical one. Philosophy is portrayed as continually invigorating and stimulating the arts. This became a pervasive medieval concept and is often depicted in iconographic representat-ions of Philosophy who is shown at the center of a diagram with seven streams flowing from her to the arts which surround her on all sides. The careful study of the arts, Boethius held, leads to philosophy and philosophy strengthens and enlivens the intellectual fiber of the arts. In I, i of the *De Arithmetica* he wrote:

„It stands to reason that whoever puts these matters aside [i.e. the disciplines of the *qua-drivium*] that person has lost the whole teaching of philosophy. This, therefore, is the *quadri-vium* by which we must travel, by which we bring a mind from knowledge offered by the sen-ses to the more certain things of the intellect. There are various steps and certain dimensions of progression for the mind which, as Plato says, is composed of many corporeal eyes and is of higher dignity than they; it seeks out the truth which demands that by its light alone it be in-vestigated and beheld. This eye, let me say, submerged and surrounded by the corporeal senses, is in turn illuminated by these disciplines."

Moreover, in the closing days of his life, in a cramped cell, awaiting execution, after hav-ing, in all probability, suffered severe torture, Boethius made a final statement about the mean-ing of philosophy. In the opening passages of the *Consolatio*, where he had every reason to speak with great earnestness, the unhappy and bewildered author is chided by Lady Philoso-phy to whom he had complained of his unhappy fate and the cutting short of his career before its full realization. While giving expression to his despair at the cruel turn of fortune, he is ac-costed by Lady Philosophy who appears larger than human, with her head reaching to the very skies, in a dress ornamented by a ladder whose rungs lead from Π to Θ; her learning extends from practical to theoretical philosophy, from the knowledge of earthly matters easily accessible

---

2   I have translated this and following passages of the *De Arithmetica* from G. Friedlein's edition (Leipzig, 1867; reprinted, 1966).

to the senses, to the sublime knowledge of abstract philosophy. Commentators and iconographers of the Middle Ages understood the rungs of the ladder to represent the disciplines of the Liberal Arts and accordingly they described Lady Philosophy as adorned with a dress ornamented by a ladder with seven rungs and on each rung the name of one of the Liberal Arts: grammar, rhetoric, logic, followed by arithmetic, music, geometry, and astronomy.[3]

In a similar way, though with less clarity of statement from Boethius, the implications of the Liberal Arts texts may be sought in his theological works.[4] The logical and rhetorical treatises fitted into the structure of the Liberal Arts curriculum as it eventually took shape. Boethius took pains to define and describe the *quadrivium* and he even coined the term. The *trivium*, a term Boethius never knew, was defined later.

When one reads the works of Boethius, particularly those designed as texts for the Liberal Arts, one develops a strong sense for the cohesiveness and continuity of ideas in his writings. This cohesiveness and continuity is illustrated by the authors of the essays in this volume. Even more significant, as may be seen in most of these essays, was the effect of the intellectual unity of the Boethian writing upon the intellectual life of Europe throughout the Middles Ages and the early Modern Era. Evidence of the intellectual milieu in the centuries immediately after Boethius' death in approximately 524 is very limited and yields little to even the most persistent efforts to discover how his texts were transmitted. Only in the 9th century does the manuscript evidence begin to illuminate his growing importance, an importance which, with some exceptions, grew continuously in scope throughout the later Middle Ages. Many scholars now realize that the Renaissance is not to be seen as the end of the Middle Ages but rather, in many ways, as an intensification and enrichment of many things essentially medieval. If we are to judge by the editions, commentaries, and citations by other authors to which scholars have drawn attention, Boethius was more popular than ever by the 16th century. This continuous growth in popularity is made apparent in several essays in this volume.

We may well understand that readers in the Middle Ages would not have grasped the significance of Boethius' writings as well as modern scholars who are able to scrutinize the texts and see them in the context of the medieval intellectual milieu. Yet his works, even with the misinterpretations to which they were subjected, exercised a considerable influence in the fashioning of the intellectual atmosphere in which the medieval thinker developed his view of the world and in which he studied art and nature. The entire body of Boethian ideas as well as their misinterpretations must be studied in their own right. A major concern, therefore, of the authors in this volume is to show the various aspects of this intellectual framework developed and to what extent non-Boethian accretions may have altered the original. To this point Professors Pizzani and Folkerts have traced, as well as the existing evidence has allowed, the complex history of the treatises on music and geometry.

The tract on geometry underwent a strange and tortuous evolution which has left us with very little of Boethius' original treatise. Though we have good evidence that Boethius did write treatises on all the Liberal Arts in the *quadrivium*—arithmetic, music, geometry and astronomy—,[5] the texts for the socond part of the *quadrivium* did not survive to the late Middle Ages.

3   For example, we may draw attention to the illustration in Leipzig, Universitätsbibliothek, 1253, f.3, reproduced in Pierre Courcelle, *La Consolation de Philosophy dans la tradition littéraire* (Paris, 1967), pl.6.

4   Given in probable order of composition, these are: *De Trinitate; Utrum Pater et Filius et Spiritus Sanctus de Divinitate Substantialiter Praedicantur; Quomodo substantiae, in eo quod sint, bonae sint, cum non sint substantialia bona; De Fide Catholica* (authenticity questioned); *Contra Eutychen et Nestorium; Hebdomades* (lost). The extant works have been edited and translated into English by H.F. Steward and E.K. Rand (Loeb Classical Library, New York, 1918).

5   Though scholars who have discussed the *quadrivium*, even in reference to Boethius, seldom seem concern-

We will have more to say on the geometry below. The astronomy has vanished without a trace and unfortunately the essays in this collection cannot touch on that important and culminating discipline in the medieval curriculum. No doubt one could derive from the *Consolatio* considerable astronomical lore and find there its application to philosophical studies. It has, for example, long been recognized that writers such as Dante and Chaucer drew heavily from the *Consolatio* for the ethical applications of astronomy. In at least two representations of Lady Philosophy with the Liberal Arts, the figure of philosophy is seen in company with a maiden who holds a scroll reading: 'Qui contemplantur celestia me venerantur.' (Those who contemplate heavenly things venerate me).[6] The Boethian text on astronomy was doubtless a compilation from the works of Ptolemy and would hardly have contained material we would not recognize from other extant treatises on medieval astronomy.

The first of the two Boethian treatises for the latter part of the *quadrivium*, geometry, presents a set of interesting and complex relationships between the transmission of geometrical studies from Euclid to the Middle Ages and the Boethian context of the Liberal Arts. Fragments of the lost Boethian work survived in parts of the two Pseudo-Boethian geometries which until modern times were taken as authentic. They may therefore be viewed legitimately as sharing in his influence in the Middle Ages. Professor Folkerts has brought to bear the results of his extensive research in the preparation of an edition of one of the treatises. The history of this text, as well as can be determined from existing evidence, contrasts with the fate of the Boethian treatise on music which exists in a large number of manuscripts. The transmission history of the tract on music is different from that on geometry, no doubt because in the centuries after Boethius the notion of a coherent body of learning which we call the Liberal Arts had not yet come together. As a result, the various treatises by Boethius were transmitted independently of each other. Only later, after the structure of the Arts had taken firm shape, was it realized that the slot for geometry was vacant, and accordingly it was filled with two pseudo-Boethian works.

The tract on music, which seems to have taken hold immediately after Boethius' time, evidently had a different history yet one which has left many unanswered questions. What, for example, happened to chapters 19-30 in the final book of that treatise, which Boethius put in his chapter list to that book? How did the complex and elaborate diagrams of the treatise evolve? Are they from Boethius' own hand? It is hoped that an eventual study of all the existing texts of the *De Musica* will provide further information on these questions. Hence the modest title of Professor Pizzani's already illuminating study: a contribution to further research.

The importance of the *De Musica* for both musical and non-musical thought in the Middle Ages and Renaissance has been long recognized. Hence it seems fitting that more than one scholar should be called upon to examine this work so that its multiple facets may be better shown. The discussion by Professor Holloway on the literary influence of Boethian music theory supplies in its footnotes some notion of the large bibliography which has grown up from the broader aspects of medieval music theory. Her study shows how music theory and literary ideas blended as a result of their Boethian orientation in the Liberal Arts structure. Professor Bower's essay on the Boethian influence in medieval music theory provides some notion of the extent of that influence in musical thought. The relationship between music practice and music theory was at times very weak, indeed, probably non existant. The actual performance of music was not as highly esteemed as the study of music theory, and the requirement of musical

ed about the order in which the disciplines are presented, it seems significant to follow, as I do here, the order Boethius emphatically outlines in the *De Arithmetica* I, i.

6   As found in Bayerische Staatsbibliothek, CLM 2955, f. 101 (c. 1200). Reproduced in M.Masi, „Boethius and the Iconography of the Liberal Arts," *Latomus*, XXXIII (1974), 57-75.

study in the curriculum of the Liberal Arts has nothing to do with learning to perform on a musical instrument. By the late Middle Ages, however, composers had begun to read the treatises carefully and even those works which discussed the practical aspects of music, such as Simon Tunstede's *Quatuor Principalia Musicae* or Johannes Gallia's *Ritus Cannendi Vetustissimus et Novus*, incorporated into their discussion of music some theoretical excepts from the *De Musica* of Boethius. In the Renaissance, music theory and composition reached a synthesis that seems to have eluded medieval musicians. But at that point Boethius was less important and was replaced by translations of Greek theoretical works which were more available than formerly.

The music and arithmetic come from two different periods in the development of Boethius' thought on the structure of the quadrivial disciplines. While it is obvious from the essays on music and arithmetic that the relationship between the first and second disciplines in the *quadrivium* is not entirely clear, the two should be seen as closely tied. Certainly in the Middle Ages the two were seen in a simpler way than Boethius may have conceived them and the first book of the *De Arithmetica* provided a useful way of organizing the quadrivial disciplines. The *De Musica* is a continuation of the *De Arithmetica* and depends on it for the development of its principles. It is assumed in the music treatise that the reader is already acquainted with number theory. He may then proceed to the study of geometry, which is, in turn, indispensable for a good grasp of astronomy.

The Boethian music is quite different from what moderns understand by the term music—it is a theoretical, almost entirely mathematical study of musical tones and their relationships. Similarly, Boethian arithmetic is philosophical number theory, very different also from the modern concept of arithmetical study. Its primary focus is on the relationship between numbers rather than on the solving of problems. All four disciplines are based on numbers, in contrast to the disciplines of the *trivium*, which are based on the word and the rules regulating its uses. In the tract on arithmetic, number is defined and rules are given for discovering the hidden orders of number in nature. Music defined the relationships between tones of the scale in terms of numbers; while arithmetic dealt with numbers in themselves, the *De Musica* concentrated on the definition of relationships between numbers. Geometry treated of relationships between figures, on a plane or extended into three dimensions, while astronomy took these relationships between figures and applied them to the study of heavenly figures. The bodies of the heavenly spheres—fixed stars, movable stars (planets), sun, and moon were as points to and from which lines were drawn that created a continually moving series of evolving figures. This is the ultimate development of number theory before the leap to moral philosophy—which does not occur within the structure of the Liberal Arts disciplines.

For Boethius, as for the ancient Greeks, there was a sharp distinction between philosophical number theory and practical mathematics, which in the Middle Ages was variously called algorism or computation. As with music, theory and practice came to be united in the treatises of the late medieval period. Quite often, texts on algorism would begin with a theoretical introduction taken from the *De Arithmetica* before going on to practical mathematics.

Another distinction which Boethius maintained rigidly throughout his writing is one between philosophical numbers and mystical numbers. All the Boethian discussions of number are in terms capable of being grasped by the intellect. Thus, perfect numbers (such as 6 or 28) are those which are precisely equal to the sum of all their dividends. Mystical numbers, such as 7, 40, 144,000 are those whose meaning is derived from Scripture or other authority but which have in themselves no particular mathematical significance. Medieval writers who commented on or cited the Boethian mathematics did not usually observe this distinction as carefully as did Boethius.

This same differentiation between revealed knowledge and an understanding achieved by the rational powers of the mind is clear in the *Consolatio*. That work presents a man confronted by the meaninglessness of death, inflicted seemingly by chance, which brings to an undeserved end a scholar's exemplary life. Such has always been the *locus classicus* for an appeal to revealed truth, to Christ, whose death and resurrection are the starting point for spiritual consolation. Not so with Boethius who appeals to reason and to the meaning of that philosophical truth which he has professed all his life, a truth derived from purely rational understanding. Because of his failure to appeal to Christ, readers considered that the author of the theological works was another Boethius, perhaps living at the same time, but not identical with the pagan author of the *Consolatio*, the mathematical works, and the logical treatises. Most authorities have come to accept all these works as coming from the author of the *Consolatio*, though the issue is not interely settled.[7] Students of medieval philosophy have perhaps not been accustomed to such rigid distinctions between religion and revelation; they may well expect a Christian appeal to God at the moment of any unhappy and tragic death, instead of to a pagan rationalism. On close examination one may see, however, that moral concepts of the *Consolatio* fit well with the teachings of Christian doctrine and at no point contradict it. Moreover, a close study of the theological works shows their intimate relationship with the methods of the logical writing. L. Minio-Paluello has shown, for example, in a discussion of the *De Trinitate*, how Boethius approaches his subject matter from the aspect of logical distinctions and definitions. Boethius is concerned about the apparently illogical concept of God's simultaneous unity and trinity. Boethius explains that the three are substantially one and that the three are three only when viewed as internal relationships. The Trinity is further discussed in terms of Aristotelian categories in the second Boethian theological treatise, *Utrum Pater et Filius et Spiritus de Divinitate Substantialiter Predicantur*.[8] In his work *Contra Eustychen et Nestorum*, Boethius takes up another logical problem in Christian theology—the double nature in the single person of Christ. By careful definition of terms, Boethius attempts a reconciliation of the singularity of Christ's person with his human and divine natures. These concepts are of immense importance in medieval theology and several major medieval writers, notably Thomas Aquinas and Gilbert de la Porrée, took up the ideas of the *De Trinitate* for further discussion.

It will be seen that practically all of Boethius' works spawned a significant *fortleben* which endured more than a thousand years. In that long period it will also be seen that while Boethius made some emphatic statements about the meaning, relationships, and purpose of the disciplines in the *quadrivium*, his ultimate intentions may not have been understood in the centuries that followed. The complex penetrations and applications made by his medieval readers into other areas of study and to other disciplines could hardly have been anticipated by him in the 6th century. In the case of the *trivium*, the situation is yet more undefined. This lack of claritiy is partly due to the position of logic in medieval studies. Unlike any of the other disciplines, logic was studied twice, once in simpler form as part of the *trivium*, later in more advanced form, after the course of the Liberal Arts was completed. When Chaucer says that his clerk „unto logyk hadde longe ygo" (*Gen. Pro.* line 286) he indicates that this dour scholastic had advanced far into philosophy—much beyond the study of the Liberal Arts.

The largest part of Boethius' writing was made up of translations and commentaries on Aristotle's logic, to which he added his own logical writing. If we are to judge Boethius by the

---

7   One may consult the discussions in E.K. Rand, *Founders of the Middle Ages* (Harvard University Press, Cambridge, Mass., 1928), pp. 135-185 and M. Cappuyns, „Boéce," *Dictionnaire d'histoire et de geographie ecclesiastique*, 9 (1936), 348-380.

8   See Rand, pp. 153-158 and L. Minio-Paluello, „Jacobus Veneticus Grecus," *Traditio*, 8 (1952), 265-304; „Boethius," *Encyclopedia Britannica*, 3 (1971).

bulk of his work, we must consider him primarily a logician. His importance in this area has long been recognized and, as Mrs. Stump's essay demonstrates, his influence was complex and uneven. It is certainly well known that his *Commentary on the Isagoge of Porphyry* stimulated the discussion of the universals, one of the more significant issues of medieval philosophy. For the study of logic in the *trivium*, selections from the longer Boethian treatises were commonly excerpted, as may be seen in Thierry's *Heptateuchon*.

Boethius gives considerable thought to the relationships between the disciplines of the *trivium*, as he did to the disciplines of the *quadrivium*, and some of his most important ideas may be gleaned from the *De Differentiis Topicis*. While he did not write a treatise on rhetoric as such, Boethius' statements on that discipline were well known and some anonymous writer, perhaps as early as the 10th century, excerpted selections from the *De Topicis*, Books I and IV under the title *Speculatio de Rhetoricae Cognatione*.9 This little treatise has all the characteristics of an introductory rhetoric text for study in the *trivium*. Professor LeMoine has drawn on the *De Topicis* for a rhetorical study of Boethius' style in terms of his own statements. Professor Uhlfelder has taken a broader view of Boethius' rhetoric and has seen its culmination in the *Consolatio*, where rhetoric and philosophy combine in a final and most eloquent statement. In both of these works we see the importance of Boethian ideas and Boethian writing. His own grounding in rhetoric was doubtless very sound and this we may judge from his mastery of the complex formalities in the proemium to the *De Arithmetica* and the refinements of style in the *Consolatio*.

In conclusion, we should take note of the fact that the medieval fascination with Boethian authority was not always beneficial to the advancement of medieval sciene. This is certainly true of the mathematics and, to a lesser extent, of the music and logic. Historians of science have looked on the Boethian works as impractical, tied to philosophical speculation and repeating—in simplified form — what had long been known to the Greeks. When the original Greek works became known, the significance of Boethius' mathematics evaporated. E.T. Bell in his well known book, *The Development of Mathematics* (New York, McGraw-Hill, 1945), had little to say for Boethius' place in the development of that science: „We therefore continue our descent to the nadir of mathematics, and follow the learned Boethius into the abyss"(p. 88). It is certainly true that the arithmetic represents no advance in the discipline of mathematics; the popularity of this work had an arresting effect on the development of mathematics and, possibly, on the absorption of Arabic mathematical knowledge. The fact that it used Roman numerals and that it was a standard text for the study of arithmetic (as Professor Kibre's essay demonstrates) meant that a student often received no practical grounding in algorism as part of his regular curriculum. Only in those instances when it was combined with practical mathematics did it make a useful text, and then merely as a short theoretical introduction. The same situation prevailed in the study of music. The learning if the Boethian *De Institutione Musica* was required for candidacy to the Master of Arts degree at Oxford well into the 18th century. It was precisely treatises of this kind which discouraged Sir Philip Sidney from completing a degree there and of which he specifically complained when he denounced the university's outmoded medieval curriculum.

Nonetheless, these works played an enormous role in the development of some significant and even creative aspects of medieval thought. From the limited point of view of the historian

---

9   This has been printed as a separate treatise in *Pat. Lat.* 64, 1217-1222. The work should be read in its original context for a real comparison of Boethian dialectic and rhetoric. See also the English translation of the *Speculatio* in *Readings in Medieval Rhetoric*, ed. Joseph M. Miller, Michael H. Prosser, Thomas W. Benson (Indiana University Press, Bloomington, 1973), pp. 69-76.

of science, the mathematical works represent no advance and hence they have been ignored. But from the cultural historian's point of view, the Boethian texts on the Liberal Arts can be seen to permeate every aspect of medieval thought—philosophy, literature, music, architecture, theology and a number of other related disciplines. Regardless of their lack of scientific advance, these texts do provide an insight into the way liberal disciplines were interpreted and how the sciences and arts were integrated. It is with the hope of advancing such an understanding that the present collection of essays is presented to the students of the Middle Ages.

Michael Masi

MYRA L. UHLFELDER

THE ROLE OF THE LIBERAL ARTS

IN BOETHIUS' *CONSOLATIO*

The word „role" in the title of this paper is intended as an active metaphor, not a faded one, since the dramatic element in the *Consolatio* is significant and altogether suited to dialogue as a genre. In developing his theme, Boethius casts his literary *persona* as Everyman and Lady Philosophy as his guide along the path of return. The opening scene portrays Boethius reenacting with his elegiac Muses the part made famous five hundred years before by the Augustan poet Ovid in his *Tristia* and *Epistulae ex Ponto* after his banishment to the Black Sea. But Ovid, despite the Pythagorean allusions intended to enhance the thematic unity of his *Metamorphoses* and to make it appear more profound, was essentially the type of the unphilosophical man who never progressed beyond the stage of lamenting Fortune's lost favors. The only return for which he longed was restoration to Rome, or at least to a civilized place where he could again hear Latin instead of barbaric Scythian dialects.[1] Boethius, on the other hand, a disciple of the Eleatic and Platonic philosophers, as his mentor reminds him, was never intended for such a role.

In driving away the mournful elegiac Muses, Philosophy uses a specifically theatrical image, denouncing them as *scenicas meretriculas*.[2] She is presumably comparing them to the *meretrices* of Roman comedy, stock characters often instrumental in bringing about the financial ruin of imprudent youths or their even more imprudent elders. Philosophy's clear moralizing implication is that these Muses encourage the passions which beguile a man into choosing the false values unmasked in the first half of the *Consolatio*. The adjective *scenicas* anticipates the later question that fortune, in a diatribe composed for her by Philosophy, addresses to Boethius: „Are you just now arriving suddenly and for the first time as a guest at this theater (*scaena*)

---

1   *Metamorphoses* 15. 60-478; *Tristia* and *Epistulae ex Ponto, passim*; of specially *Tristia* 1. 1; 5; 5. 7; *Epist. ex P.* 2. 7; 4. 9; 15.

Boethius consciously draws on the established literary tradition as one means of achieving his intended effects. Lucretian echoes, for example, induce the reader to analyze the essential difference between the views of Lucretius and Boethius. Ready-made „types", whether represented by the classical authors themselves or by figures taken from their writings, can be useful in a work like the *Consolatio*, related as it is, in some respects, to allegory. As the type of the philosopher persecuted by a tyrant, for example, Seneca has significance beyond his considerable literary influence. Earlier works in the Platonic tradition are also recognizable in the text. Cicero's *Somnium Scipionis*, Apuleius' *Metamorphoses*, and Martianus Capella's text of the Liberal Arts all make their contributions. The precise nature of Boethius' literary use of the classical tradition has not yet been thoroughly studied. It is certain, however, that he subordinates all *bravura* effects to his concern for the work as a whole, and that he does not try to display his own erudition.

2   1.P. 1. 8. References, which follow the standard practice of designating prose passages of the *Consolatio* as „P." and poems (meters) as „M", conform to the enumeration in the Weinberger-Hauler edition, *Corpus Scriptorum Ecclesiasticorum Latinorum*, 67 (Vienna 1934).

stage as the real world, not as a place of images and reflections?" The whole concept of a theater, however, implies an audience in attendance to observe a spectacle. Outside the cosmos itself, the audience can only be God, watching the drama performed by His creatures, with man as the protagonist. A view of this Divine Spectator provides a dramatic tableau at the very end of the *Consolatio*. Philosophy has fulfilled her mission of restoring Boethius to his proper mental vigor, the temporary loss of which had been the cause of his spiritual exile, and has freed him by leading him to understand and accept his place in harmony with the cosmos. With the goal achieved, Philosophy declares that all men live under a decree which demands moral conduct. At the same time, she paints a verbal picture of the Author of that decree, the Judge who looks down upon His world. In conformity with the judicial metaphor of the passage, she uses the appropriate forensic verb *agitis*. Its immediately obvious judicial connotation is, ,,You are pleading your case." More generally, it would mean ,,You engage in activity." Another possible interpretation is ,,You live;" that is, ,,You spend your allotted time." Finally, the *agitis* may extend the scenic metaphor to the very last sentence of the work. Since metaphors of parallel levels are of fundamental importance in the *Consolatio* and one sense does not preclude another, the *agitis* may be a dramatic term implying ,,You play your roles".

The opening and closing scenes are also contrasting illustrations of the frequent metaphors of looking up and looking down.[3] This metaphor, like all the abundant imagery related to light and darkness and to the visual process, is of the greatest possible significance in regard both to the work as a whole and to the specific subject of the Liberal Arts. Boethius' downcast gaze at the beginning of the *Consolatio* symbolizes his loss of the inner light of *mens*, man's likeness to God which, in Christian terms, would be called the *imago Dei*. Turned away as he is from the Source of light and life, he fixes his eyes upon the heavy and dulling element which the rays of the sun cannot penetrate. In the image perfectly suited to and implied in the *Consolatio* (although Boethius does not elaborate it in the most traditional or obvious way), Boethius or Everyman has abandoned his assigned place in the Great Chain of Being by assuming the posture of a beast, which looks downward, and ceasing to look upward like a man. The relationship to this idea of the motiv of metamorphosis in the *Consolatio* is apparent and is sometimes explicit in the text.[4]

The dejected Boethius has given up his divine birthright and so his freedom as conceived and defined in the *Consolatio*. He presumes to denounce what he regards as the flaws in God's rule and administration of justice because his morbid affections, having extinguished his mental and spiritual insight, cause him to believe that man is excluded from the general cosmic order.[5] Here, as throughout the *Consolatio*, the dark terrestrial element and darkness in general signify man's alienation from his rational nature, a state indicated by the constantly recurring metaphor of exile.

The metaphorical association between physical and mental vision (the latter of which, in Platonic terms, includes morality as well as intellect) is thoroughly familiar and seems all but

---

3   In addition to other obvious examples of the motif, the Orpheus lyric (3. M. 12), which recounts the failure of the mental ascent, expresses looking down as looking back into Hades toward Eurydice. The turning back of the gaze, away from light and toward darkness, is here a moral and spiritual relapse. The geometrical figure implied by the turn is a diameter (a 180° angle).

4   For a few especially good illustrations of these ideas and their interrelationships, see 2. P. 5. 25-29; 4. P. 3. 16 through P.4. 1; 5. M.5. The bond of Fate proceeding from Providence (4.P.6) controls natural order, one important aspect of which is the chain of being.

5   1.M.5.

universal. It is nevertheless given fresh appropriateness and force by Boethius' explicit identification of seeing with knowing.[6] *Mens* as the gift and reflection of the Divine Light is therefore no hackneyed metaphor in Boethius' work, but the basis of an epistemological theory in the Augustinian tradition.

At the close of the *Consolatio*, God is looking down upon the cosmos while the newly liberated and restored Boethius, with the recovery of *mens* at the end of his philosophical return, is looking up as far as possible toward the Divine Light, who judges His well-ordered world and perceives everything though He Himself is beyond understanding. The whole situation is now the diametrical opposite of what it had been when Boethius, at the beginning, was indulging his grief with his elegiac Muses.

The preceding example is interwoven with the important judicial metaphor in the *Consolatio*. In passing judgment on God, Boethius had been influenced at the beginning by his personal experience of suffering shameful injustice at the hands if men, experience of which the autobiographical material in Book 1 provides ample evidence. By the end, however, Boethius has ascended beyond the limits of reason to accept on faith the goodness of the Divine Judge whom, even in his affliction, he had continued to recognize as Creator and Ruler (1. P.6. 4).

In bringing about the changes so dramatically portrayed in these opening and closing scenes, the Liberal Arts make a contribution which it is the main purpose of this paper to examine.

The Trivium: Grammatica, Rhetorica, Dialectica

Of the individual arts, Grammatica appears to be absent, although appearances in this case, as so often, are partly deceptive. There are, in fact, no passages dealing with what we ordinarily mean by grammar and syntax. Literacy, and on an exeptionally high level, is rather presupposed by an author who depicts Philosophy with books in her right hand (1.P.1. 6). In the *Consolatio*, Philosophy regularly associates poetry with music, although the ancients often subsumed metrics under Grammatica in its broader sense; and sections on metrics were sometimes included in *Artes Grammaticae*. The study of literature in general was ordinarily another area introduced by the *grammaticus*. But Boethius' acquaintance with the work of classical authors is so wide and so deep that he must have achieved his intellectual growth and his knowledge of classical literature and thought largely through his own initiative and efforts.

Boethius himself, then, went far beyond any course in Grammatica; and yet his literary achievement is a personal and extraordinary product of an author first tutored in the grammatical art, as that art was understood in its broadest sense. The *Consolatio* itself as a literary work therefore proves the importance of the humble supporting role played by *Grammatica*.

Much more explicit evidence is to be found in the text about the role of the other Liberal Arts. *Rhetorica*, although popular in antiquity even to excess, never fully recovered from its early association with the Greek Sophists, who made it suspect as a participant in any search for truth. Lady Philosophy states, however (2. P.1. 8), that rhetoric can be trusted to proceed along the right path when it holds to philosophical precepts. Since Philosophy herself is the guide, no doubt remains that rhetoric serves the cause of truth on this occasion.

The influence of rhetoric in the *Consolatio* is strong and clearly perceptible from the beginning of Book 2 throughout the section of the work which ends before the revelation of the *summum bonum* in the famous cosmological poem, 3. M.9. Philosophy refers to ,,the persuasiveness of rhetorical sweetness" (*Rhetoricae suadela dulcedinis*, 2. P.1. 8), the function of which in the *Consolatio* is a negative one, namely to deny the value of Fortune's gifts by de-

6   Consider the frequent and significant use of *cernere*.

monstrating that they are never truly one's own—i.e., that they are *aliena*, not *propria*. One by one as they are paraded before us, the error of identifying any of them as the *summum bonum* is indicated. The tone of this section is reminiscent of *Ecclesiastes* and Lucretius, but negative Rhetorica does not have the last word in the *Consolatio*. With an application of his metaphor of levels to the construction of his whole work, Boethius represents Philosophy's patient, not yet in condition for her more drastic treatment, bearing the truth-serving rhetorical persuasion which deals with ethics, a branch of that practical philosophy indicated by the Π at the bottom of Philosophy's dress. This division of philosophy is relatively untaxing intellectually, and gives Boethius' *persona* an opportunity to prepare himself for the great adventure of the mental ascent.

Throughout this section dedicated to persuasion—or, to speak more accurately, to dissuasion — the author's style proves his thorough familiarity with rhetoric. Diction, figures, and tropes at once attest a mastery of the art from a stylistic point of view, and sustain the spirit of this lowest of the three stages in the recovery of *mens*. In 2. P. 1, Philosophy delivers what might technically be classified as a speech in defense of Fortune against Boethius' charges. Her real point, however, is that Boethius has erred in expecting Fortune to be consistent when she is specifically characterized by the fickleness symbolically represented by her turning rolling wheel. Philosophy's speech, an invective against Fortune in spirit if not in letter, is therefore related to the epideictic as well as the judicial branch of oratory.

In the next passage (2. P.2), Philosophy composes a speech such as Fortune might deliver in her own defense against Boethius' charges. This oration, quite different in style from the preceding one, clearly follows the pattern of a judicial speech with what is known in the rhetorical manuals as a *constitutio iuridicalis*. This kind of judicial oration is delivered when the defendant acknowledges the commission of an act with which he has been charged, and the issue centers upon the question of its legal justification. In the present case, Fortune's defense is based upon what she claims is Boethius' wrong judgment in regarding her favors as true and outright gifts rather than as loans retractable at her will. Fortune's speech is appropriately full of technical legal terminology. From one sentence, for instance, it appears that Boethius' charge against her is conceived of as a lawsuit on grounds of extortion.[7]

After Fortune's speech and the following poem, Boethius tells Philosophy that the rhetorical eloquence had had a fair outer appearance, but that it provided no real cure for one in a serious condition such as his. Philosophy agrees that the speeches and the poem were merely palliatives, and promises that she will administer more potent remedies when Boethius is strong enough for them.

The exchange between Boethius and Philosophy is significant in explicitly establishing a hierarchy of values in which *dialectica* holds a position of greater honor than *rhetorica* because, as the proper medium for rational discourse, it provides a more effective remedy against the light-quenching sickness of the mind.

Immediately after 3. M.8, rhetoric gives way to dialectic, that tough-minded discipline which makes exacting demands upon reason. In contrast to rhetoric, dialectic has been assigned the task of rationally conforming the true good rather than persuasively refuting the false. The shift from rhetoric to dialectic is a clear stylistic signal that the progress of the argument and the state of Boethius' recovery have reached the higher level of speculative philosophy, with which only trained reason can cope. Although the succeeding third and ultimate stage of

---

7   2.P.2. 3: *Quovis iudice de opum dignitatumque mecum possessione contende. Et si cuiusquam mortalium proprium quid horum esse monstraveris, ego iam tua fuisse quae repetis sponte concedam.*

speculation eludes the grasp of unaided reason, it nevertheless requires the support of reason thoroughly disciplined. That topmost level of speculative philosophy, demanding faith and supernatural insight, is represented at the beginning of the *Consolatio* by Lady Philosophy's highest stature, marked by the disappearance of her head above the clouds.

The second level of the mental ascent, expressed in the idiom of dialectic, is indicated by Philosophy's middle stature. While touching the heavens with her head, she remains fully visible under the open sky. Her height indicates that dialectic, the instrument of rational inquiry, is applied to the study of the physical sciences including astronomy which, as we shall see, has a position of special importance in this work. The association of dialectic with the Quadrivium is also appropriate because the mathematical disciplines, like all *technai* or *artes*, were originally organized by *Dialectica*, although this systematizing function of dialectic is not overtly mentioned in the *Consolatio* as it is in some ancient and medieval sources.[8]

Other usual functions and aspects of dialectic are clearly recognizable throughout the second half, especially from 3. P.9 to 4. P.6, the section of the *Consolatio* which specifically represents the second level of the mental journey.

In addition to the application of syllogistic method and form, Boethius openly alludes to various aspects of the dialectical art. A convenient example is provided by 5. M.4, a rejection of Stoic epistemology, which is judged as too passive. Emphasizing mental vigor throughout his work, Boethius, through Lady Philosophy, expresses a preference for a theory of knowledge in which *mens* responds actively to external sensory stimuli and takes a leading role in the process of cognition. In speaking of mental activities in this meter, Philosophy explicitly refers to dialectical division and collection (vv. 18-23) and to the critical function of distinguishing the true from the false (v. 25).

Technical dialectical terminology abounds throughout the second half of the *Consolatio*, as even a cursory reading shows. But even more interesting than this formal evidence of dialectical influence is the clear indication of the weight, even the cogency, attributed – on a human level, of course – to dialectical argument. In one passage, for example, Boethius is surprised at the inference drawn from the preceding argument, although he admits that the conclusion follows logically. Philosophy understands Boethius' reaction, but explains: ,,Whoever regards it as difficult to agree with the conclusion must show either that some false inference was drawn before or that the combination of proposition does not produce a necessary conclusion. Otherwise there are no grounds for assailing an inference drawn from what has been conceded previously. In fact, the point which I am about to make will seem just as strange, but it is equally necessary as a consequence of assumptions already made" (4. P.4. 9-12).

In another passage, when Philosophy states that the conclusion just reached in argument is opposed to popular belief, Boethius, now well on the way to recovery, answers: ,,It is the truth, even though no one should dare to acknowledge it" (4. P.7. 14-16).

The role of *ratio*, for which dialectic provides a method of logical thought and discourse, is thus seen to be of great importance. It may even be in a position of enhanced dignity partly because Boethius' choice of a non-Christian outer form for his work has automatically eliminated Biblical and theological *auctoritas* and so left *ratio* uncontested, as it were, in her own realm.

That Boethius assigned such important functions to dialectic is not at all surprising since we are informed by Philosophy at the very outset that he had studied the doctrines of the Eleatics and the Platonists (1. P.1. 10). The Eleatic Zeno, a younger associate of Parmenides, is named by Aristotle as the founder of dialectic;[9] and Plato's use of dialectic is a matter of

8   Cf. Cicero, *De Oratore* 1. 187-90; *Brutus* 150-53; *Martianus* Capella 4. 336-38; Augustine, *De Ordine* 2.38.
9   Diogenes Laertius 9. 25.

common knowledge from the Platonic *corpus* still extant.

Finally, a few comments may be made on the way that Boethius' literary form is influenced by dialectic. In 3. P.12. 25 Philosophy, echoing Plato, suggests that they cause two arguments to clash together in hopes of striking out a spark of truth.[10] The efficacy which is attributed to the dialectical process had undoubtedly influenced his choice of dialogue as genre.

A passage just a few sentences later than the one cited above (3. P.12. 30-38) deals specifically with relationship between content and form. When Philosophy has reached the conclusion of a short argument, Boethius addresses her as follows, in the spirit more of a charge than of a real question: ,,You are playing games with me, 'I said,' by weaving an inextricable labyrinth with your rational arguments. Now you enter where you go out, and then again you go out where you have just entered. Or are you entwining a kind of wonderful circle of the Divine Simplicity?' " Boethius explains that he is referring to the fact that Philosophy's argument is self-contained, drawing upon itself without adding new reasons from outside. In response, Philosophy affirms her seriousness of purpose, saying that her argument has been modeled on the Divine Form, which Parmenides calls a sphere. This sphere, she states, causes the universe to move but is itself motionless. She then proceeds to allude to a passage from the *Timaeus* (29b), where Plato (or rather Timaeus) says, according to her version, that words should be related to the subject of which they speak. That her interpretation of the Greek may be questionable when examined in the Platonic context is beside the point in a consideration of the *Consolatio* in its own terms.[11]

As will be mentioned later, circles and spheres are among the most frequent and important images in the *Consolatio*. The motion of the various non-divine circles and spheres, contrasting with the Parmenidean stationary One, helps to carry out the crucially important antithesis between the stability of God and the ceaseless motion of the phenomenal world. All of Boethius' images in the *Consolatio* are highly functional, evoked by and constantly recalling, in one way or another, the theme of the mind's return from slavery and exile; while the recurrent metaphors of levels sometimes openly, sometimes implicitly, suggest the mental ascent and the interrelationships of man, the physical cosmos, and God.[12]

Philosophy's reference to a significant connection between form and content is, I believe, a helpful hint from the author that his readers should carefully observe the stylistic and structural features of the *Consolatio* along with its content if they wish to extract its full meaning. The unity of the work, exceptional by any standard, makes such a study of interrelationships possible and even necessary.[13] *Dialectica* affords a good example, since it influences both style and structure while furnishing a method of logical disputation in a work which stresses the value of trained reason.

---

10 *Republic* 435a.
11 *...cognatos de quibus loquuntur rebus oportere esse sermones.* Cf. *Timaeus* 29b 3-5:
ὧδε οὖν περί τε εἰκόνος καὶ περὶ τοῦ παραδείγματος αὐτῆς διοριστέον, ὡς ἄρα τοὺς λόγους, ὧνπέρ εἰσιν ἐξηγηταί, τούτων αὐτῶν καὶ συγγενεῖς ὄντας.
As Timaeus then explains, an unquestionably true account can be given only about a certainly-known subject. His cosmology can therefore only be reasonable and probable because of the limit of human capacity to discern such matters clearly and surely. In developing his point, Timaeus makes an analogy a metaphorical proportion that as being is to becoming, so is truth to belief. (*Timaeus* 29c 3: ὅτιπερ πρὸς γένεσιν οὐσία, τοῦτο πρὸς πίστιν ἀλή ειχ.)
Cf. Boethius' metaphorical proportions in the section of this article on Arithmetica (pp. 24-25).
12 For an excellent treatment of the Neo-Platonic tradition behind the metaphor in the *Consolatio*, see V. Schmidt-Kohl, *Die Neuplatonische Seelenlehre in der Consolatio Philosophiae des Boethius* (Meisenheim am Glan, 1965).
13 The *Consolatio*, both as a whole and in its many component elements of form and content, can and should

Toward the beginning of the *Consolatio* when Philosophy is trying to decide what method of treatment to adopt for Boethius' malady, she begins by asking (1.P.6. 3): „Do you think that this world is moved by the random events of fortune, or do you believe that any ruling principle of reason is inherent in it?" Boethius then answers: „I should by no means judge that such a surely-defined pattern is produced by random fortune. Indeed, I *know* that God, the Creator, presides over what He has made; and no day will ever force me to abandon this sound view."[14] Starting with Boethius' conviction, Philosophy undertakes her course of therapy, by which she will restore him to soundness. Boethius' statement, the basic premise upon which the whole philosophical structure of the work rests, is impressively forceful. He does not talk about belief or unqualified opinion, but uses the strongest possible verb, *scio*, „I know;" and although the noun *sententia* („view") may suggest opinion rather than knowledge, the *veritate* („truth"), upon which the *sententia* depends syntactically, leaves no doubt that in this case the opinion is correct, and is regarded by Boethius as the equivalent of truth.

Philosophy than wonders how Boethius can have fallen into such a state of *lethargia* when his fundamental principle is so sound. By additional questioning she quickly finds out, and so her philosophical therapy can proceed.

The reader may rather wonder why Boethius should have remained so firm in his acceptance of a rationally planned and governed universe when his own state seemed as unwarranted as it was deplorable. How had he gained his awareness of the stability, „the surely-defined pattern"? The answer to the question comes as early as 1. M.2, Philosophy's first poem in the *Consolatio*, where she tells how Boethius, who now is downcast, used to walk as a free man under the open sky, and see the course of sun, stars, and the other natural phenomena. Her reference to *numeris* in v. 12 clearly indicates the mathematical arts of the Quadrivium, by which Boethius had won an understanding and real mastery of what meaning the phenomenal world can hold for a philosopher. That Boethius had been a student as well as a lover of nature is also indicated in vv. 22-23, where Philosophy speaks of his former activity in searching out the secrets of nature and giving a rational account of them. In short, Boethius' study of the mathematical disciplines had led him to perceive the regularity in the natural world. As he later tells Philosophy (3. P.12. 5-8), the harmonious order among the potentially discordant cosmic elements had led to his certainty that a stable and abiding One must be the Preserver and Mover of the world. This One, as he states, he designates by the usual term „God". Without Boethius' unshaken belief in a Divine Creator and Ruler, a belief which he associates with his study of the Liberal Arts, the *Consolatio* could not exist in its present form because Philosophy would have needed some other starting-point for her therapy.

be read as dynamically evolving according to the system of levels which forms the path of the mental ascent. In reaching the upper levels of the philosophical journey, Boethius does not discard already-used images or ideas, but enriches his interpretation of them as they reveal themselves anew. For this reason, point of view is of the greatest possible significance throughout the *Consolatio*. A convenient illustration is provided by the concept of *felicitas*. The first implied definition of *felix*, „blessed by Fortune" (1. 17-22), is soon rejected because of its incompatibility with philosophical conclusions. On the level of ethics, *felix* has an essentially negative meaning, e.g., „safe from harm" (2. M.4, 19-22) or „content without wealth" (2. M.5). On the next level, *felix* indicates the positive happiness resulting from awareness of divinely-granted cosmic harmony (cf. 2. M.8. 28-30); this meter looks ahead to the second level. Cf. p. 30 below. Finally, on the highest level, *felicitas* ist the joy that comes with perception of the Divine Light (cf. 3. M.12, 1-4, which looks ahead to the highest philosophical level) by rising, through reason, above reason.

14   „*Atqui,*" inquam, „*nullo existimaverim modo ut fortuita temeritate tam certa moveantur, verum operi*

Another early allusion to study of the Arts is made by Boethius in 1. P.4 when he mentions his library, where he and Philosophy had been accustomed to meet and to discourse „about the knowledge of human and divine matters" (*de humanarum divinarumque rerum scientia*). Boethius asks Philosophy: „Was this my bearing and this my countenance when I searched with you into the secrets of nature; when you marked out for me with your wand the paths of the stars; and when you formed my character and the rational principle of my whole life according to the examples of the celestial order (*...ad caelestis ordinis exempla formares*)?" The clear meaning of this passage is that the study of astronomy had revealed the orderly arrangement and movement of heavenly bodies; and that perception of this order had served as an *exemplum* for Boethius in developing a principle of order for his own life. We may advance one step further by speculating about the meaning of the phrase *caelestis ordinis exempla*. In a work so characterized by poetic ambiguity and by the coexistence of several levels of meaning, the expression *caelestis ordo* inevitably suggests an order created and maintained by God. Order, then, exists for Boethius in an interrelated way on three levels at once. God is, of course, the Cause; the heavens are orderly because God has so made them; and human life can have moral order when it adopts as an example the celestial order made by God. Reason perceives this celestial order when, trained by the quadrivial arts, it correctly interprets sensory data. Dialectic, too, participates in this process as provider of the means for organization of material and also as the source of criteria for distinguishing true judgments and inferences from false.

For the most part, allusions in the *Consolatio* to the quadrivial arts and their functions are concrete and imagistic. That is, Boethius deals here with the sensibles constituting the subject matter of the physical sciences, not with theoretical principles expressed in the technical language of the formal disciplines. So, for example, he repeatedly alludes to sun and stars rather than to astronomy or astronomical principles. From a stylistic point of view, his transformation of the discussion about the arts into images and metaphors is perfectly adapted to expression in lyric poetry. By using the same images and metaphors in the prose too, Boethius enhances the structural and stylistic unity of his work. In addition, as already noted (p. 18), he keeps reminding the reader of the main theme through the interrelated sets of images and metaphors.

As Boethius states in the Proemium of his work on mathematics, Arithmetica holds prior place in the Quadrivium since the other three mathematical disciplines depend upon it.[15] In the *Consolatio* the relationship between human knowledge of *Arithmetica* and the divine order may be indicated by the juxtaposition of two verses which include the word *numeris*. The first, mentioned just above, is from Philosophy's opening poem, in which she states that Boethius in the past had observed the stars and made numerical calculations about their orbits (vv. 10-12). The other occurrence is in the cosmological poem, 3. M.9, where, addressing God, Philosophy says: „*Tu numeris elementa ligas...*" („You bind the elements with numbers..."). The study of mathematics is thus shown to be an appropriate and direct way to progress toward a rational understanding of the cosmic order.

An implicit use of *Arithmetica* may be suggested in connection with the number five, since the *Consolatio* is comprised of five books. As Martianus Capella tells us in Book 7, *De Arithmetica* (pp. 369-70 ed. Dick), that number represents the cosmos. It is called *apocatastaticus*, „recurrent", because five to any power produces a number ending in five. As an astronomical

suo conditorem praesidere deum scio nec umquam fuerit dies qui me ab hac sententiae veritate depellat."
15 P. 10, ed. Friedlein.

term, the noun *apocatastasis* refers to the return of a celestial body to the starting point of its orbit. Finally, it is used by Proclus (*Inst.* 199) specifically to indicate „the return of the soul." Since Bothius seems to have conceived of his work as a kind of literary image of the cosmos with its disparate stylistic and structural components harmoniously blended, and since the return of the *mens* is the theme, the associations with the number may have influenced his division of the work into five books.

Other uses of Arithmetica involve metaphorical adaptations of proportions. Significantly, such usage occurs in the third stage of Philosophy's therapy—i.e., the highest level of the mental ascent, which has already passed the proper function of dialectic and the other rational disciplines, dealing as it does with the Divine, not with the physical universe. When the subject of Providence and Fate is being discussed, Boethius presents a fivefold set of ratios, the upper terms of which all relate to the phenomenal world and the lower to the Divine. The sentence reads: „As *ratiocinatio* (the rational process) is to *intellectus*, that which comes into being to what which is, time to eternity, a circle to its center, so is the mobile series of Fate to the stable simplicity of Providence."[16] A more usual pattern of metaphorical proportion, one having the same middle terms, is implicit in Book 5 (P.5. 8-12) where Philosophy indicates that God has a level of vision and knowledge surpassing the human, so that, unknown and unknowable, He is incomprehensible to man as rational man is to non-rational creatures. The implied proportion is: As sense and imagination (faculties shared by sub-human creatures) are to reason, so reason is to Divine *intelligentia*.

The relationship between music and mathematics, familiar from the time of Pythagoras, would have placed music among the quadrivial disciplines in any case; but in addition, as we noted before, Philosophy in the *Consolatio* specifically refers to poetry as *musica*, an association especially appropriate both because it is lyric and because of the quantitative nature of classical poetry denoted by the term „meter".[17]

Philosophy's attitude toward poetry seems difficult to assess. After abruptly dismissing the elegiac Muses at the beginning of the first book, she composes poems throughout the whole *Consolatio*. There is also an ambiguity in the term *vernacula* by which she refers to her poetic Muse (2. P.1. 8), an ambiguity increased by the diminutive ending suggestive of either a patronizing or an affectionate tone or of both at once. Yet Philosophy's position is not really paradoxical or incomprehensible. In referring to the Muses as „sweet to the point of destruction" (*usque in exitium dulces* 1. P.1. 11), she stresses the charm which can be used for ill as well as for good. So Orpheus, whose musical magic entrances others, defeats himself by allowing passion to overcome reason. When he laments „in tearful measures" (*flebilibus modis*, 3. M. 12. 7), he reminds the reader of the tearful Boethius who, in the opening elegy, had been compelled to take up *his* mournful measures (v. 2: *flebilis heu, maestos cogor inire modos*). On the other hand, while controlled by Philosophy and so by reason, poetry like rhetoric can perform important services in the philosophical quest, as it does, for instance, by evoking images of the divine cosmic plan (3. M. 9) and of the mental ascent (4. M.1), which cannot be visualized or properly expressed through the rational process of dialectic. That Philosophy never seems

16 *Igitur uti est ad intellectum ratiocinatio, ad id quod est id quod gignitur, ad aeternitatem tempus, ad punctum medium circulus, ita est fati series mobilis ad providentiae stabilem simplicitatem.* (4 P. 6.79).

17 The term *modi*, frequently used to designate poetry, emphasizes association with the musical art. Grateful acknowledgment is made for the invaluable help provided by Lane Cooper's *Concordance of Boethius* (Cambridge, Mass. 1928), which facilitates a study of the *Consolatio* from any point of view.

wholly comfortable about poetic music can be explained by her strong predilection for active reason, which results in her feeling that poetry is somehow not quite „serious". It would be misleading, however, to identify Boethius' own views too closely with those of Lady Philosophy, who is, after all, his literary creation.

Boethius assigns an important function to poetry by using individual poems to accentuate the tone of their immediate contexts and to point up the stage reached in the philosophical arguments. The conventional themes and spirit of some lyrics in the first half for example, are appropriate to the section dedicated to the refutation of false values. The commonplaces and attitudes reminiscent of Roman satire are at home in the province of Rhetorica, who delights in sententious moralizing. The element of the Heroic, on the other hand, is reserved for the higher levels of the second half.

Besides this harmonious combination of prose and poetry within the various divisions of the work, the poems help to harmonize the work as a whole by serving as structural and thematic links.[18] Such effective harmony of poetry and prose offers one of many indications that the *Consolatio* is made in the image of the cosmos. Boethius the artificer is following his interpretation of the Platonic injunction (*Timaeus* 29b) that the form of a *logos* should resemble its content. The cosmos about which he writes provides Boethius with the supreme paradigm of all harmony since it was formed by God's harmonious arrangement of fire, air, water, and earth so that like qualities — the appropriate combinations of dryness, heat, wetness, and cold — serve as twofold means to bind successive pairs of elements. Dryness and heat mediate between fire and air, heat and wetness between air and water, and wetness and cold between water and earth, which is cold and dry.

The image of bonds, which appears constantly and in greatly diversified forms throughout the *Consolatio*, belongs, in its positive aspects, to the concept of harmony just as, in its negative functions, it is related to the thematic motif of slavery. The bonds in the *Consolatio* are now material, now metaphorical; but they are always unmistakably clear and always deeply significant. They also illustrate how the idea of metamorphosis in the work is connected with point of view. When considered as the link between God and creation, as in the case of the chain of Fate, the same bonds which appeared to enslave are revealed as the means by which the harmonious reconciliation of opposites can be and sometimes is achieved.

Other contributions too are made to the *Consolatio* by the musical art. After mentioning the harmonious arrangement of the primary elements, the cosmology of 3. M.9 relates that the Divine Artificer had made the World Soul and diffused it through the „consonant members" of the world (vv. 13-14). The allusion to musical consonance is still another indication that Boethius is fashioning his work into a cosmic image. His two co-existent and interrelated structural principles of five divisions by books and four divisions of the argument provide the *consona membra* of the *Consolatio*, a theory supported by the fact that the numbers four and five are regularly associated with musical consonance.[19] Music is thus depicted in the *Consolatio* as an art with widely divergent possibilities. Although it can lead to disaster when its physical embodiment (*not* its theoretical principles) causes the passions to overcome reason, it is wholly and strongly positive as one of the mathematical disciplines and as the „mother" and „home" of harmony.

As for the other arts of the Quadrivium, they are so closely intertwined in function that they must be dealt with mainly together. Philosophy does make one explicit allusion to Geometry toward the beginning of the section devoted to dialectical argument about the *summum*

18   See the Appendix.
19   Martianus 9, 933-34; Boethius, *Inst. Mus.* 1.

bonum (3. P.10. 22). First she states, „Just as it is customary for geometers to draw inferences called *porismata* from propositions already demonstrated, so I shall give you a kind of corollary." Then she continues with her syllogistic argument, taking as established the conclusions drawn from preceding syllogisms. In this instance as in the metaphorical proportions mentioned above, the reader has a clear example of the way that Boethius' thought and expression are shaped by mathematical processes.

The antithesis throughout the work between stability and motion as attributes of God and creation respectively accounts for much of the astronomical and geometrical imagery. The unmoved Parmenidean Sphere, identified with God, is obviously prior in dignity, power, and importance. The single specific allusion to it in 3. P.12. 37 brings together some important associations. After Philosophy has explained that her circular argument has been modelled on the form of the Divine, she continues: „Such is the form of the Divine Substance that it neither slips away outside itself nor takes up anything from outside within itself, but, as Parmenides says: 'On all sides it is like in mass to a well-rounded sphere.' It rolls the moving orb of the universe, but remains motionless itself."[20]

This quotation, in its reference to „the moving orb of the universe", includes one of the most important of all images in the *Consolatio*, that of moving circles and spheres. The associations is often made in allusion to the sun and other planets or astral bodies, to the Wheel of Fortune in Book 2, and to the concentric, moving wheels or circles in Book 4, connected as they are to the divine, immovable center of Providence by the bonds of Fate, which are, in effect, radii of the circles. The cycles of the seasons and the inherent tendency of all creatures to revert to their true nature are other examples of metaphorical moving circles. Even in Hades, to which Orpheus has descended in his attempt to bring up the dead Eurydice, we find Ixion's wheel (3. M.12. 34-35). Although its movement is temporarily arrested by the magical charm of Orpheus' music, its usual swift though purposeless motion is emphasized by the adjective *velox*. In contrast to Ixon's wheel, an august example appears in the hexameter cosmology of 3. M.9. 14-17, where Boethius, following the account in the *Timaeus*, speaks of the cutting of the World Soul into two strips, each of which was then joined into a moving circle.[21] Many of

---

20 *Ea est enim divinae forma substantiae ut neque in externa dilabatur nec in se externum ipsa suscipiat, sed, sicut de ea Parmenides ait:* πάντοθεν εὐκύκλου σφαίρης ἐναλίγκιον ὄγκῳ, *rerum orbem mobilem rotat, dum se immobilem ipsa conservat.*

21 After much thought and hesitation, I have decided that Boethius' literary analogues of the two cosmic moving circles are (1) the five-part structure of the *Consolatio*, externally marked by the number of books; and (2) the three-level philosophical argument of Books 2-5 (see pp. 29-30 below). After telling in his cosmology how the Demiurge had compounded the World Soul, the Platonic Timaeus says: „This whole fabric, then, he split lengthwise into two halves; and making the two cross one another at their centres in the form of the letter X, he bent each round into a circle and joined it up, making each meet itself and the other at a point opposite to that where they had been brought into contact" (*Timaeus* 36b 6-c2, tr. Cornford). For some observations about 3. M.9 as the central meeting place of the two cosmic circles, see p. 31 below. The division of the *Consolatio* as a whole into two antithetically balanced halves, with the negatives of the first half corresponding to the positives of the second, supports the hypothesis. The obvious balances between Books 1 and 5, and 2 and 4 (cf. the balance between Fortuna and Providence and the corresponding imagery) all contribute to the interpretation. A stylistic circle also is made by the opening poetic passage of Book 1 and the concluding prose passage of Book 5, which closes the circle of alternating passages.

As was observed at the beginning of this paper, a clearly semi-circular pattern is traced by the *Consolatio*. This fact does not, however, invalidate the interpretation of the *Consolatio* as circular. The theme is the return of the mind, and the path of return in the *Consolatio* is consistently circular. The explanation must be, therefore, that we follow the course only of „the way up," the ascent of the mind. Boethius lets us see the results of the descent, but not the process (except insofar as the narrating of his

these moving circles and spheres in the *Consolatio* metaphorically represent the theme of the soul's return. Although the metaphor is often represented in clear images, it is sometimes only subtly implied. For example, ,,birth" is expressed by the word *ortus* because of the association of that word with the rising of the sun and stars, the courses of which provide man with natural *exempla* of the soul's return.[22] In Fortune's case, however, the connection with false values makes the erratic spinning of the wheel a symbol of instability entirely different from the orderly motion of return directed by a divine plan. In the familiar imagery of the *Consolatio*, Fortuna's blindness signifies her lack of mental and moral perception. Accordingly, through the passage about the concentric circles joined by Fate to unmoving Providence, Fortune is seen in retrospect as not really owning the wheel which she spins. Instead, she herself is held in bondage by the chain of Fate, and ultimately serves the purposes of inscrutable Providence whom, in her blindness, she will never see.[23] In fact the greatness of her distance from Providence lengthens the bond by which Fate controls her.[24] Ixion's wheel too is a symbol both of perpetual slavery and banishment within the dark earth and of the futility of incessant motion without a goal.

Combining the imagery of light and of moving circles, 3. M.11. 1-4 reads: ,,Whoever tracks down the truth with his mind's depth and will not be deceived by treacherous paths, should roll into himself the light of his inmost sight, bending the motions into a circle." In the context of the *Consolatio*, where the immediate end is the return of the inner light, the imagery of moving circles and of light have the closest possible relationship. The role of the Liberal Arts in helping to effect the return is clearly indicated in these two verses from the same poem (11-12): ,,Surely a seed of truth remains within; and this is stirred to life when the breeze of learning (*doctrina*) blows." The subject of the ,,learning" is, in fact, the Liberal Arts.

The allusion to inner light in this lyric implicity suggests the metaphor of the ascent of the mind toward the Source of all light, an association strengthened by vv. 7-8, which reads: ,,...what the black cloud of error long obscured will glow more brightly than Phoebus himself." The name of Phoebus the resplendent sun, in turn suggests the name of the True Phoebus, God. This connection between the solar body and its Creator and Exemplar is indicated clearly in the following verses from two earlier poems. In 3. M.6. 3, after mentioning the common origin of all men from one Divine Creator, Philosophy says: ,,It is He who gave Phoebus his rays and the moon its horns." In 3. M.10. 17-18, after speaking of the Divine Light that rules the heavens, Philosophy concludes: ,,Whoever can observe this Light will say the rays of Phoebus do not gleam." Finally, in an explicitly Homeric contrast between the cosmic Phoebus and the Supreme Light, Philosophy declares (5. M.2, 13-14): ,,Since He alone beholds all things, you can call Him the True Sun."[25]

---

earlier misfortunes by his *persona* serves as a flashback account). The meaning of the semi-circle and its implicitly accompanying diameter can be either conversion or relapse. For the circle of the philosophical argument, see p. 31.

22 For passages strongly suggesting such usage, cf. 3.M.2. 27; 4. M.1. 26; M.6. 30-33; 5. P.1. 30.

23 In speaking of the *series Fati*, Philosophy says (4.P.6.86): *heac actus etiam fortunasque hominum indissolubili causarum conexione constringit, quae cum ab immobilis Providentiae proficiscatur exordiis, ipsas quoque immutabiles esse necesse est.* Cf. 5. M.1. 11-12: *Sic quae permissis fluitare videtur habenis Fors patitur frenos ipsaque lege meat.*

24 Cf. 4.P.6.65: *Nam ut orbium circa eundem cardinem sese vertentium qui est intimus ad simplicitatem medietatis accedit ceterorumque extra locatorum veluti cardo quidam circa quem versentur exsistit, extimus vero maiore ambitu rotatus quanto a puncti media individuitate discedit tanto amplioribus spatiis explicatur, si quid vero illi se medio conectat et societ, in simplicitatem cogitur diffundique ac diffluere cessat, simili ratione quod longius a prima mente discedit maioribus fati nexibus implicatur ac tanto aliquid fato liberum est quanto illum rerum cardinem vicinius petit.*

25 Allusions to Phoebus throughout the *Consolatio* regularly are endowed with heroic associations, such as

28

The fully developed combination of the metaphors of lights and of levels, an extended metaphor or cluster of metaphors related to the mental ascent of the Platonic tradition, is expressed in a mystical poem (4. M.1) especially reminiscent of Lucius' cosmic journey in the rites of initiation recounted in Apuleius' *Metamorphoses*. It may also be recalled that Lucius' ritual dress as described in the novel converts him into a solar image (11. 21-22).

The three main divisions of the philosophical argument of the *Consolatio* in Books 2-5, tracing the progress of Boethius' recovery, correspond to the three levels in the mental ascent. Actually, Philosophy's guidance is the path (*via, semita*) of the ascent, which is also implicitly depicted as a dialectical process. Rising from the individual or most specific of specifics in his state of alienation represented by the metaphor of exile, Boethius reaches the most general or universal, namely, God and the cosmos. The self-absorption indicated by the autobiographical content of Book 1 is pre-philosophical, since even the lowest level of philosophical thought (the practical level of ethics presided over by Rhetorica in 2-3.8) demands that a man rise above himself as an individual and consider mankind as a whole. The next level, the stage of *ratio, dialectica*, and the Quadrivium (3.9-4.6), deals with man in relation to the physical cosmos. Finally, on the highest level Boethius is concentrating on the cosmos and its Divine Creator. Man is now seen as part of the whole.

The relationship between the mental ascent and the return of the mind is now unmistakably clear; the ascent is the process of which the return is the goal. As we have noted repeatedly, the return is presented by images of moving circles and spheres; whereas the ascent implicitly assumes the form of horizontal geometrical parallel planes, each succeeding pair of which is joined by a vertical plane. The steps on philosophy's robe represent this image, of which the iconographically familiar ladder is a variant.

It is of the greatest importance that the anagogic process, culminating in the revelation of God insofar as He can be revealed to living creatures, takes one back at the end to earth and the level of ethics, which still speaks the language of rhetoric and carries the judicial metaphor to the very conclusion of the work. By this time, however, the fuller view of the divine plan has raised the level and deepened the significance of man's motivation to lead a good life.[26] The vision of God has confirmed the belief in His goodness and in the benign order of the creation which He rules. The Divine Creator and Ruler is now acknowledged also as the Judge whose law imposes upon men an obligation to act justly. By thus returning to the level of ethics, which is seen in a new light, Boethius completes the cyclical course of his argument. So the mental ascent, which had appeared to be a graded, linear path, is finally perceived as following the course of Boethius' magic circle.

The role played by the Liberal Arts in the *Consolatio* as a whole can now be seen. The level of Dialectica and the Quadrivium, providing a mean between earth and the Creator, reveals the physical universe as a mirror of the divine plan, and so makes it possible for man to reach the third level. This consummation of the mind's ascent results directly in the return from slavery and exile to freedom and home. The true and final return can only be foreshadowed in the *Consolatio*, as it is in the mystic vision of 4. M.1, since it cannot be fully realized during life in a world of appearances, reflections, and the ceaseless flow of time.

---

dactylic meters, military metaphors, and Homeric epithets.

26   Compare the anagogic level of patristic exegesis, with its characteristic reference to Christ as Judge. Man, temporarily earth-bound, can best express his faith by following the divinely sanctioned precept that he lead a moral life. So the anagogic often leads back to the tropological, but with significant enhancement because now there is not only a backward look to Biblical teaching and example, but also a vision of the eternity into which time will be dissolved. Now in the *Consolatio* Rhetorica, supporting faith in the

The association of freedom with the Liberal Arts, inevitably suggested by the root of the adjective, is clear in the *Consolatio*, where the thematic antithesis between slavery and freedom dominates the whole work and is dealt with both explicitly and implicitly on all planes. At the pre-philosophical stage represented by the dark earth in Book 1, slavery in its most literal, physical sense continues as before. It results from Fortune's withdrawal of her favors, and can only be made more tolerable and finally reduced to insignificance by a change in point of view. When Rhetorica shows that wordly goods are never one's own, a kind of freedom is attained through release from bondage to the false values born of blind and blinding Fortune. The practical level of philosophical discourse thus paradoxically provides a *consolatio* by demonstrating that there is no need for one because no actual loss has been sustained. In the next level the mathematical disciplines, training the reason with the help of Dialectica, free the mind from the darkness of ignorance which had made man feel like an exile in the world, and make possible the ascent to the third and highest step. There, after the intellectual revelation of the cosmic order on the second level, man attains the higher revelation of faith, which assures him that God has granted the free will without which the rational faculties would be impotent and meaningless. It is through the exercise of this free will that man accepts his place in the cosmic order and so achieves his highest freedom.

Bryn Mawr College

True God, has a positive role sharply contrasting with its negative function on the first philosophical level (2-3.8).

Besides the division of the *Consolatio* into five books, the argument has four main structural divisions. The first, comprising all of Book 1, is Philosophy's pre-philosophical analysis of Boethius' ailment. The second, the rhetorical argument of ethics against the false goods of Fortune, begins with Book 2 and ends before the disclosure of the true good, the divine plan realized in the cosmology of 3. M.9. The transition is marked by Philosophy's statement (3. 9. 1): „We have drawn a clear enough picture of false happiness; and now, if you have examined it closely, we should show the form of true happiness." This transition, as indicated above, is underscored by the change from rhetorical to dialectical style and method.

The passage from the second to the third level is defined precisely by Boethius' introductory statement (4. P.6. 7): „Then, as though setting out from another beginning, she took up the argument as follows."

Boethius' explicit identification of these structural divisions of the argument proves that there are two coexistent structural principles, one based on the fivefold division into books, and the other on the fourfold stages of the „plot", with special emphasis on the threefold division of the philosophical argument.

The *Consolatio* contains thirty-nine passage of prose and the same number of poetic passages. The poems are distributed as follows:

DIVISION BY BOOKS	DIVISION INTO FOUR PARTS OF ARGUMENT
2: 8	Level 1 of philosophical argument: (2-3.8): 16
3: 12	Level 2—(3.9-4.5): 9
4: 7	Level 3—(4.6-5.5): 7
5: 5	

The center of the three philosophical levels is thus seen to be marked by 2. M.8 and 3. M.1,4. M.1, and 5. M.2. Of these poems, 2. M.8 both ends the first half of the first philosophical level and corresponds with the end of Book 2, while 3. M.1 both begins the second half of the first philosophical level and is in the opening passage of Book 3; and 4. M.1, which is in the exact middle of Level 2, occurs at the beginning of Book 4. By these correspondences, Boethius has reconciled („harmonized") the two systems of structural division by books and by philosophical levels of the argument.

In talking about the harmonious order of the cosmos, 2. M.8 anticipates the content of the next level, beginning with 3.9, which deals particularly with the physical sciences; 3. M.1 (v.v. 11-13), on the other hand, looks back to the ethical argument of Book 2, with which it is about to proceed. In this way, 2.8 and 3.1 criss-cross to form two structural links which compensate, as it were, for the division into books. The third level, attainable only through the consummation of the mental ascent, is anticipated by 1. M.1. Significantly the heroic dactylic cosmology of 3. M.9, the seventeenth of thirty-two poems in the philosophical argument of Books 2-5, marks the beginning at once of the second philosophical level and of the second half of the philosophical „path" of the *Consolatio*, as measured by the number of passages. It also is the center of the *Consolatio* as a whole, dividing as it does the negative or dark half from the positive or light half. 3. M.9, then, is the center where the two structural circles of the *Consolatio* are joined.[27] The central poem of the third level, 5. M.2, reflects the heroic associations of 3. M.9 by quoting and alluding to Greek epic in exalting God as the True Sun who far surpasses the Phoebus acclaimed by Homer.

---

27   Cf. n. 21 above.

Another obvious basis for detection of structurally significant correspondences of poems in the *Consolatio* is the variety of meters. The distribution of recurring meters is summarized as follows (see Weinberger's chart in his Index):

Glyconic — 1. M.6; 2. M.8; 3. M.12; 4. M.3; 5. M.4.
Anapaestic dimeter acatalectic — 1. M.5; 3. M.2; 4. M.6; 5. M.3.
Elegiac — 1. M.1; 5. M.1.
Choliambic — 2. M.1; 3. M.11.
Paroemiac — 2. M.5; 3. M.5.
Sapphic — 2. M.6; 4. M.7.

It may be seen at once that only glyconies occur in every book; that the anapaestic dimeters acatalectic occur once in every one of the fourfold structural divisions; that the balanced position of the elegiacs contributes to a symmetrical pattern based on the five books; that the coliambics occur near the beginning of the first and second philosophical levels respectively; that the paroemiacs both come in the first philosophical level, though in different books; and that the sapphics, which might fit into either of the two structural patterns, suggest especially a relationship to the symmetry of the structural pattern based on the division into five books and two halves. Some common features of poems written in the same meter are indicated below.

Glyconics

The glyconic poems in Books 1-4 all have variants of the topos of the *adynaton* („the impossible").[28] In 1. M.6. 7-8, the topos exemplifies the impossibility of achieving success when action is taken out of due season. In 2. M.8, *amor* as harmony — of the physical cosmos and its parts, of the social order among peoples bound by treaty, and between individuals in marriage and in friendship — is stressed and shown as interrelated in all of its aspects. The topos here (vv. 9-12) implies that cosmic order on all levels would be impossible if harmony did not prevail and keep everything within its appointed bounds. The order of the physical cosmos is seen as supplying *exempla* and *documenta* for human life. In 3. M.12, 7-41, the topos is expressed by the reversal of the usual order as everything yields to the magical charm of Orpheus' music. The transformation of the normal order culminates in surrender to pity by the ruthless king of Hades. In 4. M.3., 8-26, the *adynaton* assumes the form of physical metamorphosis caused by Circe's potions. What, then, is the relationship of these poems to 5. M.4, which refutes Stoic epistemology? The poem includes a series of three questions (vv. 10-25) which Stoic epistemology cannot explain. The cumulative effect of the topos of the *adynaton* in the preceding four glyconies intensifies the implication that the Stoic system is impossible to accept since it cannot explain mental activities.

Anapaestic dimeters acatalectic

The poems in this anapaestic meter represent all four of the structural divisions of the *Consolatio* based on the argument. The first, 1. M.5, emphasizes the extremity of Boethius' alienation when he sees the general cosmic order as excluding men. Here the regularity of natural cycles is contrasted with the capricious changes brought about by Fortune, who produces moral chaos in human lives. In 3. M.2, the universal pattern of return is explained by the controlling bond of nature. The relationship between the chain of Fate governing nature and the stable center of Divine Providence from which Fate comes, a concept elaborated imagistically in 4. P.6, is anticipated in this poem by the *provida* in v.3 modifying the *natura* in v.2. In 4.

---

28   On this topos, see E.R. Curtius, *European Literature and the Latin Middle Ages* (New York 1953), 94-98.

M.6, the bond of natural constraint emphasized in 1. M.5 (cf. v. 4, *cogis*; v. 15, *stringis*; v. 18, *tua vis*; v. 23, *nihil antiqua lege solutum*; v. 43, *rerum foedera nectis*) has been transformed into the benign bond of harmony (love). The universal process of return is now viewed as the greatest object of desire for all creatures, which find in the return to their Source their only means of survival. The awareness of divine order in *all* life (as inferred from perception by *mens* of the cosmic pattern) has been attained on the second philosophical level and is appropriately placed in this poem at the beginning of the third and steepest part of the road. In 5. M.3, the universal bond of harmony is represented (vv. 1-3) as broken by the supposed incompatibility of God's „foreknowledge" (later explained as a timeless view incomprehensible to finite human reason) and human free will. The series of questions (vv. 1-21), indicating the mental quest for the truth, leads to the conclusion that man has partial knowledge of it but that complete certainty eludes him. Now, on its highest philosophical level, the search has risen above the physical cosmos and deals with the possibility of human knowledge about the divine plan. Here, since the final return has not yet been achieved, the resolution of the questions is tentative. Human reason, dimmed by its „burial" in the living body, lies somewhere between perfect knowledge and complete ignorance.

These four poems, all dealing with the bonds of nature and the return, are thus seen to vary in their treatments according to their respective stage of the philosophical argument.

Elegiacs

Although the two elegiac poems seem so different, they have significant elements in common. In 1. M.1, the poet attributes to Fortuna the power to influence human life by granting or withdrawing her favors (17-22). Morever, the *fallaceum vultum* („deceitful countenance") of v. 19 emphasizes Fortune's treacherous nature. In 5. M.1, the courses of the Tigris and Euphrates are seen to be governed by a *defluus ordo*, „an order flowing down" (v. 10). This phrase, in addition to its obvious natural meaning, must imply the divine source of Providence from which all cosmic order flows through the natural law represented in 4. P.6 as the bonds of Fate. Now Fortune herself is revealed as held in check by cosmic order although she appears to follow her own course without restraint. The element of treachery in this poem assumes the form of an allusion (vv. 1-2) to Parthian archers, proverbial for shooting behind their backs. To summarize: in these two poems also, Boethius uses different treatment of the same motifs to represent the progress achieved through the philosophical argument. In 5. M.1, Fortune has been transformed from the ruler to the ruled.

Choliambics

The two choliambics, coming at or near the beginning of philosophical levels, also present a contrast significantly related to their respective positions. 2. M.1 deals with Fortune and the cruel game which she plays upon men (v. 7: *Sic illa ludit*), arousing their passions by suddenly reversing the order of their lives. The first verse (*Haec cum superba verterit vices dextra*) alludes to her spinning wheel. In 3. M.11, the moving circle is the course of man's turning from the outer to the inner world. Here his reason prevails and the inner light of *mens* makes him invulnerable to Fortune's assaults. It is in the following prose passage that Boethius accuses Philosophy of playing a game with him by arguing in a circle, and that Philosophy denies that she has been merely playing (3. 12. 30-36). The common though contrasting associations with moving circles, outer and inner treasures, emotion and reason, and the „game" motif all indicate that the poems have the function of stressing the difference between the first and the second philosophical levels. The harshly negative tone of the first and the positive spirit of the second also are consistent with Boethius' treatment of the two halves of the work. The negative words in 3. M.11 acquire the force of strong affirmatives by implicitly cancelling the negative qualities of Fortuna. So *nullis deviis falli* in v. 2 echoes the *fallax* describing Fortune in 2. M.1. 4. The *non* in 3. 11.9, unlike the *non* in 2.1.5, has the positive function of stating that not all the light of *mens* is extinguished because of its dwelling in the body. The Platonic association of the poem, explicit in vv. 15-16, are anticipated by the opening Platonic figure of tracking down the truth by reason. The metaphor of the part of the *logos*, assuming here the form of the circle that one bends back into himself, stresses the initiative and independence of action which is the direct opposite of passive acceptance of motion externally imposed by Fortune. Also strongly implicit is the contrast between Fortune's blindness and the inner light which is the subject of 3. M.11.

Paroemiacs

These two poems represent two stages of the argument on the first philosophical level against the true value of Fortune's gifts. In 2. M.5, conventional simple life theme leads to the idea that hope of profit can arouse an enemy to wage war. Thus avarice, rejecting the simple life, opens the door to destruction and death by tempting an enemy to covet wealth. In 3. M.5, the emphasis is upon the vanity of worldly power in contrast to self control. Both poems, then, stress the worthlessness of Fortune's favors.

The advancement of the philosophical argument on the same level is illumined by a juxtaposition of these two meters. In 2. M.5, the disadvantages of wealth are summarized in the *pretiosa pericula* of the last verse. The reader might have anticipated the more obvious *pretia periculosa*, which would imply the external dangers accompanying worldly wealth. Boethius' inversion of noun and adjective subtly indicates man's irrationality in voluntarily paying a high price for a source of danger rather than of pleasure and profit. Clever man has made an bad bargain! As so often in a conventional treatment of the „simple life" theme, human initiative is regarded as a transgression against Moire, (the Boethian *ordo*) analogous, for example, to the encroachment of sea upon land. Dangers lurk outside, ready to strike when man refuses to submit passively to the natural order. In 3. M.5, on the other hand, vigorous activity, directed inward, is depicted as a great good resulting in the moral and mental selfconquest without which freedom is unattainable.

Sapphics

As indicated above, the contrast between the negative and positive halves of the *Consolatio* is sustained by these two poems, representing respectively the anti-hero (the tyrant) and the true hero who, by subduing his own feelings, overcomes the greatest obstacles in human life. Nero's savage and selfishly-motivated parricide must be contrasted with Agamemnon's paternal grief at having to sacrifice his daughter in order to avenge his brother's honor. Ulysses, too, is depicted as mourning and avenging the comrades slain by Polyphemus. These figures as negative and positive examples of *pietas* in the Vergilian sense can hardly escape the reader.

Hercules' feats performed against destructive monsters make him unique among heroic saviors. Whereas Nero's poison (2. M.6 20) had been used to murder his brother. The poison in 4. M.7 is associated with the deadly Hydra (v. 22); Nero is fierce and bestial (*ferus*) like Polyphemus (2. 6. 3 and 4. 7. 9); Nero's *celsa potestas* („lofty power") is Fortune's gift, but the *celsa via* („the road leading to the heights") travelled by Hercules is the rough heroic path which he has chosen to pursue and from which he does not swerve. These two poems clearly form a diptych.

A future literary study must deal with other structural and thematic patterns formed by the poems and the prose, both separately and together. The almost perfect symmetry in the distribution of prose passages by books, for example (6, 8, 12, 7, 6), is too obvious to miss and reinforces the structural significance of the division into five books.

ELEONORE STUMP

BOETHIUS AND PETER OF SPAIN ON THE TOPICS

Boethius's *De topicis differentiis* is a philosophically interesting and historically influential work having to do with the art of Topics, a branch of philosophy which antiquity bequeathed to the Middle Ages but which philosophers of the scholastic period transformed almost past recognition. In this article, I want to explain briefly Boethius's art of Topics and then discuss in some detail that of Peter of Spain, which seems superficially quite similar to Boethius's but is in fact very different from it. As a result, I hope to make clearer what Boethius's method is and to chart one of the landmarks in the process by which that method was lost.

I

De topicis differentiis falls into the area of logic for the most part (it also contains some discussion of rhetoric), and specifically into that branch of logic which the ancients and medievals called 'dialectic'. Dialectic has its origins in the sort of argument by question and answer which Socrates carries on in many of Plato's dialogues; and Aristotle, the heir of that tradition, still regards dialectic as the art of being a good questioner or answerer in such a disputation. Boethius is aware of the definition of dialectic as Socratic disputation, and he pays lip service to it; but for him, as for a number of his predecessors in the long history of the subject, dialectic is primarily a discipline designed to help one find arguments. As there is a method for judging or evaluating arguments (which is what we today call 'logic'), so, Boethius thinks, there is also a method for discovering arguments. Men do often hit on arguments naturally, without the help of any art; but dialectic enables them to find arguments „without travail and without confusion"[1]; it provides a way „without wandering" and „a straight path" for the discovery of arguments.[2]

The main instrument of this method for discovering arguments is something called a Topic (in Latin, *'locus'*). 'Topic' is the standard English translation of the Greek *'topos'*, which means, literally, a place or area. A dialectical Topic is a „place" or „area" which contains arguments within it and from which a variety of arguments can be drawn out. For Aristotle, a dialectical Topic is a strategy of argumentation or a basic principle by means of which a number of particular arguments can be constructed.[3] By Boethius's time, the concept of a Topic has changed; and in *De topicis differentiis*, Boethius is working with a complicated and ingenious variant on Aristotelian Topics, namely, the Topics which he calls Differentiae.

1   *In Ciceronis Topica* (ICT), in *Ciceronis Opera*, ed. J.C. Orelli, Turin, 1833, v.5, pt.1, p.272.3; for the same text in the *Patrologia Latina* (PL) edition, see PL, vol.64, 1043 B5.
2   ICT p.271.41-43; PL 1043 A13-15.
3   See Stump, *Boethius's De topicis differentiis* (Cornell University Press, 1978), pp.159-178. For a general discussion of Aristotelian dialectic, see J. D. G. Evans, *Aristotle's Concept of Dialectic* (Cambridge University Press, 1977).

Boethius recognizes two different sorts of things as Topics. First of all, he says, a Topic is a maximal proposition (*maxima propositio*) or principle.[4] Maximal propositions are generalizations which are self-evidently true, not proved on the basis of or derived from other propositions. Boethius gives as examples of maximal propositions principles such as these:

(1) Things whose definitions are different are themselves also different. (*De top. diff.* 1185 D2)

(2) That to which the definition of a genus does not belong is not a species of the genus defined. (*De top. diff.* 1187 A13)

(3) Those things whose efficient causes are natural are themselves also natural. (*De top. diff.* 1189 C13)

(4) The properties of opposites must be opposites. (*De top. diff.* 1191 D12)

Maximal propositions have two functions in *De top. diff.* First, they are general premisses which are essential to the validity of certain dialectical arguments, though they are not always an explicit part of the argument.[5] Secondly, they help in finding arguments because in Boethius's view, they are the principles that give arguments their force and the generalizations on which arguments depend. Once one has the appropriate maximal proposition for some question, it is not hard to construct the argument or the general outline of the argument for that question. For example, given the question 'Is an envious man wise?' and the maximal proposition 'Things whose definitions are different are themselves different', an arguer has the heart of his argument; the rest of the argument will consist in giving the definitions of wise man and envious man and showing that the two are different.

Though maximal propositions play a significant role in dialectic, the real instrument of Boethius's art of discovery is the second sort of Topic, what Boethius calls a Differentia. The heart of any dialectical argument is a term intermediate between the two terms in a question; this intermediate term is a term which can be linked to each of the two terms in the question in such a way that the two terms of the question can be linked to each other in the conclusion of an argument. Differentiae are the genera of such intermediate terms. For example, Boethius presents the question whether trees are animals.[6] Here the two terms of the question are *tree* and *animal*; if we can find an intermediate term that links the two terms of the question in a certain way, we will have an argument that enables us to draw a conclusion linking the two terms of the question to each other. Boethius gives as premisses

---

4 The current term for '*maxima propositio*' is 'maxim', but I think 'maxim' is a bad translation for three reasons. (1) Though the seventeenth-century sense of 'maxim' included the meaning 'self-evident truth', the current sense of the word is restricted to 'rule of conduct' or 'moral principle'; and since *maximae propositiones* are self-evident truths applicable in a variety of sciences and disciplines, the current sense of 'maxim' is both too narrow and too broad to translate the Latin phrase. (2) The translation of '*maxima propositio*' as 'maxim' obscures the relationship of a *maxima propositio* to the two premisses of a syllogism. A syllogism has a major and a minor proposition. ('*Propositio*' is frequently used to mean premiss.) A *maxima propositio* is an extreme of major propositions; it is major in relation to all other premisses which can be coupled with it in a syllogism and thus „maximal". (3) Topics are discussed not only in dialectic but also in rhetoric. But 'maxim' is already being used as the conventional and accepted translation for the very frequently occurring γνώμη of Aristotle's *Rhetoric*.

5 They function slightly differently in hypothetical arguments, where they are used as warrants for the passage from the antecedent to the consequent in the argument's hypothetical premiss.

6 The question will seem less absurd if the reader remembers that 'animal' does not carry the same connotations for Boethius as it does for us; for Boethius, an animal is basically something that has the capacity for sensory perception, so that angels (on some accounts) are animals in this sense.

(a)   an animal is an animate substance capable of perceiving

(b)   a tree is not an animate substance capable of perceiving

and so a tree is not an animal (because „that to which the definition of a genus does not belong is not a species of the genus defined"). The intermediate term *animate substance capable of perceiving* is linked to *tree* and *animal*, the two terms of the question, in such a way that we can link them to each other in the conclusion of the argument. The intermediate term in this example is a definition; that is, the intermediate term *animate substance capable of perceiving* falls into that genus of things which we call 'definition', and so the Differentia for this argument is *definition*.

Boethius gives two different lists of such Differentiae, one taken from the Greek commentator Themistius, the other taken from Cicero. The Themistian and Ciceronian lists of Differentiae are each supposed to be exhaustive; that is, they each list all the genera of intermediate terms which could be used to make sound dialectical arguments.[7] The Differentiae in these lists aid in finding arguments because they aid in finding intermediates between the two terms in a dialectical question. A Differentia does not specify some particular intermediate to be used to join the terms in the conclusion of an argument but rather gives a genus of intermediates appropriate to the argument. So Differentiae are Topics or places for arguments, because as genera of intermediate terms they „contain" intermediate terms, which themselves „contain" and hence give rise to arguments. The complete Boethian art for using these Differentiae is complicated and spelled out in detail in *De top. diff.*[8] It makes provision for hypothetical as well as categorical arguments, and it ties together the functions of the Differentiae and the maximal propositions by making use of the four Aristotelian predicables (genus, definition, property, and accident).

II

Boethius's influence on later medieval philosophy is, of course, enormous, and his treatment of the Topics is no exception to that general rule. Later medieval philosophers had a strong interest in dialectic. The whole technique of the *disputatio*, for example, and the consequent literature on *obligationes* have their ultimate origin in dialectic; and the study of the Topics was considered a regular part of logic and treated in a section of its own in elementary logic texts. For a long time, Boethius was the most important, and sometimes the sole source for the study of the Topics, and his work remained an important indirect source even when it was superseded by later treatments of the subject. For example, three of the best known thirteenth-century logicians, William of Sherwood, Peter of Spain, and Lambert of Auxerre, all have a chapter on Topics in their introductory logic texts; and all three reproduce the Boethian list of Topics and the major Boethian categorizations or divisions of the Topics.

For the sake of putting Boethius's work on the Topics into medieval perspective and of understanding the changes and developments in the Topics, it is useful to consider the treatments of the Topics among some of these later medieval philosophers. In particular, it is worthwhile examining the discussion of the Topics in Peter of Spain's *Tractatus*,[9] which was the most widely used textbook of logic on the Continent from the late thirteenth to the end of the fifteenth century.[10]. Its discussion of the Topics is very similar to discussions found in

---

7   For Boethius's explanation of the existence of *two* lists, *each* of which is exhaustive, see the beginning of Book III of *De top. diff.*

8   For a complete analysis of Boethius's method for using Topics, see Stump, *Boethius's De Topicis differentiis*, pp. 179-204.

9   Ed. L. M. De Rijk (Assen, 1972).

10   *Ibid.*, pp. XCV-C.

several of the scholastics contemporary with or earlier than Peter. Besides being a representative and influential treatment of the Topics, Peter's discussion is heavily dependent (directly or, more likely, indirectly)[11] on Boethius's account. The chapter on dialectic in the *Tractatus* is like *De top. diff.* in organization. It begins with a series of definitions and then lists the Topics with a description and example of each. The definitions and the listing are those in *De top. diff.*, and in some places Peter's words are equivalent to a quotation from Boethius.[12] Consequently, comparison of Boethius and Peter is not difficult. Some of the recent literature has suggested that Peter's work on the Topics is simply a slightly varied compilation drawn from Boethius's *De top. diff.* Otto Bird, for example, who has published a number of very useful articles on the medieval Topics, says that Peter's discussion of the Topics „is little more than a summary of the first half of BDT [*De top. diff.*],"[13] and that „Peter of Spain made a précis of it [*De top. diff.*] (primarily of the second book) and provided additional Maxims in the fifth tract of his Summulae [*Tractatus*]."[14] But such a view shows a mistaken understanding of both Peter and Boethius. In what follows here, I will examine Peter's discussion of the Topics in considerable detail in order to exhibit with some accuracy a method for using Topics that, despite its apparent similarity to Boethius's method, is in fact very different from it; by doing so, I hope to show what Peter's method comes to and as a result to clarify the nature of the Boethian art of Topics.

III

Peter's treatise on the Topics is not an isolated work on the subject; there are many such treatises from the early scholastic period onward. To understand Peter's discussion, it is helpful to take into account treatments of the Topics in earlier and contemporary works, such as Garlandus Compotista's *Dialectica*;[15] the anonymous treatises *Introductiones Montane minores*, *Abbreviatio Montana*, *Tractatus Anagnini*, *Introductiones Parisienses*, *Logica „Ut dicit"*, *Logica „Cum sit nostra"*, *Dialectica Monacensis*;[16] William of Sherwood's *Intro-*

---

11 Cf., *Tractatus*, p. xciii, n. 5.
12 Cf., for example, Peter, *Tractatus*, p. 55.17 and Boethius, *De top. diff.*, 1180C4-5, Peter p. 55.23 and Boethius 1183A9-10, and Peter p. 56.16-18 and Boethius 1184B13-C1.
13 „The Tradition of the Logical Topics: Aristotle to Ockham", *Journal of the History of Ideas*, 23 (1962), p. 313.
14 „The Formalizing of the Topics in Mediaeval Logic", *Notre Dame Journal of Formal Logic*, 1 (1960), 140. Jan Pinborg echoes Bird's view of Peter. Cf. „Topik und Syllogistik im Mittelalter", in *Sapienter Ordinare: Festgabe für Erich Kleineidam*, ed. F. Hoffmann, L. Scheffczyk, and K. Feiereis (Leipzig, 1969), p. 164; and *Logik und Semantik im Mittelalter* (Stuttgart-Bad Cannstatt, 1972), p. 75. De Rijk, ed., *Tractatus*, p. xciii seems to agree at least in part with Bird's view: „This tract [chap. V of *Tractatus*] is not a compilation from Aristotle's *Topica* but from Boethius' *De topicis differentiis I* and *II*, with some additions from Aristotle's *Topics*." He argues in note 5 on the same page that Peter's treatment is not taken directly from Boethius: rather, he says, it is „useful to point to the treatment of the *loci* in the Logica *Cum sit nostra*, pp. 438-445 or to that in the somewhat older work, *Dialectica Monacensis*, pp. 528-555." De Rijk's point is very likely right, but what can be inferred from the claim in the text and the note is that Peter's work on Topics amounts to an indirect compilation from Boethius's *De top. diff.*
15 Ed. L. M. de Rijk (Assen, 1959), pp. 86-114.
16 For the major treatment of the Topics in these last treatises, see *Logica Modernorum*, ed. L.M. de Rijk, II (Assen, 1967), pt. 2,47-67, 85-97, 242-251, 365-371, 401-408, 438-445, 528-555 (cf. also 504-506).

ductiones in logicam;[17] and Lambert of Auxerre's *Logica.*[18] Abelard produced a very long and detailed treatment of the Topics,[19] and he also wrote a commentary on Boethius's *De top. diff.*[20] but Abelard's treatment tends to be idiosyncratic or allied to accounts of Topics in later scholastics such as Ockham.[21]

Peter's treatise on the Topics begins with a discussion of the word *'ratio'* and its different senses, because in one sense of the word, *ratio* is the genus of argument in Boethius's definition of argument.[22] According to Peter, *ratio* in that definition is a *middle* (or intermediate) entailing or implying a conclusion.[23] An argument, which is a reason (*ratio*) producing belief regarding something that was in doubt, is a middle proving a conclusion, and a conclusion is a proposition that must be confirmed by an argument.[24] To understand clearly what Peter means by 'argument' here, it would be helpful to know more precisely what he conceives of as a middle, but Peter says only that a middle is what has two extremes (p.55.22). In the context it is hard not to suppose that by 'middle' Peter means to refer to the middle term of an Aristotelian syllogism,[25] but we will see as we go on whether such an interpretation is justified.

After a brief discussion of the difference between argument and argumentation, in which Peter provides Boethius's definition of argumentation,[26] he considers the four different kinds of argumentation. Syllogisms have been treated at length in an earlier treatise (or chapter) of the book, and the bulk of this section on argumentation is devoted to the enthymeme. Peter explains briefly that an enthymeme is a syllogism with a premise missing and then shows how enthymemes are reduced to syllogisms: ,,It is important to know that every enthymeme must be reduced to a syllogism. In every enthymeme there are three terms, as in a syllogism; of these terms, two are put in the conclusion and are the extremes, and the other

---

17   *Introductiones Magistri Guilelmi de Shyreswode in logicam,* ed. Martin Grabmann, in *Sitzungsberichte der bayerischen Akademie der Wissenschaften,* Heft 10 (Munich, 1937), pp. 30-104. For corrections of Grabmann's text, see John Malcolm, ,,On Grabmann's Text of William of Sherwood," *Vivarium,* 9 (1971), 108-118, For an annotated translation, see *William of Sherwood's Introduction to Logic,* tr. Norman Kretzmann (Minneapolis, 1966).

18   Lambert of Auxerre, *Logica (Summa Lamberti),* ed. Franco Alessio (Florence, 1971). There is also an incomplete and very general commentary on *De top. diff.* by Martin of Dacia, *Martini de Dacia Opera,* ed. H. Roos, Corpus philosophorum Danicorum medii aevi (Hauniae, 1961), pp. 317-327; and a commentary by Radulphus Brito, edited by N.J. Green-Pedersen, *Cahiers de l'institut du moyen âge grec et latin* 26:1-121.

19   Peter Abelard, *Dialectica,* ed. L. M. de Rijk (Assen, 1970), pp. 253-466.

20   Peter Abelard, *Scritti di Logica,* ed. Mario dal Pra (Florence, 1969), pp. 205-330.

21   This is not to say that Abelard's treatment had no influence on the tradition of the Topics or that it bears no resemblance to the discussions of the Topics in Peter and Boethius. But Abelard's account seems in some respects more sophisticated and advanced than Peter's, so that it might be more sensible to read Abelard in the light of Peter of Spain, rather than the other way around. See Bird, ,,Tradition of the Logical Topics", pp. 317 and 320.

22   Cf. *De top. diff.* 1174D1-2.

23   ,,*Medium inferens conclusionem,*" p. 55.12-14.

24   *Tractatus,* ed. De Rijk, p. 55.13-18. Peter says, ,,*argumentum est ... medium probans conclusionem que debet confirmari per argumentum*" (p. 55.17-18). He seems to mean something like the two different definitions I suggest here and not one circular definition, for he goes on to spell out the definition of 'conclusion': ,,*Est enim conclusio argumento vel argumentis approbata propositio*" (p. 55.19).

25   In the passage on enthymemes immediately following, Peter uses *'medium'* to refer to the middle term of a syllogism.

26   ,,Argumentation is the explication of the argument in discourse ... the whole discourse composed of premises and condusion," pp. 55.23, 56.4-5; cf., for example, *De top. diff.* 1174D8-9 and 1183B4-11 in conjunction with 1184D10-14.

39

is a middle and is never put in the conclusion. Of the extremes, one is taken twice in the enthymeme and the other once. A universal proposition must be produced from the extreme taken once and the middle in keeping with the requirement of [the syllogistic] mood. In this way, a syllogism will be produced."[27] He gives the example, „Every animal is running; therefore, every man is running." The premise needed to make the enthymeme a syllogism, according to Peter's theory above, is a universal proposition composed of the middle, *animal*, and the extreme taken only once, *man*. The proposition can be negative or affirmative, and the middle can be the subject or the predicate; and so the resulting syllogism will be either first or third figure. But there is no valid third-figure syllogism with a universal affirmative conclusion; and the only first-figure syllogism with a universal affirmative conclusion is Barbara. So the missing premise will have to be a universal affirmative with the middle term as predicate, namely, ‚Every man is an animal.' Peter simply gives the missing premise in the passage without stating his reasons for choosing this combination of middle and extreme; but the reasoning I have provided to explain that choice of the missing premise seems to be what Peter has in mind when he says that the missing premise ought to be constructed „in keeping with the requirement of [the syllogistic] mood."

Peter begins his general discussion of Topics with a definition of a Topic and a statement of its function. An argument is confirmed (*confirmatur*) by a Topic, Peter says; and a Topic is the seat (*sedes*) of an argument, or that from which a fitting argument for the question at issue is drawn.[28] Since Peter has defined argument earlier as a certain kind of middle, what is drawn from a Topic is a middle of some sort. Hence a Topic functions as part of the proof for a conclusion, and it does so by providing a middle.

Included in this general discussion of Topics is some of the basic theory about Topics found in Boethius. Peter divides a Topic into maximal proposition (which he abbreviates as '*maxima*', 'maxim') and Differentia, which he defines much as Boethius does: the Differentia is a differentia (specific difference) of maximal propositions; and a maximal proposition, or maxim, is a proposition for which there is no prior or better-known proposition. The Topics are also divided into the three main groups found in *De top. diff.* Book II (the Themistian division of the Topics), namely, intrinsic, extrinsic, and intermediate, depending on whether the argument is taken from the nature of one of the terms in the argument's question or from what is external to their nature or partly from their nature and partly from without (p. 59).

The first Topic Peter gives in detail is the intrinsic Topic *from definition*. The Topic *from definition*, he says, is the relationship of a definition to what it defines (the *definitum*), and the Topic contains four arguments and four maxims (p. 60.10-12). Peter identifies the four arguments by specifying four sorts of premises for enthymemes: „First, by using the definition as the subject in an affirmative proposition; second, by using it as the predicate in an affirmative proposition; third, by using it as the subject in a negative proposition; and fourth, by using it as the predicate in a negative proposition" (p. 60.13-15). Since many things are definitions, this Topic contains not four arguments but four sorts of argument. The rest of the section on this Topic consists in examples of these four sorts of arguments and appropriate maxims for them; and the examples for this and every other Topic in Peter's treatise on the Topics are all enthymemes.

27 P. 57.3-10. „*Sciendum autem quod omne entimema debet reduci ad sillogismum. Ergo in quolibet entimemate sunt tres termini sicut in sillogismo. Quorum terminorum duo ponuntur in conclusione et sunt extremitates, et alius est medium et numquam ponitur in conclusione. Illarum autem extremitatum altera est sumpta bis in entimemate, altera semel. Et ex illa extremitate semel sumpta et medio debet fieri propositio universalis secundum exigentiam modi et sic fiet sillogismus.*"

28 P. 58.10-13; cf. *De top. diff.* 1185A4-5 and ff.

Peter does not say that his examples are enthymemes; and all the examples he gives for Topics, here and in the rest of Treatise V, differ in an important respect from the examples he gives of an enthymeme: the quantity of the propositions in all the examples for Topics is indefinite or singular rather than universal or particular. Nonetheless, I am regarding these examples as enthymemes for three reasons. First, they fit Peter's definition of enthymeme (closely paraphrased from Boethius, 1184 B13-C1) at the beginning of this Treatise: „An enthymeme is an imperfect syllogism, that is, discourse in which the precipitous conclusion is derived without all the propositions having been laid down beforehand."[29] The definition does not exclude arguments composed of an indefinite premise and conclusion. Furthermore, when Peter discusses indefinite propositions in connection with complete syllogisms, he does not exclude them altogether; he says only, „A syllogism cannot be produced from propositions which are all particular or indefinite or singular."[30] An enthymeme can be composed of an indefinite premise and conclusion and still be reduced to a complete syllogism by the addition of one premise, provided that that premise is universal. Second, at the start of this Treatise (p. 56.10 ff.) Peter gives an apparently exhaustive list of the varieties of argumentation, that is, the varieties of legitimate combinations of premises and conclusions (see p. 56.4-5); they are syllogism, induction, enthymeme, and example. It is hard to see how Peter's combinations of premise and conclusion could be classified except as enthymemes because they are more like enthymemes than they are like syllogisms, inductions, or examples; and Peter gives no other classifications into which they might fit. Third, as far as I can tell, nothing turns on the indefinite quantity of the propositions in Peter's examples; nothing explicit or implicit in Peter's account makes much of the indefinite quantity of the propositions. In the rest of my analysis of Peter, therefore, I will refer to his examples of arguments as enthymemes.

Indefinite propositions can be interpreted either as universal or as particular propositions; for example, 'a man is an animal' should be taken as a universal, but 'a man is a father' as a particular. William of Sherwood's interpretation of indefinites and singulars often seems determined more by the needs of a certain syllogistic mood than by any theory about the nature of indefinites and singulars; for example, he takes 'an animal is not a quantity' as a particular[31] and 'Socrates is included under „every man" ' as a universal.[32] In the discussion that follows, I will read Peter's indefinite propositions either as universals or as particulars, depending on what the context calls for.

The four enthymemes given for the Topic *from definition* are these:

(1) A mortal rational animal is running; therefore, a man is running.
(2) Socrates is a mortal rational animal; therefore, Socrates is a man.
(3) A mortal rational animal is not running; therefore, a man is not running.
(4) A stone is not a mortal rational animal; therefore, a stone is not a man. (p. 60)

Their corresponding maxims are:

(1') Whatever is predicated of the definition is also predicated of the thing defined.[33]

29   „*Entimema est sillogismus imperfectus, idest oratio in qua non omnibus antea positis propositionibus infertur festinata conclusio,*" p. 56.16-18.
30   „*ex puris particularibus vel indefinitis vel singularibus non potest fieri sillogismus,*" p. 45.1-2.
31   „*Animal non est quantitas,*" *Introductiones,* Grabmann, ed., p. 59.21; Kretzmann, tr., p. 76.
32   „*Sortes est sub eo, quod est omnis homo,*" *ibid.,* Grabmann, ed., p. 61.32-33; Kretzmann, tr., p. 80.
33   „*quidquid predicatur de diffinitione, et de diffinito.*"

(2') Whatever the definition is predicated of, the thing defined is also predicated of.[34]

(3') Whatever is removed from the definition is also removed from the thing defined.[35]

(4') Whatever the definition is removed from, the thing defined is also removed from.[36] [Ibid.]

If we look at the arguments given for this first Topic in the light of the introductory material Peter presents at the beginning of this Treatise, particularly the special consideration accorded to enthymemes and the method for reducing enthymemes to syllogisms, then it is easy to suppose that the Topics are the instruments for reduction to syllogism (or to syllogistic inferences). Such a view of the Topics is not uncommon among contemporary writers,[37] and is also taken by some later medievals.[38] Peter's contemporary, Lambert of Auxerre, appears to take Topical arguments in this way; at the end of his treatment of the Topics, he says,

> it can be said that [an argument depending on the Topics] is an enthymematic argumentation ... and can be reduced to a syllogistic argumentation. ... [For example,] 'a man is running, therefore a mortal rational animal[39] is running' is an enthymeme [composed of] the major [premise] and conclusion. Let the minor premise be put forward, and there will be a syllogism in the third mood of the first figure [Darii] in this way: 'Every man is running; a mortal rational animal is a man; therefore, a mortal rational animal is running.' It should not cause surprise that what is taken as an indefinite in the enthymeme is taken as a universal in the syllogism, because a syllogism cannot be produced without a universal, although an enthymeme can by itself be produced correctly without a universal.[40]

And William of Sherwood, another contemporary of Peter's, also regularly reduces Topical arguments to syllogisms.[41] In what follows, I will show the way Peter's discussions of the first five Topics lend themselves to such a view of Topics and how Topics function according to that view. I will then show how Peter's Topics cannot be considered solely or primarily as instruments for reducing enthymemes to syllogisms and that they confirm arguments in a more complicated and perhaps a looser way.

If we consider the enthymemes for the Topic *from definition* according to Peter's method for reducing enthymemes to syllogisms, we see that in each enthymeme the middle term is *mortal rational animal* and the term taken only once is *man*. No valid syllogism con-

---

34 „de quocumque predicatur diffinitio, et diffinitum."
35 „quidquid removetur a diffinitione, et a diffinito."
36 „a quocumque removetur diffinitio, et diffinitum."
37 See, for example, Jan Pinborg, „Topik und Syllogistik", p. 159.
38 See, for example, Bird, „Formalizing of the Topics", p. 146; according to Bird, Burley, for example, thinks that the Topics reduce material inferences to formal inferences, inferences that hold good solely in virtue of their form.
39 Reading *'animal'* for *'homo.'* The text as Alessio gives it is clearly mistaken.
40 „dici posset quod est argumentatio empthimemica ... et ad sillogisticam argumentationem posset reduci ... 'homo currit, ergo homo rationale mortale currit' empthimema est ex maiori et conclusione; et ponatur minor: erit sillogismus in tertio prime figure sic: 'omnis homo currit, animal rationale mortale est homo, ergo animal rationale mortale currit'; nec mirandum est si sumatur in sillogismo universalis, que sumetur in empthimemate infinita, quia sine universali non potest fieri sillogismus: empthimema vero bene potest fieri sine universali" (Logica, ed Alessio, pp. 139-140). I have no explanation for the curious assignment of quantity in the syllogism. Lambert's explanation seems both lame and artificial.
41 I do not mean to imply nor is it at all clear that either William or Lambert thinks that the *primary function* of a Topic has to do with reduction to syllogism.

tains exactly one or three negative propositions; there are three affirmative or one affirmative and two negative propositions in every valid syllogism. And every valid syllogism contains at least one universal premise. So the missing premise in each of the four enthymemes is a universal affirmative proposition whose two terms are *mortal rational animal* and *man*.

The first enthymeme will be reduced to a first-figure syllogism if we take the definition as the predicate in the missing premise and to a third-figure syllogism if we take it as the subject. The premise given in the enthymeme is the major premise since the extreme in it is the predicate rather than the subject of the conclusion and hence this extreme is the major term; so the missing premise is the minor premise of the appropriate syllogism. The syllogism, then, will be a syllogism in IAI in either the first or third figures if we read Peter's indefinites as particulars. But since there are no such valid first-figure syllogisms, the enthymeme must be reduced to the third-figure syllogism Disamis; and the missing premise is 'Every mortal rational animal is a man.'

In the second enthymeme, the missing premise is the major premise; and the appropriate syllogism is AII in the first or second figure, depending on whether the missing premise is 'Every man is a mortal rational animal' or 'Every mortal rational animal is a man.' But there are no valid AII syllogisms in the second figure; so the premise needed is again 'Every mortal rational animal is a man,' and the enthymeme reduces to a first-figure syllogism in Darii.

The third enthymeme reduces to OAO in either the first or third figures. There are no valid first-figure syllogisms in OAO; so the appropriate syllogism here is the third-figure Bocardo, and the missing premise is again 'Every mortal rational animal is a man.'

It seems clear that the propositions for the last enthymeme ought to be taken as universals, and the appropriate syllogism is one in AEE. If we add the same premise here as we did to the other enthymemes, namely, 'Every mortal rational animal is a man,' we have an invalid first-figure syllogism. The other possibility is a second-figure syllogism in AEE; and there is such a valid syllogism: Camestres. So for this enthymeme the missing premise is 'Every man is a mortal rational animal.'

The Topic following the Topic *from definition* is the Topic *from what is defined (the definitum)*; and it, too, has four sorts of arguments and four corresponding maxims. The four enthymemes and the corresponding maxims are these:

(1)   A man is running; therefore, a mortal rational animal is running.
(2)   Socrates is a man; therefore, Socrates is a mortal rational animal.
(3)   A man is not running; therefore, a mortal rational animal is not running.
(4)   A stone is not a man; therefore, a stone is not a mortal rational animal.
        [p. 61]
(1')   Whatever is predicated of the thing defined is also predicated of the definition.[42]
(2')   Whatever the thing defined is predicated of, the definition is also predicated of.[43]
(3')   Whatever is removed from the thing defined is also removed from the definition.[44]
(4')   Whatever the thing defined is removed from, the definition is also removed from.[45] [Ibid.]

42   „quicquid predicatur de diffinito, et de diffinitione.“
43   „de quocumque predicatur diffinitum, et diffinitio.“
44   „quicquid removetur a diffinito, et a diffinitione.“
45   „a quocumque removetur diffinitum, et diffinitio.“

They reduce to the same syllogisms as those from definition: Disamis, Darii, Bocardo, and Camestres. For the first three enthymemes, the missing premise is 'Every man is a mortal rational animal'; and for the last one, it is 'Every mortal rational animal is a man.'

The Topic *from explanation of the name* is the next one provided with examples. In this case, too, we are given four enthymemes with their maxims.

(1)   A lover of wisdom is running; therefore, a philosopher is running.

(2)   A philosopher is running; therefore, a lover of wisdom is running.

(3)   A lover of wisdom does not envy; therefore, a philosopher does not envy.

(4)   A philosopher does not envy; therefore, a lover of wisdom does not envy. [p. 62]

(1')   Whatever is predicated of the explanation is also predicated of what is explained.[46]

(2')   Whatever the explanation is predicated of, that which is explained is also predicated of.[47]

(3')   Whatever is removed from the explanation is also removed from what is explained.[48]

(4')   Whatever the explanation is removed from, that which is explained is also removed from.[49] [*Ibid.*]

In all four, *lover of wisdom* is the middle term, and *philosopher* is the term taken only once in the enthymeme. For the first two enthymemes, the missing premise is 'Every lover of wisdom is a philosopher'; and the enthymemes reduce to Disamis and Darii, as in the Topic *from definition* and the Topic *from the definitum*. The missing premise in the second two enthymemes is 'Every philosopher is a lover of wisdom'; and the appropriate syllogisms are Celarent and Baroco.

One enthymeme is given for the Topic *from genus* (that is, from the relationship of the genus to the species): „A stone is not an animal; therefore, a stone is not a man" (p. 63. 16-18); and two for the Topic *from species* (the relationship of the species to the genus): (1) „A man is running; therefore, an animal is running"; and (2) „Socrates is a man; therefore, Socrates is an animal" (p. 64.1-10). The missing premise for all three is 'Every man is an animal'; and the appropriate syllogisms are Camestres, Disamis, and Darii respectively.

In every one of the enthymemes considered above, the Topic is a relationship between the things referred to by the middle term of the enthymeme and one of the extremes − in every case, the extreme taken only once in the enthymeme. When the middle and the extreme taken only once are used to make a universal premise, according to Peter's method for reducing enthymemes to syllogisms, the resulting premise presents an instance of the relationship that is the Differentia, or some part of that relationship. As we have seen, Peter holds that the function of the Differentiae is to confirm arguments and that they do so by providing a middle or intermediate. We might be inclined to think that the middle provided must be a middle term; but an enthymeme already has a middle term and so cannot be provided with, or confirmed by the addition of, a middle term. What does depend on the Differentiae is not a middle term, it seems, but rather a premise that is based on the relationship that is the Differentia or some part of the relationship. That premise, made as Peter says the

46   „quicquid predicatur de interpretatione, et de interpretato."
47   „de quocumque predicatur interpretatio, et interpretatum."
48   „quicquid removetur ab interpretatione, et ab interpretato."
49   „a quocumque removetur interpretatio, et interpretatum."

missing premise for an enthymeme should be made, turns the enthymeme into a valid syllogism and by doing so confirms the inference made in the enthymeme. It seems, then, that the Differentiae provide missing premises for enthymemes and that Peter's method of the Topics is a method for reducing enthymemes to syllogisms. And the Differentiae do provide a middle as Peter's account requires, not, however, by providing a „middle" proposition (middle in the sense that it is between the premise and the conclusion of the enthymeme), but instead by providing a bridge between the lone premise and the conclusion of the enthymeme, a link that validates the passage from premise to conclusion.

In William of Sherwood's treatment of those Topics we have been considering in Peter's account, we find explicit the procedure that seems implicit in Peter. William, too, gives enthymemes as examples for Topics, and he reduces almost all his enthymemes to syllogisms. Two of his enthymemes, those serving as examples for the Topic *from species*[50] are the same as Peter's. William reduces them to syllogisms in the way I suggested Peter's enthymemes ought to be reduced. He leaves the enthymeme's propositions indefinite or singular, and he adds a universal premise taken from the Differentia. As I did with Peter's enthymemes, he takes the indefinite or singular propositions as particulars; and he claims that the enthymemes are reduced to Disamis and Darii respectively, the same two moods that Peter's method for reducing enthymemes yields for these examples.[51]

We have considered in detail, however, only the first five Topics in Peter's treatise on the Topics. The sixth is the Topic *from an integral whole*, the relationship of the integral whole to its part. One enthymeme is given for this Topic: „A house exists; therefore, a wall exists" (p. 64.12-17). According to Peter's method for reducing enthymemes to syllogisms, we pick out the middle term — *house* — and the extreme taken only once — *wall*; and we combine these two terms into a universal proposition in keeping with the requirements of the syllogistic mood to get a valid syllogism. The premise given in the enthymeme has the middle as subject, and so the appropriate syllogism cannot be in the second figure. The enthymeme's premise is also the major premise and should be read as particular (an I premise), so the first figure is ruled out since it has no valid moods with major premises in I. That leaves the third figure; the missing premise must be a universal premise with *house* as subject and *wall* as predicate; and the premise will have to be affirmative because the conclusion is affirmative. If we proceed straightforwardly to produce the needed premise as a universal affirmative with the middle as subject, we will reduce the enthymeme to a valid syllogism in Disamis. But the premise added will have to be 'Every house is a wall'; and it is absurd to suppose that the enthymeme would be confirmed by such a premise. Peter's method for reducing enthymemes to syllogisms apparently will not work in this case.

We could try to find the missing premise by working directly from the Differentia since the Differentia is supposed to provide the argument and confirm the enthymeme. The Differentia is *from an integral whole*; that is, the enthymeme depends on a relationship between

50 *Introductiones,* Grabmann, ed., p. 60; Kretzmann, tr., p. 77.
51 There are more possibilities for arguments than those generated by considering only syllogistic mood and the quality (affirmative or negative) of the propositions. The quantity (universal or particular) of the propositions can be varied, too, to provide different arguments in different moods of the syllogism. For instance, Peter's enthymemes for the Topic *from definition* reduce to syllogisms in Disamis, Darii, Bocardo, and Camestres. If enthymemes were generated by varying quantity as well, there would also be enthymemes that reduced to Darapti, Barbara, Felapton, and Baroco (corresponding to Disamis, Darii, Bocardo, and Camestres). And in a later development of the Topics, Ockham, for example, does take the quantity of an argument's propositions into account. See Otto Bird, „Topic and Consequence in Ockham's Logic," *Notre Dame Journal of Formal Logic,* 2 (1961), 69-70.

an integral whole and one of its parts. In this case, the integral whole is a house, and its part is a wall. So we might make this premise from the Differentia: 'A wall is part of a house' or perhaps even the universal, 'Every wall is part of a house.' But we cannot use either of these propositions to reduce the enthymeme to a syllogism because in the context *part of a house* would be a fourth term. Apparently this enthymeme cannot be confirmed by adding a premise according to Peter's method or directly from the Differentia. However the Topic is meant to confirm the argument here, it does not do so by reducing it to a syllogism.

For the Topic *from an integral whole*, William of Sherwood gives the same enthymeme as Peter; and he adds: „Arguments from an integral whole reduce to the third mood of the first figure [*Darii*], as follows: 'every part of the house exists (since the house exists), a wall is part of the house; therefore a wall exists.' "[52] As William gives it, the argument is this:

(1) A house exists.
(2) Therefore, every part of the house exists.
(3) A wall is part of the house.
(4) Therefore, a wall exists.

The second, third, and fourth steps constitute the syllogism in Darii, and the enthymeme's premise is not one of the premises in the syllogism. The syllogism's minor premise, step (3) in the argument, is the premise generated from the Differentia in question here, and it describes the relationship between wall and house, the particular whole and part in the enthymeme. The syllogism's major premise, step (2), is the conclusion of an enthymeme very similar to the original enthymeme 'A house exists; therefore, a wall exists.' The maxim William gives for this Differentia is „What goes together with an [integral] whole in respect of proportional and perceptible parts (*secundum partes proportionales et notabiles*) goes together with a part."[53] And the inference from step (1) to step (2) in the argument above seems to depend on this maxim, which attributes certain predicates of an integral whole to any and every part of that whole. The inference from (1) to (2) seems to go like this:

(A) What goes together with an integral whole in respect of proportional and perceptible parts goes together with every part of that whole.
(B) Every house is an integral whole.
(C) Existence goes together with some house in respect of proportional and perceptible parts.
(D) Therefore, existence goes together with every part of that house.

Steps (C) and (D) are equivalent to steps (1)[54] and (2) in William's argument; (B) is the premise related to the Differentia; and (A) is the Differentia's maxim.

So in the argument William provides to show that the enthymeme for this Differentia can be reduced to Darii, one premise of the syllogism in Darii comes from the Differentia (the relationship involved in the enthymeme). The other premise is derived from the enthymeme's premise (premise C above), a premise related to the Differentia (premise B above), and the maxim for the enthymeme (premise A above). The valid inferring of the conclusion depends on the enthymeme's premise, the Differentia, and the maxim.

---

52   „*Et reducuntur argumenta iuxta hunc locum in tertium prime sic: quelibet pars domus, quia domus est, est. Paries est pars domus quia domus est* [sic!]. *Ergo paries est.*" *Introductiones*, Grabmann, ed., p. 61.6-9; Kretzmann, tr., p. 79.
53   *Ibid.*, Grabmann, ed., p. 60.32-33; Kretzmann, tr., pp. 78-79.
54   Except, of course, for the qualification about proportional and perceptible parts, which seems to be taken as understood in (1).

The Topic *from an integral whole* is typical of most of the remaining Topics in Peter's treatise. Take, for example, the Topic *from a material cause*. One of the enthymemes for that Topic is 'There is no iron; therefore, there are no iron weapons', or more conveniently, for present purposes, 'Iron is not; therefore, iron weapons are not' (p. 68.4-5). The enthymeme's premise is the major premise and *iron* is the middle term; so the appropriate syllogism for this enthymeme must be a first- or third-figure syllogism in OAO. The only combination that gives a valid syllogism is the third-figure syllogism Bocardo; but that mood requires the blatantly false premise 'Everything that is iron is iron weapons.' The proposition describing the relationship that is the Differentia here would have to be something like 'Iron is the matter (or material cause) of iron weapons'; such a proposition would introduce a fourth term if it were added to the enthymeme in order to produce a syllogism.

William of Sherwood gives a similar enthymeme for this Topic: „the Moors do not have iron; therefore they do not have iron weapons."[55] And he says the enthymeme is to be reduced to Ferio in this way: „no people who do not have iron are people who have iron weapons, the Moors are people who do not have iron; therefore the Moors are not people who have iron weapons."[56] The syllogism's minor premise is the premise in the enthymeme; the major premise, however, seems to depend on or be drawn from the maxim for this Differentia: „Where the matter is lacking, what depends on that matter is lacking (*deficiente materia deficit materiatum*)".[57] That maxim and a proposition drawn from the Differentia stating that iron is the matter of iron weapons (the *materiatum*, what depends on the matter) yield the conclusion that all people who lack iron lack iron weapons and so also that no people who lack iron are people who have iron weapons, which is the major premise of William's syllogism.

In much the same way, the maxims and Differentiae in Peter's treatise can be combined to confirm arguments, even for the arguments of Topics that can be confirmed by reduction to syllogisms. For example, the Topic *from definition* has as its first enthymeme 'A mortal rational animal is running; therefore, a man is running' and the corresponding maxim „Whatever is predicated of the definition is predicated also of the *definitum* (the thing defined)" (p. 60). The enthymeme, as we saw above, can be confirmed by reducing it to the third-figure syllogism Disamis, adding a premise describing the relationship of the Differentia. But it can also be confirmed without reduction to a syllogistic mood, by using the maxim and the Differentia:

(1) Whatever is predicated of the definition is predicated of the *definitum*.
(2) Mortal rational animal is the definition of the *definitum* man.
(3) Running is predicated of a mortal rational animal.
(4) Therefore, running is predicated also of man.

The first premise is the maxim; the second is the premise drawn from the relationship in the Differentia; and (3) and (4) are equivalent to the premise and conclusion of the original enthymeme.

Or, for another example, the Topic *from a quantitative whole* has as its first enthymeme „Every man is running; therefore, Socrates is running"; and the corresponding maxim is „Whatever is predicated of a quantitative whole is also predicated of any part of that whole"

---

55 *Introductiones*, Grabmann, ed., p. 63.29-30; Kretzmann, tr., p. 85.
56 *Ibid.*, Grabmann, ed., p. 63.32-34; Kretzmann, tr., p. 85.
57 *Ibid.*, Grabmann, ed., p. 63.30-31.

(pp. 64.24-65.5). If we take this as the premise from the Differentia: 'Every-man is the quantitative whole of which Socrates is a part,' then we can make a valid argument that yields the enthymeme's conclusion as we did above, from the premise drawn from the Differentia, the maxim, and the premise in the enthymeme.

Furthermore, of the different discussions of the Topics taken into account here,[58] when enthymemes and their confirming Topics are given, William's treatise is the only one to add appropriate syllogisms and to show that the enthymemes can be reduced to syllogisms. All the other discussions of the Topics, including Lambert's, leave syllogisms out of consideration and give only the enthymemes and their maxims. Peter himself, who spends some time explaining how to reduce enthymemes to syllogisms, makes no attempt to do so for his examples and presents enthymemes and maxims without any mention of corresponding syllogisms.

Peter's main interest, then, is not in confirming enthymemes by reducing them to syllogisms; and though such confirmation by reduction works for the arguments exemplifying the first Topics, it does not work for many of the enthymemes Peter gives. The reason Peter introduces his method for converting enthymemes to syllogisms and the way he means it to relate to confirmation by maxims are not clear. It seems likely that there is a disparity between Peter's theory and his practice with respect to the Topics. Peter inherits the Topics from logicians such as Garlandus and Abelard, who use them to validate conditional inferences.[59] But, like other terminist logicians, Peter's interest in conditional inferences is minimal by comparison with his interest in Aristotelian syllogistics, which he considers *the* fundamental system of logic. Fitting the Topics into a system of logic so dominated by the Aristotelian syllogism is not an easy job, and also apparently not one of primary concern to the terminists, whose interests centered more on the properties of terms than on the warrants for inferences. What seems to have happened in the case of a terminist such as Peter is that he reproduced and developed treatments of the Topics which he inherited from his predecessors, but gave an explanation of their function and purpose which was in accord with Aristotelian syllogistics, namely, that Topics confirm enthymemes. The resulting theory of Topics is not altogether coherent, and it was not long-lived. By the early fourteenth century in the works of logicians such as Burleigh and Ockham, Topics are again conceived of as providing warrants for conditional inferences and in fact become part of scholastic theories of consequences, or conditional inferences.[60]

In any case, the method of confirmation that seems to work for all the Topics in Peter's account is that using both maxims and Differentiae. The maxims are general principles that specifically validate enthymematic inferences for a certain relationship. They serve as specific inference warrants for certain enthymemes, and the Differentiae provide the information needed to apply them.

Otto Bird argues that many of the maxims work with the Differentiae to validate enthymemes because the maxims in question are laws of class logic. One of Peter's enthymemes for the Topic *from genus* is „An animal is not running; therefore, a man is not running," and

---

58   See the beginning of this chapter.
59   See my paper „Dialectic in the Eleventh to Thirteenth Centuries: Garlandus Compotista" in *History and Philosophy of Logic*, forthcoming.
60   See my paper „Topics: Their Development and Absorption into Theories of Consequences" in *The Cambridge History of Later Medieval Philosophy*, ed. Anthony Kenny, Norman Kretzmann, and Jan Pinborg, forthcoming.

its maxim is „What is removed from the genus is also removed from the species."[61] Bird thinks that the enthymeme's conclusion is validly inferred from the enthymeme's premise, the maxim for the enthymeme, and this premise drawn from the Differentia: 'Animal is the genus of the species man', and he formalizes the argument in this way. Let a and β be classes, and let M be the class of men and A the class of animals. Then,

$$(1) \quad ac\beta \rightarrow ((x) \sim (x\epsilon\beta \wedge \phi x) \rightarrow (x\epsilon a \wedge \phi x))$$
$$(2) \quad McA$$
$$(3) \quad \therefore \quad (x) \sim (x\epsilon A \wedge Rx) \rightarrow (x) \sim (x\epsilon M \wedge Rx)$$

And if the enthymeme's premise is added, the argument yields the conclusion of the enthymeme.[62]

Peter's enthymemes, then, work because there is a certain relationship between what is signified by the middle term and what is signified by one of the extreme terms (namely, the relationship spelled out in the Differentia) and because certain inferences are valid given that relationship (those falling under the maxim for a Differentia). Theoretically, a maxim is a self-evidently true generalization;[63] and so the inference in the enthymeme is shown to be valid once the enthymeme has, with the help of the Differentia, been shown to fall under the generalization that is the maxim. And it should be clear now what the middle is that the Differentia provides to confirm arguments: it is the relationship that holds between the middle term and one of the extremes in the enthymeme, on the basis of which the maxim can be applied. So in the first enthymeme for the Topic *from definition* – „A mortal rational animal is running; therefore, a man is running" – the relationship between the middle *mortal rational animal* and the extreme *man* is spelled out in the Differentia *from definition*. Given this relationship, those inferences that fall under the maxim for the enthymeme are valid. The maxim is „Whatever is predicated of the definition is predicated also of the *definitum*"; applied to the enthymeme, it validates the passage from premise to conclusion, and it can be applied to the enthymeme because the middle and extreme have the relationship of definition to *definitum*, which is the Differentia for this example. So the enthymematic argument is „confirmed," as Peter says it is, by the twofold Topic consisting in the Differentia and maxim for this argument.

IV

The method found in Peter's treatment of the Topics, then, is very different from that in Boethius's *De top. diff.* In Peter's treatise, the Topics are almost completely divorced from the predicables and from the dialectical dispute. There is no discussion of the question going with each Topic or of anything related to disputation; and there is no evidence here of the technique of arguing by question and answer, which Boethius thinks is characteristic of dialectic. For Peter, the Differentia is the *relationship* between the things referred to by a middle term and an extreme in the conclusion of an argument (for example, the relationship

---

61 In fact, neither the enthymeme nor its maxim is given in the text of De Rijk's edition of Peter's *Tractatus*, though both are in the apparatus as variants (p. 63). De Rijk's edition was not available at the time Bird was writing.

62 Bird, „Topic and Consequence in Ockham's Logic," p. 73.

63 See Peter, p. 59.

of definition to *definitum*).[64] For Boethius, the Differentia is simply the sort of thing that the middle term refers to (for example, a definition); and when he thinks of a relationship involving the middle term (or what it refers to), he thinks of it as the relation between the things referred to by the middle term and one of the terms in the *question*. The function of the Differentiae in the two methods is different, too. For Boethius, a Differentia provides a middle term or an intermediate between the two extremes in order to *produce* an argument. For Peter, a Differentia provides a premise or information needed in order to apply the maxim that *validates* the enthymeme's inference. And finally, Boethius's main purpose in *De top. diff.* is to teach the art of obtaining an argument for and belief in a certain conclusion; Peter's main interest is in explaining and justifying the validity of obvious and readily granted inferences that are enthymemes. Boethius explains at length that the method for the Topics belongs to the art of finding arguments rather than to the art of judging them. For Peter, the reverse is true; the function of the Topics in his treatise is solely to confirm arguments, to manifest and guarantee their validity. In Peter's treatment of the Topics, they are an interesting and important part of scholastic logic, but the Boethian art of discovering arguments has been lost.[65]

Virginia Polytechnic Institute

---

64 When Peter is giving Boethius's definitions of key terms in the introductory section of this treatise, he says that arguments may be taken from things that agree with the terms posited in the question (p. 59.28-31). But when he discusses the relationships that are the Differentiae, the relationships are those holding between a term in an enthymeme's premise and another term in that enthymeme's conclusion; see, for example, p. 61.21-25. See also *Dialectica Monacensis*, p. 528, where the point is discussed in some detail.

65 See, for example, Ernest A. Moody, *Truth and Consequence in Medieval Logic* (New York and Amsterdam, 1953).

FANNIE J. LEMOINE

THE PRECIOUS STYLE AS HEURISTIC DEVICE: THE FUNCTION OF INTRODUCTIONS TO THE ARTS IN MARTIANUS CAPELLA AND BOETHIUS

The first two books of Martianus Capella's *De Nuptiis Philologiae et Mercurii* and the introductory portion of each of the following seven books on the liberal arts are written in a style that is markedly different from the plain, unadorned language used for the didactic material of the handbooks themselves. The highly mannered style which Martianus employs in the first two books of the myth and in the introductory portraits of each of the Arts exhibits many of the faults and some of the virtues of the preciosity found in certain writers of the Late Empire.[1] On quick reading the style does not appear to agree with the theory of *elocutio* which Martianus himself expounds in the handbook on rhetoric. Neither does an extremely ornate and complicated introductory description seem an appropriate beginning for a manual of instruction.

The apparent discrepancy between Martianus' rhetorical theory and his stylistic practice could be dismissed as one more sign of the author's careless manner of compilation and general incompetence. Similarly, the joining of the highly figured language of the introductory descriptions to the compendia of the seven liberal arts might be waived aside as a conventional opening device designed to charm the reader and gain his goodwill. Certainly this is part of the argument Martianus himself cites at the beginning of the third book, before introducing each of the Arts in allegorical dress. And *satura*, the genre he claims for his work, can perhaps hold the *farrago* of philosophical fable, allegorical description and plain handbook that Martianus serves up in the *De Nuptiis*.

The same type of elaborate introduction followed by increasingly plain exposition may be found in Fulgentius' works. Both in the *Mythologies* and the *Exposition of the Content of Virgil* the openings turn upon the introduction of allegorical figures. The introduction of the *Mythologies* follows the mixed pattern of prose and verse used by Martianus and Boethius in the *Consolation*. In the *Content of Virgil* the personification of that poet appears as the major interlocutor of the following dialogue on the true meaning of the *Aeneid*.

In the works of Boethius the stylistic distance between elaborate introduction and plain

---

1   Although in English usage the term „precious" almost always has a derogatory connotation, I wish to avoid that implied evaluation as much as possible in the present paper. The traits of the precious style which I consider of particular importance for this study are:

        a. consistent choice of unusual, rare, or poetic vocabulary;
        b. frequent use of the most daring figures of speech and thought; and
        c. elaborate, repetitive prose rhythms.

    Certainly Latin writers of the Late Empire show features of preciosity associated with the *kakozelia* of the decadent period: an excessive attention to detail, an outrageous penchant for verbal pyrotechnics, and a monotonous repetitiveness of verbal trickery. A good discussion of these negative features of the precious style may be found in André Loyen's *Sidoine Apollinaire et l'esprit précieux en Gaule aux derniers jours de l'Empire* (Paris: Société d'édition „Les belles lettres", 1943).

exposition is much more skillfully bridged, but a certain distance still exists. The dedicatory letter to Symmachus that prefaces the *De Arithmetica* is the most obvious example of Boethius' use of a very highly polished, if not completely precious, style, and the allegorical setting with which the *Consolation* opens certainly stands within the figured tradition already exploited by Martianus and Fulgentius.

Clearly, then, by the sixth century such highly ornamented introductions have become part of accepted literary convention, convention that contrasts noticeably with the leisurely, pleasant *exordia* of, for example, Cicero's rhetorical or philosophical dialogues. However, to point to the convention is only the first step toward investigating the way in which the convention is used and the reasons for its popularity. Of course to a certain extent literary conventions are repeated because they lie ready to hand and are frequently selected for service without any conscious effort; but the choice of a stylistic opening that requires a great deal of effort presupposes other factors at work. To examine some of the reasons for this choice and some of the indirect factors that may have influenced the stylistic change is the concern of this paper.

One of the most obvious reasons for ornamentation is the need of charming the audience, of seizing and holding attention. However, in the works of Martianus Capella and Fulgentius few would doubt that the stylistic virtue of decorum is on occasions sacrificed before uncontrolled desire for decoration that does little to charm the audience. Another possible reason for the joining of allegorical personification and educational handbook is a derivative of the need to hold the audience's attention, that is the need to fill a locus of the memory. The fully developed allegorical figure may serve as a means for anchoring attention and focusing memory of the art.

This function of the elaborate introduction is linked to a philosophical and religious attitude toward the arts and learning that contrasts sharply with the less spiritualized and more practically political attitude found in Cicero or other classical writers. In many ways the allegorical introductions of the arts in the *De Nuptiis* may be compared to *agalmata*. They are ornaments but they function as testimonial statues adorning an area marked off from the profane crowd. They serve a symbolic as well as a purely decorative or a merely allegorical function. The elaborate stylistic devices, especially the use of word play, allegory and paradox, are not just ends in themselves but may well lead the reader to discovery of knowledge and insight not possible for those who spurn the liberal path.

Although the liberal arts are frequently seen as propaedeutic to philosophy or theology, the propaedeutic and heuristic function of certain aspects of the precious style has not been examined.[2] In this paper I intend to show that the precious style may be employed to foster the intellectual pursuit which frees the mind from the literal and leads to a discovery of a higher order. I also hope to suggest that in theory as well as in practice the Aristotelian stylistic virtue of *to prepon* is modified and undercut by the Latin writers of the Late Empire. That Augustine revolutionized rhetorical theory has long been acknowledged;[3] that this revolution falls within an entire pattern of change has perhaps not been sufficiently emphasized. Conse-

2   Jean Pépin has written an excellent article on the protreptic function of allegory. He does not, however, consider the full range of the figured style, of which allegory is only a part, nor the literary implications of the theory which he examines so well. See „Saint Augustin et la fonction protreptique de l'allégorie," *Recherches augustiniennes* I (1958), pp. 243-286.

3   One of the best discussions of Augustine's transformation of classical rhetorical theory is by Erich Auerbach in his *Latin Literary Language and its Public in Late Latin Antiquity and in the Middle Ages*, trans. Ralph Manheim (New York: Random House, 1965), pp. 27-66. For a more sober assessment of Augustine's contributions, see James J. Murphy, *Rhetoric in the Middle Ages* (Berkeley, Calif.: University of California Press, 1974), pp. 47-64.

quently a consideration of the theory of *elocutio* which Martianus gives in his handbook on rhetoric will be the first concern. It will be followed by an examination of Martianus' stylistic practice in the introduction to the art of rhetoric and a short investigation of aspects of the precious style which appear in Boethius' introduction to the *De Institutione Arithmetica* and in the *Consolatio Philosophiae*.

The fifth book of the *De Nuptiis Philologiae et Mercurii* is devoted to the art of rhetoric. The handbook offers an interesting combination of both major ancient traditions of rhetorical theory, the Isocratean and the Aristotelian, as Solmsen has pointed out in his deservedly famous article on the Aristotelian tradition:

> Martianus Capella obviously knew both traditions and was anxious to give each of them its due; in his book on rhetoric (V) he first presents us with a discussion of the lines of the quinquepartite system, refraining from any reference to the *partes* in the *inventio* (although he makes extensive use of the *status*) and treating the *dispositio* very briefly (30), yet after finishing this he adds a full treatment of the alternative system beginning with the proem and ending with the epilogue (44-53). This is a unique procedure, and it is interesting to see that in the „Aristotelian" part of the book he preserves some elements of that tradition which the majority of rhetorical theorists no longer know (namely, his inclusion of ἦθος and πάθος). Another curious fact is that he deals with argumentation in both parts of the book but treats it differently.[4]

Studies of the probable sources for Book V by Hinks[5] and Fischer[6] suggest that Martianus was indebted to a surprisingly large number of earlier writers on rhetoric. He seems not only to have used a wider range of sources than he does for most of the handbooks on the other arts; his choice of sources was also quite good. Most prominent among the sources are Cicero's *De Inventione*.[7] Martianus also draws from the *De Oratore* and the *Orator* for the treatment of stylistic expression (*elocutio*), memory (*memoria*), and delivery (*actio*). For his treatment of *elocutio*, the aspect of rhetoric of special interest in this paper, Martianus also borrows a long passage on figures from Aquila Romanus (523-537) as well as some material from Donatus and minor grammarians.[8]

Martianus may have known the commentaries by Marius Victorinus on Cicero's *De Inven-*

---

4   Friedrich Solmsen, „The Aristotelian Tradition in Ancient Rhetoric," *AJP*, 62 (1941), p. 50.

5   David A.C. Hinks, „Martianus Capella on Rhetoric," Vol. II of „The Rhetoric of Hermagoras of Temnos: Its Origins and Development," Diss. Trinity College, Cambridge 1935.

6   Hans W. Fischer, *Untersuchungen über die Quellen der Rhetorik des Martianus Capella*, Diss. Breslau 1936 (Breslau: special printing, 1936).

7   The importance of Cicero's *De Inventione* as a source for Martianus' work has long been recognized. In addition to the authors cited above, see L.W. Conklin, The Fifth Book (*De rhetorica*) of the *De nuptiis Philologiae et Mercurii et de septem artibus liberalibus* of Martianus Capella. A Translation with an Introduction and Notes," M.A. Thesis Cornell 1928; and D.E. Grossner, „Studies in the Influence of the *Rhetorica ad Herennium* and Cicero's *De Inventione*," Diss. Cornell 1953. Of course Martianus' reliance on and indebtedness to Cicero is sometimes indirect. For any author in the compendium tradition the possibility that epitomes served as the immediate sources must always be kept in mind.

8   Martianus' treatment of *elocutio*, the figures of thought, and the *clausulae* was particularly popular among Northern Italian humanists of the fourteenth through the sixteenth centuries. For a listing of the relevant manuscripts, see C. Leonardi, „I codici di Marziano Capella," *Aevum*, XXXII (1959), pp. 433-89; XXXIV (1960), pp. 1-99, 411-524. A summary of Leonardi's findings on the manuscripts of the fifth book may be found in W. Stahl, R. Johnson, and E.L. Burge, *Martianus Capella and the Seven Liberal Arts* (New York: Columbia University Press, 1971) I, p. 120.

tione and *Topics*.[9] For his theory of constitution, Martianus apparently relied upon three sources: one Ciceronian, one Theodorean not found elsewhere in Latin, and one Hermagorean, probably Marcomannus, the source common to Martianus, Fortunatianus, and Sulpitius Victor.[10] Finally, for the sections on the *genera causarum* (447-48), it has been argued that Martianus draws upon an unidentified Greek source since his work here shows a better understanding of Aristotle's theory on the *genera causarum* than other extant Latin rhetoricians.

From this brief summary of the *Quellenforschung* it is apparent that Martianus had access to a number of good rhetorical treatises and included within his handbook a considerable amount of material not otherwise known. Johnson, after his discussion of the sources of the fifth book, concludes with what may be a somewhat harsh judgment: „It would appear that Martianus used a wider range of sources for his discourse on rhetoric than for most of his other handbooks, and attempted with neither success nor consciousness of failure, to combine

---

9   Fischer, pp. 123-124, doubts that Martianus knew Victorinus' commentaries and lays great stress upon
     the second-hand nature of Martianus' knowledge of all the sources of classical rhetoric such as the
     works of Cicero:

        ...komme ich auch zu dem Schluss, dass ebenso wie ich es für Celsus vermuten muss, dessen
        Lehre uns ja im Wortlaut nicht vorliegt, auch die in Frage kommenden rhetorischen Schriften
        Circeros M.C. nicht direkt vorlagen, sondern dass es sich hier als notwendig erweist, eine Zwi-
        schenstufe einzuschalten. Möglicherweise, ja wahrscheinlich – eine unwiderlegliche Ansicht zu
        gewinnen und zu vertreten ist hier unmöglich! – war dieses Filter in diesem Falle, wenn man sich
        den tatsächlich starken Einfluss von Cicero de inventione und seinen rhetorischen Lehren über-
        haupt vergegenwärtigt, jene vulgär-rhetorische τέχνη selbst, in die auch Ansichten z.B. des C.
        Victorinus eindrangen, wohingegen es unmöglich ist, einen Kommentar ähnlicher Art zu Ciceros
        Schriften als Quelle für M.C. in Ansatz zu bringen, ist es doch schon m.E. unmöglich, die direk-
        te Benutzung des C. Victorinus anzunehmen, da sich nur sehr wenige Berührungspunkte erge-
        ben; ein Schriftsteller vom Schlage des M.C. aber, der eine Encyclopädie schreiben will, wird
        nicht ein immerhin so umfangreiches Werk wie das des C. Victorinus wegen einer dann so gerin-
        gen Beute durcharbeiten, sondern sich an Stoffsammlungen halten, die ihm in konzentrierter
        und epitomierter Form möglichst viele Ansichten und Lehren übermitteln, wie dies in einer
        Schul-τέχνη der Fall war, die ihm ja sogar so wegweisend erschien, dass er seine Gesamtgliede-
        rung nach ihr ausrichtete.

     Although this criticism of Martianus is to some extent justified, Fischer holds it with such tenacity that
     he fails to see almost any virtues in Martianus' work. For example, on one of the rare occasions when Fi-
     scher is willing to credit Martianus with an improvement upon a known source, Aquila Romanus, he
     immediately undercuts the praise with a slighting remark:

        Das Beispiel zur παλλιλογία hat er nicht abgeändert, sondern ein neues gebracht (Cat. 13) 265,
        6, ebenso wie er es noch einmal 266,16 beim πολύπςωτον macht. Wir werden gerechterweise zu-
        geben müssen, dass beide Beispiele treffender als die von A.R. gebrachten sind: ihrer kurzen
        Form nach können sie Schuldbeispiele sein, die also M.C. von Jugend auf geläufig waren (p. 88).

10   It is interesting to note the parallels between the Hermagorean material found in Martianus and in the
     Aurelii Augustini *De rhetorica*, for example Martianus' discussion of the determination of the *status* (5,
     455) and Aug. *rhet.* 11 in K. Halm, *Rhetores Latini Minores* (Leipzig: Teubner, 1863), p. 144. Were the
     Aurelii Augustini *De rhetorica* generally accepted as a work by Saint Augustine, the two treatises would
     provide intriguing suggestions on the influence of Hermagoras in North African rhetorical schools of the
     fourth century as well as a firm starting point for comparing the rhetorical theory of Saint Augustine
     and Martianus Capella. For a summary discussion of the question of authorship and a translation of the
     Latin text, see O. A. L. Dieter and W.C. Kurth, „The *De rhetorica* of Aurelius Augustine," *SM*, 35
     (1968), pp. 90-108. For Karl Barwick's extensive work on the topic, see especially „Augustine Schrift
     de rhetorica u. Hermagoras von Temnos," *Philologus*, CV (1961), pp. 97-110; „Zur Erklärung u. Ge-
     schichte der Stasislehre des Hermagoras von Temnos," *Philologus*, CVIII (1964), pp. 80-101; and „Zur
     Rekonstruktion der Rhetorik des Hermagoras von Temnos," *Philologus*, CIX (1965), pp. 186-218.

conflicting theories."[11] Although Martianus is perfectly capable of including two different expositions of the same thing within the confines of his work, as he does for example for argumentation, and of conflating or confusing numerous points, I would still judge the handbook to be a clear and even a rather interesting presentation of the rhetorical art. Both the quantity and quality of his sources obviously suggest that Martianus had considerable interest and some expertise in the handling of rhetorical theory.

Also when Martianus comments on the course of his own narration in the *De Nuptiis*, he displays his familiarity with rhetorical terms and shows his own conscious reliance upon rhetorical principles of composition. The clearest example of this is found in the poems at the end of the first two books of the myth (ii. 219-220) and the beginning of the first book of the liberal arts, *De Arte Grammatica* (iii. 221-222). The opening lines of the concluding poem of the second book introduces a play on the *ductus causae* and the following poem continues with punning references to rhetorical color.[12]

Martianus' special concern for style can be seen from the length of the section devoted to *elocutio* in the fifth book. Indeed, Hinks, in his excellent study of the sources of the fifth, remarks especially on the length of Martianus' discussion and its inappropriateness:

> Martian's treatment of the province of expression is extensive for one of the minor rhetoricians, who commonly pass it by as quickly as they can. So many sober Ciceronian precepts of style come ridiculously enough from such a writer. It is difficult to imagine how he could in all seriousness have set them down; but it is not the less true that he thought it worth while to do so at some length.[13]

The discussion comprises almost a fifth of the handbook (508-537) and shows an interesting departure from the four virtues established by Aristotle and Theophrastus, namely, correct usage, clarity, appropriateness, and ornateness. In the opening discussion (508) Martianus makes a distinction between *elocutio* and *eloquentia* and then divides the needed qualities of *elocutio* into the two fundamental virtues of correct usage and clarity and the two higher virtues of richness and ornateness. In setting forth this division Martianus draws upon the common comparison of architecture and rhetoric, correct usage and clarity are the basic supports upon which the edifice of full and ornate speech must be built:

> 508 duabus his officii partibus absolutis elocutionis cura est intimanda. quae cum constet in singulorum animadversione verborum, hoc ab eloquentiae nomine separatur, quod illa totius operis oratorii virtus est, haec pars habetur officii, cuius Cicero duo quasi fundamenta, duo dicit esse fastigia. fundamenta sunt latine loqui planeque dicere, quorum unum Grammatice loquente didicistis, cum eius vobis insinuata subtilitas, fastigia vero sunt copiose ornateque dicere, quod non ingenii sed laboris est maximi, exercitationis etiam diuturnae, qua non solum uberior, sed ilustrior quoque facultas adquiritur.

11   W. Stahl, R. Johnson, and E.L. Burge, p. 119.
12   ii. 219 (Dick, p. 79, 20-23): Transcursa, lector, parte magna fabula,
                    quae tam morosis implicata ductibus,
                    tenui lucernam palpitare lumine
                    coegit instans crepusculum.
All references to the text of Martianus Capella are from the 1925 edition by A. Dick, with additions by J. Préaux (Stuttgart: Teubner, 1969). The citations refer to the section numbers indicated in the margin of the printed text. If further precision is required, the section number will be followed by the page and line reference from the Dick edition. For a longer discussion of Martianus' play on rhetorical terms in these two poems, see my work *Martianus Capella: A Literary Re-evaluation*, Münchener Beiträge zur Mediävistik u. Renaissance-Forschung, 10 (Munich: Arbeo-Gesellschaft, 1972), pp. 107-122.
13   Hinks, p. 71.

Fischer[14] traces the distinction between *elocutio* and *eloquentia* back to Fronto who, along with Cicero and Pliny, is named as one of the major representatives of Latin rhetoric in the introductory allegorical description of the Art and her accompanying band of followers (431-432). The explicit reference to Fronto and Pliny at the beginning of the handbook clearly suggests the deference Martianus felt was due not only to Fronto but also to Pliny, that original practioner of the *genus pingue et floridum*.

Martianus' attitude toward Cicero is more complex. Cicero is portrayed as the incomparable leader of the long procession of Latin orators in the allegorical proem, and he is cited much more frequently than any other author in the text of the handbook itself. Yet in the section devoted to *clausulae* (519-522) Martianus records some sharp criticisms of Cicero's practice. Here in the opening discussion of the virtues of *elocutio* Martianus gives a reference to Cicero for which no exact parallel has been found. Although Martianus appears to be following Cicero's more extended comments in the third book of the *De Oratore*,[15] his omission of any mention of the stylistic virtue of decorum is a noticeable deviation from the pattern of the four virtues given by Cicero. While Cicero, in his discussion of style in the *De Oratore*, clearly separates correct usage and clarity from the more complex virtues of decorum and embellishment, much of Cicero's discussion concerns the appropriate, and in the *Orator* he lays even more emphasis upon the fundamental importance of this virtue:

> sed est eloquentiae sicut reliquarum rerum fundamentum sapientia. ut enim in vita sic in oratione nihil est difficilius quam quid deceat videre. πρέπον appellant hoc Graeci, nos dicamus sane decorum.[16]

Although Martianus retains the Ciceronian linking of grand, middle, and low style to corresponding grand, middle, or low subject matter, it is a point mentioned almost in passing in the introductory description of Lady Rhetoric.[17]

In the subsequent paragraphs (509-513) Martianus continues his discussion of *elocutio* with some interesting remarks[18] on the choice of vocabulary and the use of words in a proper or metaphorical sense. Through the entire discussion the influence of Cicero can be seen both in the precepts given and the examples chosen to illustrate the precepts. Martianus begins with a brief mention of the common belief that the ancients especially used words in their proper sense either because they did not know how to use the ornaments of style or they did not dare to do so. He then moves to a discussion of archaisms:

> 509 sed quia uerborum ueterum iam exoleuit usus, non sunt audacius usurpanda illa, quae cum aetate mutata sunt. itaque ‚alucinari' et ‚cerritum' et ‚caperratum' similiaque praetereuntes utemur his, quae consuetudo recipiet, nec tamen sordidis, nisi cum rei sententiaeque uis exigit, ut, cum Cicero uolens crudelitatis inuidiam facere ait ‚gurgulionibus exsectis reliquerunt' et ‚uirgis plebem Romanam concidere'. nec indecore Vergilius uitandae humilitatis aucupio ‚lychnos' pro lucernis ait.

As this passage and the following sections on *elocutio* plainly show, *humilitas* is no virtue for Martianus. After his remarks on archaisms, Martianus turns to new coinages and outlines the various means of compounding from current words, forming by derivations or borrowing from another language. Finally in this category he discusses words with transferred meanings, which,

---

14   Fischer, p. 73. Fischer believes this statement is a distant echo, not a direct borrowing from Fronto.

15   See *De Oratore* 3, 37-90. For specific verbal similarities, see *De Oratore* 2, 63; 3, 91; and 3, 151.

16   *Orator* 70.

17   428 denique exilis in modicis, in mediocribus facilis, in elatione flammatrix (Dick, p. 212, 14-16).

18   Hinks, pp. 72-75, rightly points to the confusion Martianus introduces here in regard to the earlier discussion of the virtues and the subsequent sections on diction.

he says, occur when the subject treated has no term proper to itself or when we wish to express the ideas in unusually striking terms.

Martianus then gives examples of metaphor where the meaning has been transferred „because of the poverty of the language" or „for the sake of beauty." C. Iulius Victor, who cites some of the same examples as Martianus in his discussion of this aspect of *elocutio*, does not treat the subject at nearly as great a length. He also mentions both the need to keep to the appropriate and the need to avoid obscurity in the use of *aenigmata* (Halm, pp. 431-2). On the other hand Martianus stresses ornament and clearly finds the examples of metaphor „for the sake of beauty of great interest, if length of treatment is any fair indication.

512   ... decoris uero, ut ,bellum subito exarsit', cum potuerit dici extitit. et item possumus ab omnibus sensibus mutuari, ut ab oculis ,luce libertatis et odore legum', et (ab auribus) ,silent leges inter arma' et a gustu ,o nomen dulce libertatis'. uerum non debet haec translatorum alienorumque uerborum affectatio sine moderatione captari. nec longe petita debent esse translata, ut si dicas ,luxuriosam Charybdim'. uitandum quoque, ne turpis sit similitudinis usurpatio, ut si dicas ,castratam Africani morte rem publicam' aut ,clodium stercus senatus'. in hoc genere transferendi etiam allegoriam poetae praecique nexuerunt; et Cicero cum dicit ,cum senatum a gubernaculis deiecisses, populum Romanum e naui exturbasses, ipse archipirata cum grege praedonum impurissimorum plenissimis uelis nauigares'; et in Pisonem ,ut qui maximis tempestatibus ac fluctibus rei publicae nauem gubernassem saluamque in portu collocassem, frontis tuae nubeculam et collegae tui contaminatum spiritum pertimescerem?' usurpatis ergo his similiter, pluribus uerbis elocutus est, quae suis fortasse angustius aut humilius diceret.

After discussing other types of metaphor, synecdoche and metonymy, Martianus passes to a rather lengthy exposition of composition. He begins with proscriptions against a list of compositional faults such as *homoeoprophoron* or *hiulcae* and then proceeds to a discussion of prose rhythm. In his treatment of *clausulae* from 517 onward, Martianus is following a tradition noticeably critical of Cicero's rhythmical practice. The amount of attention Martianus devotes to this topic is a clear indication of his concern for and interest in prose rhythm. Indeed, throughout the *De Nuptiis* Martianus shows his ability to handle metrics and prose rhythms with competence.

The final section of Martianus' treatment of *elocutio* is a list of figures of thought and speech which corresponds almost exactly with the list of figures given by Aquila Romanus. Martianus either omitted or did not possess the opening sections as given by Aquila and he changed details of vocabulary or construction in the parts which do correspond. The changes in diction or construction show at least a certain desire for originality. From a comparison of the two texts Fischer concludes that Martianus was a very careless copyist in the large overview but showed a slavish fidelity to his text in smaller details.[19] Although Martianus' text on *elocutio* can be faulted at many points, Fischer's judgment is in my view a bit severe. Martianus does improve on Aquila Romanus in one instance.[20] His changes in vocabulary and construction are consistent, and some of his large omissions may quite as easily be due to a defective copy text as to hasty reading.

Martianus' treatment of *elocutio* is indeed far below the standard of the great texts of Cicero or Quintilian, it is by no means as clear as the *Auctor ad Herennium*, and it lacks the schematic brevity of Cassiodorus or the great insight of Augustine. Yet both the sheer bulk of

19   Fischer, p. 88.
20   See note 9 above.

material Martianus includes in his discussion of *elocutio* and the variety of his sources indicate the importance of this topic for him. That so much of his discussion is concerned with the rhythmic and figured embellishments of style also suggests that his emphasis upon the copious and ornate and his omission of the appropriate as a stylistic virtue are not accidental.

By stressing fullness and ornateness and modifying or omitting entirely the virtue of appropriateness Martianus departs not only from Cicero but also from the authors of other later Latin handbooks of rhetoric. For example, *to prepon* plays an important role in the discussions of style in Sulpitius Victor, in C. Julius Victor, and in Isidore.[21] This departure is particularly significant in view of the mixed form of Menippean Satire in which the *De Nuptiis* is composed and in view of the transformation of the principle of *decorum* in Augustine's discussion of style in the *De Doctrina Christiana*.

More than any of the other stylistic virtues decorum stands in a middle ground and constantly involves relationships and comparisons that connect the persona of the author, the reader, and the subject and creation of the text. Like correct speech it is a virtue which disappears when present and becomes strikingly visible when absent. In the *De Nuptiis* it is patently absent. Whether by ineptitude or conscious design Martianus forces the reader to consider questions of decorum from the beginning to the end of the work. The question of the appropriate voice for delivering the text is raised directly by the persona of the author in the uneasy, broken dialogue which the author undertakes now with his son, now with Camena, now with the personification of the work *Satura* and always either directly or indirectly with the listener. Since Martianus introduces at least three fictive authors for the text (himself, Camena, and Satura) and a multiple audience (his son, the heavenly assembly and the addressed reader) within the frame of his work, his struggles with the appropriate level of address are hardly surprising. Not only are the speakers and those addressed complicated, if not confused, over the entire span of the work but the message itself frequently seems to be out of context in the most basic sense of the phrase.

Decorum may be difficult to achieve in a dramatic dialogue, but the problem is especially acute in the *De Nuptiis*. The author's consciousness of the problem can be seen at a number of points in the course of the work. The question of decorum is raised prominently in the opening prose paragraph in which the author's son discovers his old, white-haired father singing a wedding song. Since the son does not understand the true significance of the poem that has just been sung, he finds the light little verses to the god of weddings highly inappropriate for the advanced age of his father and interrupts the performance:

> dum crebrius istos Hymenaei uersiculos nescio quid inopinum intactumque moliens cano, respersum capillis albicantibus uerticem incrementisque lustralibus decuriatum nugulas ineptias[22] aggarrire non perferens Martianus interuenit dicens ,quid istud, mi pater, quod nondum uulgata materie cantare deproperas et ritu nictantis antistitis, priusquam fores aditumque reseraris, quin potius edoce quid apportes, et quorsum praedicta sonuerint reuelato'. ,ne tu' inquam ,desipis admodumque perspicui operis ἐγέροιμον[23] noscens creperum sapis? nec liquet Hymena-

---

21   For examples, see Sulpitius Victor, *Institutiones Oratoriae* 15 (Halm, pp. 320-21); C. Julius Victor, *Ars Rhetorica* 22 (Halm, p. 440); Isodore, *De Rhetorica* 16 (Halm, p. 515).

22   Following the emendation suggested by J.G. Préaux, ,,un nouveau mot latin, l'adjectif *nugulus*," *Revue de Philologie*, XXXV (1961), pp. 225-231. Dick reads *nugulas ineptas* (p. 4, 8). According to Préaux, *nugulus* is a new coinage with the diminutive suffix *-ulus* from the rare adjective *nugus*. Its formation is similar to another new coinage found in the parallel passage in Book VIII discussed below, *cerritulus* – somewhat mad, foolish (*quemquam velut cerritulum garrientem*, Dick, p. 426, 3).

23   Also following the emendation suggested by Préaux, *ibid*. Dick conjectures ὑμνολογίζεις (p. 4, 11). If the emendation by Préaux is accepted, the text would contain an explicit reference to the type of *exercita-*

eo praelibante disposita nuptias resultare? si uero concepta cuius scaturriginis uena profluxerint properus scrutator inquiris, fabellam tibi, quam Satura comminiscens hiemali peruigilio marcescentes mecum lucernas edocuit, ni prolixitas perculerit, explicabo.[24]

In this opening paragraph the author not only indicates the higher, revelatory nature of the philosophical fable he is about to undertake, he also suggests an answer to the apparently inappropriate form in which his celebration of a divine union has been cast. Very simply stated, the answer is that things are not always exactly as they appear to be; what may seem to be madness or folly may be true wisdom; the apparent babbling of trifles may conceal an attempt at something never before conceived. The son, and by extension the reader, is directed to assume the role of seeker or investigator in order to hear the instruction which Satura taught the author. Thus in the opening prose paragraph the author meets the charge of lack of decorum by asserting the hearer's need for investigating what lies behind the literal interpretation of the words of the text.

The answer to the charge is framed and reinforced by a number of contrasting motifs which are repeated frequently in the discussions between the author and Satura or Camena interspersed in the course of the work and between the author and his son in this opening prose paragraph and in the concluding poem. Some of the most prominent of these include the doubleentendres upon *desipis* and *sapis* and the recurrent motif of foolish babbling. By designating the work as *satura* and by couching it throughout in the allegorical form of the philosophical fable, Martianus suggests that there will be no simple relationship between the outer form and the inner meaning. In such circumstances, paradoxically, wisdom may appear as folly and the apparently inappropriate be the most appropriate form. Such a philosophical position complicates the pursuit of the appropriate as a major stylistic virtue and increasingly tends to invest the obscure enigmas of a text with a propaedeutic and heuristic value.

In the discussions between the author and Camena at the beginning of the third book and between the author and Satura in the eighth book Martianus introduces another argument for the mixed style and varying tone he has adopted throughout the work. The charm of allegorical dress and the inclusion of laughter amidst the sober discourses of the liberal arts are means of relieving the tedium of the weary listener. The discussion in Book VIII provides a good illustrative example of Martianus' use of puns and doubleentendres as well as his continuation of the motif of babbling folly:

> 806 hac iocularis laetitiae alacritate fervente Satura illa, quae meos semper curae habuit informare sensus ,ne tu'ait ,Felix, vel quisquis es non minus sensus quam nominis pecudalis, huius incongrui risus adiectione desipere vel dementire coepisti? ain tandem non dislensas in Iouiali cachinnos te mouisse concilio verendumque esse sub diuum Palladiaque censura assimulare quemquam vel (ut) cerritulum garrientem?'[25]

After an intervening discussion in prose and verse, the author concludes his disagreement about the decorum of the work with a question and a quotation in which laughter and the charm of fiction are seen not as mad folly but as the means of recovery of one's senses.

> 809 ergone figmenta dimoueam, et nihil leporis iocique permixti taedium auscultantium recreabit? Peligni de cetero inuenis versiculo resipisce et, ni tragicum corrugaris, ,ride, si sapis, o puella, ride!'[26]

---

tio mentis which is linked with figured language and allegorical interpretation.

24 Dick, p. 4, 5-20.
25 *Cerritulus* is the diminutive of one of the archaic words which Martianus suggests should be avoided in his discussion of archaisms in Book V (509) (Dick, p. 250, 21).
26 Dick, p. 428, 3-7.

The final poem introduces a last apology for the form of the work and reveals the author's lack of satisfaction with the text. The author begins with a summary description of the confused agglomeration of the work which he attributes to Satura, and Satura concludes by attributing the faults to the author's drowsy incompetence. The summary and the concluding lines show Martianus' acute awareness of the uneasy elements he has placed in juxtaposition and his uncomfortable recognition of the justness of the charge of babbling folly in an attempt to teach wisdom:

> 998 haec quippe loquax docta indoctis aggerans
>   fandis tacenda farcinat, immiscuit
> ˙   Musas deosque, disciplinas cyclicas
> ˙   garrire agresti cruda finxit plasmate.
>   ....
> 1000 ab hoc creatum Pegaseum gurgitem
>   decente quando possem haurire poculo?
>   testem ergo nostrum quae ueternum prodidit
>   secute nugis, nate, ignosce lectitans.

The numerous debates about form included in the course of the *De Nuptiis* and the final recognition of failure of decorum implied in the words *decente poculo*[27] clearly suggest Martianus' consciousness of the claims of decorum and his lack of satisfaction with the answers or the attempts he has made to resolve his dilemma within the text. The omission of decorum as a major stylistic virtue and the stress upon the ornate indicate the direction Martianus attempts to follow in the resolution of his difficulty. The arguments from necessity and delight, as well as the call to look beyond the literal level of the text, place Martianus within the same broad philosophical and literary tradition as, among others, the quite diverse figures of Porphyry, Julian the Apostate, Macrobius, Origin, Clement, and Augustine. Within this tradition allegory, paradox, and other aspects of the figured style are seen as the vehicles and gymnastic aids by which the intellect passes from a profane lack of understanding to an intuition of higher mysteries, mysteries which ultimately transcend any verbal expression. Every speaker or author within this tradition is thus involved in the paradoxical act of constructing a ladder of language which leads to silence and can never be appropriate.[28]

Augustine, in the *De Doctrina Christiana*, breaks the strong joining of appropriate style and subject matter established by Cicero. By linking the choice of style to the purpose of the speaker rather than the topic of the speech, Augustine transforms the principle of stylistic decorum and makes his rhetorical theory conform to his more comprehensive doctrine of *uti* and *frui*. Martianus, however, finds no consistent resolution to the problem of an appropriate language for expressing both the multiplicity of the world and the fundamental harmony of the universe which lies beyond human powers on conception. By omitting the appropriate as a stylistic virtue and by stressing the full and ornate in his discussion of *elocutio* Martianus indicates the solution he attempts to make in the presentation of his myth and in the integration of the liberal arts as a propaedeutic to the higher vision. Thus in many ways Martianus' pursuit of the precious style is diametrically opposed to Augustine's advocacy of the sublime

---

27   *Decens* is a word Martianus employs frequently throughout the *De Nuptiis* from the opening song to the concluding prose paragraph. Although the word is often used without any necessary implication of its proper meaning of harmonious, fitting, or appropriate, here in the final poem the proper force seems quite pronounced.

28   An interesting discussion of the importance of decorum in ancient rhetorical criticism and its transformation in the commentaries of the later Neo-Platonists may be found in James A. Coulter's *The Literary Microcosm: Theories of Interpretation of the Later Neoplatonists* (Leiden: Brill, 1976).

humility of Biblical style and Biblical truth; yet it is important to recognize that Martianus and Augustine both undercut and transform the classical principle of decorum in theory as well as in practice.

In speaking of the *De Nuptiis* James Murphy makes an apt comment about the precepts on which Martianus' rhetorical theory rests: „But the disciplines of Martianus are still the amoral precepts of the Roman schools, without an explicit theological or even philosophical base."[29] The statement serves as a particularly fit contrast to what could be said about the rhetorical theory of Augustine. But it also obscures the fact that Martianus was indeed attempting to give those drab and amoral precepts color and substance by placing them within the framework of his philosophical fable. A perceptive reader such as Murphy may see the contrast between allegorical figure and plain precept and yet fail to recognize the synthesis Martianus was attempting to create. In Augustine's *Confessions* and in Boethius' *Consolation of Philosophy* the partners in the dialogue maintain a consistent but by no means static relationship. Any fundamental breach of decorum in the development of the dialogue is not admitted. In the *De Doctrina Christiana* and in the *De Arithmetica* the inconsistencies of tone are either removed by the philosophical consistency of the teacher in the one case or by the balanced use of conventional forms of address and instruction in the other.

In the *De Nuptiis* as a whole and in the introductions to the Arts Martianus is clearly attempting to sketch in concrete terms what the absorption and complete internalization of the dry principles of the arts would produce. Each introduction is intended as a demonstration of the art in its fullness. Although what he produces is not a golden metamorphosis of precept into practice, the allegorical figures do stand as emblems of the arts and well stocked places for the memory. In each of the descriptions Martianus tends to stress qualities that are more usually associated with the appearance of a divine being such as great height or shining brillance of face, eyes, or raiment. Although these „divine" qualities become more pronounced in the descriptions of the Arts of the quadrivium, especially Arithmetic and Astronomy, they may also be found in the earlier portrayals, as for example, in the introduction of Rhetoric in the fifth book.

The book begins with a hexameter poem, the opening lines of which echo Vergil's *Aeneid*. The choice of hexameter points to the epic or mock heroic tone in which the entire allegorical depiction of Rhetoric is cast. The first lines of the poem also suggest the military and arming metaphors which will be carried throughout the description.

> 425 Interea sonuere tubae raucusque per aethram
> cantus, et ignoto caelum clangore remugit:
> turbati expauere dii, uulgusque minorum
> caelicolum trepidat, causarum et nescia corda
> haerent, et ueteris renouantur crimina Phlegrae.

A quick reading of the entire poem would reveal a remarkable number of spondees, which give an air of expectancy to the lines and thus heighten the reader's anticipation of Rhetoric's entrance. The frequent displays of alliteration, the numerous instances of the artful interplay of meter and meaning and the repetition of vocabulary are all examples of the complex art and perhaps excessive attention to sound associated with the precious style and frequent in Martianus' poetry.

The epic catalogue of gods and weapons builds to the final words of the poem *tela Tonantis* and thus establishes a rather clever link to the comparison of Rhetoric's arms and Jupiter's thunderbolts in the following prose section:

29   Murphy, *Rhetoric in the Middle Ages*, p. 46.

426 sed dum talibus perturbatur multa terrestrium plebs decorum, ecce quaedam sublimissimi corporis ac fiduciae grandioris, uultus etiam decore luculenta femina insignis ingreditur, cui galeatus uertex ac regali caput maiestate sertatum, arma in manibus, quibus se uel communire solita uel aduersarios uulverare, fulminea quadam coruscatione renidebant. subarmalis autem uestis illi peplo quodam circa humeros inuoluto Latiariter tegebatur, quod amnium figurarum lumine uariatum cunctorum schemata praeferebat, pectus autem exquisitissimis gemmarum coloribus subbalteatum. haec cum in progressu arma concusserat, uelut fulgoreae nubis fragore colliso bombis dissultantibus fracta diceres crepitare tonitrua; denique creditum, quod instar Iouis eadem posset etiam fulmina iaculari.

In the prose section the same almost poetic interweaving continues. *Perturbatus* picks up *turbati* of the third line of the poem and shows the typical love of play on verb and compound found frequently in Augustine and other late Latin authors. In the phrase *sublimissimi corporis fiduciae grandioris* is found chiastic arrangement slightly distorted by the difference between the comparative and superlative degree. The description of the garments shows Martianus' obvious delight in wordplay. The passage quoted and the long opening description which follows (427-438) are filled with examples of poetic vocabulary and artful figures, such as simile, balance and climax. The verbal echoes of Cicero and the references to other famous practitioners of the art who form the long troup accompanying Rhetoric suggest the great value of the art (and display Martianus' erudition). The recollection of her immortal glory and the depiction of her queenly position point to the exalted ideal eloquence represents. In short, the entire personification may be seen as a type of divinization of the art. Yet such an elevation clearly contrasts with the exposition of precepts which follows and to an even greater extent with the humorous, almost burlesque conclusion of the fifth book. There (565) Rhetoric is described as incapable of doing anything silently—even of bestowing a silent kiss.

Martianus' characteristically inappropriate contrasts and uneasy stylistic juxtapositions are especially noticeable when the *De Nuptiis* is placed beside Boethius' treatises on arithmetic and on music or beside the *Consolation of Philosophy*. Yet the introductions in his work do afford excellent points of comparison with those of the Boethian texts. In his personifications Martianus creates figures that serve partly as mere devices in an allegorical game, ornaments that occasion delight, but more importantly as transitional bridges that anchor the divine aim to the human effort and thus provide a means of union between the drudgery of learning and the blessed joy of wisdom. As such, they aid the reader in internalizing both message and material, they assist him in focusing his memory, and they impress upon him the glorious end of the long art. Although Martianus' Arts are static, immobile statues, they have a vividly visual quality that in great part accounts for their successful survival and influence in the iconographic tradition. Similarly, although Martianus retains many conventional elements of earlier educational treatises, such as the dialogue framework between father and son, he has a rightful claim to originality, not just by the fact that he presents the arts in allegorical guise, but by the way in which that presentation changes the very evaluation of the arts' worth. That the arts are graphically portrayed as assistants to the apotheosis of the human intellect and are glorified and adorned with all the devices of rhetorical skill suggests the substantive contribution stylistic embellishment has wrought.

Boethius' dedicatory letter to Symmachus that prefaces the *De Arithmetica* offers the most conspicuous example of Boethius' use of stylistic embellishments associated with the precious style. The letter falls within the elaborately figured epistolary tradition of the later Empire. In later Latin and in early Byzantine Greek the art of letter writing comes to show the worst features of the precious style all too frequently. The vain complexities and highly artificial constructions of Sidonius Apollinaris are by no means the exception in both formal and purportedly casual correspondence.

Although Boethius' dedicatory epistle to Symmachus displays some of these faults of excess, it also shows Boethius' early mastery of the stylistic virtues as well. For example, the opening sentences, and many that follow, reveal artful parallels and balance:

> In dandis accipiendisque muneribus ita recte officia inter eos praecipue, qui sese magni faciunt, aestimantur, si liquido constabit, nec at hoc aliud, quod liberalius afferret, inventum, nec ab illo unquam, quod iucundius benevolentia conplecteretur, acceptum. Haec ipse considerans attuli non ignava opum pondera, quibus ad facinus nihil instructius, cum habendi sitis incanduit, ad meritum nihil vilius, cum ea sibi victor animus calcata subiecit, sed ea, quae ex Graecarum opulentia litterarum in Romanae orationis thesaurum sumpta conveximus.[30]

The text is also filled with vivid metaphorical expressions and highly colored vocabulary, as for example in the phrases quoted above, *cum habendi sitis incanduit* and *cum ea sibi victor animus calcata subiecit.* Throughout the letter may be found instances of subtle and not so subtle flattery that are at times accompanied by an artful verbal repetition. The following sentence provides an example of this in the phrase *quae ex sapientiae doctrinis elicui, sapientissimi iudicio conprobentur.* Boethius also embellishes his gift with a copious use of other devices, including comparative analogies drawn from other arts such as sculpting or war. He also shapes his narrative to build toward artfully arranged stylistic points as in the following sentences from the end of the first paragraph:

> Tam multis artibus ars una perficitur.... Quamlibet enim hoc iudicium multis artibus probetur excultum, uno tamen cumulatur examine.[31]

In brief then, as the examples show, Boethius presents us with the type of elaborately prepared preface that polite conventions demanded. As would be expected, the letter contains much flattery and many artful comparisons.[32] The most extreme appears near the very end of the text. There Boethius says:

> Recte ergo, quasi aureos Cereri culmos et maturos Baccho palmites, sic ad te novi operis rudimenta transmisi. Tu tantum paterna gratia nostrum provehas munus. Ita et laboris mei primitias doctissimo iudicio consecrabis et non maiore censebitur auctor merito quam probator.[33]

To be sure, the parallel drawn between Symmachus and the deities of Bacchus and Ceres is not an unusual or even exaggerated form of praise by late Latin standards. To a certain extent Boethius is here merely demonstrating his ability to play upon various connotations of *munus* and thus turn a fine compliment as part of the conclusion. From the opening of the letter through seemingly intentional puns on *munusculo* and *munimenta,*[34] to the conclusion Boethius exploits a good part of the semantic range of the term. Yet the analogy drawn between the dedication of his work to Symmachus and an offering made to the gods also suggests that the gift offered and the favor granted are set within an elevated, if not a sacred context. So, just as in Martianus' *De Nuptiis,* the precious style in this introductory letter is decorative but also marks a definite substantive change in attitude, a quality of glorification, if not sanctification that places the arts literally and metaphorically within a new setting.

Not infrequently this new setting is accompanied by an appeal to the discovery of wisdom. This appeal underscores the philosophical scales upon which authors like Martianus and

---

30 Boethius, *De Institutione Arithmetica*, ed. Godofredus Friedlein (Leipzig, 1867; rpt. Frankfort a.M.: Minerva G.M.B.H., 1966), p. 1.
31 *Ibid.*, p. 2.
32 There is, however, no question of his sincerity.
33 *Ibid.*, p. 5.
34 *Ibid.*, p. 1, 20-21.

Boethius weigh the value of learning and the liberal arts and provides the larger context within which the glorification of the arts acquires meaning. Boethius sounds the theme in the opening sentences of the Proemium to the *De Institutione Arithmetica*. Later he elaborates more fully on the role of the quadrivium not only for understanding the full cosmic design but also for the illumination of the mind's eye, the eye far more precious than a multitude of bodily eyes:

> Constat igitur, quiquis haec praetermiserit, omnem philosophiae perdidisse doctrinam. Hocigitur illud quadruvium est, quo his viandum sit, quibus excellentior animus a nobiscum procreatis sensibus ad intellegentiae certiora perducitur. Sunt quidam gradus certaeque progressionum dimensiones, quibus ascendi progredique possit, ut animi illum oculum, qui, ut ait Plato, multis oculis corporalibus salvari consitiuique sit dignior, quod eo solo lumine vestigari vel inspici veritas queat, hunc inquam oculum demersum orbatumque corporeis sensibus hae disciplinae rursus inluminent.[35]

In the following sections of the Proemium Boethius asserts the philosophical principles by which the smallest arithmetic precepts are related to the grandest cosmic design and by which each of the arts of the quadrivium is related one to the other and to the attainment of enlightenment. Although Boethius does not present an elaborate personification of Arithmetic in the Proemium of his treatise, the philosophical, even somewhat mystical context, the use of embellishment to glorify the art, and similar appeals to authority underline the changed perspective on learning and the liberal arts found in both authors.

Within this philosophical perspective, the arts, especially the arts of the quadrivium, become the means by which the intellect discovers a true vision of the cosmos and knowledge of its own worth. The arts act as symbolic guides to the ascent and ultimate attainment of the human pilgrim in search of enlightenment. As such, then, the arts themselves tend to become symbols that constantly point beyond their literal value or even any value that can be expressed discursively. Within this philosophical framework stylistic ornament and especially the use of the allegorical mode invests the arts with qualities of an enigmatic religious vision that requires mental effort to penetrate. Understanding of the art is thus changed by the altered context and purpose.

The use of stylistic ornament to glorify, justify, even sanctify the arts can not then simply be dismissed as inconsequential ornament or purely conventional detail. It clearly reflects a perceived need to defend the value of the arts and corresponds to some recognition, however dim, that the arts had to be placed in a new order and given a value more intrinsically dependent upon the individual and his progress toward enlightenment than upon the community and the communal benefits that might be derived from their mastery. Finding appropriate language is always hard but under such circumstances it is notably so. The development of aspects of the precious style, especially poetic enigma as the means by which the reader may progress toward discovery of a new order, is no small literary gift.

Although Boethius' Philosophy provides the outstanding example of this development, she arises within a complex stylistic tradition that is more than cosmetic. Indeed, Philosophy fulfills many of the same functions as the allegorical figures of the arts and the precious complexities of the introductory laudation. She is an ornament and a place for fixing the memory of the ideal of philosophy. She is that idealization and the embodiment of the gift. Her description and entrance clearly mark off a special, if not a sacred province. To be sure, by localizing the dramatic action of the *Consolation* within the confines of the human soul, Boethius avoids the more obviously inappropriate disruptions within his narrative frame.

35   *Ibid.*, pp. 9-10.

Boethius' Philosophy also participates in the instruction and righting of the fallen Boethius far more dynamically than any of Martianus' figures perform in their educative roles. Philosophy serves as both physician and physic for the mind and actively assists it to reascend to its rightful place in the universe. Yet Boethius comes to the discovery of health and wisdom first by focusing attention on the external vision of Philosophy, then by internalizing the philosophical vision. In the course of the *Consolation* the reader must both literally and metaphorically trace the same path.

University of Wisconsin, Madison

PEARL KIBRE

THE BOETHIAN *DE INSTITUTIONE ARITHMETICA* AND THE QUADRIVIUM IN THE THIRTEENTH CENTURY UNIVERSITY MILIEU AT PARIS

Although the Boethian *Arithmetica* has already received attention from scholars concerned with Boethius' place in the cultural history of western Europe in the middle ages,[1] the specific role that this work played in the framework of the *quadrivium* in the thirteenth century French university milieu has so far not been set forth. It is this lacuna that the present study would endeavor to fill. Before turning to this task, however, a brief review or account of the nature of the work and of its history in the west before the close of the twelfth century may be in order. The so-called Boethian *Arithmetica* is the Latin translation or paraphrase by Anicius Manlius Boethius of the Greek text of the *De Institutione Arithmetica* of Nicomachus of Gerasa, who flourished about 100 A.D., and was a popularizer of neo-Pythagorean doctrines.[2] Like the Pythagoreans he stressed the importance of the theory or philosophy of numbers

---

[1]   The most comprehensive work on Boethius in the Middle Ages is that of H.R. Patch, *The Tradition of Boethius: A Study of His Importance in Medieval Culture* (New York: Oxford University Press, 1935). Professor Patch has incorporated the information of the chief writers on the subject who wrote before him on Boethius. Although Professor Patch brought his account up through the fifteenth century his focus was general and literary in nature and he did not relate the work specifically to the thirteenth century university milieu. For recent estimates of Boethius, see the article by Lorenzo Minio-Paluello in the *Dictionary of Scientific Biography*; also, William H. Stahl, *Roman Science* (Madison: The University of Wisconsin Press, 1962), pp. 198 ff. and Gillian R. Evans, articles, especially Introductions to Boethius's „Arithmetica" of the 10th to the 14th century in *History of Science*, 16 (1978), 22-41.

[2]   See especially Nicomachus of Gerasa, *Introduction to Arithmetic*, trans. by M.L. D'Ooge, with studies in Greek arithmetic by F.E. Robbins and L.C. Karpinski (*University of Michigan Studies*, Humanistic Series, XVI; New York: Macmillan, 1926); David Eugene Smith, *History of Mathematics* (2 vols., New York: Ginn and Co., 1951-53), I, pp. 127-29, 178-79; also Sir Thomas Heath, *A History of Greek Mathematics* (2 vols., Oxford: Clarendon Press, 1921), I, pp. 10 ff. A critical edition of Boethius' *De Institutione Arithmetica* by G. Friedlein (Leipzig, 1867; reprinted: Minerva G.M.B.H., Frankfurt a.M., 1966), pp. 3-173, was made on the basis of eight MSS from Bamberg and Munich of the 12th century. The text is also included among Boethius' *Opera omnia* in Migne's *Patrologia latina* (1860), LXIII, col. 1079-1168. A new edition of the *Arithmetica* has been announced by Professor Jean Schilling of Nancy as forthcoming in 1970, but so far has not appeared. MSS of the work are fairly numerous. In addition to the eight MSS utilized by Friedlein, and those listed by L. Thorndike and P. Kibre, in *A Catalogue of Incipits of Mediaeval Scientific Writings in Latin* (Cambridge, Mass.: Mediaeval Academy of America, new and revised edition, 1962, henceforth designated as TK), col. 465, 768, 959, 991; as well as those noted by Menso Folkerts, in his edition of „*Boetius" Geometrie II* (Wiesbaden: Franz Steiner Verlag GMBH, 1970), the following MSS have been noted: London, British Library (henceforth designated as BL) Arundel 339, 13th cent., ff. 1r-31r; Harleian 549, 10th cent.; 1737, only a part of the *Arithmetica*; 2510, 13th cent., ff. 136-167r; 3595, 10th cent., ff. 1r-48v; Lansdowne 842 B., 15th cent., ff. 1r-50v; New York, Columbia Univ. Plimpton MS c. 1294, indicated by D.E. Smith, I, 180; Paris, Bibliothèque Nationale (henceforth indicated as BN) 6401, 9th cent., ff. 15-138v; 6639, 10th cent., ff. 73-151; 7039, 10th cent., f. 95, incomplete; 7185, 9th cent., ff. 1-40v, Gloss, 12th cent., ff. 41r-47r; 7189, 12th cent., ff. 1-50; 13020, 9th cent.; 14064, 9th cent.; 14065, 13th cent.; 16201, 13th cent., ff. 6v-34; 17858, 10th cent., ff. 3ra-36ra; and it was also included in the library of Richard de Fournival 39, c. 1250 (Delisle, *Le Cabinet des MSS*, Paris, 1874, II, p. 526; Folkerts, p. 38).

under the Pythagorean principle that „all things that can be known have number" and „all things are numbers."[3] Under this aegis arithmetic was taken out of the realm of practical utility or commercial transactions and was raised to the level of speculative thought.

In preparing the *De Institutione Arithmetica* for Latin users, Boethius asserted that he had not made a literal translation of the Greek text but had rather given a free interpretation. He had condensed where Nicomachus was diffuse and expanded where further explanatory information seemed essential, adding formulas and demonstrations familiar to Latin scholars.[4] However, Boethius adhered to the general Pythagorean or neo-Pythagorean character of the Nicomachean text. That is he retained the philosophical rather than the mathematical side of arithmetic. In general, the work therefore had less appeal or application to mathematicians and those concerned with numerical calculation or simple reckoning than to philosophers and philosophy. The *De Institutione Arithmetica* in its Greek form had earlier drawn the attention of the second century Platonist, Apuleius of Madaura, who is credited with having translated it into Latin, although no trace of this version has as yet been found; also among others, of the fourth and fifth century neo-Platonists, Iamblichus and Proclus, both of whom commented on it, as well as of Martianus Capella, who cited the work possibly secondhand.[5] Moreover, in the Boethian translation or paraphrase, the Nicomachean *De Institutione Arithmetica* came to provide the basic text in western Europe for the study of arithmetic in its philosophical or theoretical rather than practical aspects. By its content Latin scholars were introduced to the divisions of numbers and their nature and properties, and were provided with a vocabulary and descriptive account of mathematical forms and terms. These comprised, among others, even and odd numbers, numbers separate and unified, absolute and relative, prime, deficient or defective numbers, perfect, abundant or redundant or overperfect numbers, linear numbers, rectalinear, polygonal, triangular, quadratic, pentagonal, hexagonal, heptagonal numbers, also solids, cubic, pyramidal, and circular or spherical numbers, as well as the ratios or proportions and proportionalities of numbers. In addition there were descriptions of the relation between arithmetic and geometry, or arithmetical geometry, and of harmonic proportion in the sense of Pythagoras and Plato.[6]

Boethius' translation of the *De Institutione Arithmetica* may well have been part of his general plan to make available in Latin the Greek writings essential for the study and mastery of the seven liberal arts as a prelude to the quest for wisdom or philosophic truth. In the schema canonized in the medieval schools, the four mathematical arts, arithmetic, music, geometry, and astronomy, or the *quadrivium*, generally followed the first three of the arts,

The Arithmetica was first printed separately at Augsburg, Ratdolt, 1488 (Arnold C. Klebs, *Incunabula Scientifica et Medica*, Bruges: The Saint Catherine Press, 1938, henceforth cited as Klebs, 191.1); and with the *Opera* (Venice: Gregoriis, 1491, 1492, Klebs 192.1; and Venice: Gregoriis, 1497, 1499, Klebs 192.2). An *Epitome in duos libros arithmeticos Boethii* by Jacques Lefevre d'Etaples, was printed with Jordanus Nemorarius, *Arithmetica*, at Paris: Higman and Hopyl, 1496 (Klebs 563.1). The commentary on Boethius' *Arithmetica* by Jean de Muris was printed in 1515 (Cf. TK 959).

3   Heath, p. 67.
4   *De arith.*, Praef.: „... paululum liberius evagatus alieno itineri, non vestigiis, insisto. Nam et ea, quae de numeris a Nicomacho diffusius disputata sunt, moderata brevitate collegi et quae transcursa velocius angustiorem intellegentiae praestabant aditum, mediocri adiectione reseravi, ut aliquando ad evidentiam rerum nostris etiam formulis ac descriptionibus uteremur." Friedlein, pp. 4-5: 29-4.
5   Heath, pp. 10 ff., 66 ff., 98-99; William H. Stahl, Richard Johnson, and E.L. Burge, *Martianus Capella and the Seven Liberal Arts*: Volume I: *The Quadrivium of Martianus Capella* (Records of Civilization: Sources and Studies, LXXXIV; New York and London: Columbia University Press, 1971), p. 156.
6   *Boetii de Institutione Arith.*, Libri duo ed. G. Friedlein, 1966, pp. 3-173. For the definitions of the mathematical terms, see Heath, pp. 74 ff., 91-112; and D.E. Smith, *History of Math.*, II, 1953, pp. 16 ff.

designated as the *trivium* at a later time, comprising grammar, rhetoric, and dialectics. Although Boethius is believed to have coined the term *quadruvium* or *quadrivium*, the actual grouping of the four branches went back to Plato, as well as to Archytas, in the fourth century before Christ.[7] Plato, as Professor Merlan has noted, represented the two aspects of the four mathematical arts, namely their elementary character (in the *Laws*) as grammar school subjects taught for practical purposes only, without any claim to being philosophical in nature or intent, and their position in the *Republic*, as preparation for philosophy or wisdom, the highest form of knowledge.[8]

In the differing interpretations of the role of the subjects of the quadrivium, Professor Merlan has drawn attention to the fact that the transition from the belief that they were elementary branches of learning to the view that they were philosophical in intent was made smoothly for arithmetic, geometry, and astronomy. But for the fourth branch, music, this was not so easy, since music as performed, or as produced in composition, or as enjoyed esthetically and so on, had little necessarily to do with music as the philosophy of sound or of acoustics.[9] Boethius, following Nicomachus, had adhered to the concept of not only the philosophic importance of the four branches of the quadrivium but also of their close interrelationship since as *mathematica* their common subject was quantity. And this quantity was either discontinuous or continuous, that is discontinuous either per se as in arithmetic, or in relation to another, as in music or harmony; and continuous either without motion as in geometry, or in motion as in astronomy. Thus the quadripartition was specifically that of quantity.[10]

In addition to this quadripartition, the *mathematica* or *quadriviales* were also encompassed within the Aristotelian concept of the tripartition of theoretical knowledge, corresponding to the tripartition of being, into physical, mathematical and theological, or the three states or spheres of being, namely of ideas (theological), mathematical, and physical. As Professor Merlan has noted, this theory of the tripartition of being into theological, mathematical and physical, persisted through the Middle Ages and was clearly set forth in the thirteenth century by St. Thomas Aquinas. It was also in evidence in the tripartite character of the curriculum of the Faculty of Arts at Paris, in the three divisions of natural philosophy into *physica, mathematica,* and *metaphysica* (the divine science).[11]

As set forth by Boethius and before him by Nicomachus and Plato, the four branches of *mathematica*, whose common constituent was quantity, were intimately connected in the quadrivium. They were said to constitute the fourfold or fourpronged road toward philosophical truth. Without knowledge of all four of them the seeker for truth would find it impossible

---

7   Heath, I, pp. 10 ff., citing Plato's *Republic* (VII.522C, 525A, 526B); and F.S. Benjamin Jr., and G.J. Toomer, editors and translators of *Campanus of Novara and Medieval Planetary Theory: Theorica Planetarum* (Madison, Milwaukee, and London: The University of Wisconsin Press, 1971), p. 372. On Boethius and the quadrivium, see also Etienne Gilson, *La Philosophie au Moyen Age: Les Origines Patristiques à la Fin du XIVe Siècle* (2nd ed., Paris: Payot, 1947), pp. 140-41.

8   P. Merlan, *From Platonism to Neoplatonism* (2nd ed., The Hague, 1960), pp. 88 ff., citing the *Protagoras* (318E), the *Laws* (817E), and the *Republic* (VII 530 D). In regard to the Platonic curriculum and the quadrivium, see the appendices to the *Republic*, Book VII, in *The Republic of Plato*, ed. by James Adams, 2nd ed. by D.A. Rees (Cambridge: University Press, 1969), pp. 164 ff.

9   Merlan, pp. 94-95.

10   *Ibid.*, pp. 89 ff., 94-95. *Boetii Inst. Arith.*, I. 1: „Horum ergo illam multitudinem, quae per se est, arithmetica speculatur integritas, illam vero quae ad aliquid, musici modulaminis temperamenta pernoscunt, immobilis vero magnitudinis geometria notitiam pollicetur, mobilis vero scientiam astronomicae disciplinae peritia vendicat...." Friedlein, 1966, p. 9: 1-6.

11   Merlan, p. 224; and see below.

to reach his destination or achieve his goal.[12] Yet, despite this emphasis upon the interrelationship of the four branches, it is impossible to determine with any degree of certainty, in the present state of our knowledge, whether the four were in fact studied with equal attention and devotion either in the earlier schools or in the universities of the thirteenth century. For purposes therefore of this study we shall concentrate on one of the four branches, namely on arithmetic, which, in the opinion of Boethius, was the one that should be studied first,[13] since all the other branches are dependent upon it and it alone was independent of the others. Boethius in placing arithmetic first, was, it might be recalled, following the Nicomachean progression of arithmetic, music, geometry, and astronomy, rather than that of the Varronean arrangement of geometry, arithmetic, astronomy, and music.[14]

The adoption of the *De Institutione Arithmetica* as the basic textbook on the theory of numbers in areas and times far removed from Ostrogothic Italy of the early sixth century provides an interesting illustration of the propagation of texts derived from the Greek. Beginning with the utilization of the work by Cassiodorus for his *Institutiones* or *Introduction to Divine and Human Readings*, the work was looked upon as the principal source from which knowledge of the art or theory of numbers might be derived. It thus accompanied the more practical abacus arithmetics and other texts on calculation. As Professor Patch and others before him have shown, the work was incorporated into the teaching of the cloister and cathedral of St. Gall, Reichenau, Laon, Hildesheim, Rheims, Chartres, Paris, and so on, or wherever the curriculum was organized on the plan of the seven liberal arts. Moreover, such prominent early scholars as Bede, Alcuin, Rabanus Maurus, Gerbert, Helperic, Hroswitha and many others had culled pertinent information from the *De Institutione Arithmetica*.[15] In the twelfth century, Boethius and arithmetic appeared in the allegory, attributed to Honorius of Autun, of the return of the soul from its exile of ignorance to its true homeland by means of the ten arts depicted as cities through which the soul must pass on its way to its true homeland. Arithmetic, the fourth city, was portrayed with Boethius teaching the art of even and odd numbers.[16]

---

12 *Boetii Inst. Arith.* I.1: „...haud quemquam in philosophiae disciplinis ad cumulum perfectionis evadere, nisi cui talis prudentiae nobilitas quodam quasi quadruvio vestigatur...." (ed. Friedlein, 1966, p. 7: 23-26); and *ibid.* „Quibus quatuor partibus si careat inquisitor, verum invenire non possit, ac sine hac quidem speculatione veritatis nulli recte sapiendum est. Est enim sapientia earum rerum, quae vere sunt, cognitio et integra comprehensio.... Constat igitur, quisquis haec praetermiserit, omnem philosophiae perdidisse doctrinam. Hoc igitur illud quadruvium est, quo his viandum sit.... (ed. Friedlein, 1966, p. 9: 6-10, 26-29).

13 *Boetii Inst. Arith.*, Praef.: „Cum igitur quattuor matheseos disciplinarum de arithmetica, quae est prima, perscriberem..." (ed. Friedlein, 1966, p. 5: 6-7).

14 See my article, „The *Quadrivium* in the Thirteenth Century Universities (with special reference to Paris)," in *Actes du Quatrième Congrès International de Philosophie Médiévale: Arts Libéraux et Philosophie au Moyen Âge* (Montreal: Institut d'Etudes Médiévales, and Paris: Librairie Philosophieque J. Vrin, 1969, henceforth to be cited as *Actes*, 1969), p. 181; also W.H. Stahl, *Martianus Capella and the Seven Liberal Arts*, 1971, pp. 154-55.

15 Patch, pp. 36 ff., citing the earlier literature on the subject. See also H.L. Heiberg, *Geschichte der Mathematik und Naturwissenschaften in Altertum* (Munich, 1925), pp. 49ff.; and the brief historical survey of the quadrivium, and of arithmetic in particular, in W.H. Stahl, *Martianus Capella and the Seven Liberal Arts*, 1971, pp. 154 ff.

16 *Ibid.*, Patch, pp. 36 ff. and the „De animae exsilio et patria, alias, De Artibus," attributed to Honorius of Autun, in which the exile is ignorance and the fatherland, wisdom. Migne, *Patrologia*, CLXXII, col. 1243-1246: 1244, „cap. v. Quarta civitas arithmetica.... In hac, Boetio docente, par et impar numerus..." See also Eva Matthews Sanford, „Honorius, presbyter and scholasticus," *Speculum*, 23 (July, 1948), p. 419.

Furthermore, Professor Patch drew attention to the indebtedness to Boethius of such prominent thirteenth century scholars as Alexander Neckam, Albertus Magnus, Thomas Aquinas, Michael Scot, Roger Bacon, and Robert Grosseteste, all of them associated at one time or another with the University of Paris.[17] However, he made no attempt to single out for specific study the use of the *De Institutione Arithmetica* by these authors, nor the continued presence of the work as a textbook for the study of arthmetic among the quadrivial arts in the university curriculum.[18] This then is the twofold task toward which this study is directed, with particular emphasis upon the Parisian university milieu.

Although there were in the thirteenth century several other French as well as non-French university centers, none of these could be considered as representative of the era as Paris. The University at Paris was a truly international association and was acknowledged as the intellectual center of Europe in the thirteenth century. It drew scholars not only from all parts of the French kingdom but also from the British Isles and continental Europe as well.[19] And insofar as the scholars whose works are to be considered were at one time or another in Paris, their writings may be examined for our purpose without regard to whether they were of English, German, Hungarian, Italian, Spanish, Scandinavian or of any other origin.

In general, as suggested earlier, little attention until recently had been drawn to the fate of either the Boethian *Arithmetica* or the quadrivial arts in the University of Paris in the thirteenth century. As noted in my previous study on the quadrivium in the thirteenth century University of Paris,[20] this neglect may be accounted for in part by the paucity of information on the subject in the thirteenth century university documents. However, as also suggested earlier, there are other available sources that may be tapped. The latter comprise student manuals or guides and the writings of either professors or scholars known to have been associated with the university as well as others in the immediate vicinity whose direct connection cannot be ascertained but who in all likelihood came in close contact with the community of scholars in the rather restricted geographical confines of the city of Paris. In addition, there is the evidence provided by extant manuscripts of texts either of earlier vintage or by contemporary authors who were regent or teaching masters in the university.[21] A sampling of only a portion of such resources has been possible for this study. But these few have reinforced the views earlier expressed. The mathematical or quadrivial arts were being taught within the larger and more comprehensive framework of the three philosophies, rational, natural, and moral, that made up the Faculty of Arts, which at Paris as elsewhere had taken over the task of providing the basic groundwork of the university educational program. As noted earlier, the quadrivial arts constituted one of the three divisions of natural philosophy, under the heading of *mathematica*, the other two being *physica* and *metaphysica.*[22]

---

17   Patch, pp. 39 ff.
18   For recent suggestions in this regard, see my earlier study in *Actes*, 1969, pp. 175 ff.; also the brief summary on the quadrivium by Mgr. Glorieux, *La Faculté des Arts*, (Paris: J. Vrin, 1971), pp. 33-34.
19   See my *Nations in the Mediaeval Universities* (Cambridge, Mass.: Mediaeval Academy of America, 1948), pp. 14 ff. and the references there noted.
20   *Actes*, 1969, pp. 175-91; also, Philippe Delhaye, „Arts libéraux et Programmes scolaire au XIIIe siècle," *Actes*, 1969, pp. 162-73; and Glorieux, *La Faculté des Arts*, 1971, pp. 33-38.
21   *Actes*, 1969, p. 176, and n. 8.
22   *Actes*, 1969, pp. 180-81; and St. Thomas Aquinas, *The Division and Methods of the Sciences: Questions V and VI of his Commentary on the De Trinitate of Boethius*, translated with introduction and notes by Armand Maurer (3rd rev. ed., Toronto: The Pontifical Institute of Mediaeval Studies, 1963), pp. xiv-xv. As indicated in my article named above, St. Thomas had asserted that the old divisions into trivium and quadrivium were no longer adequate to comprise the whole of speculative philosophy. And in the tripartite division into mathematical, natural, and divine or metaphysics, he had held that the mathematical

Moreover, for the teaching of the first of the quadrivial arts, arithmetic, the Boethian *De Institutione Arithmetica* appears to have maintained its position as a basic text, and this was the case despite the fact that there were available for the study of arithmetic in the thirteenth century, in its various practical as well as other aspects, a wealth of materials both old and new. To the many tracts on calculation, abacus arithmetic, mathematical games, and simple reckoning, of earlier vintage, there had been added the treatises on algorisms where Hindu-Arabic numerals made an early appearance, as well as other practical treatises and pedagogical instruments, as Guy Beaujouan has shown in his account of elementary texts for the teaching of arithmetic in the universities.23 However, despite this abundance of practical materials, the Nicomachean *Arithmetica* in the translation or paraphrase by Boethius was named as the text in arithmetic by the anonymous Paris master in the examination manual dated between 1230 and 1240 prepared for students coming up for examinations for degrees or for the license in arts at Paris.24 The Boethian *Arithmetica* had similarly been named together with Euclid, that is apparently the sections on numbers of the *Elements*, in an earlier list of textbooks prepared probably by Alexander Neckam at the close of the twelfth century while he was teaching the quadrivial arts at Paris.25

Furthermore, the tendency to relate or combine the Boethian *Arithmetica* with the new Hindu-Arabic mathematics26 is illustrated in the *Algorismus Vulgaris* of John Halifax or Sacrobosco.27 Although the name of John of Sacrobosco, an English scholar who taught at

arts should precede studies in natural philosophy or physics. In his opinion, the mathematical arts among which he placed arithmetic first, would prepare the mind, or open the way for the apprehension and understanding of the other physical or natural sciences. For a slightly different division of the three philosophies, see Father James A. Weisheipl, „The Place of the Liberal Arts in the University Curriculum during the XIVth and XVth Centuries," *Actes*, 1969, p. 210. See also above for the tripartition of theoretical knowledge.

23 For the place and importance of arithmetic in the university curriculum, see my previous study in *Actes*, 1969, pp. 181 ff.; also Guy Beaujouan, „L'enseignement de l'arithmétique élémentaire à l'Université de Paris aux XIIIe et XIVe siècles. De l'abaque à l'algorisme," in *Homenaje à Millas-Vallicrosa* (Barcelona: Consejo superior de investigaciones cientificas, 1954), I, pp. 93-124. Beaujouan's recent study, „L'enseignement du Quadrivium," Estratto da Settimane du Studio del Centro italiano di studi sull'alto medievo, XIX, *La Scuola nell'occidente Latino dell'alto medioevo* (Spoleto, 1972), pp. 639-723, relates in large part to music and to treatises other than those of the *Arithmetica*. For another indication of the variety and amount of mathematical literature available to the student in the later thirteenth century, see the introduction to Roger Bacon, *Communia mathematica*, ed. by Robert Steele in *Opera hactenus inedita* (Oxford: Clarendon Press, [1909-42]), fasc. 16, pp. viii-ix.

24 „Huius vero scientie auctor est Nicomachus, Boetius vero translator:" Barcelona Archivio de la Corona de Aragon Ripoll 109, f. 134v. This MS was discovered by Mgr. Martin Grabmann, „Eine für Examina-zwecke abgefasste Quästionensammlung der Pariser Artistenfakultät aus der ersten Hälfte des 13. Jahrhunderts," in *Mittelalterliches Geistesleben: Abhandlungen zur Geschichte der Scholastik und Mystik*, II(1936), 189; and my article in *Actes*, 1969, p. 181 and note 40; also Delhaye, *loc. cit.*, p. 166.

25 „Institutis arismetice informandus, arismeticam Boecii et Euclidis legat:" Charles Homer Haskins, *Studies in the History of Mediaeval Science* (2nd ed. Cambridge, Mass.: Harvard University Press, 1927), p. 374; also Mgr Glorieux, *La Faculté des Arts*, p. 33.

For the combination in the teaching of arithmetic of the Nicomachan arithmetic with the section on numbers from Euclid's *Elements*, book VII, see W.H. Stahl, *Martianus Capella and the Seven Liberal Arts*, pp. 156-157; also Father J.A. Weisheipl, „Curriculum of the Faculty of Arts at Oxford in the early Forteenth Century," *Mediaeval Studies*, XXVI(1964), p. 170.

26 See my article in *Actes*, 1969, p. 182.

27 *Ibid.*, p. 183 and n. 53. For 13th century MSS of the *Algorismus*, see TK 991. To the 13th cent. MSS there listed might be added: London BM Harley 3353, 13th cent., ff. 76r-86v. The work was printed with the title: *Tractatus de arte numerandi*, together with an English translation, by J.O. Halliwell, *Rara mathematica* (2nd. ed., London: Maynard, 1841), pp. 1-26.

Paris, nowhere appears in the university documents of the thirteenth century, his presence is attested by another master, Bartholomew of Parma, who commented on Sacrobosco's *Sphere.* [28] The prose tract on the *Algorisms* as well as Sacrobosco's tract on the *Sphere*, both of which became basic textbooks for the teaching of two of the quadrivial arts, that is arithmetic and astronomy, are extant in thirteenth century manuscripts.[29] The *Algorismus*, a comparatively short tract which treated of various arithmetical operations and included the new Hindu-Arabic numerals from zero through nine was composed between 1220 and 1245 and constituted one of the major textbooks popularizing the new Arabic arithmetic. Yet it opened with the well known phrase from the second chapter of the first book of the Boethian *Arithmetica*: „All things that proceed from the first origin of things are formed in numerical ratio," and followed this with the definition of number as multitude composed of collected units and materially as a collection of units added one to another.[30] The *Algorismus* deals with the nine operations of the art of numeration, namely: addition, subtraction, halving, doubling, multiplying, dividing, progression, and extraction of cubic and square roots.[31] John of Sacrobosco also drew from Boethius his discussion of the extraction of roots and the explanation for the correspondence of numbers to geometric figures, and he summarized what Boethius had said of linear numbers.[32]

In addition to John of Sacrobosco's own citations and borrowing from the Boethian *Arithmetica* in his *Algorismus*, there were citations to the *Arithmetica* by the commentators on Sacrobosco's other popular university textbook, the *Sphere*. In one of these commentaries dated 1271, the author, Robertus Anglicus, a professor at Montpellier and also probably at Paris,[33] in his discussion of the number and position of the elements, recalled both the doctrine of Plato on means and proportion and the assertion of Boethius that „All things which proceed from the primeval origin of things are formed in numerical ratio."[34] And in another commentary, which is anonymous, the author drew from Boethius in the introduction to his translation of Nicomachus, the statement that: „Among all the sciences the quadriviales are the most suited for bringing one to wisdom" and the assertion, from the first chapter of Boethius' *Arithmetica*, that if anyone should neglect the four sciences that make up the quadrivium he would be unable to discover the truth. And further, that no one ignorant of these

28 As noted in the introduction to *The Sphere of Sacrobosco and its Commentators*, edited and translated with introduction by Lynn Thorndike (Chicago: University of Chicago Press, 1948), p. 2, n. 4.

29 For 13th cent. mss of the Algorismus, see note 27 above and for the *Commentary* by Petrus Philomenus de Dacia, found in 13th and 14th century mss, TK 681. Even more numerous are the 13th cent. mss of the *Sphere*, as indicated in TK 1524, 1577. The *Sphere* was also printed frequently by incunabula presses. See Klebs, 874, 1-30; and in Portugese 875.1.

30 „Omnia quecumque a primeva rerum origine etc." as in *Arith.* I.2, ed. with slight editions, Friedlein, p. 12: 14-15. „Omnia quaecumque a primaeva rerum natura constructa sunt, numerorum videntur ratione formata." And for the definition of number: „Numerus est unitatum collectio, vel quantitatis acervus ex unitatibus profusus..." *Ibid.*, p. 13; *Arith.* I-3: 10-12.

31 See Halliwell, pp. 1-26, for the text of the *Algorismus* or „Art of Numeration."

32 *Ibid.*, also Beaujouan, in *Homenaje à Millas-Vallicrosa*, 1954, p. 16. Cf. Boethius, *Arith.* ed. Friedlein, pp. 86 ff; 90 ff.

33 Thorndike, *The Sphere of Sacrobosco*, especially pp. 1-2; also P. Duhem, *Le Système du monde* (Paris: Hermanns, 1958), III, pp. 291-298 and for MSS, TK 337, 1596. The *Commentary* in both Latin and English translation is printed by Thorndike, pp. 143-98, 199-246.

34 „Lectio II," *Ibid.*, pp. 149-150; and p. 204: „.... sicut dicit Boetius, Omnia que a primeva rerum origine processerunt ratione numeri sunt formata." Cf. *Arith.* I,2. ed. Friedlein, p. 12: 14-17: „Omnia quaecumque a primaeva rerum natura constructa sunt, numerorum videntur ratione formata. Hoc enim fuit principale in animo conditioris exemplar."

four sciences is suited to philosophizing.[35] The author then, probably to prove that he was not wanting in this regard, went on to repeat from Boethius the assertion that mathematical science relates to quantity which is dual in nature, that is either discontinuous or continuous. The discontinuous comprises number considered in itself, which is arithmetic, and number in relation to another which is music; and quantity that is continuous and unmoved which is geometry or quantity that is continuous and moved which is astronomy.[36]

Moreover, the Boethian *Arithmetica* provided the basis for another thirteenth century work on arithmetic, that of Jordanus Nemorarius, who may possibly be the same as the Jordanus of Saxony, who was a master of arts at Paris, a member of the Dominican Order, and the author of a number of mathematical tracts.[37] Although his *Arithmetica* was based on the Boethian work, Jordanus had expanded the two books of that text into ten books, of which the first treated the common attributes of numbers, their parts and composition; the second, proportions and common attributions of proportionalities; third, of the first composition of numbers and proportions; fourth, of proportionality; fifth, of addition, subtraction, and parts of proportion; sixth, of numbers squared and cubed; seventh, of odd and even or equal and unequal numbers; eighth, of the forms of numbers; ninth, of equality and inequality; and tenth, of the median or arithmetical music. However, the *Arithmetica* of Jordanus differed from that of Boethius since it made use of letters instead of concrete numbers. Jordanus had also incorporated a number of additional demonstrations and examples into his work, a procedure for which he was criticized by his contemporary, Roger Bacon.[38]

In all probability the continued use of the Boethian *Arithmetica* in the thirteenth century was due to its philosophical tenor and the degree to which the work lent itself to the speculative aspects of mathematical and scientific exposition. In the thirteenth century the work was cited by several theologians. One of these, Robert Grosseteste, bishop of Lincoln (d. 1253), primarily an Oxford scholar, had nevertheless spent some time in Paris.[39] He is moreover

35 Anon. Comm. on John of Sacrobosco's *Sphere*: Thorndike, *The Sphere of Sacrobosco*, Appendix II, p. 451: „Nota quod inter omnes scientias quadriviales maxime sunt appetenda que maxime faciunt ad sapientiam, quod patet per Boetium primo arismetrice sue ubi dicit quod sunt quatuor partes exponentes se, id est, quadrivium, quia si quis caret verum inveniri non potest et sine quorum speculatione aliquis non potest habere speculationem veritatis. Et etiam dicit alibi, Hiis quatuor ignoratis nullum dico aptum ad philosophandum." Cf. Boethius' *Arithmetica*, ed. by Friedlein, 1966, p. 9: 5-8: „Quibus quattuor partibus si careat inquisitor, verum invenire non possit, ac sine hac quidem speculatione veritatis nulli recte sapiendum est...." (*Ibid.*, p. 9: 10-13) Quod haec qui spernit id est has semitas sapientiae ei denuntio non recte esse philosophandum, siquidem philosophia est amor sapientiae, quam in his spernendis ante contempserit."

36 „Modo ille scientie quadriviales sunt mathematice que diversificantur, quia mathematica scientia est de quantitate. Modo duplex est quantitas, discreta et continua. Discreta que est de numeris est duplex. Vel numerus consideratur in se ut unus duo est, vel in alio ut duplum triplum. Sic quantitas continua est duplex, quedam est immota et de illa est geometria, quia est de magnitudinibus etc. que sunt absoluta ab omni motu et materia saltem secundum rationem. Quedam est quantitas que est continua mota et de illa est astronomia...." Lynn Thorndike, ed., *The Sphere of Sacrobosco*, Appendix II, pp. 451-52. Cf. Boethius' *Arithmetica*, ed. by Friedlein, 1966, p. 9: 1-6, cited above n. 10.

37 For Jordanus Nemorarius, see my article in *Actes*, 1969, pp. 182-83, and notes; also. E.A. Moody and Marshall Clagett, *The Medieval Science of Weights* (Madison: The University of Wisconsin Press, 1960), pp. 3-4. For his many mathematical works, see the index to TK under Jordanus Nemorarius, and especially for the *Arithmetica*, ibid., 1600. Another 13th century MS of the *Arithmetica Jordani (de Nemoraria)* is at Paris: BN 16644, 13th cent., ff. 2r ff. This MS was deeded to the Sorbonne by Gerard of Abbetsville. Jordanus also has an *Algorismus*: TK 237, 431.

38 Paul Abelson, *The Seven Liberal Arts* (New York, 1939; reprinted New York: Russell and Russell Inc., 1965), p. 105, and my article in *Actes*, 1969, p. 183; for Roger Bacon's criticism, see below.

39 For his Paris sojourn see Ludwig Baur, „Die Philosophie des Robert Grosseteste Bischofs von Lincoln (d. 1253)," *Beiträge z. Geschichte d. Philosophie des Mittelalters*, Münster, XVIII, Heft 4 (1917), 4-5, n. 1.

associated specifically by Professor A.C. Crombie with the development of a new scientific procedure, through the utilization of mathematics. Without this discipline, upon which the investigation of natural phenomena is dependent, according to Grosseteste, man cannot achieve a scientific understanding of nature. Mathematics, in his view, provides the means to throw light on nature and natural phenomena.[40] However, although Grosseteste cited the Boethian *Arithmetica* in his tract on „Lines, angles, and figures,"[41] he relied more heavily on geometry than on the *Arithmetica* for his demonstrations.[42] He also gave considerable attention to the other two mathematical arts, that is to music and astronomy.[43]

On the other hand much more extensive use was made of the Boethian *Arithmetica* by Roger Bacon, Grosseteste's disciple. Bacon, a member of the Franciscan Order, as well as a master of arts, probably in the University of Paris, appears in any case to have spent a goodly part of his academic career in Paris.[44] Although generally outspoken in his criticism of contemporary mathematicians, Bacon expressed agreement with the views set forth in the Boethian *Arithmetica* and cited it frequently. He placed Boethius first among authorities on the subject and cited him for the statement that if the seeker after truth should lack knowledge of the four branches of *mathematica* (the quadrivium) he would be unable to achieve his goal; and for the further assertion that „without this speculative knowledge nothing of the truth could rightly be known."[45] Bacon had explained that the *mathematica* comprise the four sciences of geometry, arithmetic, music, and astrology, placing under the latter both the judicial and operative aspects of the science.[46] And he repeated the statement from Cassiodorus that these four sharpen our perception and are instructive for all other sciences which indeed cannot be taught without mathematics, as Boethius had suggested in the prologue to the *De Arithmetica.*[47] Bacon also repeated the phrases from the *Arithmetica* that among all

40   For Robert Grosseteste, see especially A.C. Crombie, *Robert Grosseteste and the Origins of Experimental Science*, 1100-1700 (Oxford, Clarendon Press, 1953), pp. 44 ff., with references to earlier bibliography in note 1; also *ibid.*, p. 50; my article in *Actes*, 1969, p. 185; and Ludwig Baur, „Die philosophischen Werke des Robert Grosseteste, Bischofs von Lincoln (d. 1253)," *Beiträge zur Geschichte der Philosophie des Mittelalters*, Münster, IX (1912), 59-60: „Utilitas considerationis linearum angulorum et figurarum est maxima, quoniam impossibile est sciri naturalem philosophiam sine illis."

41   „De lineis, angulis et figuris," ed. Baur, *Beiträge z. Gesch. d. Philosophie*, IX (1912), p. 61: „Item, linea recta habet aequalitatem sine angulo; sed melius est aequale quam inequali, ut dicit Boethius in arismetica sua." (Boethius, *Arith.* I,32; II,1; Friedlein, pp. 66, 77.)

42   Crombie, pp. 32 ff., 50, 59; „De Natura locorum," ed. Baur, *Beiträge z. Gesch. d. Philosophie*, IX (1912), pp. 65-66: „His igitur regulis et fundamentis datis ex potestate geometrie diligens inspector in rebus naturalibus potest dare causas omnium effectuum naturalium per hanc viam." See also *Actes*, 1969, p. 185.

43   *Ibid.*, pp. 186, 189. See „De Artibus liberalibus," ed. Baur, *Beiträge* IX (1912), 1-5, for music; p. 5 for astronomy; and p. 4 for arithmetic and geometry.

44   *Ibid.*, p. 177; also Lynn Thorndike, *A History of Magic and Experimental Science* (New York, 1923), II, chap. LXI.

45   Roger Bacon, „Communia mathematica," in *Opera hactenus inedita*, ed. by Robert Steele (1909-42), fasc. 16 (1940), p. 7: „Incipio a Boetio. Dicit enim in prologo Arismetrice secundo mathematice ,Quatuor partibus si careat inquisitor, verum minime invenire potesta sine hac quidem speculatione veritatis nulli recte sapiendum est.' " Cf. Friedlein, p. 9: 6-8; *Arith.* I. 1. For the lines quoted, see n. 12 above.

46   Bacon here follows the Varronean order, transmitted by Martianus Capella, which differed from the Nicomachean order of arithmetic, music, geometry (or in the variant, geometry, music), and astronomy. L. Baur, „Die Philosophie des Robert Grosseteste Bischofs von Lincoln (d. 1253)," *Beiträge z. Gesch. d. Philosophie des Mittelalters*, XVIII, Heft. 4 (1917), pp. 17-18. Grosseteste followed the unusual order of music, arithmetic, geometry and astronomy. *Ibid.*, 1917, p. 18.

47   Roger Bacon, *Opera hactenus inedita*, ed. by Robert Steele (Oxford: Clarendon Press), fasc. V, pp. 2-3; „... et dicitur hec mathematica dicitur doctrinalis vel disciplinalis quia omnes alie sciencie per hanc docentur et sine illa non possunt doceri. Quod etiam Boethius in prologo Arithmetice..." Boethius, *Arith.*

those of ancient authority who under the leadership of Pythagoras sought to attain the pinnacle of perfection in the disciplines of philosophy none could do so without the knowledge of the four mathematical sciences.[48]

Roger Bacon furthermore gave preference in the *Communia mathematica* to the Boethian work over that of his contemporary, Jordanus Nemorarius, whose *Arithmetic* in ten books, as previously noted, was largely based on that of Boethius. As between Jordanus and Boethius, Bacon asserted, the latter's *Arithmetica* is the better of the two and more useful. Jordanus, in Bacon's opinion, had included a superabundance of demonstrations, a failing that Bacon asserted, wasted too much time.[49] So many demonstrations were superfluous and unnecessary, he insisted, and if it were not for them and the difficulties they create, one could within a year know as much as anyone would learn in the course of twenty years, as experience has clearly shown.[50] Bacon further cited, on the subject of proportionality, Boethius and Jordanus as well as Adelard (Alardum) of Bath in the commentary on five of the *Elements* of Euclid that he had translated.[51]

Roger Bacon's agreement with the views expressed in the Boethian *Arithmetica* was further exemplified in several other instances. Although he had not followed Boethius' lead by placing geometric progression before that of arithmetic, Bacon made clear his adherence to the view expressed in the Boethian *Arithmetica* that without the speculation engendered by arithmetic, which teaches the species of numbers and the reasons for their operations, attainment of wisdom would be impossible.[52] Moreover, in his *Questiones altere supra libros prime philosophie Aristotelis (Metaphysica I-IV)*, Bacon referred to Boethius' *Arithmetica*, in the course of a discussion of the question whether numbers are the foundations of things as the Pythagoreans and Platonists had asserted. He agreed that they were, „since Boethius has written in the *Arithmetica*, ,whatever is has proceeded from the primeval origin of things, therefore numbers are the beginnings of things...' "[53] He similarly acquiesced in the application of the term wisdom or philosophy to mathematics since „as is written in the *Arithmetica*; ,Wisdom is made up of those things that are true.' "[54] In sum, Bacon was articulate in his conviction, expressed at great length in the *Communia mathematica*, and the *Opus maius*, part four, as well as in other of his works, that the Boethian *Arithmetica* was of great importance

I, 1; Friedlein, pp. 7 ff. See also Bacon, *Opus maius*, ed. by J.H. Bridges (reprinted Frankfurt/Main: Minerva G.M.B.H., 1964), I, pp. 103 ff.

48 „Inter omnes prisce auctoritatis viros qui Pictagora duce... haud quemquam in philosophie disciplinis ad cumulum perfectionis evadera nisi cui talis prudentie nobilitas quasi quadrivio vestigatur..." *Opera hactenus inedita*, ed. by Robert Steele, fasc. XVI (1940), p. 7; Boeth. *Arith*. I.1, ed. by Friedlein, p. 7: 21-25.

49 „Communia mathematica," *Opera hactenus inedita*, ed. by Robert Steele, fasc. XVI, p. 47; „Jordani ex fontibus Boetii oriuntur. Unde optimus liber est *Arismetica* Boetii et utilior quam liber Jordani, quia pauca de numeris demonstranda sunt..."

50 For Bacon's criticisms of the mathematical teaching of his day, see *ibid.*, pp. xi, 117-18.

51 *Ibid.*, p. 83: „hec tres proportionalitates sunt medietates et secundum Boetium et Jordanum in Arismetica et secundum Alardum Batoniensem in expositione quinti Elementorum Euclidis quam tradidit..." and again *ibid.*, p. 86, „Sed continua proportionalitas potest esse in Arismetica medietate et in musica sicut in geometrica ut patet in exemplis et Boetius hoc edocet in Arismetica." Adelard of Bath made his translation of Euclid in the twelfth century. See *ibid.*, introd., p. ix.

52 See above note 45.

53 Ed. Robert Steele with the collaboration of F.M. Delorme, O.P., *Opera hactenus inedita* (Oxford: Clarendon Press, 1932), fasc. XI, p. 81. Cf. *Arith*. I.2, as cited in note 29 above.

54 *Ibid.*, p. 111: „Mathematica dicitur sapientia vel philosophia videtur; scribitur in Arismetica ,Sapientia est eorum que vere sunt." Cf. *Arith*. I.1: „Est enim sapientia earum rerum quae vere sunt..." Friedlein, p. 9: 8-9.

and also that mathematics was necessary and useful in every science including the divine science.[55]

The Boethian *Arithmetica* was also utilized by another member of the Franciscan Order, Saint Bonaventura (d. 1274), who taught in the University of Paris between 1248 and 1255.[56] Bonaventura has been shown to have been very much interested in the significance of numbers. The recent editor and translator of his „Collations on the Six Days" asserts that „In almost every one of his works and frequently in the present one, there are elaborate references to the numbers 3, 6, 7, 12, 144, 666, and 1000, in which he sees logical links with the realities of heaven and earth."[57] It is not surprising therefore that Bonaventura found much of interest to him in the Boethian *Arithmetica*. For example, in the „Third Collation" of the „Six Days of Creation," which he used as a literary and symbolic framework, Bonaventura referred to the Boethian *De Arithmetica* among other authorities for his expressed views „on oneness." „Indeed if oneness were able to know the sum total of its potencies, it would know all the lines passing through the center. Oneness, however, is more a principle than the mathematical point, for oneness is an essential part of number, while the point is a principle but not a part."[58] Furthermore, he utilized the Boethian *Arithmetica* among other works in the „Fourth Collation" in referring to mathematics. „Now these sciences prepare for the understanding of Scripture, as is clear in the case of perfect numbers, and of the decreased and increasing number, as it appears with the perfection of the number six which is perfect of itself... Likewise, concerning the two first cubic numbers, 8 and 27: twice two times two equals 8, and three times three times three equal 27, and they can be related through no other numbers than 12 and 18, for 12 is to 18 as 18 is to 27, in the proportion of one and a half, which contains the whole and its intermediate."[59]

Finally, Bonaventura utilized Boethius' *Arithmetica* in the „Eleventh Collation" on the vision of God's Trinity. „According to Boethius, inequalities have their origin from equality. Likewise if something essentially different is produced by God, by necessity there must be produced first something substantially the same, for before the extrinsic there is in the intrinsic, as is evident."[60]

Boethius' *Arithmetica* was similarly utilized by another contemporary of Roger Bacon, the learned and sainted Albertus Magnus, of the Order of Preaching Friars, whose intellectual activities are closely associated with Paris although his native home was in the Germanies. Albertus, too, like Bacon, expounded mathematics at considerable length in several of his writings, and is the author of a commentary on Euclid as well as of other mathematical writings.[61] He is credited further by the *Histoire Littéraire* with a commentary on the *Arithmetica Boetii.*[62] However, diligent search focused at the Bibliothèque Nationale in Paris has not so far led to success in locating such a work. Nevertheless Albertus has in his own writings exemplified both his interest in the quadrivial or mathematical arts and his use of the Boethian *Arithmetica.*

55 *Opus maius*, ed. J.H. Bridges (reprinted, 1964), I, pp. 97 ff.; 175 ff.
56 Etienne Gilson, *La Philosophie au Moyen Âge: Des Origines Patristiques à la Fin du XIVe Siècle* (2nd ed., Paris: Payot, 1947), pp. 439 ff.
57 „V. Collations on the Six Days," *The Works of Bonaventura, Cardinal, Seraphic Doctor, and Saint*, trans. form the Latin by José de Vinck (Paterson, New Jersey: Anthony Guild Press, 1970), introduction.
58 *Ibid.*, pp. 43-44; cf. *Arith.* I.7. Ed. Friedlein, p. 16.
59 *The Works of Bonaventura*, 1970, pp. 66-67. Cf. *Arith.* I. 20, ed. Friedlein p. 41 ff.
60 *The Works of Bonaventura*, 1970, p. 162. Cf. *Arith.* I. 32, Friedlein, p. 66.
61 B. Geyer, „Die mathematischen Schriften des Albertus Magnus," *Angelicum*, XXV (1958), 159-175, including the text of the Commentary on Euclid at pp. 170-175.
62 *Histoire littéraire de la France*, Paris, 1824, XVI, 113. The statement is also repeated by Mgr. P. Glorieux in *La Faculté des Arts et ses Maitres au XIIIe siècle*, 1971, p. 76.

In addition to citing the *Arithmetica* specifically on the subject of the science of numbers, in his *Commentary on the Sentences*,[63] Albertus Magnus drew attention to the quadrivium and to the four mathematical disciplines in his work on *Metaphysics*.[64] He there took care to make clear the liberal and speculative rather than utilitarian character of the mathematical sciences of the quadrivium, that is of arithmetic, music, geometry, and astrology (*sic*). They are called liberal, he held, when they are exercised not for any utilitarian purpose but for themselves alone, since in the same way as man is free, that science is termed free or liberal that has no other utility than that of the science itself.[65] Similarly, the mathematical sciences are speculative, he continued, when they are pursued wholly for knowledge or for the science itself. Albertus had already affirmed the principle that the aim of all speculation is to know the truth, whereas the aim of practice is the work itself.[66] He also went on to assert that the speculative character of the mathematical sciences is not based on opinion but entails the speculative intellect. They are thus designated as true sciences and are distinguished as *doctrinales* and *disciplines*. They do not require experience and are taught simply by the master's demonstration. Hence inexperienced youth could greatly excell in them. This differentiates them from the physical sciences where experience is necessary. For unlike the *physicales* which are concerned with matter and hence are subject to motion, change, or both in time, the *mathematicales* which are not constituents of physical matter have their definitive form through demonstration.[67]

Furthermore, in his discussion of the Pythagorean doctrine that numbers are the beginnings of things, Albertus quoted the passage from the Pythagorean *Arithmetica* to the effect that unity is that by which each thing is one.[68] He went on then to assert that unity is in no way joined to number and to draw attention to the fact that Boethius, in transferring the substance of the words of Pythagoras into his discussion of the substance of number in the second chapter of the *Arithmetica*, had asserted that „Everything that proceeds from the primeval nature of things has been formed in numerical ratio" for this was the principal exemplar in the mind of the Creator.[69] But as Albertus explained in his *Summa Theologia*, the number which attended the divine ratio is not the number of forms; it is the number of proportion where the two extremes, as Boethius says, are connected by arithmetical means.

63 Albertus Magnus, *Commentarius in Sententias*, ed. A. Borgnet (Paris, 1890), XXVII, 15 (II Sent. Dist. 1, Art. 5): 2. Item Boetius in prohemio primi Arithmeticorum dicit sic: Numerorum scientiam ille hujus humane molis conditor Deus primam (*sic*) suae habuit rationis exemplar, et ad hanc conjuncta constituit quaecumque fabricante ratione, per numeros assignati ordinis invenire concordiam."
64 Albertus, *Metaphysicorum Libri XIII*, ed. A. Borgnet, Paris, 1890, VI, 1 ff., 32.
65 *Ibid.*, VI, 31-32 (Metaph. I.II.6-7): Scientie methematicae formas stantes habentes quae principium liberorum sunt sciendi in ipsis...hoc modo enim liberalis dicitur quae non alterius utilitatis causa quaeritur. Et hec modo sunt liberales illae quae dicuntur esse de quadrivio scilicet arithmetica, musica, geometria, et astrologia..."
66 *Ibid.*, VI, 31: „Finis autem omnis speculationis est scire et veritas: et praxis omnis finis est opus: ergo scientiae sunt speculativae: hi ergo prosecuti sunt scientiam propter notitiam simpliciter: non causa alicuius utilitatis...."
67 *Ibid.*, VI, pp. 1-2 (Metaph. I, 1, 1).
68 *Ibid.*, VI, p. 62 (Metaph. I.IV.2): „Pythagoras in Arithmetica, unitas est quaelibet res una est...." Cf. *Arith.* I. 7, ed. Friedlein, p. 16.
69 *Ibid.*, VI, 64 (Metaph. I.IV.2): „Et hoc quod dixit Boetius substantiam verborum Pythagorae transferens, et de substantia numeri in principio *Arithmeticae* loquens: ‚Omnia quae a primaeva rerum natura constructa sunt, numerorum videntur ratione formata: hoc enim fuit principale in animo conditoris exemplar...' " Cf. *Arith.* I. 2, ed. Friedlein, p. 12. See note 34 above, for the citation.

He noted too that Boethius had similarly asserted that this number cannot be understood as mathematical number but rather as ideal number.[70]

The views expressed by Albertus Magnus regarding the mathematical or quadrivial arts were similarly expounded by his disciple, St. Thomas Aquinas. St. Thomas asserted that arithmetic formed the principal part of mathematics and should precede geometry as well as astronomy or astrology, and music.[71] He had also in the *Commentary on the Ethics* outlined the order of learning or teaching as logic first, since it taught the method of all philosophy; and next the mathematicales or quadriviales, arithmetic, music, geometry, and astronomy, since as indicated by Albertus, they require no experience; thirdly, natural philosophy; fourthly, moral philosophy; and finally, divine philosophy or metaphysics.[72]

For another order of learning, it may be of interest to note that in a work entitled *Liber de Apprehensione* attributed to Albertus Magnus that is probably not by him, but is printed with his other works by Borgnet,[73] the recommendation to students is that they first study *physics* (natural philosophy) then *mathematica* (the arts of the quadrivium), and finally complete their studies in the divine science or metaphysics. The reason given for this order is that it corresponds to the order of nature in which sense apprehension is first, then the intellect receives the *mathematica* abstracted from sensible matter.[74]

This same order of study is also found in the section on the mathematical sciences by Vincent of Beauvais, the learned Dominican friar who was closely associated with the French monarch Louis IX as royal chaplain, librarian, and tutor to the royal children, for whom he composed an educational tract.[75] Although Vincent of Beauvais cannot be directly associated with the University of Paris, his three or four part *Speculum* indicated that he was apparently in close rapport with the intellectual and scholarly community in Paris.[76] He devoted one entire book (Liber XVI) to *mathematica* in the second part of the *Speculum*, that is the *Speculum Doctrinale*.[77] And he there asserted that mathematics should be read or studied after natural philosophy or natural science because the latter considers form as it is in matter, whereas the former or mathematics is abstracted by the intellect. And since sense apprehension is prior to intellectual apprehension it should come first.[78]

70 Borgnet VI, 61 (Metaph. I.IV.2); also *Summa Theologiae* II, tract. I, Q. 4, m. 2, ad 3, ed. Borgnet XXXII, 76: „Numerus quem attendit ratio divina in constituendo res, non est numerus formarum, sed est numerus proportionis...." See also Albertus, In II Sentent. Dist. 1, A. Art. V, Borgnet XXVII, 15: „Boetius in prohemio primi Arithmeticorum...constat autem quod de numero mathematico istud non potest intelligi: ergo necesse est, quod intelligatur de numero ideali qui praecessit omnia ideata."

71 St. Thomas Aquinas, „In XII libros Metaphysicorum," *Opera Omnia*, Paris, 1875, XXIV, 468b. (Metaph. IV, lect. 1).

72 St. Thomas Aquinas, „In X libros Ethicorum ad Nicomachum," *Opera Omnia*, 1875, XXV, 503-504 (Ethica VI, lect. 7).

73 Borgnet, V, 556 ff. „Liber de Apprehensione a quibusdam adscriptus." Preceding the above text which is in the form of a dialogue, is the statement that the work is ascribed by some to Albertus, but is rejected as not authentic by others, among them J. Quetif and J. Echard, *Scriptores ord. Praed.* (2 vol., Paris, 1719-21; new ed., I-VI, Paris, 1910-1913).

74 Borgnet, V, 607: Liber de apprehensione Pars VI.5: „Ideoque bene studentes primo in physicis, postea ad mathematica venerunt, et tandem in divinis finiunt vitam in ipsis felicitati cupientes...."

75 L. Thorndike, *History of Magic and Experimental Science*, II, 458.

76 Vincentius Bellovacensis (Vincent de Beauvais), *Speculum quadruplex sive Speculum maius naturale/ Doctrinale/ Morale/ Historiale*. Photocopy of the edition of 1624: Ex officina typographica Baltozaris Belieri, Duac. Photocopy made in Graz, Austria, 1965. For incunabula editions, see Klebs 1036.1-3, 1037.1-3.

77 „Tomus secundus: *Speculum Doctrinale*. Liber Decimus sextus. De mathematica."

78 *Ibid.*, end of cap. 1, 1504: „Haec scientia [id est mathematica] post naturalem legenda est, quia naturalis

Vincent of Beauvais described mathematics as the discipline which considers abstract quantity and deals with invisible forms of visible things just as *physica* deals with the visible causes of visible things. He then went on to explain in the fashion of the Boethian *Arithmetica* the fourfold aspect of quantity as either separate and permanent, that is arithmetic or number; or successive, that is music, the number of sounds; or quantity continuously mobile, that is astronomy; or immobile, as geometry.[79] The authority to whom Vincent of Beauvais turned after Boethius was Michael Scot, the noted scholar, translator, and astrologer, whom Professor Lynn Thorndike characterized as „the leading intellectual in Western Europe during the first third of the thirteenth century."[80] Boethius' *Arithmetica*, Book One, was cited not only for the above fourfold aspect of quantity but also for the statement that no one can attain the pinnacle of perfection in the disciplines of philosophy unless he is possessed of the nobility of intellect achieved through the comprehension of truth. And without knowledge of the four parts of the *mathematica* as noted above, the seeker for truth would be unable to find it.[81]

Vincent of Beauvais further cited Boethius on the primacy of arithmetic, among the mathematical arts, and he repeated the statement that arithmetic is the discipline of numbers, about which the first Greek to write was Pythagoras. And he was followed by Nicomachus, whose work was translated into Latin first by Apuleius and then by Boethius.[82] He reported from Boethius the well known phrase „All things which were constituted from the primeval origin of things seem to have been formed from the ratio of numbers"[83] and cited him on several other occasions as well.

With this encyclopedia we may bring to a close our brief foray into some of the evidence reflecting and exemplifying the continuity of interest in, and utilization of, the Boethian *Arithmetica* and the quadrivium in the university milieu at Paris. The survival of interest in these relics of Greek antiquity particularly among philosophers and theologians is an interesting demonstration of the persistence of the Greek elements in western intellectual history and the extent to which they were adapted and molded to the new interests of medieval scholars.

Hunter College and The Graduate School CUNY.

considerat formam prout est in materia: haec autem prout est abstracta, scilicet intellectu, apprehensio enim sensus prior est, quam apprehensio intellectus."

79   *Ibid.*, cap. 1, 1503; *Arith.* I.1, ed. Friedlein, pp. 8-9.
80   *Ibid.*, cap. 1, 1503. For Michael Scot, see Lynn Thorndike; *Michael Scot*, (London: Thomas Nelson and Sons Ltd., 1965), and especially pp. 54 ff. for his interest in numbers.
81   Vincent de Beauvais, *Spec. doct.* cap. II, 1504; *Arith.* I.1, ed. Friedlein, p. 9. See n. 12 above for the quotation.
82   Vincent de Beauvais, Spec. Doct., cap. V, 1506: „*Isid. in lib. 3 Etymo.* Arithmetica est disciplina numerorum. Graeci namque numerum a *Rythmom* dicunt. Hanc apud Graecos primum conscripsisse Pithagoram autumant, et postmodum a Nicomacho diffusius esse dispositam, quam apud Latinos primus Apuleius, deinde Boetius transtulerunt."
83   Vincent de Beauvais, *Spec. doct.*, cap. VI, 1507: „Boetius ubi supra. Omnia quaecumque a primaeva rerum natura constituta sunt, numerorum videntur ratione esse formata..."; also *ibid.*, cap. vii, 1507, et passim. For the citation from Boethius, *Arith.* I, 2, see n. 30 above.

MICHAEL MASI

THE INFLUENCE OF BOETHIUS' *DE ARITHMETICA* ON
LATE MEDIEVAL MATHEMATICS

In another essay of this collection, Professor Ubaldo Pizzani has made a study of the Boethian *De Musica* and how it was disseminated throughout Europe until the High Middle Ages. He has made clear that the history of the *De Musica* was closely tied with the spread of the *De Arithmetica* which seems to have been intended--or at least to have served in the medieval schools--as an introduction to the music theory. It is my intention in this chapter of the collection to extend Professor Pizzani's survey to the late history of the *De Arithmetica*. We should be able to see that the history of the Boethian mathematics underwent several interesting developments, most of these quite apart from its connection with the music theory. First and most significantly it must be noted that the Boethian arithmetic did not lose its importance after the influx of Arabic mathematics and the re-introduction of Greek number theory. If we are to judge from the number of extant manuscripts which contain the *De Arithmetica*, by the frequency of citations in other treatises (with or without the mention of Boethius' name) and by the number of early printed editions through the 16th century (at least 25),[1] we must conclude that the Boethian mathematics enjoyed an extraordinary increase in popularity and influence between 1200 and 1600.

That Boethius' mathematics should have become so widely used may seem surprising since the superior texts of Euclid, Nicomachus (Boethius' source) and Archimedes were available, could be read by many scholars, and were being translated. Moreover, as all students of the period are aware, the nature of mathematics was undergoing thorough and wide reaching changes at this time. The needs of a growing merchant trade which demanded efficient book-keeping were responded to by an increasingly more sophisticated computational mathematics couched in the recently adapted Arabic number system. Though the new mathematical techniques were initially slow to grow in European soil, by the 15th century hundreds of computational works[2] were available for those who wanted to learn. The ascendency of the Boethian mathematics in this context indicates a far more interesting aspect about the development of mathematics in the Middle Ages than that it was simply evolving into modern algebra and trigonometry. An examination of the various texts dealing with mathematics shows that this discipline was becoming highly diversified in nature by the late Middle Ages.

Until the late Middle Ages, a large portion of the mathematics studied in the schools and universites was a carry-over of earlier number theory, unoriginal and impractical. It was a mathematics which oriented the student to philosophical study and was imbued with the terminology of logic. As a preparation for higher philosophical study, it had once served its purpose well, but it had long since ceased to grow by the 15th century. But practical and computational mathematics slowly broke with the old number theory and began a new strain

---

1   In the introduction to my translation of the *De Arithmetica* (to be published soon by Rodopi, Amsterdam), I have listed almost 200 manuscripts of the *De Arithmetica* extant. A list of printed editions may be found in David Eugene Smith, *Rara Arithmetica* (Boston: Ginn & Co., 1908), p. 27.
2   Descriptions of many such works may be found in Smith's *Rara Arithmetica*.

of mathematics. This break occurred outside the universities and probably began very early in the Middle Ages. It was a new strain of mathematics that lived in the counting rooms of merchants and its greatest exponent was Fibonacci, the son of a trader. Certainly much of the computational mathematics was as servile to the merchant as the older number theory was to the philosopher. Some few thinkers, subtle and perceptive in their study of both Greek and Arabic numbers, such as Bradwardine, Nicholas of Oresme and Fibonacci, achieved a scope of mathematical vision not fully appreciated until recent times.

By the late Middle Ages the *De Arithmetica* had become moribund, and the widespread popularity of Boethius served, perhaps, to slow down the progress of mathematical innovation. The text of the *De Arithmetica* was inherited by the universities as a scrap from that vast learning of Greek thinkers and had become fossilized as part of the Liberal Arts curriculum, a once vital program of studies. But, for a small number of original thinkers (whose proportion among mathematicians has perhaps remained a constant even to our own times) Boethian definitions of numbers, the classification of number and ratio, and the definitions of the types of proportionalities were the starting points for new understandings.

I have accordingly divided my study into two parts. Initially I will survey the evidence which makes the Boethian treatise the best known mathematical work of the Middle Ages. Without attempting to evaluate the works cited, I will review a few treatises which show the way in which Boethius was adapted. When the *De Arithmetica* was not used directly as a text, it appeared in shortened form (an *epitome*) or merely excerpted to reduce its length. In the second part of the essay I will attempt to demonstrate how Boethian ideas provided seeds for more original thought in the works of a small number of innovative mathematicians. The most important of these are Thomas Bradwardine, Albert of Saxony (whom he influenced), Roger Bacon and Nicholas of Oresme.

A good example of the kind of treatise derived directly and uncritically from Boethius is the *De Arithmetica* of Johannis De Muris (c. 1300-1351). De Muris is known now chiefly for his work as a writer of musical theory and he would be expected to be interested in number theory since those two disciplines were closely tied in the Middle Ages. His short treatise on arithmetic does not mention Boethius by name but it is clearly taken from the Boethian *De Arithmetica*.[3] Its main purpose is to present the essentials of Boethian number theory in simplified and shortened form. The resemblance to its source is obvious from the verbatim transcriptions of many definitions as well as in the identical arrangements of topics. Unlike the work of other mathematical writers who resemble Boethius (such as Jordanus Nemorarius, below, who completely reorganized his discussion of number theory) De Muris follows Boethius slavishly. Here, for example, are some of his definitions.

Boethius: Numerus est unitatum collectio vel quantitas acervus ex unitatibus professus. (Friedlein ed., p. 13)

De Muris: Numerus est collectio unitatum vel quantatis acervus ex unitatibus profusus (p. 4).

Here is the definition of even number:

Boethius: Par numerus est, qui in duo aequalia et in duo inaequalia partitionem recipit, sed ut in neutra divisione vel imparitati paritas vel paritati imparitas misceatur, preter solum paritas principem, binarium numerum, qui in aequalem non recipit sectionem, propter quod ex duobus unitatibus constat et ex prima duorum quommodo paritate (p. 14).

De Muris: Numerus par est qui in duo aequalia et in duo inaequalia recipit divisionem ita ut in neutra divisione vel imparitati, vel paritati imparitas misceatur. Praeter solum paritatis princi-

---

3   The *De Arithmetica* of Johannis de Muris was last published in 1538 and I cite that edition. It is descri-
     bed in Smith, p. 119.

pem binarium qui in aequalem non recipit divisionem (p. 5).

As another from many such examples we may note De Muris' explanation of the „crib" of Erothosthenes (whom he, unlike Boethius, does not mention). This procedure need not delay us with its particulars but may be pointed out in De Muris as much reduced from Boethius. Boethius ends his exposition with a stern warning to the student that he proceed with care: Sed id non vulgo neque confuse. Nam primus numerus illum, qui est post duos secundum se locatos, per suam quantitatem metitur (p. 34). De Muris has made his own adaptation of this warning: Et hoc non inordinate et confuse traditur, quia primum quem numerat per se ipsum numerat, secundum quem numerat per secundum imparem numerat (p. 16).

Finally, we may see from the following outline that the structure of the two works is precisely identical. (I have included some verbatim repetition between the titles as useful for the comparison.)

De Muris	*Boethius*
Part I	
Tractatus I.	
Chap. I. Substance of number; its definition and division.	Book I, chap. 2-7.
Chap. II. Even number and its types	Book I, chap. 8-12.
Chap. III. Odd number and its types.	Book I, 13-18.
Chap. IV. Perfect, superfluous and diminished numbers.	Book I, 19-20.
Tractatus II.	
Chap. 1. On proportions: the multiplex.	Book I, 21-23.
Chap. 2. On the Superparticular.	Book I, 24-27.
Chap. 3. On the Superpartient.	Book I, 28.
Chap. 4. Multiplex Superparticular.	Book I, 29-30.
Chap. 5. Multiplex Superpartient.	Book I, 31.
Chap. 6. A Demonstration of the Minor Inequalities.	Book I, 32.
Part II.	
Chap. I, Inequalities are reduced to equalities.	Book II, 1.
Chap. II. De Inveniendo in unoquoque numero quot numeros eiusdem proportionis possit praecedere (p. 47).	Book II, 2. De inveniendo in unoquoque numero quot numeros eiusdem proportionis possit praecedere eorumque descriptio, descriptionis expositio (p. 80).
Chap. III. Quod multiplex intervallum ex quibus superparticularibus medietate intervallis fiat.	Book II, 3. Quod multiplex intervallum ex quibus superparticularibus medietate possita intervallis fiat eiusque invenienda regula (p.83).
Chap. IV. Considering numbers absolutely.	II, 4-9; 22.
Chap. V. On solids.	II, 23-28.
Chap. VI. De Natura Rerum quae dicitur eiusdem naturae et de ea quae dicitur alterius naturae et qui numeri cui naturae coniuncti sint (p. 65).	II, 31. De ea Natura rerum, quae dicitur eiusdem naturae et de ea quae dicitur alterius naturae et qui numeri cui naturae coniuncti sint (p. 122).
Chap. VII. On Proportions.	II, 40.
Chap. VIII. Geometric Proportions.	II, 44.
Chap. IX. Harmonic Proportions.	II, 47.

Chap. X.   Seven other Medial Proportions.   II, 51-53.
Chap. XI.   Perfect Symphony.   II, 54.

I have found no clear indication of how popular or influential the treatise of De Muris may have been. It can hardly be considered a major work in the medieval mathematical repertory. Its significance resides more in the fact that it represents the many individual adaptations of the Boethian mathematics.

Another such representative work, an anonymous treatise from Italy in the 15th century, may be found in the Plimpton collection of Columbia University Library.[4] This work is entitled *De Commutata Proportione* and is part of a volume which contains various mathematical and astronomical works. Such collections are commonly found in this period. These pages on number theory may well be some scholar's notes taken from a lecture or from some other written source. The ideas, however, are clearly drawn, directly or indirectly, from the first part of the Boethian treatise on arithmetic with some few excerpts taken from the second book of the same treatise. It is in the first part of the *De Arithmetica* where Boethius outlines and defines the five types of ratios between unequal numbers: the multiplex, superparticular, superpartient, multiplex superparticular and multiplex superpartient. In this anonymous manuscript the author calls these ratios „proportions," a confusion of terms also found in Boethius. Most mathematicians consider ratios as relations between numbers and proportions as relationships between ratios; proportions are ratios of ratios.

The organization and chapter titles of the Columbia University treatise are somewhat haphazard, but they follow approximately the Boethian order. Chapter titles are not numbered but they may be identified by the folio page on which they occur.

f. 13:   *De Commutata proportione*. This title of the first chapter has been used by Smith (the only scholar to describe this manuscript in detail) to identify the entire treatise. The opening part, not taken from the *De Arithmetica*, is simple enough. It explains the conversion or reduction of proportions (that is, ratios) such as 2:4 which is as 4:8, or 3:9 which is as 2:6.

The discription of how ratios are transferred is followed by a definition of the five types named above (*De Arithmetics* I, 23).

f. 15v: *Quid sit numerus superparticularis et quod subsuperparticularis (De Arithmetica* I, 24).

f. 16:   *Numerorum Superpartientium (D. A.* I, 28). This section contains the following diagram:

I	II	III	IIII	V	VI	VII	VIII	IX	X
III	VI	IX	XII	XV	XVIII	XXI	XXIIII	XXVII	XXX
II	IIII	VI	VIII	X	XII	XIV	XVI	XVIII	XX

This set of numbers is used to develop the sesquialter superparticular ratios and is found in Friedlein, p. 50. On f. 16v there is another set, used to develop the sesquitertial superparticular numbers.

1	2	3	4	
4	8	12	16	etc.
3	6	9	12	

---

4   Described by Smith, *Rara Arithmetica*, p. 477-78.

This diagram is from Boethius I, 24 (Friedlein, p. 51) but is put into Arabic numbers in this manuscript and is extended one set further to

11.

44

33

f. 16 v: *Quid sit numerus superpartiens et subsuperpartiens. (D.A.* I, 31).

f. 19 v: Here is displayed the following diagram:

1	7	9	11	13	15	17	19	21	23
3	4	5	6	7	8	9	10	11	12

In this fashion are generated the multiplex superpartient ratios. While this diagram is not found in the Friedlein edition it may well be derived from another Boethian manuscript tradition than is represented in the Friedlein edition. In any case, the ratios it describes are defined in the *De Arithmetica.*

f. 19v: *Numerorum superpartientium et subsuperpartientium radix et precreatio. (D.A.* I,31).

f. 20v: *Numerorum superpartiens proprietates, (D.A.* I, 31).

f. 21v: *De Multiplici superparitente et submultiplici superpartiente. (D.A.* I, 31).

f. 22: This chapter presents the diagram of square numbers in a scheme of 10 by 10:

1	2	3	4	5	6	
2	4	6	8	10	12	etc.
3	6	9	12	15	18	
4	8	12	16	20	24	
5	10	15	20	25	30	
	etc.					

This diagram comes directly from *D.A.* I, 27.

f. 24v: *Expositio quadratorum equalilaterum. (D.A.* II, 10)

Expositio altera parte longiorum. (D.A. II, 26) This section contains diagrams not found in the Friedlein edition but which appear in the *De Arithmetica* as edited in the *Patrologia Latina* (vol. 63, col. 1135) and hence probably belong to one of the manuscript traditions which may be considered authentic but different from that of the Friedlein manuscript.

f. 26v: *Quod omnis inequalitates ab equalitate mediate vel immediate procedit.* (D.A. I, 32)

The treatise ends imperfectly, in the middle of an exposition. It is followed by a 17 line fragment of a treatise on the squaring of the circle. *Aristoteles in eo quod Cathegoriis libro inscribitur quadratura circuli....*[5] The remainder of f. 26v is blank.

It must be said on behalf of the anonymous Columbia manuscript that while it is clearly derived from Boethius, it is not a slavish copy of his text (as is De Muris' above). The author does amplify with considerable detail a text probably already lucid, but a close reading of particular definitions shows considerable variation from the *De Arithmetica.* Nor does this text match Boethius' Greek source, Nicomachus, which was appearing in Greek editions about this same time. Departures in the Columbia ms may be due to an intermediary source or to its own author's inventiveness. We may cite some examples from the superparticular ratio for comparison:

Columbia ms: Numerus superparticularis sic species est numerus maioris inequalitatis et ille quod ad alium comparatus hoc eum totum et cum aliquam illius parte aliquot (f. 15v).

Boethius (I, 24): Superparticularis vero est numerus ad alterum comparatus, quotiens habet in se totum minorem et eius aliquam partem (p. 49).

5   Companus of Novara, *De Quadratura Circuli,* cited in Lynn Thorndike and Pearl Kibre. A Catalogue of Incipits of Mediaeval Scientific Writings in Latin (Cambridge, Mass., 1937; revised, 1963), col. 136.

In his description of how to construct the diagram which illustrates the superparticular ratios on f. 16 the anonymous author is considerably more detailed:

Ad inveniendum sesqualteros prius in superiore ordine disponatur numerus secundum ordinem suum naturalem deinde sub illo ordine ponatur triplices omnis secundum ordinem suum sibi in ordine succedentes et sub ordine illo ponatur omnes duplices sibi succedentes. Describatur igitur tres ordines modo qui sequitur:

I	II	III	IIII	V	VI	VII	VIII	IX	X
III	VI	IX	XII	XV	XVIII	XXI	XXIV	XXVII	XXX
II	IIII	VI	VIII	X	XII	XIIII	XVI	XVIII	XX

Boethius presents the same diagram but with a much simpler, less verbose description:

Primus igitur versus continet numerum naturalem, secundus eius triplicem, tertius vero duplicem (p. 50).

Unlike some more original medieval mathematicians, Jordanus Nemorarius has received scant attention from modern historians of science and no recent editions of his work are to be found.[6] His most important work is in the study of statics which he elaborated in the treatises *Elementa super demonstrationem ponderum* and the *Liber de ratione ponderis*. He has also written a *De Arithmetica* and a *Planispherium* as well as other mathematical treatises. Jordanus was very important during the Middle Ages and Renaissance when his work was widely read and studied. If we may judge from the interest taken in the 15th century by Jacques LeFèvre d'Étaples, Jordanus' arithmetic embodied the best that medieval mathematics could offer to his times. LeFèvre edited, summarized and wrote a lengthy commentary for the Jordanus arithmetic so that his own students might make good use of this text.[7] LeFèvre was also interested in the Boethian mathematics which he considered of almost equal importance. It is clear that Jordanus and Boethius covered essentially the same material in their works on number theory as may be seen in a diagram drawn up by LeFèvre and published with his commentary on Jordanus' arithmetic in 1494. It is presented here with some corrections and abbreviations.[8]

Topic	Boethius		Jordanus	
	Book	Chap	Book	Proposition
Numerus	1	7	1	2
Numerus Par	1	5	7	2
	2	46	7	10, 12
Numerus Impar	1	5	7	3
	2	46	7	11, 16
Numerus Pariter Par	1	9	7	29, 31, 32, 54
Numerus Pariter Impar	1	10	7	33-35
			1	2,3
Numerus Impariter Par	1	11	7	37, 40

6   Jordanus flourished in the second half of the 13th century. See Edward Grant's article in *Dictionary of Scientific Biography*, Vol. VII (1973), 171-179.

7   My study on LeFèvre's mathematical interests, especially as carried on by his student, Gerard Roussel, appears in the *Sixteenth Century Journal*, (1979), 23-41.

8   The Boethian references at to the Friedlein edition; the Jordanus references are to the 1494 edition. The text of the Jordanus arithmetic has not been established, though there is an edition in progress. LeFèvre's work is described by Smith, p. LeFèvre has not been published since the 15th century.

Topic	Boethius		Jordanus	
	Book	Chap	Book	Proposition
Numerus Perfectus	1	20	7	60
Numerus Primus et compositus	1	17	3	1
			7	25
Numerus ad alterum Primus	1	17	3	12
	1	18	3	15
Equalitas/Inequalitas	1	32	9	70
	2	1	9	75
Multiplex	1	23, 26	9	30, 37, 52
	1	27	9	70
Species in Multiplex	1	23	9	38
Superparticularis	1	24	9	37, 52
Species Superparticularis	1	24	9	38
Superpartiens	1	28	9	42, 52
Species Superpartientis	1	28	2	7
Multiplex Superparticularis	1	29	2	7
Multiplex Superpartiens	1	31	2	7
Species Numeri Plani	2	9	8	1
Numerorum Proprietates	1	27	9	38
	2	12	7	26
	2	18	8	5
	2	38	6	10
	2	46	6	10
	2	46	6	4
	2	46	6	14
	2	46	6	26
	2	46	6	26
	2	14	8	12
	2	15	8	14
	2	18	8	14
	2	16	8	21
Parte altera longior	2	25	7	27
	2	28	9	·38
	2	33	6	31
	2	34	8	11
Pyramis	2	23	8	28, 27
Cubis	2	39	7	28
	2	46	6	4, 16
Medietas Arithmetica	2	43	10	1
Medietas Geometrica	2	44	2	1, 3, 5, 25, 26
			10	20
			9	30
Medietas Musica	2	45, 47, 50	10	34, 37, 40
Medietas Quarta	2	51	2	7
Medietas Quinta	2	51	2	7

The most notable difference between the Boethian treatise and the arithmetic of Jordanus is in their format, each of which is governed by the purpose for which the two authors intended their works. For Boethius, a pedagogue, the *De Arithmetica* was a textbook for the beginner, filled with explanation and example. Jordanus was a scholastic, writing in the tradition established by the *Sentences* of Peter Lombard. The explanations of Boethius are, in Jordanus, replaced with concise mathematical statements (at least as found in the manuscript for the 1494 edition). Jordanus also treats of several points not found in Boethius. Most of the non-Boethian material occurs in chapters four and five: *De Numeris Continue Proportionalibus Conmensurabilibus et Inconmensurabilibus* and *De Additione, Subtractione, et Partitione Proportionum*. These chapters are drawn from other sources, ancient or contemporary.

Without entering on a detailed description of each of the remaining treatise which have come to my attention, it may be more practical to survey a number of works of the kind which could be found in any sizable library in Europe today and which typify the Boethian mathematics as it developed in the later Middle Ages.

The earliest of such Boethian mathematical works is in a manuscript which was written as early as the 9th or 10th century, now catalogued as Vatican Ottob. Lat. 1631, entitled *Wirceburgensis Rithomachia.*[9] On ff. 4-27, this manuscript contains a treatise on practical mathematics with a short introduction on number theory. Although it does not mention Boethius by name, the list of proportions and their types must certainly have come from the *De Arithmetica*, perhaps through some other compilation. *Quinque genera inequalitatis ex equalitate procedere manifestum est ex libris arithmetica: multiplex, superparticularis, superpartiens, multiplex superparticularis, et multiplex superpartiens. Sed reiectus duobus compositis ex tribus simplicibus huius modo conflictum quidam ex clero Wirziburgensi si periti iudicent, dabit posteritati.*

From the later Middle Ages (S. XIII-XIV) comes a collection of mathematical and astronomical works which contains another practical mathematics with an introduction from number theory (Reginensis 1268, ff. 43-44). The number theory is essentially a compilation of definitions which are derived from Boethius. *Numerorum imparium alius est primus et incompositus, alius secundus et compositus, alius partim compositum. Proportio alia multiplex, alia superparticularis, alia superpartiens....*

Vatican manuscript 1108 contains two treatises based on Boethius and both were written in the 15th century. The first of these, on ff. 126-131, mentions Boethius by name and follows the Boethian model although it also cites Aristotle. It clearly owes more to the *De Arithmetica* than to the works of the two Greek writers. *Proportio secundo elementorum Euclidis et primo ab Aristotele et Boecii sic definitur. Proportio est duarum eiusdem generis ad invicem habitudo.* The second treatise in Vat. 1108 (ff. 140-143) may have been intended as part of an earlier work but is given a separate title: *Textus Proportionum*. It is essentially Boethian in character but with some resemblances to the work of Bradwardine (see below). *Omnis proportio vel est communiter dicta vel proprie dicta. Communiter dicta est duarum rerum comparatorum ad invicem habitudo. Proprie dicta est duarum quantitatum eiusdem generis.*

Another 15th century manuscript, Ottob. 1484[10] contains a simple description of

9   I wish to express my gratitude to the custodians of the Vatican Microfilm Library at the University of St. Louis who made it possible for me to examine the mathematical holdings of the Vatican collection. Of particular help to anyone wishing to search out mathematical treatises in the Vatican Library is the computer index compiled by Father John Daly as yet unpublished but available to those who visit the microfilm collection in St. Louis. Father Daly did publish a two part article which surveyed some of the material itemized in his lengthy compilation in John F. Daly and Charles Ermatinger, „Mathematics in the Codices Ottoboniani Latini," *Manuscripta*, VIII (1964), 3-17; IX (1965), 12-29.

10   Daly, VIII, 14-15.

number theory in the Boethian manner which then proceeds to describe some practical mathematical procedures (ff. 1-11). *Tractatus de Proportionibus Numerorum. Quinque sunt genera proportionum scilicet...* Of a similar nature is the short treatise in Reg. Lat. 1146 (ff. 7-9), also anonymous. *De Proportionibus. Proportio est quadam habitudo duorum terminorum ad invicem vel distantiam duorum terminorum inter se. Sed notandum est quod aliud est proportio et aliud est proportionalitas...* The distinction between proportion and proportionality is a distinction found most notably in Bradwardine and this work probably shows his influence.

Dozens of similar treatises could be found in the libraries of Paris, Vienna, Munich, Florence or Berlin. One essay cannot attempt to catalogue every treatise of this sort but may merely indicate with brief comments the nature of the Boethian influence typically found through the Middle Ages.

Certainly of greater interest to the historian of mathematics are not the pedestrian copiers of older works but rather the original thinkers who, beginning with traditional mathematics, went on to devise new mathematical ideas. There can be little doubt that Thomas Bradwardine was among the most original and perceptive thinkers on number theory of medieval writers. He lived from about 1290 to 1349 and distinguished himself in a variety of ways. He was known as a teacher, first at Balliol College (c. 1321) and at Merton College (c. 1323). He became important as a churchman as well, and received the archbishopric of Canterbury, only to succumb forty days later to the plague. Theology was his main interest but he composed a number of treatises on mathematics as well as on controversial religious topics. He wrote the *Tractatus de Proportionibus* in 1328.[11] The treatise was almost immediately recognized as significant and it gave impetus to much of the succeeding mathematical and philosophical thought at Merton College.[12] This treatise became important enough, in fact, that it was made required reading for the B.A. degree at Vienna and Freiburg.[13] Bradwardine's recognition among the intellectual public may be judged by the citation of his name in Chaucer's work, the *Nun's Priest Tale*. In a discussion of necessity and God's foreknowledge, Bradwardine's name appears in the same line with Boethius and immediately after St. Augustine:

> But I ne kan nat bulte it to the bren [sift it to the bran]
> As kan the hooly doctour Augustyn,
> Or Boece, or the Bisshop Bradwardyn,
> Wheither that Goddes worthy forwityng
> Streyneth me nedely for to doon a thyng.[14]

Bradwardine's treatise on proportions has enjoyed a good scholarly edition with translation by H. Lamar Crosby, on which I have depended heavily for this discussion. In his treatise, Bradwardine develops the Boethian number theory beyond the system of simple proportionalities which he inherited from the Greeks. More significantly for his time, Bradwardine exemplifies how a fertile mind may examine traditional material and transcend the dry textbook explanations we find more commonly derived from Boethius.

Although Bradwardine utilized traditional terminology for the mathematical ratios and proportions, he achieved some understanding of what we now grasp in terms of modern mathe-

11 Aside from his work on proportions, his other writings include: *De Causa Dei adversus Plagium; De Arithmetica Speculativa; De Geometria Speculativa.* For bibliography, see E. Gilson, *History of Christian Philosophy in the Middle Ages* (Random House, New York: 1955), pp. 770-771.

12 Marshall Clagett, *Science of Mechanics in the Middle Ages* (U. of Wisconsin Press, Madison: 1959), p. 186.

13 H. Lamar Crosby, ed. Bradwardine, *Tractatus de Proportionibus* (U. of Wisconsin Press, Madison: 1955), p. 4.

14 Lines 3240-44. Ed. F. Robinson (Houghton Mifflin, New York: 1958).

matical symbols. Naturally he was thinking in only approximately what our modern symbols signify and he lacked the broader mathematical context which gives full meaning to our notions of exponentials, roots, and powers. (I think it is important to be aware of this anachronism as we read expositions such as Crosby's introduction to the edition of the *Tractatus*.) Thomas Bradwardine was interested in the proportional relations between velocities, and he searched in Boethius' work for the language to express the results of his thinking. Boethius provided the beginnings of problems which Bradwardine pursued to his own solution. Aristotle, and Boethius after him, declared that there could be a proportionality only between things of the same genus or between things as seen under the same aspect. Thus there may be a univocal proportion between two cats or two dogs, but not between a dog and a tree. As Aristotle explained, ,,Thus horse and dog are so commensurable that we may say which is the whiter, since that which primarily contains the whiteness is the same in both, viz. the surface; and similarly they are commensurable in respect of size. But water and speech are not commensurable in respect of clearness, since that which primarily contains the attribute is different in the two cases."[15]

According to this traditional attitude, there can be a proportionality between numbers or between velocities, but there can be no proportionality between number and velocity. It would be possible to arrange a proportional series of numbers to express relationships between velocities; but such a series could never express the relationships between two continuous velocities if they are of different genera, e.g. locomotion and alteration, or if seen as different species, e.g. rectilinear and circular motion.[16] Bradwardine countered the traditional view by observing that two kinds of proportionality may be found. There is first a proportionality of the rational order which is denominated by a number and which we may express by a ratio or fraction: 2/1, 4/2 (double); 3/1, 6/2 (triple) etc. It is with such proportionalities that Boethius and the traditional Greek number theorists were concerned. There is another order of proportionality, a non-rational order denominated medially by a first order proportionality. So, Bradwardine explains, the proportion of a diagonal of a square to its side is not able to be expressed in a single, simple proportion of integers, but rather must be expressed as one ratio denominated by another. In modern mathematical terms the ratio of a diagonal of a square to its side would be expressed thus for a figure whose side is a unit of 1:

$$\left(\frac{2}{1}\right)^{\frac{1}{2}} \quad \text{or} \quad \sqrt{2}$$

The Greeks, and Boethius, knew of irrational numbers but they were assigned to the realm of geometry where irrational relationships are grasped in terms of sides on a triangle. Bradwardine has succeeded in drawing this concept under the concept of ratios and proportions, which is the realm of arithmetic. In so doing he was able to express the notions of powers and roots.

,,The second order comprises those proportions which are called ‚irrational' by a given proportion, which is, in turn, immediately denominated by a number. Of this sort is the square root of the proportion of two to one, which is the proportion of the diagonal of a square to its side, and the square root of the proportion of nine to eight, which constitutes a musical half-tone."[17]

---

15 *Physics*, VII, ch. 4; trans. R.P. Hardie and R.K. Gaye, in *The Basic Works of Aristotle*, ed. R. McKeon (Random House, New York: 1941), p. 350.
16 Crosby, p. 19.
17 Secundum vero gradum illa tenet quae irrationalis vocatur, quae non immediate denominatur ab aliquo numero, sed mediate tantum (quia immediate denominatur ab aliqua proportione, quae immediate denominatur a numero; sicut medietas duplae proportionis, quae est proportio diametri ad costam et

By extending the meaning of terms of the Boethian treatise and of the traditional mathematics, Bradwardine has made a new application of the concept of proportionality. While traditional writers, for example, used the term „denominate" to signify multiplication or division, Bradwardine uses it to express the raising of a number to a power or extracting its root. So, above, when trying to express the idea of an exponential, he says that a number is „denominated medially" by another.

But perhaps the most notable concept which Bradwardine develops from Boethius comes from the distinction between proportions and proportionality which Bradwardine develops with care. He begins his discussion of proportionality with an extensive list of the types, drawn directly from the Boethian *De Arithmetica*.[18] A ratio is a relation between two terms, as 1:2, or as expressed in a fraction, $\frac{1}{2}$ and the relationship is called a rational number in its fractional form. A proportion is a ratio between ratios, as when 1 compared to 2, which is as 2 is to 4 (1:2 as 2:4). Proportions may be set up in series, as a series of duplex, triple, or quadruple proportions: 1:2 as 2:4 as 4:8, etc. This is the beginning of a duplex series. Bradwardine extracts the idea of proportionality from the Boethian conception of proportion. Proportionality, then, signifies the formal aspect of a series, the laws which may be deduced from the series to show the relationships between terms of the series.

Bradwardine adapted, also from Boethius, the idea that the the most important proportionalities are the arithmetic, geometric, and harmonic.[19] He then analyzed these three proportions accordingly as they are continuous or discontinuous. When Bradwardine says that the arithmetic proportionality is continuous he means that the equal differences possess common terms, so in the proportional set 3:2 as 2:1, the common term is 2. Yet these two ratios have a common difference (one), the requirement for an arithmetic proportionality. We also see the common terms in the arithmetic proportionalities 8:6 as 6:4 or 6:4 as 4:2. Discontinuity in the arithmetic proportionality signifies a lack of a common term, as in 6:4 as 3:1.

In the geometric proportionality, the common term occurs in a set of ratios such as 4:2 as 2:1 (or 4/2 as 2/1). As may be seen, for a geometric proportionality, the product of the two ratios must be the same. Conversely, the following are discontinuous geometric proportions: 14/7 as 6/3 as 2/1. The distinction between continuous and discontinuous proportionalities is crucial in Bradwardine and it is closely tied with what Crosby considers the Aristotelian bent of the Bradwardine number theory.[20] This Aristotelianism is important to Bradwardine's conviction that the physical correlations between velocities can be expressed in mathematical terms,[21] and in making this observation he uses the Aristotelian notions of continuous and discontinuous quantities. Bradwardine brought Boethian proportionality away from Boethian Platonism which understood the world in terms of numbers, to be somehow made up of numbers. He was more interested in stating a law of motion and a principle of mechanics, not a philosophical number theory.

However, in order to work out in greater detail the question of whether a proportion of forces may legitimately be used to express a proportion of velocities, Bradwardine had to look

medietas sesquioctava proportionis, quae toni medietatem constituit). (Crosby, p. 66).

18   *Ibid.*, pp. 22-24.
19   Boethius lists ten, but these are, he explains, derived from the first three. Cf. *De Arithmetica* II, 53.
20   Crosby, p. 26.
21   Cf. *Physics* VII, 4.

elsewhere. Among other works which he consulted is the *Epistola de Proportione et Proportionalitate* by Ahmad Ibn Jusuf.[22] From that point, clearly in non-Boethian territory, Bradwardine demonstrates that discontinuous proportionality may obtain even between proportions of heterogeneous kinds, as between two variable velocities. By that point Bradwardine has developed an exponential series to solve the problems posed by the traditional notion that velocities could not be measured by commensurable proportionalities.

Perhaps as an appendix to the discussion on Bradwardine's treatise on proportions it should be pointed out that Albert of Saxony wrote a similar work. This treatise, *De Proportionibus*, was clearly derived from the Bradwardine treatment of the Boethian proportionalities. Albert's work was not unknown among medieval and early Renaissance mathematicians, and several printed editions of the treatise appeared during the 16th century.[23] Though his work was not of great importance to medieval philosophy generally, it does have some relevance for the historian of medieval mathematics since it embodies a number of Boethian elements. Some of these elements do not appear in Bradwardine but come directly from the *De Arithmetica*. Such is certainly the case with the diagram taken from Boethius I, 26 which is used to explain the types of inequalities:

```
1   2    3    4     5     etc.
2   4    6    etc.
3   6    12   etc.
4   8
5
etc.
```

Other sections of Albert's treatise are closely modeled on Bradwardine's work, such as his distinction between continuous and discontinuous proportions. His definition of *proportio*, also, while incomplete, clearly reflects the definition given by Bradwardine.

Albert: *Proportio communiter duorum est duorum comparatorum.*

Brandwardine: *Proportio est duorum comparatorum, in aliquo in quo comparatur, unius ad alterum habitudo.*[24]

The name of Roger Bacon (c. 1220-1292), scientific innovator and stern critic of the *status quo*, would not at first be thought associated with the Boethian arithmetic–a conservative document even by the standards of the 13th century. But Boethius and Bacon had one significant interest in common, and that is a philosophy of education which is solidly based on a knowledge of mathematics. In his *Opus Maius*, Bacon expends considerable energy criticizing the current status of the educational system in Europe. He feels that mathematics is being neglected and that it is a learning absolutely essential for the study of all other disciplines in the liberal arts. But more significantly, it is also required for studies beyond the realm of the liberal arts, for philosophy and theology as well.[25]

Bacon draws his argument for the importance of mathematics from the *proemium* of the *De Arithmetica* and cites Boethius *verbatim*. He gives a very strong approval to the Boethian theory of education; while he does not advocate the study of Boethian number theory, he does

22   Ahmad Ibn Jusuf, *Epistola de Proportione et Proportionalitate*, not edited but found in Bodleian, Ashmole Ms. 357. Cf. Crosby, p. 19.

23   L. Hain, *Repertorium Bibliographicum* (cottae, Stuttgart: 1826) *583. Frederick R. Goff, *Incunabula in American Libraries* (Kraus, New York: 1973), col. 341.

24   Crosby, p. 66.

25   In my discussion of Roger Bacon I am much indebted to the essay by Pearl Kibre, „The Quadrivium in the Thirteenth Century Universities (with special reference to Paris)," in *Arts libéraux et philosophie au moyen-âge* (Montreal, Canada: 1969), pp. 175-191.

support the Boethian attitude toward the fundamental importance of mathematical discipline. Bacon insists that those who know the four mathematical sciences will make progress in all other studies without difficulty.[26] He is particularly concerned with the importance of mathematical learning for all other study and with the relationship between mathematics and the other disciplines. In two consecutive chapters, Bacon cites Boethian texts and especially emphasizes this passage: „If someone is lacking these four elements [quadrivial disciplines] he is not able to find the true, and indeed without this kind of speculation, nothing of the truth is rightly known. It is the wisdom of those things which truly are, their knowledge and complete comprehension. Because he who spurns these things, that is the paths of wisdom, by that denunciation he does 'not philosophice rightly–if indeed philosophy is the love of wisdom, which he has already shown contempt for in spurning these."[27]

Bacon expands and repeats these ideas in several places: „There are four great sciences, without which the other sciences cannot be known nor a knowledge of things secured...." „Since he who is ignorant of this cannot know the other sciences nor the affairs of this world ...." „For without these neither what precedes nor what follow can be known; whence they perfect what precedes and regulate it, even as the end perfects those things pertaining to it, and they arrange and open the way to what follows...."[28]

Bacon also supports his arguments on behalf of mathematics for progress in philosophical study by demonstrating how illustrious philosophers such as Robert Grosseteste (Bacon's teacher) and Friar Adam Marsh based their learning on mathematics. It was their certain grasp of numbers which made it possible to excell in other more difficult disciplines. It is not Boethius alone whom Bacon calls upon to support this point of view but he cites Aristotle as well as Alfarabi to demonstrate that the basis of all philosophy is *mathematica.*[29] But it is particularly interesting that Bacon puts the study of mathematics before logic. In this, as Professor Kibre points out (p. 179) he differs from most of his contemporaries and goes as well against the traditional order of the liberal arts disciplines in which logic appears with the verbal disciplines in the trivium, along with rhetoric and grammar. Arithmetic was the first of the mathematical disciplines of the quadrivium which constituted a more advanced stage of studies. Boethius says nothing about the relationship between the trivium and quadrivium and, in fact, he does not even use the term *trivium*. But his sense of the relationship between the arithmetic and logic must have been close to Bacon's since he was preoccupied with the logical works at the same time that he wrote the arithmetic.[30] Bacon had an intense feeling for the relationship

26   *Opus Maius* IV, Dist. 1, chap. 1 and 2. ed. J.H. Bridges (Oxford, Clarendon Press: 1897), Vol. 1, pp. 97 ff; trans. R.B. Burke (Philadelphia, U. of Penn. Press: 1928), p. 116.
27   Quibus quattuor si caret inquisitor, verum invenire non possit, ac sine hac quidem speculatione veritatis nulli recte sapiendum est. Est enim sapientia earum rerum, quae vere sunt, cognitio et integra comprehensio. Quod haec qui spernit id est has semitas sapientiae ei denuntio non recte esse philosophandum, siquidem philosophia est amor sapientiae, quum in his spernendis ante contempserit. (*De Arithmetica*, Friedlein ed., p. 9; my translation above.)
28   Et sunt quattuor scientiae magnae, sine quibus caeterae scientiae scire non possunt, nec rerum notitae haberi.... Quoniam qui ignorat eam non potest scire caeteras scientias nec res hujus mundi.... Sine his enim nec praecedentia nec consequentia scire possunt; unde perficiunt priora et regulant, sicut finis ea quae sunt ad finem, et disponunt et aperiunt viam ad sequentia. Pas. IV, chap. I, Dist. 1. Burke, pp. 116-117; Bridges, pp. 98-99.
29   *Opus Maius*, Dist. 1, Chap. 2.
30   Although the chronology of Boethius' works has not been clearly established, most scholars agree that the arithmetic was written within a few years of the time Boethius was writing his commentaries on Aristotle's logic, the work on syllogisms, and the commentary on Porphery. See A.P. McKinlay, „Stylistic Tests and the Chronology of the Works of Boethius," *Harvard Studies in Classical Philology*, XVIII (1907), 123-156 and L.M. De Rijk, „On the Chronology of Boethius' Works on Logic," *Vivarium*, II (1964), 1-49; 125-162.

between mathematics and logic, one not apparently shared by all his contemporaries but which may well come close to the Boethian feeling for logic. This is significant because Boethius was more a logician than a mathematician if we are to judge by the size of his written works in those two areas. Bacon wrote that „not only does a knowledge of logic depend on mathematics because of its end, but because of its middle and heart, which is the book of *Posterior Analytics*, for that book teaches the art of demonstration. But neither can the fundamental principles of demonstration, nor conclusions, nor the subject as a whole be learned or made clear except in the realm of mathematics, because there alone is there true and forceful demonstration, as all know and as we shall explain later. Therefore of necessity logic depends on mathematics." (Burke, pp. 119-120)

There are, of course, some critical areas in which Boethius and Bacon cannot be reconciled. Bacon does not pay close attention to the order of the quadrivial disciplines, an order to which Boethius devoted some careful and prolonged explication. For Boethius the disciplines of arithmetic and music deal with number; geometry and astronomy consider numbers in quantity. Students must proceed from one to the other; one depends on the other. Bacon differs from Boethius, however, in that he presents the peculiar order of arithmetic, geometry, music and astronomy.[31]

A more important difference between Bacon and Boethius is in their conceptions of the kind of mathematics to be studied. Certainly Bacon was not speaking of number theory when he urged the study of mathematics; he meant the study of practical computation. He says that „one should know how to compute, add, subtract, halve, multiply, divide and extract roots." (Burke, I, 242) It is safe to assume that Bacon was familiar with the nature of the entire Boethian treatise on arithmetic and no doubt there may have been feelings of antipathy on Bacon's part for the traditional character of Boethian mathematics. Yet it is notable that Bacon chose the emphatic statements about the importance of mathematical studies from the proemium to use in his almost vehement attack on the established educational system. As Professor Kibre has pointed out, the actual status of mathematical studies may not be precisely discernable from Bacon's comments since „one may venture to suggest that since he appears to have been of a highly irascible and critical turn of mind, he may have been exaggerating the actual neglect." (Kibre, p. 179) Thus, as the evidence in Kibre's article indicates, and as other sources might also suggest, in fact Boethian mathematics were widely studied, yet Bacon cites the Boethian passages for purposes of his own, not necessarily to complain of the neglect of Boethian mathematics in itself.

To conclude with a brief glance at the computational and practical mathematicians, we may note that neither the name nor the theories of Boethius have much place in their works. It is worthy of mention that the Boethian music theory received more attention among the practical musicians than did the number theory among the computational or pracitcal mathematicians. It was the definition of various proportionalities (that is, of the medial proportions) which especially attracted the musicians and which played an increasingly important role in the evolution of music theory late in the Middle Ages and into the Renaissance.

It seems appropriate to take some notice of the works of Fibonacci, however (who was also known as Leonardo di Pisa). Certainly among modern students of mathematics, he is the best known medieval mathematician. The celebrated Fibonacci series is an extension of a proportionality, but it is not a Boethian proportionality since it constitutes a series of irrational

---

31 The order is peculiar because it does not conform with the other commonly found order, derived from the *De Nuptiis Philologiae et Mercurii*, which ends with music. For the problem of order in the representation of the liberal arts disciplines, see my article „Boethius and the Iconography of the Liberal Arts," *Latomus*, XXXIII (1974), 57-75.

relationships.[32] The Boethian proportions, as found in the *De Arithmetica*, are based on true ratios; it is only in the treatise on geometry where irrational proportions, such as the Golden Mean, are to be found.

In a few places, Fibonacci does touch on elements of number theory in the Boethian sense. In the *Liber Abbaci*, for example,[33] he defines the perfect number. He is also interested in medial proportionality (p. 388). But it is hardly an interest which he derived from Boethius since he cites Euclid as his source. Altogether we cannot consider Leonardo of Pisa as one of Boethius' heirs. The entire temper of mathematical thought as seen in these two men is at variance–both in the way they conceive of numbers and in the purpose to which they feel mathematical learning should be put. For Boethius, the study of number was a means to other learning; it was a part of an educational plan which he called the *quadrivium* and which was a preparation for philosophical study. In the first chapter of Book I in the *De Arithmetica* he says that without this discipline no other study can be undertaken successfully, but with it, all others are easily undertaken. It is to this particular aspect of Boethian thought that Bacon responded. But for Fibonacci, numbers are to applied to practical matters, especially money and mercantile matters. The computation of interest, the exchange of rates within differing monetary systems, the multiplication of objects–usually objects which have commercial value, such as livestock–these are the purposes for which he elaborates his mathematics. Most of the examples in the *Liber Abbaci* are filled with details of these interests.

The place of Boethius in medieval thought has never been a matter for hot debate. Intellectual historians of the medieval period have always noted the importance of the *Consolation of Philosophy* for the literature and philosophy of Europe into the Renaissance. Historians of mathematics have merely acknowledged the existence and significance of the Boethian treatises on arithmetic and geometry. With the publication of the three essays in this collection on arithmetic and geometry, it is our hope that the truly fundamental nature of Boethian mathematics in medieval number theory will be attested. It is very possible that a number of treatises cited in this essay will never be read seriously–they are part of a vast body of medieval scientific and mathematical writing that is justifiably ignored. But it is also to be hoped that future research will bring to light more original signs of Boethian influence, such as that of Bradwardine. These future studies should show that medieval mathematics were a complex, varied and fascinating land of number theory.

Loyola University, Chicago

---

32   In the *Liber Abbaci* Fibonacci poses a seemingly simple problem: „A certain man put a pair of rabbits in a place surrounded by a wall. How many pairs of rabbits can be produced from that pair in a year if it is supposed that every month each pair begets a new pair which from the second month become productive?" To find the number of pairs which would be produced by the end of 12 months, Leonardo proceeds a month at a time: the first month and the second month, 1 pair, by the 3rd month there are two pair then 5, 8, 13, 21, 34, 55, 89, 144, 233 and 377. This recursive number sequence has since been found in many numbered series occurring naturally, in the spirals of seed patterns in sunflower heads, in the leaf buds on a stem, on cones, on daisy florets. Cf. Joseph Gies, *Leonard of Pisa and the New Mathematics of the Middle Ages* (New York, Cromwell, 1969), pp. 53-54 and Kurt Vogel, „Fibonacci," *Dictionary of Scientific Biography*, IV (1971), 604-613. The works of Fibonacci have been edited by B. Boncompagni, 2 vols. (Rome, 1857-62).

33   Chap. XII, p. 283.

UBALDO PIZZANI

THE FORTUNE OF THE *DE INSTITUTIONE MUSICA* FROM BOETHIUS TO GERBERT D'AURILLAC: A TENTATIVE CONTRIBUTION

Among those writings of Boethius which transmitted to the Middle Ages so much of the ancient culture, the *De Institutione Musica* must certainly occupy a place of special prominence. The second treatise of the *quadrivium*, according to the outline apparently sketched by Boethius himself in the first chapter of the *De Institutione Arithmetica*,[1] its fame is attested not only by the great number of manuscripts in which it has reached us,[2] but also (and above all) by the imposing mass of scholia–largely unpublished[3] –preserved in those manuscripts, as well as by the flourishing medieval musicological production that found inspiration in Boethius as the most learned and reliable authority on the ancient musical culture.[4]

It is mainly to this last aspect that scholars as a rule have directed their attention,[5] owing partly to the fact that Boethius, with his approximations and misunderstandings, did not always have a positive and stimulating effect on the musical theories of the Middle Ages.[6] But there is another factor, no less important, in the continuous good fortune of this treatise: its influence, together with that of the *De Institutione Arithmetica*, and the lost treatises *De Institutione Geometrica* and *De Institutione Astronomica*,[7] on the didactic applications of the *quadrivium*. Here the medieval schools did not have in Boethius their exclusive and unchal-

---

Note: the editor is grateful to Mr. Peter Gimpel who translated this essay from the Italian, working in close collaboration with the author.

1   *De Institutione Arithmetica* I, 1. All citations from the Boethian treatises on arithmetic and music are taken from the edition of G. Friedlein (Leipzig, 1867; reprinted, 1966) and cited hereafter as *DIA* and *DIM*.

2   A nearly complete list has been furnished recently by M. Masi, ,,Manuscripts Containing the *De Musica* of Boethius," *Manuscripta*, 15 (1971), 89-95 and ,,A Newberry Diagram of the Liberal Arts," *Gesta*, XI/2 (1973), 56.

3   As far as I know, the only scholia to have yet been published are two by Gerbert d'Aurillac (N. Bubnov, *Gerberti Opera Mathematica* [Berolini, 1899] pp. 28-31), one on the harmony of the spheres (R. Bragard, ,,L'harmonie des sphères selon Boèce," *Speculum*, 4 [1929], pp. 206-13, and some others in my article, ,,Uno pseudo-trattato dello pseudo-Beda," (*Maia*, I [1957], 36-48). It should be noted, however, that a substantial mass of scholia has been packed into this so-called treatise attributed to the Venerable Bede, as we shall see in the course of this study.

4   The texts are assembled in good part in the fundamental though somewhat obsolete collections of M. Gerbert, *Scriptores Ecclesiastici de Musica Sacra Potissimum* (Typis San Blasianis, 1784; reprinted, 1931) and E. Coussemaker, *Scriptores de Musica Medii Aevi*, 4 vols. (Paris, 1864-76). More up-to-date on the critical and textual level is the *Corpus Scriptorum de Musica*, but the latter is still far from completion.

5   See the ample bibliography after the article on *Boethius* by R. Wagner in the great German encyclopedia, *Die Musik in Geschichte und Gegenwart*, Band II (Kassel und Basel, 1952), col. 49-57.

6   See for the bibliographical references the above-cited article by R. Wagner, coll. 54-55; see also my observations in ,,Studi sulle fonti del *De Institutione Musica* di Boezio," *Sacris Erudiri*, 16 (1965), 87, 128 ff.

7   That Boethius completed the entire cycle of the *quadrivium* is deducted from incontestable evidence. (See the article, ,,Severino Boezio" in the *Dizionario Biografico degli Italiani*, 11 [Roma, 1969], 142-65.)

lenged master, but turned, as well, to the great syntheses of such teachers as Martianus Capella, Cassiodorus, and Isidor of Seville, not to mention the *De Musica* of St. Augustine. Nevertheless, there is no doubt that the Boethian corpus, with its greater amplitude, and with the prestige conferred upon its author by his logical and theological works, played a decisive and pre-eminent role. This is true especially in the Carolingian[8] and post-Carolingian periods, whence derive most of the *codices* bearing the treatises in question.[9] It is more difficult to determine the role they played in the nearly three centuries intervening between their composition and the Renaissance prompted by Charlemagne.

The fact is that the influence of Boethius on the authors of that period–particularly Cassiodorus and Isidor of Seville, who both dealt with the *artes* of the *quadrivium*–is not conclusively demonstrable, particularly as far as music is concerned. An exceptional case is that of the Venerable Bede, under whose name we have a *Musica Theorica* that is definitely linked to Boethius, but which, as I have demonstrated elsewhere[10] and will illustrate later in this essay, came into being under very particular circumstances that do not allow us to attribute it to the Monk of Jarrow *sic et simpliciter*. An investigation into this matter, culminating, as we shall see, in a proposal for a new form of edition for that unique work, will give us an opportunity to survey the mass of scholia relating to the *De Institutione Musica* (for, indeed, the *disiecta membra* of the so-called *Musica Theorica* are nothing more than scholia); to examine some of the complex problems attending the preparation of such an edition and the identification of sources; and lastly, to ascertain the potential role of these scholia in clarifying in what forms and ways the Boethian text was used in medieval scholastic activity. At that point, with a brief survey of the coeval musicological production, we shall bring our investigation to a close. Our purpose is not so much to obtain definitive solutions to individual problems as to define their terms and to establish the areas of research and the methodological criteria while trying to trace an outline–however tentative and problematical–of the fortune of the *De Institutione Musica* from Boethius to the scholastic activity of Gerbert d'Aurillac. In the absence of a thorough documentation, it is the history up to the 9th century, at least, that will prove hard to grasp in even its most essential stages. But the problems that it poses, whether in philology, strictly speaking, or in the history of culture, cannot be evaded by anyone who wishes to understand through what adventures the *De Institutione Musica* passed so decisively into the scholastic and musicological traditions of the Middle Ages–after a period, as it would appear, of total eclipse.

* * * *

At the root of our investigation is a problem whose solution cannot but have a conditioning influence on the investigation itself: what was the real position and function of music in the *quadrivium* of Boethius, and just what did the *quadrivium* signify to Boethius himself? We must not forget that the term *quadrivium* first appears, in the canonical sense it was to acquire (together with the *trivium*) in the medieval scholastic tradition, in Boethius, himself:

---

8   Our most ancient voice, in that sense, is perhaps that of Aurélien de Moutier-St. Jean (Aurelianus Reomensis), who lived in the first half of the 9th century and was the author of a *Musica Disciplina*, largely inspired by Boethius, whom he cites and exalts as *vir doctissimus* (p. 41, Gerbert) and *eruditissimus* (Gerbert, p. 32).

9   None of the extant manuscripts of the *De Institutione Musica* dates from before the 9th century.

10   U. Pizzani, „Uno pseudo-trattato."

in the proem of the *De Institutione Arithmetica*. [11] It is thus logical to ask how far and within what limits did the arrangement given by Boethius to his corpus of the four *matheseos disciplinae* influence the medieval school?

The question is not easy to answer because, among other things, it is not always easy to distinguish in Boethius what is due to his own personal initiative and what is merely a plodding repetition of his sources. For instance, it is commonly thought that in his writing Boethius followed a carefully detailed plan in which the actual works of philosophy were to be preceded by treatises on the four disciplines of the *quadrivium*, which in the venerable tradition of the ἐγκύκλιος παιδεία [12] were supposed to be preparatory to all true speculative activity. The assumption itself remains valid even for those who accept the theory of a less than perfect correspondence between the logical and chronological order of Boethius' writings. Those who wish to do so may date the composition of the more properly philosophical works between the *De Institutione Arithmetica* and the *De Institutione Musica*. [13] The fact remains that the intention of dealing with the four disciplines of the *quadrivium*, and the greater ambition of translating and annotating all of Aristotle and all of Plato so as to demonstrate the substantial unity of their views, were proclaimed in two distinct moments of Boethius' activity, [14] and definitely in that order.

11   *DIA* I,1, p. 7, 21-26: *Inter omnes priscae auctoritatis viros... constare manifestum est, haud quemquam in philosophiae disciplinis ad cumulum perfectionis evadere, nisi cui talis prudentiae nobilitas quodam quasi quadruvio vestigatur, quod recte intuentis sollertiam non latebit; Ibid.* p. 9, 28-10,1: *Hoc igitur illud quadruvium est, quo his viandum sit, quibus excellentior animus a nobiscum procreatis sensibus ad intellegentiae certiora perducitur.* Originally, the term denoted an intersection of four roads, as in Catullus (*Carmina* LVIII, 4: *in quadriviis et angiportis*) and Juvenal (*Satirae* I, 63-64: *Nonne libet medio ceras implere capaces/Quadruvio*). If Friedlein's reading is correct, the Boethian codices use the spelling *quadruvium*, while those of Catullus and Juvenal waver between *quadruvium* and *quadrivium*.

12   By ἐγκύκλιος παιδεία we must understand that cycle of studies which, having acquired its definitive characteristics in the Hellenistic age, was to assure on the one hand an independent and autonomous function comparable to the modern concept of general culture, while preserving, in the ambit of philosophical studies, the propaedeutic function of a preparatory introduction to philosophy itself. Its original nucleus, which goes back to Architas (fr. 1 Diels), may be identified with the four disciplines of the *quadrivium*: arithmetic, music, geometry and astronomy. To these were successively added rhetoric, with Gorgias, dialectic, with Aristotle, and, finally, grammar, with Dionysius Thrax. The first known formulation of the propaedeutic value of these disciplines in respect of philosophy is in Plato (*Republic* 533 cd), who assigns to the mathematical sciences the function of προπαιδεία in respect to διαλεκτική. By dialectic Plato means „the coping stone (θριγκός) in which human knowledge culminates: no other science can be added to it, or come above it" (Werner Jaeger, *Paideia: The Ideals of Greek Culture*, trans. Gilbert Highet [Oxford, 1939] II, 312) i.e., philosophy itself. But only with the Hellenistic age do the liberal arts, as the seven disciplines are commonly called, acquire the aspect which they were to preserve through the centuries in the teaching of the schools of the Middle Ages.

        Fundamental for a knowledge of this subject are the numerous contributions of H.I. Marrou „Doctrina et disciplina dans la langue des Pères de l'Église," *Archivum Latinitatis Medii Aevi*, 9 (1934), 5-25; *Saint Augustin et la fin de la culture antique* (Paris, 1938; 1958[2]); *Histoire de l'éducation dans l'antiquité* (Paris, 1955[6]); „De Philostrate à Saint Augustin," *Revue des Études Augustiniennes*, 10 (1965), 223-28; „Les arts libéraux dans l'antiquité classique," *Arts libéraux et philosophie au moyen-âge* (Montréal-Paris, 1969), pp. 5-27. Other contributions include: H. Koller, „Enkyklios Paideia," *Glotta*, 34 (1954-55), 174-189; F. Kuhnert, *Allgemeinbildung und Fachbildung in der Antike* (Berlin, 1961), (reviewed by Marrou in *Gnomon*, 36 [1964], 113-116); L.M. de Rijk, „Enkuklios paideia," *Vivarium*, 3 (1965), 24-93; M.N. Alexandre, intro., notes, and trans. *Philon, De Congressu Scientiarum Eruditionis Gratia* (Paris, 1967).

13   Such is the thesis of A. Patch McKinlay, „Stylistic Tests and the Chronology of the Works of Boethius," *Harvard Studies in Classical Philology* 18 (1907), 123-156.

14   Boethius, *DIA* I, 1; *Anicii Manlii Severini Boetii Commentarii*, ed. K. Meiser (Leipzig, 1877, 80), p. 70, 22.

But if from this overall view[15] we go on to examine what Boethius actually says about the function of the *quadrivium* in the above-mentioned proem of the *De Institutione Arithmetica*, we realize that the proposed scheme seems somehow to have eluded him; the mathematical disciplines comprising the *quadrivium* (arithmetic, music, geometry, astronomy) would seem to be presented as rather an integral part of philosophy than a propaedeutic introduction to it.[16]

The conflict between these two different postures might easily be resolved if Boethius had only prefaced his treatment of the four mathematical disciplines with an original *praefatio* illustrating the meaning and motives of his *opus*. In actuality the *praefatio* of the *De Institutione Arithmetica* is just a translation, albeit with several cuts and abbreviations, of the corresponding *praefatio* of the Ἀριθμητικὴ εἰσαγωγή of Nicomachus of Gerasa, which Boethius translated into Latin as the *De Institutione Arithmetica*. Suffice it to note that the very sentence of the said *praefatio* in which Boethius presents the *De Institutione Arithmetica* as the first treatise of the *quadrivium*, appearing thus to herald the composition of an entire corpus (p. 12, 11-12: *quare, quoniam prior, ut claruit, arithmeticae vis est, hinc disputationis sumamus exordium*) is no more than an almost literal paraphrase of a corresponding sentence in his source (p. 11, 19-23, Hoche). This, not to mention that the very term *quadrivium* presumably derives from Nicomachus, if it is true that the word was modeled on the τέσσαρες μέθοδοι of Nicomachus (*Introductio Arithmetica*: I, 4, p. 9, 5-6). If we did not know by other means that Boethius really devoted separate treatises to the four arts of the *quadrivium*, we might even doubt whether he actually planned such a corpus. Thus we shall have to undertake a comparative reading of the texts of Boethius and Nicomachus--not so much to discover some supposed originality of Boethius in relation to the Greek model as to determine what Boethius understood by it and how he presented it to his own readers.

Next we shall try to determine whether, and if so to what extent, the *De Institutione Musica* fits into the scheme of the *quadrivium* as outlined in the arithmetical treatise. We shall see that the music treatise does not have the appearance of being the second part of an organic encyclopedia, but rather looks more like an autonomous and independent work. This will permit us to draw some significant conclusions about the chronology of the work and, more pertinently, about its fortune through the centuries.

Our investigation must therefore begin with the *praefatio* of Nicomachus. Inspired by typically Pythagorean concepts filtered through the experience of Plato and Aristotle, Nico-

---

15   Courcelle, for example, limits himself to an overall view when he says (see P. Courcelle, *Les lettres grecques en Occident de Macrobe à Cassiodore* [Paris, 1948], p. 260), that in Boethius the *matheseos disciplinae* „constituent le quadrivium par lequel on accède à l'etude de la philosophie."
     He then tries to endorse this thesis of a propaedeutic value of the four disciplines of the quadrivium as handled by Boethius by observing unassailably that „Une fois ce travail préalable terminé, Boèce passe à l'étude de la philosophie." But this is to transfer onto a chronological and practical level an abstract scheme of which not even Boethius seems to have been fully aware, as we shall see.

16   I refer the reader to the excellent enunciation of this problem by G. Federici Vescovini, in „L'inserimento della ‚perspectiva' tra le arti del quadrivio," *Arts libéraux*, 1969, pp. 969-74. In her own words (p. 971): „Boezio nel classificare le discipline matematiche nel *De Institutione Arithmetica* aveva chiaramente fatto intendere che esse non sono nè discipline di insegnamento elementare, né diverse dalla filosofia, anzi che esse sono le discipline filosofiche che ci conducono alla conoscenza del vero." It should be noted that in the above-cited paper by Marrou, addressed to the Montréal congress, there is no such qualification of Boethius (p. 26), while the author merely notes that the teacher of Boethius, Ammonius, son of Hermias, was very well versed in the liberal arts and might well have transmitted this passion to his pupil. As we shall see, it was just from Ammonius that Boethius might have derived a very different conception of the liberal arts.

machus begins[17] by defining φιλοσοφία as φιλία σοφίας a definition that a long tradition attributed to Pythagoras. Immediately afterwards he explains what he means by σοφία ἐπιστήμη τῆς ἐν τοῖς οὖσιν ἀληθείας,[18] which Boethius renders literally: *rerum, quae sunt suique immutabilem sentientiam sortiuntur, comprehensio veritatis.*[19] Philosophy is thus, both to Nicomachus and to Boethius, the science of what really is, of the Platonic ὄντως ὄντα, which they list in order as follows: ποιότητες (*qualitates*), ποσότητες (*quantitates*), σχηματισμοί (*formae*), μεγέθη (*magnitudines*), μικρότητες (*parvitates*), ἰσότητες (*aequalitates*), σχέσεις (*habitudines*), ἐνέργειαι (*actus*), διαθέσεις (*dispositiones*), τόποι (*loca*), χρόνοι (*tempora*).[20] At this point, however, it is helpful to note that while Boethius seems to limit himself to the ὄντως ὄντα, to which he gives the name of *essentiae*, Nicomachus extends the realm of philosophy to another category of ὄντα, which he calls καθ᾽ ὁμωνυμίαν, or ὁμωνύμως, „existing under the same name." In other words, Nicomachus distinguishes between τὰ κυρίως ὄντα, i.e. the true essences or immaterial forms listed above, and τὰ μετέχοντα αὐτῶν, i.e. the material bodies which share those essences and receive their names from them. To both spheres Nicomachus refers the two basic concepts of the four mathematical disciplines, μέγεθος (*magnitudo*) and πλῆθος (*multitudo*): τῶν τοίνυν ὄντων τῶν τε κυρίως καὶ τῶν καθ᾽ ὁμωνυμίαν, ὅπερ ἐστὶ νοητῶν τε καὶ αἰσθητῶν, τὰ μέν ἐστιν ἡνωμένα καὶ ἀλληλουχούμενα οἷον ζῶον, κόσμος, δένδρον καὶ τα ὅμοια, ἅπερ κυρίως καὶ ἰδίως καλεῖται μεγέθη, τὰ δὲ διῃρημένα τε καὶ ἐν παραθέσει καὶ οἷον κατὰ σωρείαν, ἃ καλεῖται πλήθη, οἷον ποίμνη, σωρός, χορός καὶ τὰ παραπλήσια.[21]

In Boethius too we find the same distinction between *magnitudo* and *multitudo*, and the same type of examples: *Essentiae autem geminae partes sunt, una continua... ut est arbor, lapis, et omnia mundi huius corpora, quae proprie magnitudines appellantur. Alia vero disiuncta... ut grex, populus, chorus, acervus.... His proprium nomen est multitudo.*[22] Only, in Boethius, the missing distinction between the two types of being given by Nicomachus gives rise to a pointed incongruity when the former, after having spoken exclusively of immaterial essences and having distinguished between *magnitudo* and *multitudo* in the context of such *essentiae*, gives us only the concrete and material examples thereof, as found in his source.

17 *Introductio Arithmetica* I, 1; p. 1, 7 ff. Greek edition by R. Hoche (Leipzig, 1866). For an English translation see *Introduction to Arithmetic* by Martin Luther D'Ooge, with commentary by F.E. Robbins and L.C. Karpinski (New York, 1926).
18 *Ibid.*, p. 2, 8-9.
19 *DIA* I, 1; p. 7, 26-8, 1.
20 Nicomachus, *Introductio Arithmetica*, I, 1; p. 2, 21-3, 2 = *DIA* I, 1; p. 8, 4-7. For the origin and significance of this list see the acute observations of Robbins and Karpinski in the above-cited translation of *Introduction to Arithmetic*, pp. 94-95. „In listing these abstracts, Nicomachus is apparently giving random examples, with no serious attempt to cite only the higher and more general ideas; in general they seem to represent only predicables, doubtless suggested by the Aristotelian categories but neither identical with them nor employed in the same way; Nicomachus speaks of them in a manner that reminds one rather of the independently and eternally existing Platonic ideas. In this detail of his system he has probably united Platonic and Aristotelian theory, but in general, hitherto, Platonic terminology and doctrine have predominated."
21 Nicomachus, *Introductio Arithmetica* I, 2; p. 4, 13-20; I do not think we shall be far from the truth if we attribute Boethius' lack of distinction between the two modes of being to a gross misunderstanding. It is clear that the Boethian expression *Horum igitur, id est, quae sunt propriae quaeque suo nomine essentiae nominantur* (p. 8, 13-15 Friedl.) serves exclusively to clarify that Boethius uses the word *essentiae* to denote things which are in true opposition to material bodies. But it is also clear that the same expression is nothing but a strained translation of the Nicomachean τῶν τοίνυν ὄντων τῶν τε κυρίως καὶ τῶν καθ᾽ ὁμωνυμίαν where the distinction is expressed in the clearest terms and further explained in the parenthetical ὅπερ ἐστὶ νοητῶν τε καὶ αἰσθητῶν.
22 *DIA* I, 1; p. 8, 15-23.

In any case, what is identical in the two authors is the criterion of classification applied to the four *disciplinae*. The first two, arithmetic and music, are concerned with the *multitudines,* considered, respectively, *per se* (*per se* = καθ᾿ ἑαυτό) and in relation to another, *ad aliquod* (*ad aliquod* = πρὸς ἄλλο). Hence, their objects are, respectively, numbers and relationships. Geometry and astronomy, in contrast, deal with the *magnitudines* considered at rest (*immobilis magnitudo* = ἐν μονῇ καὶ στάσει) and in motion (*mobilis magnitudo* = ἐν κινήσει καὶ περιφορᾷ).[23]

We have here a rigid and abstract scheme, to which neither Nicomachus nor, of course, Boethius can long adhere. Only observe how Nicomachus, after he has restricted the object of arithmetic to ποσὸν καθ᾿ ἑαυτό in his introduction (p. 6,2) and dealt with this in chapters 1-16 of Book I, goes on from chapter XVII to deal exclusively and at his own explicit proposal, with that very ποσὸν πρός τι (προτετεχνολογημένου δὲ ἡμῖν περὶ τοῦ καθ᾿ αὐτὸ ποσοῦ νῦν μετερχόμεθα καὶ ἐπὶ τὸ πρός τι) which he had earlier (Intro. p. 6, 2-3) designated as the sole object of music. The same contradiction appears in Boethius (*DIA* I,1, p. 9, 1-3): *illam multitudinem, quae per se est, arithmetica speculatur integritas, illam vero, quae ad aliquid, musici modulaminis temperamenta pernoscunt;* and (*DIA* I, 20, p. 45, 7-9): *Sed quoniam de ea quantitate, quae per se fit, dictum est, operis sequentiam ad illam, quae refertur ad aliquid, transferamus.*

Boethius might have found an identical precedent schematically outlined in a work with which he was perhaps familiar before he ever saw the text of Nicomachus, and which already presented the same contradiction in an even more macroscopic form: the commentary of Ammonius on the *Isagoge* of Porphyry.[24] Here, the dependency of the mathematical disciplines on philosophy is stated in clear terms (p. 11, 6-7; 22-23, Busse): Διαιρεῖται οὖν ἡ φιλοσοφία εἰς τὸ θεωρητικὸν καὶ πρακτικόν ...Πάλιν τὸ θεωρητικὸν διαιρεῖται εἰς θεολογικόν, μαθηματικὸν καὶ φυσιολογικόν. Identical, too, is the fourfold classification of the mathematics, though differing in order from that of Nicomachus-Boethius (p. 13; 11-12): τὸ δὲ μαθηματικὸν διαιρεῖται εἰς τέσσαρα, εἰς γεωμετρίαν καὶ ἀστρονομίαν καὶ μουσικὴν καὶ ἀριθμητικήν.

As far as the objects of the single disciplines are concerned, Ammonius presents two successive formulations. The first series of definitions identifies, in detail and without establishing any mutual relationships, the material of each single discipline: ἡ μὲν ἀριθμητικὴ τοὺς ἀριθμοὺς ἐπισκέπτεται....ἡ γεωμετρία τὰ μεγέθη καὶ τὰ σχήματα, ἡ δὲ μουσικὴ τὰς τῶν χορδῶν συμφωνίας....ἡ δὲ ἀστρονομία μεταγίγνεται περὶ τὰς ἐποχὰς τῶν ἀστέρων. (*Ibid.*, p. 13, 12-31.) Following the definition of arithmetic is a long parenthesis (p. 13, 12-18) emphasizing the divine nature of the ἀριθμητικὰ θεωρήματα and pointing out that the „number" with which arithmetic is concerned does not coincide with the number commonly used in calculation. Arithmetic is more properly the study of relationships between numbers (Θεωρεῖ ἡ ἀριθμητικὴ... τὰ εἴδη τοῦ ἀριθμοῦ ὁποίαν σχέσιν ἔχουσιν πρὸς ἄλληλα, οἷον ὁ ἐξ πρὸς τὰ τρία κτλ.) and of the genesis of the various types of number (ἄρτιος, περισσός, περισσάρτιος).[25]

23   Nicomachus, *Introductio Arithmetica* I, 3; p. 5, 13-6, 7 = Boethius, *DIA* I; p. 9, 1-6.
24   Such is the thesis of McKinlay (*op. cit.*), who suggests that Boethius attended to the translation and commentary of the *Isagoge* of Porphyry–in manifest emulation of Ammonius (cf. P. Courcelle, *Les lettres grecques*, pp. 264-78)–before he ever began work on the Arithmetic.
25   It should not be forgotten that, according to the testimony of Joannes Philoponus (*In Nicomachi Introductionem Arithmeticam*, p. 7 ff. Hoche), Ammonius wrote a commentary on the Arithmetic of Nicomachus, which leads one to believe that he may also have known the music treatise of the Gerasene–which treatise served Boethius for the first three books of his own treatise on music. Confirmation of this hypothesis might be: (1) the presence of the psychagogical motive in the proem of the *De Institutione Musica*, which proem derives, at least in part, from Nicomachus, and, (2) the reference by both Ammonius (p. 13, 25-27 Busse) and Boethius (pp. 184, 10-185, 9) to the well-known episode of the raving youth whom Pythagoras soothes with music (despite the possibility that for this episode Boethius may have had a Latin source in mind as well, as I have attempted to demonstrate in my „Studi sulle fonti," pp. 162-63).

102

Analogously, after a general definition of music in terms of tonal consonance, we are apprised of its psychagogical qualities (ἐπιτηδεύει δέ, i.e. ἡ μουσική, καί τινα μέλη κομίζοντα μὲν τὰ τῆς ψυχῆς πάθη, διεγείροντα δὲ αὐτὴν ἐπὶ ἀρετήν), and in illustration of this new aspect we are told the well-known story which is also related by Boethius in the proem of his treatise on music.

Having thus marked out the territory of the four διαιρήσεις τοῦ μαθηματικοῦ, Ammonius explains why they are four and not more than four (p. 14, 1 ff., Busse); and now, in this second formulation, it is the Nicomachean scheme that reappears, in flagrant contrast with the preceding: the object of arithmetic is the ποσὸν καθ᾽ αὐτό of music, it is the ποσὸν πρὸς ἕτερον.[26] In other words, the same σχέσις πρὸς ἄλληλα which the first scheme had formulated for arithmetic is now contradicted.

This is not the proper place to discuss whether this obvious anomaly is to be attributed to Ammonius or whether we can eliminate it by blaming the parenthesis on some learned interpolator.[27] The truth is that the contradiction was already to be found, as we have seen, in the treatise of Nicomachus, which Ammonius definitely knew and commented on. Later, Boethius, with his plodding fidelity to his sources, reproduced the anomaly without innovation. But what we now want to establish is the relationship of the music treatise of Boethius to the initial scheme of the *quadrivium*, which in practice, already in the arithmetic treatise, he had so patently disregarded.

The first thing that strikes one while reading the sizeable proemial chapter–which in Boethius' original intention included chapter II[28] –is the lack of any explicit reference to the distinction between *multitudo per se* and *multitudo ad aliquid*, which in the proem of the arithmetic treatise is the basis for the distinction between music and arithmetic. The differentiation between the two disciplines is here entrusted to a new basis. The prime function of music is the scientific study of the relationships between tones (*quali inter se coniunctae sint*– i.e. *cantilenae–vocum proportione.*) Already in this formulation, which brings to a conclusion the first part of the original proem, i.e. what has come down to us as the first chapter, it is clear that music is not regarded as studying the laws regulating the relationships between numbers as such, but only insofar as they refer to sounds. But the most insistent point in the proem is another–the ethical implications of music: *unde fit ut, cum sint quattuor matheseos disciplinae, ceterae quidem in investigatione veritatis laborent, musica vero non modo speculationi verum etiam moralitati coniuncta sit.*[29]

Thus, according to Boethius, music has two faces; on one side it is a mathematical science, studying the relationships between the different tones perceived by the human ear and reducing them to numerical ratios; on the other side it is concerned with the effects produced by sounds and melodies on the human psyche and with the relationship between music and human behavior. Thus, the study of music goes well beyond the confines of an abstract exposition of numerical ratios, even considering only those which refer to a musical reality.

To be sure, the ethical aspect turns out to be a bit less productive than it would seem to promise. We have already noted[30] that the ample space devoted in the proem to the psychago-

26   It seems clear, after the preceding note, that this second formulation of Ammonius derives *recta via* from Nicomachus.
27   The presence of numerous interpolations in this text of Ammonius is underlined by Busse in the introduction to his edition, though not in specific reference to this passage.
28   Only at the end of what is now the second chapter do we read (p. 189, 12): *Sed proemii satis est,* while in the codices the title of proemium applies only to the first. It would seem, therefore, that the division into chapters is posterior to Boethius.
29   *DIM* I, 1; p. 179, 20-23.
30   Pizzani, „Studi sulle fonti," pp. 159-60.

gical function of music serves no other purpose than to illustrate the great importance of that discipline, and hence to justify its being thoroughly studied. Just what kind of study is clearly indicated at the beginning of the chapter and repeated at the end: the aim of science is not just to observe the phenomena, but to fathom their underlying nature and to study their causes. Just as a scholar who is worthy of the name will not be content to contemplate forms and colors, but will look for their underlying properties, so one must not passively accept the sweetness of a melody without exploring the numerical proportions of which it is composed.

That exploration is the exclusive object of the five books of the treatise and, except for the proem, the psychagogical aspect has no further part in it. However that may be, it is yet well to point out that the wonderful correspondences Boethius brings to light between musical intervals and numerical ratios--increasingly complex as we proceed from consonance to dissonance--testify to the intimate bonds existing between the physical-mathematical laws and the world of the spirit.

Needless to say, nothing or almost nothing, in the *De Institutione Musica* is due to the independent speculation of Boethius. The most we can say is that, in an opinion I have already put forth, the ample space devoted in the proem to the psychagogical aspect might be due, at least in part, to Boethius' having enriched the material obtained from the direct source of the first three books--i.e. Nicomachus' *opus maius* on music--with a series of *exempla* taken from a Latin source.[31] This would explain the perhaps abnormal emphasis on that part of the proem, leaving us free to presume that in Nicomachus the psychagogical part was more restricted and perhaps more fully integrated with the general context. But again, this is not the place to discuss that possibility. What is most important of all for the objectives of our study is the fact that the proem of the *De Institutione Musica* contains not a single explicit element that would tend to substantiate the presentation of the treatise as the second part of a corpus of the *matheseos disciplinae* outlined in the introduction to the arithmetic treatise. There is no reference to that treatise's definition of music in relation to arithmetic. The question of the nature of the musical science is taken up from scratch, and so is that of its proper method of study. Thus if we are to judge by the proem, the *De Institutione Musica* was conceived by Boethius as an autonomous and self-sufficient work, not necessarily part of a *corpus* on the *quadrivium*.

The problem of its relationship to the *De Institutione Arithmetica*, and to the *quadrivium* in general, becomes more complicated if we leave the first book with its descriptions and enunciations, and take a look at the second, in which Boethius proposes to demonstrate rigorously (*diligentius demonstrare*)[32] what he has enunciated in the first. With this proposal in mind, Boethius now feels he should preface his demonstrations with a few observations intended to help the reader understand more fully what is to follow: *pauca praemittam, quibus elucubratior animus auditoris ad ea quae dicenda sunt accipienda perveniat.*[33] And here we recognize, in an abbreviated and compendious form, what Boethius had said in the proem of the *De Institutione Arithmetica* about the fourfold division of the mathematical sciences and the sphere of each. Thus the arithmetic-music relationship, too, remains unchanged: *per se vero discretae quantitatis arithmetica auctor est, ad aliquid vero relatae musica probatur obtinere peritiam.*[34]

---

31 *Ibid.*, pp. 160-64.
32 *DIM* II, 1; p. 227, 14-15: *Superius volumen cuncta digessit, quae nunc diligentius demonstranda esse proposui.*
33 *Ibid.*, p. 227, 17-18.
34 *DIA* II, 3; p. 229, 7-9.

Having gone through the preliminaries and assured us that *de ... quantitate discreta, quae per se est, in arithmeticis sufficienter diximus*,[35] Boethius starts on a whole series of discussions and demonstrations concerning mathematical relationships, as though forgetting that he has already discussed them in depth (and broken the initial scheme to do so!) in the arithmetical treatise. But in reality, he has not forgotten; every time he touches on something already discussed in the earlier work, he never fails to refer to it. Once again the old contradiction emerges in all its obviousness: the initial scheme induces Boethius to describe his propositions as belonging to the sphere of music, inasmuch as they are founded on *discreta quantitas ad aliquid relata*, and to view them in opposition to arithmetical propositions concerning only *discreta quantitas quae per se est*; but then, in practice, he himself is forced to admit that already in the *De Institutione Arithmetica* both aspects were discussed. The important thing to realize however is this: the present series of propositions, constituting a true *introductio arithmetica*[36] to problems exclusively musical, while seeming on the one hand to re-establish between music and arithmetic the connection that is ignored in the proem, on the other hand exempts the reader of the *De Institutione Musica* from an acquaintance with the earlier treatise on arithmetic. So, once again, the music treatise looks like something autonomous and self-sufficient. That this might be due to the possibility that Nicomachus, too, conceived his *opus maius* on music as something independent from the *Introduction to Arithmetic* is an observation worthy of all respect; but this does not change the fact that the *De Institutione Musica* can stand perfectly well on its own, and in many respects eludes the abstract scheme of the *quadrivium*.

From what has been said so far I think we can now arrive at some conclusions which should help fix the course our exposition must take from here:

1) Boethius' plan, conceived in two successive moments and consisting of two separate projects, the first of which being the four disciplines of the *quadrivium* and the second, the commentary on the complete works of Plato and Aristotle, does not necessarily derive from the traditional scheme of the ἐγκύκλιος παιδεία in which the study of the liberal arts (including the four mathematical disciplines of the *quadrivium*) was to serve as a preparation for philosophy. According to the source Boethius used, the mathematical disciplines appear as an integral part of philosophy enabling the student to *evadere ad cumulum perfectionis*.[37]

35   *DIA* II, 4; p. 229, 11-12.
36   On the structure and sources of this *introductio arithmetica* see my „Studi sulle fonti," pp. 66 ff.
37   There are several indications that the concept of the propaedeutic function of the liberal arts was anything but rigid—even in the minds of those philosophers who practiced them—especially in the last centuries of the ancient world. It is enough to consider that St. Augustine's partly executed scheme of a liberal arts corpus in a propaedeutic capacity numbered philosophy among the various disciplines. Marrou (*St. Augustin et la fin de la culture Antique*, pp. 193-94) goes to great lengths to resolve this singular anomaly in which philosophy is inserted among those disciplines propaedeutic to it. He postulates two types of philosophy in Augustine: one, the supreme goal, the highest level of the activity of the spirit; the other, a kind of preparatory philosophy consisting of „a first initiation into the vocabulary and problems of philosophy," and of a primary exercise in discussing the opinions of the various schools. But Marrou himself considers this hypothesis not wholly satisfactory, concluding wisely that (p. 194) „la distinction entre les études préparatoires et les études propres au philosophe accompli est beaucoup moins nette, moins accusée dans la pensée d'Augustin." On such premises it is perhaps difficult to say whether Boethius adhered to the thesis which considered the mathematical disciplines a part of philosophy, or whether, in the term *quadrivium*, at least, we may descry a momentary concession to the thesis regarding the mathematical disciplines as the four roads leading to the gates of philosophy. On that point, the Boethian text is a bit vague (p. 7, 21-25): *Inter omnes priscae auctoritatis viros... constare manifestum est, haud quemquam in philosophiae disciplinis ad cumulum perfectionis evadere, nisi cui talis prudentiae nobilitas quodam quasi quadruvio vestigatur.* Boethius says here that to reach the highest peaks in the realm of philosophy it is necessary to travel the four roads of the mathematical disciplines,

2) Notwithstanding the scheme articulated at the beginning of the *De Institutione Arithmetica*, the four treatises pertaining to the disciplines of the *quadrivium* do not seem to have been conceived by Boethius as part of a single corpus, or at least not as far as form is concerned. Not only did he draw on different sources for each of them (Nicomachus for arithmetic; Nicomachus, Ptolemy, Euclid,[38] and others for music; Euclid for geometry; and, again, Ptolemy for astronomy), but any attempt to organize his material into an organic and coherent corpus seems alien to his intentions. In other words, it is a far cry from an encyclopedic work along the lines of the *Disciplinarum Libri* of Varro or the *De Nuptiis Mercurii et Philologiae* of Martianus Capella!

3) The *De Institutione Musica* was conceived by Boethius as an autonomous and self-sufficient work embracing subject-matter and problems that go well beyond the abstract scheme of a *discreta quantitas ad aliquid relata*.

This last conclusion, founded on an examination of content and structure, confirms and finds confirmation in the thesis put forward by McKinlay who suggested that a large part of the logical writings of Boethius were drafted during the period intervening between the *De Institutione Arithmetica* and the *De Institutione Musica*, except for the translation and two commentaries on Porphyry which, McKinlay claims,[39] were written even before the arithmetic treatise. Without going into all the stylistic reasons adduced by McKinlay, it is not difficult to see, even from a preliminary, cursory reading that the *De Institutione Musica* shows a polish of style, a clarity of expression, and an elegance of diction completely lacking in the arithmetic treatise, with its more laborious and artifical manner. That this change might be due to an acquaintance with Cicero[40] is not an improbable hypothesis, and in any case, the fact remains that (for once) both stylistic and other considerations discourage us from seeing any bonds of necessity between the musical treatise and the arithmetical, whether chronological or structural.

This original autonomy of the two treatises brings us to a point where we may formulate our initial hypothesis, i.e. that right from the start, the diffusion and influence of each progressed independently of the other, and that we are therefore justified if, in order to study the *Fortleben* of the musical treatise, we prescind, at least within certain limits, from the arithmetical work.

The first significant confirmation of our hypothesis comes from a fundamental liberal arts treatise which followed by not many years the productivity of Boethius: the *Institutiones Humanarum Litterarum* of Cassiodorus.

The reader will remember that Cassiodorus expressly intended this work for the instruction of the Monks at Vivarium, the religious community which he himself founded in Calabria

---

but it is not clear whether these roads lead to or coincide with the main arteries of true philosophical speculation.

38 I refer to the *Sectio Canonis* attributed to Euclid, published by C. Jan in *Musici Scriptores Graeci* (Leipzig, 1895), pp. 148-66. Boethius paraphrases the first eight paragraphs of this work in *DIM* IV, 1-2 (see my „Studi sulle fonti," pp. 105 ff). On the attribution of this work to Euclid, see the recent *Pitagorici: Testimonianze e Frammenti*, ed. M. Timpanaro Cardini, 3 (Firenze, 1962), 194 ff.

39 „Stylistic Tests."

40 McKinlay actually speaks of a Ciceronian phase, embracing, in addition to the *DIM*, the commentary on the *Topica* of Cicero, the *De Differentiis Topicis*, the *Opuscula Sacra*, and still more (op. cit., p. 154). There no longer seems to be an obstacle to McKinlay's thesis in the early date (507) traditionally applied to Epistle I, 45 of the *Variae* of Cassiodorus, which letter marks the *terminus ante quem* for the composition of the four treatises of the *quadrivium*: L.M. De Rijk („On the chronology of Boethius' works of logic," *Vivarium* [1964] pp. 142-3) postdates the letter, with good arguments, to 515-516, a considerably advanced phase in the production of Boethius.

(not far from the modern town of Squillace), after failing in his attempt to establish in Rome, under the auspices of Pope Agapitus, a Christian university of the kind then existing in Alexandria and at Nisibis.[41] Much has been said on the structure and genesis of this treatise, whose manuscript tradition is among the most complicated and problematical to have been studied. Of the two books of which it is composed, only the first, *Institutiones Divinarum Litterarum*, expressly concerning religious instruction, presents a certain unity of tradition. The second, *Institutiones Humanarum Litterarum*, devoted to the seven liberal arts, has come down to us in at least three different redactions. The first of these is represented by a group of codices designated Ω by Mynors, to whom we owe the most important edition of the *Institutiones*.[42] In the Ω codices, the two books are combined in a single unity, as appears from the preface joining the second book to the first[43] and from the conclusion of the second, in the form of a prayer, analogous to that of the first. Linked with this redaction is a subgroup (Σ) of manuscripts which, though lacking Book I, retain the second book together with the above-mentioned preface, the final prayer, and above all, an *incipit* announcing the *Institutiones Humanarum Litterarum* as a second book. The other two redactions (Φ and Δ in Mynors) contain as a complete work the second book alone, minus the part of the preface linking it to the first book and minus the final prayer, but with several lengthy interpolations, some considerable textual divergences, and alterations in the order of the various parts.

It is not our intention to go into the details of this complex question nor to take a stand on the issue of the two main conflicting theses: that of Mynors,[44] who regards only the first redaction as authentic, and that of Courcelle,[45] who put forward the attractive hypothesis that Cassiodorus first drew up a type of outline of the second book, without preface or conclusion, and only later published the official edition in two books, having tacked on the first, and touched up the second; meanwhile the rough draft was preserved at Vivarium, even after the official publication of the work, and subsequently received successive additions and rearrangements at the hands of both Cassiodorus and the monks of the monastery: hence the formation of the two groups Φ and Δ (Courcelle uses ω to indicate the text of the original rough draft and ψ the same text as modified by Cassiodorus).

However this may be, we have to bear in mind the formation of the two groups when making our deductions. But it does not appear that the double redaction can affect our understanding of the purpose of the work. From the numerous indications that can be extracted from both Books I and II (including some parts common to both redactions) it can be ascertained with absolute clarity that for Cassiodorus the study of the liberal arts is totally subordinate to that of the sacred scriptures—contrary to Boethius, who held that the disciplines of the *quadrivium* were valid in and for themselves, as direct sources of knowledge. The most eloquent formulation of this view is perhaps from *Institutiones* I, 28, 3, p. 70, 8-19 (Mynors); *Verumtamen nec illud Patres sanctissimi decreverunt, ut saecularium litterarum studia respuantur, quia non exinde minimum ad sacras Scripturas intellegendas sensus noster instruitur: si tamen divina gratia suffragante, notitia ipsarum rerum sobrie ac rationaliter inquiratur, non ut in ipsis habeamus spem provectus nostri, sed per ipsas transeuntes desideremus*

41 Cassiodori Senatoris, *Institutiones*, ed. R.A. B. Mynors, 3rd ed. (Oxford, 1963), p. 3.
42 *Ibid.*
43 Cassiodorus, p. 89, 2-3; 7-9: *Superior liber, Domino praestante completus, institutionem videlicet divinarum continet lectionum.... Nunc tempus est ut aliis septem titulis saecularium lectionum praesentis libri textum percurrere debeamus.*
44 *Institutiones*, p. ix.
45 P. Courcelle, „Histoire d'un brouillon cassiodorien," *Revue des Études Anciennes*, 44 (1942), 65-86.

nobis a Patre hominum proficuam salutaremque sapientiam debere concedi. Quanti enim philosophi haec solummodo lectitantes ad fontem sapientiae non venerunt, et vero lumine privati ignorantiae caecitate demersi sunt! quoniam, sicut a quodam dictum est, numquam potest plenissime investigari, quod non per viam suam quaeritur. As can be seen, no concession whatever is made to the autonomous study of the profane disciplines. On the contrary, such studies should be moderate and reasonable, and no real progress can be got from them. They are only a means for ascending to true knowledge. The position of Boethius, or rather that which he assumed from his pagan sources, is challenged and surpassed in its entirety by Cassiodorus: not by the *matheseos disciplinae* are we led to the *cumulum perfectionis*, but by the word of God as expressed in the Scriptures. Yet a knowledge of those disciplines is useful, not to say indispensable, for gaining access to the Scriptures themselves. We find the same thoughts again in the *Institutiones* (II, 7, 4, p. 157, 19-22): *His igitur breviter de doctrinis saecularibus comprehensis, ostenditur quia non parvam utilitatem ad intellegentiam divinae legis afferre noscuntur, sicut etiam a quibusdam sanctis patribus indicatur.*

These words introduce the final part of the second book and hence are to be found only in redaction Ω. Their sense, however, is typical of the whole second book, including those parts which may be found in all three redactions. It will be sufficient for us to consider a passage common to almost all the codices,[46] and immediately preceding the sentence quoted above: *Nobis autem sufficit, quantum in Scripturis sacris legitur, tantum de hac parte sentire, quia nimis absurdum est hinc humanam sequi sententiam, unde, quantum nobis expedit, divinam noscimur habere doctrinam* (p. 157, 14-18). It would be hard to express more clearly the limits imposed by Cassiodorus on the *humanae litterae*. Their study comes to an end as soon as the student, with all the limitations of human capacity, achieves a knowledge of the divine. From that moment on, their further study is unjustified.

Thus, even if we accept Courcelle's reconstruction, we still have to recognize that the original rough draft—which invested only the *humanae litterae* and whose concluding words we have just had occasion to examine—was conceived in the same spirit and with the same objectives as the so-called official edition in two books. This is substantiated by the numerous references to the Scriptures contained in the discussion of each single *disciplina*.

The assessment made by Cassiodorus of the study of the liberal arts, an assessment in harmony with the venerable tradition—which he embraces—of the Church Fathers, is thus at total odds with Boethius. But in spite of this contrast, the incontestable fact remains that the author who most closely preceded Cassiodorus in the treatment of at least some of the liberal arts—belonging, moreover, to the same circles—was Boethius.

That circumstance has not failed to influence the scholars, many of whom have taken for granted Boethius' influence on the *Institutiones* of his contemporary, sometimes without even reading or making a critical analysis of the texts. But, in reality, how consistent is that influence, and what are its limits? Simon, for example,[47] has recently suggested that Boethius furnished Cassiodorus not only with material for his dissertations on dialectic, arithmetic and geometry, but with the *Gesamtaufbau* of his compendium, or, more appropriately, the respective order of the arts of the *quadrivium*. The fact that Simon excludes Boethius' *Musica* and *Astronomia* from the possible sources of Cassiodorus is indicative of more caution than we find in certain wild theories that have been held in the past.[48] However, we cannot exclude the possibility

---

46   The codices of Δ end with *sentire*; those of Φ have the entire sentence, up to *doctrinam*.

47   Manfred Simon, „Zur Abhängigkeit spätrömischer Enzyklopädien der Artes liberales von Varros Disciplinarum Libri,‟ *Philologus*, 110 (1966), 88-110.

48   See, for example, L.M. Capelli, „I fonti delle *Institutiones Humanarum Rerum* di Cassiodoro,‟ *Rendiconti dell'Instituto Lombardo* (1898), pp. 1549-57 where Boethius' dependence on the music section of the *Institutiones* is sustained without proof.

that Boethius' influence was even smaller, or at least that the Cassiodorean *ordo* was not so much derived from the Boethian *quadrivium*—which, as we have seen, may not have constituted a true corpus—as from the naked scheme of the proemial chapter of the *De Institutione Arithmetica*. But there is more: the Cassiodorean order of the four mathematical sciences appears for the first time in a scheme pertaining to the various divisions and subdivisions of philosophy inserted into the rhetorical section of the *Institutiones* (p. 110, 10-14). Now this scheme, as Mynors justly notes, could not have come from any other source but, *recta via*, the commentary of Ammonius on the *Isagoge* of Porphyry,[49] which passage we have already examined. It follows that Cassiodorus could have taken the scheme for the mathematical part of his compendium from Ammonius before he ever found it in Boethius.[50]

We come now to a more detailed analysis. As we know, the various sections of the *Humanae Institutiones* consist of brief discussions on the main aspects of each single discipline, plus some pertinent bibliographical indications for the benefit of the monks. This bibliography, which has justifiably earned for the opusculum the nickname of *Bibliographie Analytique*,[51] is of vital importance to our research. On the one hand it tells us what, in the opinion of Cassiodorus, were the essential texts on each subject, enabling us to hypothesize the probable, sources of each section; on the other hand, since the bibliographical notes were intended for the monks, we may deduce the identity of some of the books in the *Vivarium* library. The utility of the bibliographical notes is compromised, however, by the fact that they vary—sometimes significantly—from redaction to redaction. In the case of the section on dialectic, for example, the Ω redaction contains a much longer list of works than redaction ω. In the former, alongside of the Boethian version of the *Isagoge* of Porphyry and of the logical works of Aristotle, with their respective comments, we find a precise reference to the translations and commentaries of Marius Victorinus; but in the latter redaction, only Boethius is mentioned. Courcelle has shown that this redaction, i.e. that of the rough outline, is the original, on the premise that Cassiodorus in his dialectic section, manifestly avails himself of Boethius and not Marius Victorinus. Later, having read the work of Victorinus, he made what additions he felt were needed in the official edition. As the reader can see, this reconstruction is quite complicated (and, as a matter of fact, is even more so in the particulars);[52] but whatever we may think of it, the fact remains that for the dialectic part, Boethius is the essential source of Cassiodorus.

Concerning the disciplines of the *quadrivium*, the situation looks a bit simpler in the main, but conceals some facets which are disconcerting, to say the least. Suffice it to say that Boethius is evoked in connection with both arithmetic and geometry, but not once in the section dedicated to music and astronomy. Thus, in the *De Arithmetica*, we read (p. 140, 17-20): *Quam* (i.e. *arithmeticam*) *apud Graecos Nicomachus diligenter exposuit. Hunc prius Madaurensis Apuleius, deinde magnificus vir Boetius Latino sermone translatum Romanis contulit lectitandum.* Analogously in the *De Geometria*: (p. 152, 10-13): *Cuius disciplinae apud Graecos Euclides, Apollonius, Archimedes nec non et alii scriptores probabiles exti-*

49 Cf. p. 11, 6-7; 22-23; p. 13, 8-11.

50 It should be noted, however, that Ammonius never enumerates the four mathematical disciplines in the Nicomacheo-Boethian order, although that order could be perhaps logically deduced from his exposition (cf. P. Courcelle, *Les lettres grecques*, p. 325).

51 P. Courcelle („Histoire d'un brouillon"): „les *Institutiones Humanae* sont, avant tout, une bibliographie analytique" (p. 85).

52 According to Courcelle („Histoire d'un brouillon" p. 78 ff), Cassiodorus retouched the *brouillon* once again, after the official edition, completing the list of logical works by Boethius and eliminating the residual references to Marius Victorinus.

terunt; ex quibus Euclidem translatum Romanae linguae idem vir magnificus Boetius edidit. More generic is the bibliographical notice from *De Astronomia* (pp. 155, 23-156,3): *De astronomia vero disciplina in utraque lingua diversorum quidem sunt scripta volumina; inter quos tamen Ptolomeus apud Graecos praecipuus habetur, qui de hac re duos codices edidit, quorum unum minorem, alterum maiorem vocavit astronomum.* As we can see, no mention of Boethius. In fact, the only Latin author mentioned during the whole discussion is Varro (pp. 155, 11 and 157, 11). If, however, in the case of the *De Astronomia* we could understand Boethius' work to be tacitly included among the *diversorum scripta volumina*, referring to the abudant astronomical writings in *utraque lingua* extant at the time of Cassiodorus, we cannot say as much for the *De Musica*, where the name of Boethius is omitted even though the bibliographical data in this section are much more complete and detailed than in the other three disciplines of the *quadrivium*.

Already in the beginning of the exposition we find a precise bibliographical reference (p. 142, 13-17): *Gaudentius quidem, de musica scribens, Pythagoram dicit huius rei invenisse primordia...quem vir disertissimus Mutianus transtulit in latinum, ut ingenium eius assumpti operis qualitas indicaret.* But it is at the end of this section that we encounter a true bibliography of music (p. 149, 12-150,3): *Quam* (i.e. *musicam*) *apud Graecos Alypius, Euclides, Ptolomeus et ceteri probabili institutione docuerunt; apud Latinos autem vir magnificus Albinus librum de hac re compendiosa brevitate conscripsit, quem in bibliotheca Romae nos habuisse atque studiose legisse retinemus. Qui si forte gentili incursione sublatus est, habetis Gaudentium, quem si sollicita intentione relegatis, huius scientiae vobis atria patefaciet. Fertur etiam latino sermone et Apuleium Madaurensem instituta huius operis effecisse. Scripsit etiam et pater Augustinus de musica sex libros, in quibus humanam vocem rithmicos sonos et armoniam modulabilem in longis syllabis atque brevibus naturaliter habere posse monstravit. Censorinus quoque de accentibus qui voci nostrae valde necessarii sunt, subtiliter disputavit, quos pertinere dicit ad musicam disciplinam; quem vobis inter ceteros transcriptum reliqui.*

As we can see, the number of authors referred to is quite considerable, but no sign of Boethius. Redactions Φ and Δ, too, merely integrate what has been said about Gaudentius in ω, recalling his translation into Latin by Mutianus (the codices of both redactions have: *habetis hic Gaudentium Mutianilatum*, presumably to be corrected to *Mutiani Latinum*, but say nothing about Boethius).

The silence of Cassiodorus in regard to the astronomical and, especially, the musical work of Boethius is all the more disconcerting in view of the fact that none other than Cassiodorus gives us conclusive proof, in an epistle definitely anterior to the *Institutiones*, that Boethius completed all four treatises on the *quadrivium*.[53] The most logical deduction one can draw from this is that Boethius' treatise on music never reached Vivarium, and that Cassiodorus preferred to pass it over, not having been able to procure it.[54] This would be a further con-

---

53 Cassiodorus, *Variae* I, 45: *Translationibus enim tuis Pythagoras musicus Ptolomaeus astronomus leguntur Itali, Nicomacus arithmeticus, geometricus Euclides audiuntur Ausonii* (ed. Th. Mommsen [Berolini, 1894] p. 40).

54 Courcelle, „Histoire d'un brouillon," pp. 84 ff., reminds us that in the Codex Valentian. 195 and in the Parisini 8679 and 12963, at the end of the music section of Cassiodorus, we may read the following gloss: *De huius disciplinae studio et Dionysius Alicarnasseus diversa volumina graeco sermone conscripsit: de hoc et Boetius in latino opusculum composuit.* Courcelle definitely identifies the Dionysius Halicarnasseus mentioned here with the homonymous musicologist of Hadrian's reign cited in the Suda and by Porphyry in his commentary on the *Harmonica* of Ptolemy (pp. 37, 15; 92, 28; 94, 25; 96, 11; 104, 14, in the edition of Ingemar Düring [Göteborg, 1930]) and holds, furthermore, that the gloss is the handiwork of none other than Cassiodorus, on the premisse that „Une telle glose suppose une connaissance de l'Antiquité dont un scoliaste médiéval aurait été bien incapable."

firmation of what we observed to begin with, i.e. that the four treatises on the arts of the *quadrivium* were neither originally conceived as, nor subsequently united in, a single corpus. Especially the *De Institutione Musica*, owing both to its particular structure and to the lateness of its composition in respect to the arithmetical work, must have met with a completely independent fate, as seems to be borne out by the manuscript tradition of that work.

But before approaching this theme, we shall have to clarify one further and no less fundamental question; prescinding from the bibliographical data, to what degree were the Boethian treatises used as a source for the *Institutiones*? And, specifically in the case of the music treatise, did Cassiodorus make no use of the latter for the musical section of his compendium, or did he indeed use it only to exclude it from his bibliography?

Actually, an objective analysis[55] of the texts brings us to an even more surprising conclusion: not only did Cassiodorus not utilize the *De Institutione Musica*, but the arithmetical section as well seems to have been derived not so much from the *De Institutione Arithmetica* of Boethius as from the treatise of Nicomachus, whether directly or via another Latin translation, such as that of Apuleius, mentioned by Cassiodorus together with that of Boethius.

It is surprising that this inescapable conclusion seems until now to have eluded Simon who, in the article cited above, takes the arithmetical work of Boethius to be the direct source of the corresponding part of the *Institutiones*.[56] In truth, the reasons adduced by Courcelle do not seem to leave room for doubts. He demonstrates that already in the initial part of the arithmetic section, the concept of the ordinal precedence and propaedeutic priority of arithmetic among the other mathematical disciplines is much closer to the text of Nicomachus than to the epitome of Boethius.[57] But the point most emphasized by Courcelle is the difference in the translation of some of the terminology. Most significant of all seems to be the reference to the fourth scheme of Cassiodorus, dividing numbers into *lineales, superficiosi* and *solidi* (p. 139, 3 Mynors). This division corresponds perfectly to Nicomachus (p. 82, 21 ff. Hoche: περί τε γραμμικῶν ἀριϑμῶν καὶ ἐπιπέδων καὶ στερεῶν).

In Boethius (p. 86, 11-16) it is expressed discursively without assigning a precise label to each term: *Nunc etiam nobis de his numeris sermo futurus est, qui circa figuras geometricas et earum spatia dimensionesque versantur, id est de linearibus numeris et de triangularibus vel quadratis caeterisque q u o s s o l a p a n d i t p l a n a d e m e n s i o* (the doublespaced words indicate the periphrasis by which Boethius renders the Nicomachean ἐπιπέδων, which Cassiodorus translates exactly as *superficiosi.*

It does not seem likely, however, that Cassiodorus would use the word *opusculum* for a large work in five books, such as the *De Institutione Musica* of Boethius. As far as Dionysius is concerned, the reference is, without question, of learned, though presumably second-hand, origin. It should be noted, too, that Mynors (p. xxxviii) refers this gloss to *Institutiones* II,5,11, where the discussion already centers on geometry.

55 *Les lettres grecques*, pp. 329-30.

56 J. Fontaine (*Isidore de Séville et la culture classique dans l'Espagne wisigothique* [Paris, 1959] p. 354) mistakenly credits Courcelle with the thesis of the total dependence of Cassiodorus on the Arithmetic of Boethius.

57 Cf., for example, the following passage from Nicomachus (p. 10, 10-13, Hoche): οὔσης μὲν γὰρ γεωμετρίας ἀνάγκη καὶ τὴν ἀριϑμητικὴν συνεπιφέρεσϑαι· ἅμα γὰρ ταύτῃ τρίγωνον ἢ τετράγωνον... ἢ ἄλλο τι τοιοῦτον, which Boethius renders in the interrogative (p. 10, 28-30): *Si enim numeros tollas, unde triangulum vel quadratum vel quicquid in geometria versatur*? In Cassiodorus we read (p. 132, 16-18): *geometria vero quod habet trigonum, quadriangulum vel his similia, idem indiget arithmeticam.* Anyone can see that *trigonum* and *quadriangulum* are closer to the text of Nicomachus than the *triangulum* and *quadratum* of Boethius and that the expression *his similia* is a more literal translation of ἄλλο τι τοιοῦτον than Boethius' *quicquid in geometria versatur*. The fact that this passage appears only in φ and Δ substantiates the thesis of Courcelle on the priority of the *brouillon*.

111

If, however, in the composition of the arithmetic section Cassiodorus might have mainly taken into account the text of Nicomachus, and perhaps as well, the Apuleian version, without altogether ignoring, at least as a control, the Boethian reduction (with which he was familiar, as he elsewhere shows),[58] in the music section he appears to have excluded Boethius completely.

The Cassiodorean treatise begins by recalling the well-known story of the anvils, with a specific indication of its source, Mutian's Latin translation of the musical treatise of Gaudentius (p. 142, 13-17, Mynors): *Gaudentius quidam, de musica scribens, Pythagoram dicit huius rei invenisse primordia ex malleorum sonitu et cordarum extensione percussa. Quem vir disertissimus Mutianus transtulit in latinum, ut ingenium eius assumpti operis qualitas indicaret.* The text of Gaudentius, which has luckily reached us in the Greek, corresponds completely: Τὴν δὲ ἀρχὴν τῆς τούτων εὑρέσεως Πυθαγόραν ἱστοροῦσι λαβεῖν ἀπὸ τύχης παριόντα χαλκεῖον τοὺς ἐπὶ τὸν ἄκμονα κτύπους τῶν ῥαιστήρων αἰσθόμενον διαφώνους τε καὶ συμφώνους ... Δύο γὰρ ἐξάψας χορδὰς ... καὶ κρούσας κτλ. (p. 340,4 ff. Jan).

After a brief etymological disquisition inspired by Clement of Alexandria (*Protrept.* 31) and a bibliographical reference to Censorinus (p. 142, 17-143,6, Mynors), Cassiodorus goes on to consider the ethical and religious implications of music. Here, indeed, it would appear that we have come upon some trace of Boethius. The Cassiodorean expression, *Musica ergo disciplina per omnes actus vitae nostrae hac ratione diffunditur* (p. 143, 7-8, Mynors) seems to echo a passage from Boethius' proem to the *De Institutione Musica* (I, 1, p. 179, 23-26): *Nihil est enim tam proprium humanitatis, quam remitti dulcibus modis, adstringi contrariis, idque non sese in singulis vel studiis vel aetatibus tenet, verum p e r c u n c t a d i f f u n d i t u r studia.* Analogously the reference to cardiac rhythm (p. 143, 10-12, Mynors): *quidquid enim loquimur vel intrinsecus venarum pulsibus commovemur, per musicos rithmos armoniae virtutibus probatur esse sociatum* corresponds in Boethius (p. 186, 4-5) to: *Nam ut sese corporis affectus habet, ita etiam pulsus cordis motibus incitantur.* But such correspondence is only illusory. As far as cardiac rhythm is concerned, the Boethian expression is textually closer to a passage from the *De Die Natali* of Censorinus, whom Cassiodorus cites just a little earlier (p. 22, 18-19, Hultsch): *Herophilus... v e n a r u m p u l s u s r h y t h m i s m u s i c i s a i t m o v e r i.* Concerning the other generic expression, the correspondence may be judged to be purely accidental, especially since it is really limited to the use of only one verb.[59]

Furthermore, it might be added, the whole passage is full of other tidbits taken from the opusculum of Censorinus (cf. Cassiodorus' definition of music as *scientia bene modulandi,* which we find again in Censorinus [p. 16, 23, Hultsch], and the theme of universal harmony, which also appears in Censorinus [p. 22,22]).

Thus it does not seem reasonable to postulate even a minimal contamination with the Boethian text. The passage in question can be explained very satisfactorily as a re-elaboration of the corresponding passage of Censorinus, in a more spiritual and Christian form (note the observations on the Ten Commandments and on the Psaltery).

After this passage comes the definition of music previously given by Cassiodorus in two other places, in accordance with that given by Nicomachus in the proem of the *Introduction to Arithmetic: musica (scientia) est disciplina quae de numeris loquitur, qui ad aliquid sunt his*

---

58 Cf. Cassiodorus, *Expositio Psalmorum* 34 C, where we find under the name of Nicomachus a faithfully transcribed passage from the *DIA* of Boethius (p. 13, 11). Courcelle reminds us, however (*Les lettres grecques,* p. 330) that in this same commentary on the Psalms there are paraphrases of passages from Nicomachus which Boethius omitted in his treatise (cf. Nicomachus p. 84, 8-11 and p. 135, 10-13 = Cassiodorus, *Expositio Psalmorum* 34 C and 79 B). This circumstance is conclusive evidence that Cassiodorus was wont to turn to Nicomachus even without the mediation of Boethius.

59 The presence of music in all aspects of life was a commonplace which could be got, in substance, from the text of Censorinus.

qui inveniuntur in sonis (cf. *Institutiones*, p. 111, 17-19 and p. 131, 3-5). With this definition Cassiodorus begins the more technical part of the music section, and also the part that is most controversial as far as sources are concerned. Aside from the above-mentioned definition, the subjects touched on in this part boil down to the following:

1) Three-fold division of music, into harmony, rhythm, and measure;
2) Three-fold division of musical instruments into *percussionalia, tensibilia, inflatilia*;
3) Ordered description of the six consonances;
4) Ordered description of the fifteen tones.

Needless to say, none of these arguments finds a true counterpart in the work of Boethius. Instead of the division of music into harmony, rhythm, and measure, which Cassiodorus might have taken from Alypius, Boethius offers a more comprehensive division into universal, human and instrumental (*DIM* I,2). As to the *genera instrumentorum*, we have seen that they are three in Cassiodorus, but Boethius, *au fond*, counts four (p. 189, 7-10): *Haec vero-sc. musica quae in quibusdam consistere dicitur instrumentis–administratur aut intentione ut nervis, aut spiritu ut tibiis, vel his, quae ad aquam moventur,*[60] *aut percussione quadam, ut in his, quae in concava quaedam aerea feriuntur.* Note too that Cassiodorus lists a whole series of instruments that he could not have read in Boethius. Again, from Gaudentius and not Boethius, presumably, derives the discussion of the six consonances. Indeed, in the second book (ch. 18-20), Boethius counts only five, appearing to adopt the Pythagorean thesis which excludes from the number of consonances the interval of an octave plus a fourth. Only in the fifth book (ch. 9) does he expound the thesis of Ptolemy, which includes this interval among the consonances, but he does not expressly adhere to this thesis. As to the fifteen *tonoi*, we may suppose them to have come from Alypius, who, indeed, lists fifteen of them, though not in the same order as Cassiodorus, but they could also have come from the compendium of Albinus who, we have reason to believe, may have utilized the work of Aristides Quintilian,[61] who lists the fifteen *tonoi* in the same order as Cassiodorus (pp. 20-21, Winnington-Ingram). It should be remarked that both Alypius and Albinus are mentioned in the bibliographical excerpt quoted above. In any case, we shall have to exclude the possibility of an influence from Boethius, who considers (IV, 16-17) only the eight *tonoi* listed by Ptolemy.

Having finished the technical part, Cassiodorus completes his exposition by returning to the initial theme of the power of music. Here, too, we must reject any connection with Boethius. Cassiodorus combines the independent elements, taken, as usual, from Censorinus, with echoes from the Bible (see, for example, the references to David and Saul), but he does not reveal any clear debt to Boethius. We now come to the bibliographical essay which ends the music section of the *Institutiones*. After what we have said about the sources of the exposition itself, it is not surprising that Cassiodorus should not mention the treatise of Boethius. But this omission cannot be explained unless we suppose that the treatise travelled a very different path from that of the rest of Boethius' writings. It would be quite wrong to imagine that other considerations--political, for instance–induced Cassiodorus to avoid this mention. The fact is that not only is Boethius constantly referred to in the *Institutiones*, but, as we have said, his influence on the logical section is huge, while, even if his influence on the arithmetic must be

---

60   In reality, the hydraulic organs were a sort of subclass of wind-instruments (Boethius introduces them with a *vel* and not with *aut*), even though the term *spiritus* does not seem suitable for them, if by *spiritus* we are to understand the emission of air from the lungs.

61   One of the two Boethian testimonials on Albinus (I,12)–the other (1,26) concerns the Latin names of the musical notes—credits this obscure author with the theory of *voces mediae*, which completes the traditional division of the voice into συνεχής and διαστηματική found in Aristides Quintilian (*De Musica Libri Tres*, ed. R.P. Winnington-Ingram [Leipzig, 1963], I, 4, p. 5,26).

reevaluated, it cannot be excluded from the geometry or the astronomy, as Courcelle has demonstrated.

A confirmation of all this is furnished by considerations of a different order. We have already mentioned that the *Institutiones* have reached us in three different redactions, and that two of them, ϕ and Δ are characterized by a whole series of interpolations of considerable size. That a large part of the interpolations of both groups is the handiwork of the monks of Vivarium has been claimed by Courcelle[62] in opposition to previous scholars, but Lehmann[63] had already recognized the Vivarian origin of group ϕ at least, thanks to the presence in this redaction of an Easter computation from the year 562.

At this point the facts speak for themselves. A conspicuous portion of the material used by the interpolators to broaden the text of the *Institutiones* derives from Boethius, but no interpolations appear in the sections on music and astronomy. Suffice it to say that excerpts from the *De Differentiis Topicis* of Boethius appear in both ϕ and in Δ in place of the original *topica* of Cassiodorus; that excerpts from the *De Institutione Arithmetica* turn up in Δ in an appendix to the arithmetic section; and, lastly, that the geometry section closes, in Δ, with a fragment bearing the titles of *Principia Geometrica Disciplinae*, which Courcelle[64] believes, with good reasons, to derive from Boethius' lost treatise on Geometry. It is clear from all this that the corpus used by the interpolators–who could only have lived before the ninth century, since even redaction Δ was fairly widespread in that period–did not include the *De Institutione Musica*, though it still contained, besides the *De Institutione Musica*, the lost treatise on Geometry, i.e. Boethius' Latin reduction of the *Elements* of Euclid.

Thus, the fate of the *De Institutione Musica* immediately after the death of its author remains, at this point, mysterious and obscure, while the latter's renown for his great knowledge of music, praised by none other than Cassiodorus in a famous epistle,[65] seems to have been eclipsed at the very moment when the rest of his writings were becoming the foundations of western scholarship.

* * * *

After Cassiodorus we must wait until Isidor of Seville for a new systematic treatment of the liberal arts. Before him, only Gregory of Tours shows an interest in this type of study, despite his vociferous claim of ignorance; but he does not go beyond a simple definition of each discipline in terms of practical utility.[66] Isidor dedicated three[67] of his twenty *Etymologiarum Libri* to the ordered exposition of the seven liberal arts, endowing the medieval scholastic tradition with another key text whose influence was to last for several centuries.

The reader may turn to the fundamental volumes of Fontaine[68] for the general questions regarding Isidor and his writings. We shall limit ourselves to an examination of his relationship to Boethius. Our task is greatly simplified by the fact that the source Isidor used for his com-

62   „Histoire d'un brouillon," p. 70 ff.

63   P. Lehmann, „Cassiodorstudien," *Philologus*, 71 (1912), 294.

64   „Histoire d'un brouillon," p. 72.

65   *Variae* II, 40.

66   Gregory of Tours, *Historia Francorum*, X, xxxi. Cf. R. Riché, *Éducation et Culture dans l'Occident barbare*, 2nd ed. (Paris, 1962), pp. 237-38.

67   The division into twenty books was posterior to Isidor and due to the attentions of Braulion of Saragossa, while in some old mss the seven liberal arts are vivided into four books. For the entire question, see M.C. Díaz y Díaz, „Les arts libéraux d'après les écrivains espagnoles et insulaires aux VIIe et VIIIe siècles," in *Arts Libéraux*, p. 40.

68   *Isidore de Séville, etc.* [2vols.].

pendium can be identified almost exclusively as the *Institutiones* of Cassiodorus, of which Isidor's work is not so much a paraphrase as a transcription, though with additions, variations, and cuts–the latter sometimes of considerable length. It is mainly to these additions and modifications that we shall have to pay attention. What we want to determine is whether they perchance reveal a process of contamination between the text of Cassiodorus and other sources –Boethius, for example.

First of all, it seems we may exclude the possibility of Isidor's having had before his eyes, during the drafting of his dialectics, the corpus of Boethius' logical works. This has been shown by the solid arguments of Fontaine[69] and we shall not question their validity. However, we cannot say the same about the arts of the *quadrivium*–and particularly the arithmetic. In this case too, of course, the basic text is Cassiodorus, nor does there seem to be any need to challenge Fontaine's hypothesis that the chapter on the three media–without parallel in Cassiodorus–derives not from the rich and articulate expositions of Boethius, but from „une tradition plus simple, de nature scolaire."[70]

A Boethian influence, however, can indeed be seen, it appears, in certain minute additions or variants that have subtly insinuated themselves into the literal transcription of the text of Cassiodorus, and do not seem to be explicable unless we postulate that Isidor was contemporaneously looking at the Boethian treatise on arithmetic. For the sake of clarity, the passages in question, indicated by Fontaine,[71] are compared below with the corresponding passages of Boethius and Cassiodorus. Those textual correspondences peculiar to Isidor and Boethius which appear to establish their dependency have been *brought out by italics*.

Isidor	*Boethius*	*Cassiodorus*
III,3,1	p. 13, 11-12	p. 133, 12-13
Numerus autem est multitudo *ex unitatibus* constituta.	Numerus est unitatum collectio, vel quantitatis acervus *ex unitatibus* profusus.	Numerus autem est ex monadibus multitudo composita.
III, 5, 2	p. 13, 13-16	p. 133, 20-23
Par numerus est, qui in duabus aequis partibus dividi potest, ut II, IV et VIII. Inpar vero numerus est, qui dividi aequis partibus nequit, *uno medio* vel deficiente vel superante, ut III, V, VII, IX et reliqui.	Et par quidem est, qui potest in aequalia duo dividi, *uno medio* non intercedente, impar vero, quem nullus in aequalia dividit eo quod in medio praedictus unus intercedat.	Par numerus est qui in duabus partibus aequalibus dividi potest, ut II, IIII, VI, VIII, X et reliqui. Impar numerus est qui in duabus partibus aequalibus dividi nullatenus potest, ut III, V, VII, VIIII, XI, et reliqui.
III, 5, 3	p. 17, 9-17	p. 133, 23-134, 3.
Pariter par numerus est, qui secundum parem numerum pariter dividitur, *quousque ad indivisibilem perveniat unitatem; ut* puta *LXIV habet me-*	Pariter par numerus est, qui potest in duo paria dividi, eiusque pars in alia duo paria partisque pars in alia duo paria, ut hoc totiens fiat, *usquedum*	Pariter par numerus est cuius divisio in duabus aequalibus partibus fieri potest usque ad monada (ut) verbi gratia LXIIII dividuntur in XXXII, XXXII

69   *Ibid.*, pp. 615 ff.
70   *Ibid.*, p. 365.
71   *Ibid.*, pp. 356, 360, 362.

Isidor	Boethius	Cassiodorus

Isidor

dietate *XXXII, hic autem XVI,* XVI *vero VIII,* octonarius IV, *quaternarius II, binarius* unum, qui *singularis* indivisibilis est.

Boethius

divisio partium *ad indivisibilem* naturaliter *perveniat unitatem. Ut LXIIII* numerus *habet me-dietatem. XXXII, hic autem* mediatatem *XVI,* hic *vero VIII.* Hunc quoque *quaternarius* in aequa partitur, qui binarii dup-lus est; sed binarius unitatis me-dietate dividitur, quae unitas naturaliter *singularis* non reci-pit sectionem.

Cassiodorus

in XVI, XVI in VIII, VIII in IIII, IIII in II, II vero in I et I.

III, 5, 4

Pariter impar est, qui *in partes aequas recipit sectionem, sed partes eius mox indissecabiles permanent,* ut VI,X et XXXVIII, L. *Mox enim hunc numerum divideris, incurris in* numerum *quem secare non possis.*

p. 21, 24-22,7

Pariter...impar...est, qui... *in partes aequales recipit sectio-nem, partes vero eius mox... insecabiles permanebunt,* ut sunt VI, X, XIIII, XVIII, XXII, et his similes. *Mox enim hos numeros si in gemina fueris divisione partitus, incurris in* imparem *quem secare non possis.*

p. 134, 4-6

Pariter impar numerus est qui similiter solummodo in duabus partibus dividi potest aequali-bus ut (X in V) XIIII in VII, XVIII in VIIII et his similia.

III, 5,5

Impariter par numerus est, cuius partes etiam dividi pos-sunt, *sed usque ad unitatem* non perveniunt, ut XXIV. Hi enim in medietatem divisi XII faciunt rursumque in aliam medietatem VI, deinde in aliam tres; *et ultra divisionem non recipit sectio illa, sed ante unitatem invenitur terminus, quem secare non possis.*

p. 25, 5-29

Impariter par numerus est... qui dividitur in aequas partes ... *sed non usque ad unitatem* progreditur...ut sunt XXIIII ...Hi enim possunt in medieta-tes dividi et eorum rursus par-tes in alias medietates sine ali-qua dubitatione solvuntur... *et usque ad unitatem sectio illa non pervenit, sed ante unitatem invenitur terminus, quem secare non possis.*

p. 134, 6-10

Impariter par numerus est qui plures divisiones secundum ae-qualitatem partium recipere potest, non tamen ut usque ad assem perveniat; ut verbi gratia XXIIII in bis XII, XII in bis VI, VI vero in bis III et ampli-us non procedit.

III, 5, 7

Simplices sunt qui *nullam aliam partem habent nisi* so-lam *unitatem,* ut ternarius so-lam tertiam, et quinarius solam quintam, et septenarius solam septimam. His enim una pars sola est. Compositi sunt qui *non solum unitate metiuntur, sed etiam alieno numero* pro-

p. 30, 16-17

...incompositus est, qui *nullam aliam partem habet nisi* eam... ut ipsa pars non sit nisi *unitas.*

p. 32, 12-13

Secundus autem vocatur hic numerus (sc. compositus),

p. 134, 10-15

Primus de imparibus et sim-plex numerus est qui monadi-cam mensuram solam recipere potest, ut verbi gratia III, V, VII, XI (XIII), XVII et his si-milia. Secundus et compositus numerus est qui non solum monadicam mensuram, sed et arithmeticam recipere potest,

116

Isidor	Boethius	Cassiodorus
creantur, ut novem, XV et XXI. Dicimus enim ter terni et septies terni, ter quini et quinquies quini.	quoniam *non sola unitate metitur sed etiam alio numero.*	ut verbi gratia VIIII, XV, XXI et his similia.

There is more than enough to permit us to maintain without fear of rebuttal that in several places Isidor padded out the succinct exposition of Cassiodorus with material obtained from the *De Institutione Arithmetica* of Boethius. Such, at least, is the thesis put forward on various occasions by Fontaine. Nevertheless, I dislike to have to point out that there is one detail which seems to have escaped this eminent scholar, and which threatens the validity of his reconstruction: all the passages from Boethius in correspondence with the text of Isidor belong to that group of chapters from the *De Institutione Arithmetica* (I, 1-3; 6-11; 13-18) which are collected in the *Breviarium ex libro arithmeticae disciplinae*, appendixed to the *Institutiones* of Cassiodorus in redaction Δ. Obviously, it is not possible to deduce from this that Isidor modelled himself on redaction Δ! The text used by Isidor was indisputably that of redaction Ω and any contention to the contrary would be critically unfounded.[72] Nevertheless, we cannot exclude *a priori* the possibility that Isidor knew redaction Δ *as well*, or, better still, that the *Breviarium* somehow fell into his hands separately. However this intricate question may be resolved, the fact remains that Isidor was familiar, either directly or through excerpts, with the Arithmetic of Boethius.

The situation is analogous for the brief space dedicated by Isidor to geometry. Fontaine has had occasion to point out many of the extravagances in which the compendium abounds[73] and which are largely due to Isidor's lack of familiarity with this branch of mathematics. But where the text wanders from Cassiodorus without becoming unacceptable, the source, once again, is a text which may be linked, directly or indirectly, to the lost geometrical treatise of Boethius, i.e. the *Principia Geometricae Disciplinae*, which redaction Δ of the *Institutiones* contains as an appendix to the section on geometry, and which Courcelle attributes to Boethius. The connection is unequivocal. Indeed, the following definitions lack any correspondence with the authentic text of Cassiodorus:[74]

Isidor, III, 12, 7
Prima autem figura huius artis punctus est, cuius pars nulla est. Secunda linea, praeter latitudinem longitudo. Recta linea est, quae ex aequo in suis punctis iacet. Superficies vero, quod latitudines et longitudines solas habet. Superficiei vero fines lineae sunt.

Princ. Geom. Disc. (ap. Cass.), p. 169, 2-7
Punctum est cuius pars nulla est. Linea vero praeter latitudinem longitudo.... Recta linea est quae ex aequo in suis punctis iacet. Superficies vero quod longitudinem ac latitudinem solas habet. Superficiei fines lineae sunt.

We have thus reached conclusive proof that, for arithmetic and geometry, Isidor, like Cassiodorus, was able to employ the work of Boethius, albeit only to a small degree. Whether he had access to the complete work or, as is more probable, to mere compendia, is a question

---

72 The variants of φ and Δ judging from the apparatus of Mynors, do not seem to influence the Isidorian text.
73 *Isidore de Séville*, pp. 393 ff.
74 This connection is also noted by Courcelle, who erroneously cites Isidor, *Etymologies* III, 13, instead of III, 12, 7.

which can be examined in other circumstances. What is certain is that the Geometry and the Arithmetic of Boethius continued to exert influence even in the cultural environment of Visigothic Spain.

As for astronomy, we obviously lack the terms for a sure comparison, but with music we are in the same position as before: Isidor's compendium concerning music, even where it abandons Cassiodorus—as it often does—reveals not the slightest Boethian influence.

We arrive at this conclusion of necessity, whether we accept the old thesis of Schmidt,[75] postulating a common source for St. Augustine, Cassiodorus and Isidor, or the new orientation started by Stettner[76] and taken up by Courcelle[77] and Fontaine,[78] which takes Cassiodorus to be the primary source of Isidor. Since Isidor was not dependent on Boethius, as we have seen, a knowledge of the DIM could be attributed to him only on the basis of what non-Cassiodorean material has run together in his exposition, and this offers no element that would permit us to make such an attribution. The technical aspects are almost completely eluded, and are reduced to mere definitions. And the definitions turn out to be imprecise, generic, and often erroneous just where Boethius would have furnished the correct one. Compare, for example Isidor (III, 20,5) *Diastema est vocis spatium ex duobus vel pluribus* (sic!) *sonis aptatum*; Boethius (p. 195, 6): *Intervallum vero est soni acuti gravisque distantia*; Isidor (III, 20, 6): *Diesis est spatia quaedam et deductiones modulandi atque vergentes de uno in altero sono*; Boethius (p. 213, 17): *diesis autem est semitonii dimidium*; Isidor (III, 20, 7): *Tonus est acuta enuntiatio vocis*; Boethius (p. 201, 5-202,2): *Nam si vox voce... proportione... sit... sesquioctava acutior graviorque...tonum consonantiam reddet.*

Notice, too, that Isidor, in contrast to Boethius, dwells long on the biblical and mythical origins of music, and on its employment in civil and religious life (III, 16, 1-3), on the human voice and its different inflections and characteristics, as well as on the different timbres of musical instruments (III, 20, 11-14), on musical instruments (III, 21, 1-8), and on rhythm and rhythmic instruments (III, 22, 1). As for the last chapter, on the harmonic mean (III, 23, 1), the example it employs is different from that used by Boethius in the corresponding section of his *De Institutione Musica* (II, 12), and is rather an enlargement on what Isidor had already written, with the help of some source other than Boethius, on the three means in the arithmetic section (III, 8). Only in the chapter on the power of music is there something like an echo of Boethius, where Isidor speaks of the capacity of music to inflame the temper for warfare (Isidor, III, 17,2 = Boethius, p. 186, 28-30) and of the relation of musical rhythm to cardiac rhythm (Isidore III, 17,3 = Boethius p. 186, 4-5). In reality, however, the former is a commonplace which may be found in Censorinus (XII, 12), Macrobius (*Ad Ciceronis Somnium Scipionis* II, 3, 9) and Martianus Capella (p. 492, 5-6, Dick), while the latter comes almost word for word from Cassiodorus (p. 143, 10-12).

The absence of the *De Institutione Musica* from the collection of writings consulted by Isidor during the compilation of his musical compendium is all the more conspicuous for the comparatively large number of excursions which distinguish it from the rest of the corpus of the liberal arts. Nor is it enough to explain the omission to say that Isidor's treatment reveals a reawakening interest in the practical side of music, in contrast with the mathematical and speculative nature of the Greek-Hellenistic tradition to which Boethius ultimately belongs. Aside from the more strictly technical discussions, Isidor would still have been able to find

75   C. Schmidt, *Quaestiones de Musicis Scriptoribus Romanis, Inprimis de Cassiodoro et Isidoro* (Diss. Giessen, Darmstadt, 1899).
76   Th. Stettner, „Cassiodors Enzyklopädie, eine Quelle Isidors," *Philologus*, 85 (1926), 241-42.
77   *Les Lettres Grecques*, pp. 330-32.
78   *Isidore de Séville*, pp. 415 ff.

innumerable tips in Boethius, both for his historical digressions, and for the ethicopsychological implications to which Isidor was so attracted. Everything leads us to believe that Isidor had no more access to the Boethian text than Cassiodorus had. Again we are forced to conclude that structural peculiarities and the more recent date of composition must have contributed in some manner to a temporary eclipse of the *De Institutione Musica* and to its relative unpopularity beside works such as the *De Institutione Arithmetica* and perhaps even beside the *De Institutione Geometrica,* which a later age was to lose forever.

The manuscript tradition of the Boethian treatise on music offers eloquent confirmation of what we have been saying. By this I do not mean to refer so much to the fact that the treatise has come down to us in no manuscript that can be dated earlier than the ninth century, as to another solid fact which can be deduced with almost absolute certainty from the status of the tradition: there was a time prior to the Carolingian Renaissance when all that remained of the music treatise of Boethius was a single copy in an unidentifiable library of the West.

Our reasons for making this statement are quickly told: we shall see that in all the codices we know of, excepting some mutilated manuscripts, our text ends with the words *in diatonicis generibus nusquam una,* cut off in the middle of a sentence, in chapter xiv of Book V. Now, there are at least two reasons that prevent us from thinking that Boethius left his work unfinished: 1) Cassiodorus, in a letter cited above, refers to the treatise of Boethius as a finished work;[79] 2) in several codices, what is left of Book V is preceded by a table of contents of thirty chapters--eleven more than have come down to us. Moreover, the objection that Boethius could have drafted this *index capitum* himself and then not have been able to carry out his design is also easily overruled. There are, in fact, clear indications that the titles for the chapters of the *De Institutione Musica* are not Boethius' own, while it is no less clear that whoever redacted the chapters of Book V had before him the complete work.

How so? We have already had occasion to observe (*supra,* p. 103) that the title *Proemium* which the codices give to what is now the first chapter arose through an oversight: Boethius meant the proem to last until the end of what has reached us as chapter two, at the end of which we read the eloquent: *Sed proemii satis est* (p. 189, 12). It is hard to believe that Boethius himself would have made such an obvious mistake. But the most conspicuous incongruity is the title of chapter iii of Book IV: *Musicarum notarum per graecas ac latinas litteras nuncupatio.* After such a title we would expect Bothius to give us, besides an ordered exposition of the Greek system of notation based on the alphabet, another system based on Latin letters. But nothing of the kind! The text does indeed give us the signs of the Greek notation, but all it gives us in Latin is a translation of the names of the various notes alongside of the Greek terms conveniently translitterated (e.g. *Proslambanomenos, qui adquisitus dici potest... hypate hypaton quae est principalis principalium,* etc.).[80] Here, too, Boethius cannot be held responsible for such flagrant lack of precision.

Thus Boethius is not the author of the names of the chapters in the *De Institutione Musica.* But neither can we attribute to the pure fantasy of whoever named them the titles of the missing chapters of the fifth book. Indeed, as we have already shown,[81] those chapters continued the interrupted paraphrase of the first book of the Ἁρμονικά of Claudius Ptolemy from the point where it breaks off in our manuscripts, furnishing clear evidence that the exclusive source of the last book of Boethius' treatise was none other than the first book of Ptole-

79   *Variae* I, 45.
80   For this whole question see U. Pizzani, „Studi sulle fonti," p. 96.
81   *Ibid.,* pp. 152-56.

my's. The conclusion can be only one: whoever penned those titles had access to the complete treatise of Boethius.

The fact that in all our manuscripts the text breaks off at the same point gives us the absolute certainty that they all derive, more or less directly, from a single archetype from which the last folia were lost.

The reason for this disappearance may have been the usual detachment of the binding, followed by the loss of the final gathering. As a matter of fact, it is difficult to decide just how to evaluate a type of *explicit*, occurring in several manuscripts, which attributes the loss to the vandalism of the Lombards. In most cases this closure has been added by a hand slightly posterior to that of the original scribe, and yet its wide diffusion cannot be due to mere accident. For example, in ms. 236 of the Avranches library, dating from the 11th century, we read at the end of the *De Institutione Musica*, in a slighty more recent hand: *Longobardorum invidia non explicit musica*. The same formula appears in ms. Vaticanus Reginensis 1005, from the fifteenth century. The tenth-century ms. 531 of the Public Library of Bruges has: *Explicit musica Boetii nondum finita italorum invidia/Langobardorum invidia non explicit musica*—also in a second hand. Likewise, in the Oxoniensis Collegii Corpus Christi CCXXIV (13th-14th century), we read: *Longobardorum invidia non finita. Explicit musica*. We may presume that the same formula reappears in some manuscripts I have not yet examined.

If this notice has some foundation and is not the invention of a learned amanuensis, we may believe that the last refuge of the last surviving copy of Boethius' treatise was one of those Italian libraries destroyed by the Lombards. But which library? We might be tempted to hypothesize that our codex was one of the mass of manuscripts which, in the reconstruction of Mercati,[82] flowed into the Bobbio legacy from various Italian cities such as Piacenza, Pavia, Milan, Ravenna and Verona. Unluckily, however, the *De Institutione Musica* is not to be found in the famous Muratori Catalogue among the first 479 titles which refer to the ancient collection of the Bobbio Library, though we find the item *Libros Boetii III de Arithmetica et alterum de Astronomia* (nos. 384-87). Thus Bobbio still owned a copy of the astronomical work of Boethius, as Gilbert d'Aurillac verifies in a letter dated August, 988,[83] and as many as three copies of the *De Institutione Arithmetica*, but not the *De Institutione Musica*. Later, the musical treatise was to enter the Bobbio library among the donations of one Petrus Presbyter (no. 615, *Expositio in Somnio Scipionis et Boetii de musica...quas non reperimus*: the book, it appears, vanished from the library!) and of a Fulgentius (no. 622, *Librum boetii de musica*). It should be noted that the fragment from the *De Institutione Arithmetica* usually identified with the ancient relic preserved in the Biblioteca Nazionale di Torino (F IV 1/3) and consisting of only two folia, did not belong to the ancient collection, but to the donation of a certain Frater Smaragdus. Listed in the Muratori Catalogue as no. 657, *Quaedam pars de arithmetica Boetii*, the manuscript possibly, but not certainly, dates back to the sixth century. In any case, it is definitely the oldest codex in existence of any work by Boethius. In it the division into chapters with titles had already made its appearance, which is some justification for assuming, by analogy, a relatively early date for the same phenomenon in the music treatise.

The Muratori Catalogue reveals another hardly negligible circumstance: the treatises of the Boethian *quadrivium* appear in isolated manuscripts and not as part of a single corpus. Also

---

82   G. Mercati, *M.T. Ciceronis de re publica libri e codice rescripto Vaticano latino 5757 phototypice expressi. Prolegomena de fatis monasterii S. Columbani Bobiensis et de codice ipso Vat. Latino 5757* (Roma, 1934), pp. 14-18. The old thesis of R. Beer, who tried to trace the ancient Bobbio legacy back to Vivarium, may now be considered wholly obsolete (Cf. Courcelle, *Les lettres grecques*, pp. 342 ff.).

83   Gerbert, *Epistolae Ante Summum Pontificatum Scriptae*, no. 130.

important is the information that the astronomical treatise of Boethius was extant as late as the tenth century. If this were not true, it would have been fairly easy to challenge what we have been saying till now, with the hypothesis that a codex originally containing the four treatises in the order described in the proem of the *De Institutione Arithmetica* (arithmetic, music, geometry, astronomy) came to be shorn of its latter half at the point where the music treatise breaks off in the fifth book. This would explain very well the loss of the missing chapters, together with that of the other two treatises. But, as we have seen, everything signifies the contrary. At Vivarium, the Arithmetic survived together with the Geometry and perhaps the Astronomy as well, but not the Music. Astronomy and Arithmetic seem to have belonged to the ancient collection of Bobbio, but not the Music or Geometry. Nor must we forget that in almost none of the most ancient codices of the musical treatise do we find that work coupled with the Arithmetic: witness the 9th-century Bambergensis H J IV 19 containing, in addition to the *De Institutione Musica,* the *Musica Enchiriadis* and Book IX from Martianus Capella; witness the Paris BN 13020, also from the 9th century, combining the Boethian music with Bede's *De Temporibus;* and so on for dozens and dozens of codices. True, Arithmetic and Music do appear together in a substantial part of the manuscript tradition, but this is apparently a late marriage, and, in any case, neither conclusive nor sufficient as a basis for defying the rest of the evidence. In short, the *De Institutione Musica,* presumably written some time after the Arithmetic, had no diffusion whatever during the period immediately following the death of its author. Only one copy of the work was extant, probably in an Italian library, at the time of the Lombard invasion. To that copy we owe our entire tradition of the work, going back to the very moment when a reviving interest in both the mathematical sciences in general and musical theory in particular led to the rediscovery of its significance and potential.

* * * *

But what was the ambience for the launching of our treatise, and what cultural center became the epicenter of its diffusion? Indeed, already in the 9th century the *De Musica* was quoted and utilized by Aurelien de Moutier-St. Jean (Aurelianus Reomensis),[84] the first musicologist of the Carolingian era of whom we know with certainty both production and origin. We do not find much help in recent studies on the influence of the liberal arts on the insular culture of the 7th and 8th centuries, to which we owe the preservation and transmission of so many famous texts, and to which, as we shall see, there has been a tendency to tie the name of Boethius in one way or another.

As far as Ireland itself is concerned, it seems that the liberal arts did have some influence, if it is true, as has been demonstrated by M.C. Díaz y Díaz,[86] that the works of Isidor of Seville were not unknown in the Irish monasteries. But there does not seem to be any trace of Boethius. For instance (as Díaz has pointed out),[87] in the letter to Cuimnanus, published by Bischoff[88] –one of the most important documents in this field of research–the brief section touching on music, while faithful to Isidor, yet contains some elements of a different origin. These boil down to a single parenthesis *(et interpretatur carmenalis)* referring to music. We can

---

84   Cf. n. 8.
85   For an up-to-date survey of this problem, see M.C. Díaz y Díaz, *op. cit.*
86   In addition to the article already cited, see, by the same author, „Isidoriana II, sobre el liber de ordine creaturarum," *Sacris Erudiri,* 4 (1954), 147-66.
87   M.C. Diaz y Diaz, „Les arts libéraux," p. 43.
88   B. Bischoff, „Eine verschollene Einteilung der Wissenschaften," *Archives d'histoire doctrinale et littéraire du moyen-âge,* vol. 25 (1958), pp. 5-20.

at least appreciate the erudition of this unknown letter-writer who gives a new interpretation to the etymology *musica e Musis*[89] of Cassiodorus-Isidor, by noting that in Rome the muses also took the name of Camenae. But in the *De Institutione Musica* Boethius never even mentions the Camenae! Two other documents cited by Díaz y Díaz turn out to be mere lists of the arts, and do not concern us.[90]

The picture becomes still less encouraging if we go from Ireland to England, where Aldhelm of Malmesbury, who does refer several times to the liberal arts,[91] does not conceal his limitations in the field.[92] The other great representative of the Anglo-Saxon culture of this period, the Venerable Bede, not only abstains from the study of such disciplines, but in several instances explicitly condemns it.[93] Riché[94] has shown that the Monk of Jarrow, despite a tendency then still surviving in the exegesis of Irish monks, saw no utility in resorting to scientific notions in order to explain the sacred texts. If he had an interest in arithmetic, it was only ecclesiastical arithmetic, i.e. the series of calculations needed to establish the dates of the religious holidays, particularly Easter,[95] and whether he read Isidor or not, he always showed a frank distrust of his work.[96]

And, yet, in spite of all this, a series of coincidences arose which bound the name of Bede to the musicological tradition deriving from the *De Institutione Musica* of Boethius. First of all, we may observe that Bede cannot have been totally unexposed to the mysteries of music, at least in its practical, performing aspects. We learn from him that a teacher of his, the famous Benedict Biscop, was supposed to have once brought over from Rome the choirmaster of the Basilica of St. Peter to instruct his own monks, as well as any others who would listen, in the art of the chant.[97] Again, speaking of his fifty years of activity in the Jarrow monastery, he refers to the *quotidiana cantandi in ecclesia cura*[98]--which cannot have been a secondary aspect of his full life. But there is more: the choirmaster brought over from Rome by Benedict Biscop did not merely teach Jarrow's monks to sing, but also added not a few musical treatises to its library: *Qui illo* (i.e. at Jarrow) *perveniens non solum viva voce quae Romae didicit ecclesiastica discentibus tradidit sed et non pauca etiam litteris mandata reliquit quae hactenus in eiusdem monasterii bibliotheca memoriae gratia servantur.*[99] Riché[100] minimizes the import of this testimony, cautioning that ,,la seule allusion à un ouvrage musicale nous vient de Bède.''

89 Cassiodorus, *Institutiones*, p. 142,18 = Isidor, *Etymologiae* III, 15, 1.

90 The two documents are contained in the codices Vat. Pal. Lat. 1746, f. 62 and Bernens. 123 f. 35. Cf. M.C. Díaz y Díaz, ,,Les arts libéraux,'' pp. 43-44.

91 See Aldhelm, *De Virginitate*, 59, p. 320; 35, p. 277 and *De Metris et Enigmatibus ac Pedum Regulis*, p. 71 in *Aldhelmi Opera*, ed. Rudolfus Ehwald (Berolini, 1919).

92 Aldhelm openly admits to his difficulties in learning arithmetic (Epistl. p. 477, Ehwald): *De ratione vero calculationis quid commemorandum? ... Difficillima rerum argumenta et calculi supputationes quas partes numeri appellant, lectionis instantia repperi.* See P. Riché, ,,Education et culture,'' p. 434.

93 Cf. especially Bede, *In Samuelem* IX: *Et nobiles saepe magistri Ecclesiae magnorumque victores certaminum ardentiore quam decet oblectatione libros gentilium lectantes culpam quam non praevidere contrahebant (P.L.* XCI, 589 B). For another significant testimony see P. Riché, *Education et Culture*, pp. 438-41.

94 P. Riché, p. 441.

95 Cf. especially the *De Temporibus* and the *De Temporum Ratione*.

96 Cf. P. Riché, pp. 440-441.

97 *Historia Ecclesiastica* IV, 18.

98 *Ibid.*, V, 24.

99 *Vita Beatorum Abbatum*, ed. J.A. Giles in *The Complete Works of Venerable Bede*, 4 (London, 1843), 368.

100 Cf. P. Riché, p. 436.

But we must not overlook the fact that Bede speaks of a sizeable collection (*non pauca*), and that the texts might not all have been the work of the choirmaster, but could have included other musical treatises brought over from Rome. The clause, *non pauca litteris mandata reliquit* can mean simply „left several written works with Jarrow," with no indication of their authorship. Indeed, it seems that *reliquit*, in this case, does not mean „left to posterity," as it often does in the biographies of men of letters, since there is no indication that this choirmaster died at Jarrow.

In relation to this bit of information, we cannot avoid mentioning the fact, already noted,[101] that two works on music have been transmitted under the name of Bede since the very first edition of his *opera omnia*, which first saw light in 1563 in Basel. These works bear the respective titles of *Musica Theorica* and *Musica Quadrata seu Mensurata*. The latter also bears the subtitle *Musica Practica* inscribed at the top of each page. Where these works came from is hard to say, so much the more since the publisher, one Iohannes Hervagius, says in a brief preface to the reader at the front of Volume I that he has only carried on the work of collection begun by his father.

Furthermore, it does not appear to me, at this stage of my research, that these two treatises were transmitted together or under the name of Bede in manuscripts dating before the first printed edition. Definitely posterior is ms. 19 A 33 of the library of the Liceo musicale di Bologna, in which the two treatises occupy ff. 78r.-96r., as I have had occasion to observe in person.

The posteriority can be deduced both from the fact that the two treatises are preceded on f. 77 v by a note taken from a book by Oudinus, published in 1722,[102] and from an infallible clue which permits us to identify the printed edition from which the treatises were copied as that of Colonia, 1612, and not, therefore, the *editio princeps*. The clue is the *intitulatio* of the first treatise–*Bedae Presbyteri/Musica Theorica/ext. Tom.Ipag. 344*–which explicitly refers to the page on which the treatise begins in the Colonia edition (in the Basel edition of 1563, the treatise begins on p. 403).

Another manuscript is listed in Eitner's *Quellen-Lexikon* under the entry *Beda Presbyter*, which reads „Die B.B. besitzt im ms. 21 am Tinctor die Abhandlung Musica theorica." I have not been able to find this volume in the present catalogues of the Biblioteca Regia of Berlin, to which the abbreviation B.B. refers, according to Eitner's own index of abbreviations posted in the front of his *Lexikon*. But presuming that the codex really existed and still does exist somewhere, the fact that it contains the works of Giovanni Tintori, who lived in the second half of the 15th century confirms the lateness of this document, which might even be posterior to the *princeps* edition. Thus our point of departure can be none other than the Basel edition of 1563.

The authenticity of the two treatises began to be questioned early on. Already Oudinus[103] drew attention to the fact that the second opusculum contains some *exempla prosarum* that could not have been in use *in officiis ecclesiasticis missarum* before the 12th century. This excludes the paternity of Bede for at least one of the two booklets. After Oudinus, it was realized that the text published by Hervagen, though spoiled by several omissions, could be identified with a treatise preserved anonymously in five manuscripts,[104] but whose author is

101 Cf. J.D.A. Ogilvy, *Books known to Anglo-Saxon Writers from Aldhelm to Alcuin (670-804)*, (Cambridge, Mass., 1936), p. 55.
102 C. Oudinus, *Commentarius de Scriptoribus Ecclesiae Antiquis* (Francofurti ad Moenum, 1722), I, 1685 (=*P.L.* XC, 76).
103 *Ibid.*
104 Three are preserved in Paris (BN lat. 6755², 11266, and 15128 [S. Victor 659]), one at Erfurt (Wiss. Bibl. 94) and one at Siena (L.V. 30).

taken to be the same *Aristoteles*[105] Jacob von Lüttlich writes about in his *Speculum Musicae*.[106] A contemporary of the famous Francone of Colonia (or by a few years his elder), and associated with him for the diffusion of mensuralism, he was not actually named Aristotle, according to a recently accepted thesis,[107] but *Lambertus* (the pseudonym is supposed to have arisen out of a banal misunderstanding). In any case, by reason of its contents, the treatise cannot be dated earlier than the 13th century, which rules out its having anything to do with the Venerable Bede.

The other treatise (the first) entitled *Musica Theorica*, is a different matter. Its authenticity has not been completely ruled out by even the most recent scholars, including Hüschen, the author of the article on *Beda Venerabilis* in the German encyclopedia, *Die Musik in Geschichte und Gegenwart*. But the true nature of the treatise had already been understood by Quintin, who in his article on *Bède* in the *Dictionnaire d'Archéologie chrétienne et de Liturgie* (III, 646) noted that the work „n'est pas un traité mais, au moins dans sa première partie, un recueil de gloses sur un texte absent." I have already demonstrated elsewhere[108] that Quintin's intuition is perfectly correct, that it is also true of the entire treatise, and that the „absent text" is none other than the *De Institutione Musica* of Boethius.

This deduction arises not only from the observation that the disconnected parts of the so-called treatise conveniently make sense when referred to clearly identifiable and successive points in the Boethian treatise, but also, and mainly, from the fact that the text itself reappears in near totality in the form of marginal and interlinear scholia in not a few manuscripts of the *De Institutione Musica*. In my discussion of these matters, I have named two such manuscripts which I have consulted directly: the Paris BN Lat. 7200 and 10275, to which I assigned the letters A and B, and five more which I was able to consult either only in part–the Monacenses 6361 and 18480 (ms. h and f in Friedlein's edition)–or to identify indirectly–ms. 40 of the library of Autun and Monacenses 367 (o in Friedlein) and 18478 (h in Friedlein). I am now able to indicate four more, of which I own microfilms: Paris BN Lat. 7297, Vaticanus Reginensis Lat. 1638, Ambrosianus Mediolanensis C 128 inf., and Chicago, Newberry Library f. 9.

The dates of all these manuscripts vary between the 9th and 11th centuries, with the possible exception of Monacensis 367, Newberry f. 9, and Autun 40, which may belong to the 12th century. It follows that the *Musica Theorica*, for all the absurdity of its publication as a treatise, is of still older origin than its companion.

But before jumping to conclusions about the value and chronology of the *Musica Theorica*, we ought to examine one question which the present state of our knowledge may not

---

105 Under the name „*cuiusdam Aristotelis*" the *opusculum* was published in the already cited Coussemaker collection (I, 251-281). It should be noted that the editor, though he does repair the lacunae of the printed edition by consulting two mss in the Bibliothèque Nationale de Paris (BN lat. 11266 and 15128: the latter, however, appears to be unusable), resorts to the Hervagen edition in order to reconstruct the first part of the treatise, physically missing in the two codices.

106 *Speculum Musicae* VII, 1. In the Coussemaker collection, the work is still published under the name of Johannes de Muris, a false attribution arising from the fact that in the Paris BN lat. 7207, the *Speculum Musicae*, lacking an *explicit*, is followed by the *Musica Speculativa* of J. de Muris, whose *explicit* was falsely attributed to the former treatise as well. A new edition, correctly attributing the work to Jacobus Leodiensis, has begun to appear with the publication of some volumes by Roger Bragard in the *Corpus Scriptorum de Musica*.

107 Cf. the entry on *Lambertus* by G. Reaney in the oft-cited *MGG*. The misunderstanding to which the author of the *Speculum Musicae* (the only source for the name Aristotle) fell victim probably arose from the fact that the ms. Paris lat. 6755 contains, in addition to our treatise, the *Secreta Secretorum*, presented as the work of *cuiusdam Aristotelis*.

108 U. Pizzani, „Uno pseudo-trattato."

suffice us to answer. What we must try to determine is whether the scholia distributed among the various manuscripts derive from what was originally a commentary or scholiastic corpus formed in a definite environment, perhaps by the hand of a single author, and substantially identical with the *Musica Theorica*; or vice-versa, whether the latter resulted from a more or less random collection of scattered scholia. In the first case, we should still have to reckon with the question of the validity of its attribution to Bede, whereas, in the second case, such an attribution would obviously be false and another solution would have to be found.

Now, though we do not have elements to exclude the first hypothesis with absolute certainty, nevertheless there are several indications that we can lean toward the second with some confidence. We have seen that while A (9th to 10th century) seems to offer us a corpus of scholia still in the process of completion (the scholia are less numerous and are distributed both in the margins and between the lines), in B the corpus has been enlarged with additional scholia, and all have been disposed in the margins, almost so as to assume the appearance of an organic commentary, which happens to coincide, save for a very few omissions, with what we read in the so-called treatise attributed to Bede. Now we should add that in the Paris BN lat. 7297, which, if not even older, cannot be later than the 10th century, the scholia are still scarser than in A, while in a manuscript almost certainly posterior, the Ambrosianus C 128 *inf.*, the scholia are disposed in a manner very similar to that of B. This tends to bear out the hypothesis that the corpus gradually took shape through successive additions and integrations. Moreover, the problem of how a corpus of scholia can come to be mistaken for a treatise is easily explained if we consider that both the Ambrosianus–which we shall call M–and, even more, B, present margins full of scholia in such a manner as to look like a continuous whole, as though it were an independent text, separate from that of Boethius. As for its attribution to Bede, this might be due to the possibility that our collection of scholia appeared in some codex together with works authentically his, or at at least bearing his name.

If this reconstruction is correct, we can see how the study of the so-called treatise and the codices containing the scholia that comprise it, not to mention the other scholia to be found in the margins and between the lines of the same codices (sometimes the „extra“ scholia are in the same hand as those of the *Musica Theorica*, other times not)...becomes intertwined with the study of the influence of the *De Institutione Musica* in the period between the 9th and 12th centuries. Besides the rich documentation we have just surveyed, no research in that direction can prescind from the general notions contained in works like the *De Institutione Clericorum* of Rhabanus Maurus, or from the musicological literature itself, beginning with the above-mentioned Aurelianus Reomensis.

Nevertheless, it is the scholia themselves that furnish the clearest illustration of how the Boethian text was read and commented on from the Carolingian era and after. A clear picture of this intensive exegetic activity will be available only after the scholia have been systemtically published and someone has attempted, within the often insuperable limits which this kind of research naturally imposes, to identify their various currents, to define the various manners and localities in which they were formulated, and to ascertain the contaminations, the reciprocal interferences, the sources, the more or less explicit quotations–in a word, the cultural substratum underlying this particular type of literature. But the scholia of the *Musica Theorica* themselves already give us a sample of the cultural interests awakened by the resumption of the diffusion of the Boethian treatise.

At the beginning of our exposition we referred to the manner in which the Nicomacheo-Boethian definition of music as the science of *multitudo ad aliquid relata*, implying a conception that was strictly mathematical even though formally part of a philosophical framework, was eventually superseded by the musical treatise, both through the introduction of ethical aspects and through the limitation of the arithmetical ratios to those actually found in music.

125

This restriction implies, in turn, that a strict correlation between arithmetico-musical ratios and auditory sensations of consonance and dissonance had now been established. In short, the study of music was now broaching the more complex question of the relationship between the senses and the intellect.

Boethius, presumably on the example of Nicomachus, did not venture to offer a very thorough discussion of this theme, but he did make some very precious, isolated remarks. At the beginning of the proem he limits himself to emphasizing the difference between the mere recognition of sensory activity (*inlaboratum est enim quod sensum percipiendis sensibilibus rebus adhibemus*) and the scientific study of the same (*quae vero sit ipsorum sensuum secundum quos agimus natura*), which, as such, involves *conveniens investigatio* guided by *veritatis contemplatio*.[109] He also attests the sometimes controversial explanations that were given of certain sensory mechanisms (*adest enim cunctis mortalibus visus qui utrum venientibus ad visum figuris an ad sensibilia radiis emissis efficiatur inter doctos quidem dubitabile est*),[110] but he immediately goes on to consider the ethical implications of the musical phenomenon, with an historical and anecdotal digression on the powers and prodigies of music. To the problems of sensation Boethius returns only in passing, in I, 14, where we find the well-chosen simile of the concentric waves occaisioned by a stone falling into a pond, and in I, 30-31, where Boethius compares the conflicting opinions of Plato and Nicomachus on the perception of consonance.

Apparently, the amount of space Boethius devoted to the topic of sensation must have seemed too little to the scholiasts, because the first extensive scholia, occupying nearly a fifth of the *Musica Theorica*,[111] and the host of shorter ones that crowd the margins and interlinear spaces of the first folio in the various codices all strive to amplify this very aspect.

After a brief note on the wholly rational nature of the musical science, which note we find even in those codices least rich in scholia,[112] the discussion for a long time concerns only the senses and their activity.

Obviously, what we have is not a discussion conducted along rigorously logical lines, arising as it does from the juxtaposition of different scholia; but these scholia are all more or less related to each other and without exception refer to one brief context, as we have said. The various annotations regard: the division of the senses into external–sight and hearing, and internal–taste and touch, while the sense of smell is left undefined (cc. 403,61-404,4, Herv. = c. 909A, Migne); the definition of sense as *vinculum corporis et animae* (c. 404,4-5, Herv. = c. 909B, Migne); the classification of the senses, defined as *corporales* and *invisibiles*, as an intermediate *quid* between spiritual entities, *incorporea et invisibilia*, like the soul, and material bodies, *corporalia et visibilia* (c. 404,5-10, Herv. = c. 909B, Migne), the inability of the senses to perceive themselves (c. 404,11-15, Herv. = c. 909B, Migne); the identification of the object of hearing as *aer commotus et percussus*, and hence something furnished, like the senses, with the characteristics of invisibility and corporeality (c. 404, 21-27, Herv. = c. 909C, Migne). The long series of annotations, whose source is presumably to be identified with Claudian Mamertus,[113] closes with a lengthy quotation explicitly from the *De Trinitate* of St. Au-

---

109 pp. 178, 24-179,8.
110 p. 179, 8-11.
111 From c. 403,55 to c. 405,45 (Hervagius)= cc. 909A-910D (Migne)(the two musical treatises attributed to Bede were reprinted, as is known, in vol. XC of the *Patrologia Latina* of Migne).
112 *Notandum quod, cum omnis ars in ratione contineatur, musica quoque in ratione numerorum consistit atque versatur.* From this point, when quoting the text of the scholia, I have emended the Hervagian text, where corrupt, on the basis of the codices.
113 The correspondences appear to be irrefutable:

gustine (XI, 1, 57-115) which illustrates in great detail the familiar doctrine that the object of sensation is not the material body but the form it impresses on our perceptions.

As we can see, scholia tend not so much to clarify the various points arising in the Boethian treatise as to constitute a separate gnoseological discussion for which the treatise merely offers pretext and inspiration. The same can be said of the brief explanatory note to the term αἰσθητήριον[114] à propos of the already mentioned passage of Boethius (I,14) where the auditory phenomenon is explained by the waves-in-pond image. Here, too, only a slender thread–the concept that air is the reason for hearing–unites the scholion with the basic text.

Contrarily, another series of scholia is eminently explanatory and integrative in character. The material is taken not infrequently from the various parts of the treatise itself. Such is the case, for example, with the long scholion preceded by the erroneous title *quid sit tonus* (in reality, the heading corresponds only to the first clause) and covering 74 lines in the Hervagius edition (cc. 407,58-409,9 = cc. 913 A - 914 B, Migne).

Regarding this particular scholion, the presence of a title, however improper, plus the size and compendious nature of the scholion itself induced Quintin to suggest the hypothesis that only the first part of the so-called treatise is composed of scholia, where „the first part" evidently signifies everything preceding the title. In truth, c. 409,9, Herv. begins a new series of shorter scholia. The first of these, which starts with the words *Quaeritur quare prius posuit diapason, diapente, diatessaron, nunc aliter incipit ordinem ipsarum consonantiarum vertere. Quod sic solvitur eqs.*, clearly (and explicity) refers to *De Institutione Musica* I, 16 (p. 202, 13-15), where the three consonances are listed in the reverse order to that given in the earlier part of the chapter. Hence the need for the clarification. Right afterward, we have (c. 409,20-21, Herv. = c. 914 B, Migne) the etymological glosses on the name Nicomachus (*Nicos victor, machia pugna*), which appears for the first time in *De Institutione Musica* in I, 20, p. 205,28, and on that of Orpheus (c. 409, 21-22, Herv. = c. 914 BC, Migne: *orea graece pulchra, phone vox, inde Orpheus pulchra vox dicitur*)[115] whom Boethius mentions immediately after (DIM, I, 20, p. 206, 2).

To return to the long scholion which we were discussing, one must concede that it is a sort of compendium, a treatise in miniature. On the other hand, it does not even have a constant collocation in the codices of the Boethian treatise. In A it is distributed among the upper and lower margins of two folio pages (8v and 9r) containing chapters 9 and 10 of Book I. But,

Musica Theorica c. 404, 5-14, Herv. = c. 909 B, Migne.	Claudius Mamertus, *De Statu Animae* I, 6 (ed. A. Engelbrecht [Wien, 1885], pp. 43-44).
Quaedam sunt incorporalia et invisibilia, ut anima vel deus, et quaedam corporalia et visibilia ut sunt corpora, quaedam invisibilia et corporalia ut sensus corporei. Corporalia sunt quia corpori administrantur, et invisibilia quia illud quod dicitur auditus vel visus non potest videri. Unde fit ut cum quinque corporei sensus alia exteriora sentiant, se ipsos non sentiant. Visus enim se ipsum non videt, gustus se ipsum non gustat, quod si faceret nunquam ieiunus esset.	Nam cum omne incorporeum invisibile sit, non omne invisibile incorporeum est...animus qui sentit in corpore, etsi per visibile sentit, invisibiliter sentit. Aliud enim est visus aliud oculus, aliud aures aliud auditus, et nares aliud aliud odoratus, et os aliud aliud gustus. Nec hoc idem manus et tactus...et gustatu dulcia atque amara sentimus, sed gustatum gustare non possumus... coloratas oculis formas adspicimus...sed visum...non videmus...aliud est ergo membrum per quod sentimus, et sensus aliud quo sentimus, quia inter invisibile incorporeum et corpus visibile est illud invisibile corporeum, quod in nobis visus, auditus, odoratus, gustus et tactus est.

114 This passage, too, except for the Greek term, seems to derive from Claudian Mamertus, *De Statu Animae* (I, 7).

115 Cf. Fulgentius, *Mitologiarum* III, 10: *Orpheus enim dicitur orea fone, id est pulchra vox* (ed. Rudulfus Helm [Leipzig, 1898], p. 77, 16-17).

though still attached to chapter 9 in the Ambrosian, in B it is clearly linked to chapter 16. The latter collocation would seem the more logical. Indeed, the scholion touches successively on the tone and its divisions (*semitonium maius* and *semitonium minus* or *diesis*), the three kinds of tetrachord (diatonic, chromatic, enharmonic), the three principal consonances (fourth, fifth and octave), the concepts of *intensio* and *remissio*, the practical realization of the four principal intervals (tone, fourth, fifth, octave) through the *sectio canonis*. With one exception, all these topics develop what is actually expounded in chapter 16, which discusses the consonances and intervals, and explains the concept that the tone *in aequa dividi non potest*, while, as for the three genres (diatonic, chromatic, enharmonic) the discussion pertains to a reference in chapter 15.

In any case, all the foregoing comments are developments of concepts expressed in the Boethian text: the term *diesis* given to the *semitonium minus* is mentioned by Boethius in III, 5 in reference to Philolaos. The relationships between the notes of the three canonical tetrachords (diatonic, chromatic, enharmonic) are in agreement with those given by Boethius in I, 31, in spite of some vagueness of expression on the part of the scholiast, and the attributes given to each also derive from Boethius. Indeed, when the scholiast defines the diatonic genus (*diatonos melodia*) as *antiquior* and *subasperior* and the chromatic as *posterior* while characterizing it as having a more pleasing quality (*ad delectationem aurium sua varietate permulcet animos*) as well as a certain frivolity (*nimiis minutiis tinnule fertur*), this derives from the fact that Boethius, beyond characterizing the former as *durius* (p. 212, 26) and the latter as *mollius* (p. 213,1), also notes that the second is a more recent invention (p. 184,4-5), stressing its diseducative nature, while he explicitly proclaims the superiority of the enharmonic genus (*totam possidet armoniam et sui dignitate alias praecellit*), in keeping with a judgment he expresses on another occasion (p. 213, 1-2): *enarmonium optime atque apte coniunctum*. Needless to say, Boethius is also the source for the numerical ratios underlying the three canonical consonances (I, 16) and for qualifying the octave ratio (or *diapason*) as *aequisonantia* (V, 12). Also Boethian are the functions *intentio-acumen* and *remissio-gravitas*. Finally, as for the *sectio canonis*, with which the scholion concludes (division of the string into three, five, seven and ten to produce, respectively, the intervals of octave or *diapason*, fifth or *diapente*, fourth or *diatessaron* and tone), the scheme is identical with that described more analytically in the last chapter of *DIM*, Book IV.

Despite the fact that the scholiast obtains his technical material from the very text he is annotating, one has to admit, as comparison will show, that he maintains a certain freedom of expression. We are no longer looking at an obsequious transcription of texts whose meaning is not always fully understood, as in the case of Isidor. The scholiast shows a complete understanding of the works lying open before him and moves with ease through their various complexities.

As we have said, moreover, here and there we find true effort of integration. For example, on the subject of the harmony of the spheres, Boethius does not go beyond observing (I, 2) that it is not perceptible to the human ear, *quod multis fieri de causis necesse est* (p. 187, 28-29). The scholiast takes the trouble to specify these reasons in a long note in which, among other things, he gives us the canonical example of the inhabitants of an Egyptian town near the Nile cataracts, who are so used to the roar of the waters that they don't hear it any more;

---

116 Cf. c. 108, 10 ff. (Hervagius) = c. 913 B (Migne): *Chromatica...constat...ex tono et tribus semitoniis vel tribus semitoniis et tono* (actually, he ought to have said: *ex semitonio, semitonio et tribus semitoniis vel tribus semitoniis et semitonio et semitonio)...Enharmonium...constat ex duobus diesis et duobus tonis vel duobus tonis et duobus diesis* (more properly: *ex diesi, diesi et duobus tonis vel duobus tonis, diesi et diesi*). It should be noted, however, that the definitions of the scholiast would make sense if we presumed him to have some notion of πυκνόν.

thus we do not perceive the harmony of the spheres, having been inured to it since birth.[117] It is interesting to note that the waterfall is indicated by the Greek word καταβαθμός which in this particular sense is found only in a passage of Aeschylus (*Prometheus*, 811). Usually it is found as a place-name for a locality on the borders between Egypt and Cyrenaica near present-day Aqaba (cf. Sallust, *De Bello Iugurth.*, 17,4; 19,3; Ponponius Mela, *De Chorographia in Senecam Rhetorem*, I, 8, 1; I, 9, 1; Pliny, *Natural History*, V, 5, 5, 32). The cataracts near Syene, to which the scholion most likely refers, are usually designated by the term κατάδουπα as in Cicero (*Somnium Scipionis*, 3, 5, 19). This divergence in toponymy might be worth further investigation.

Still other scholia, as we have seen, are of an etymological character and serve to clarify or anticipate explanations that Boethius is either too hasty or too slow to handle in due fashion. But in my opinion, by far the most significant, apart from those of gnoseological import, are the scholia found in the last part of the so-called treatise and which reveal the commentator's obvious pechant for mathematics.

Let us take one example. In *DIM*, II, 9, Boethius demonstrates that 58/53 < 55/50 and that 53/48 > 55/50. More exactly, he wants to show that if the difference between two numbers (in this case, 58-53=5) does not go into each of them an exact number of times, but with a remainder that is the same in both (in our case 3: 58/5 = 11, r. 3 and 53/5 = 10, r. 3), then the ratio of the two numbers will be smaller than that of the same two numbers when each has been dimished by that remainder (i.e. 58/53 will be smaller than 55 [= 58-3]/50 [53-3]). Conversely, if the difference between two numbers (in our case, still 5) does not go into each of them an exact number of times and the number needed to round off to the next highest integral quotient is the same for both (in this case 2: 53/5 = 11, r. -2; 48/5 = 10, r. -2), the ratio of the two original quantities will be greater than that of the same two quantities when each has been augmented by that needed number (53/48 will be greater than 55 [=53+2] /50 [= 48+2]). To prove this theorem, Boethius invokes the general principle that *in minoribus numeris maior semper proportio repperitur* (p. 238, 32). This he illustrates with a series of *superparticulares proportiones*, which become smaller and smaller as their terms grow larger (e.g. 3/2 > 4/3 > 5/4, ...ad inf.).

The scholiast begins (cc. 409, 47-410,21, Herv. = cc. 914 D- 915 B, Migne) by stating the problem posed by Boethius: *Hic quaeritur quomodo minor proportio est in LIII et LVIII quam in L et LV et quomodo iterum maior proportio est in XLVIII et LIII quam in L et LV. Sic respondendum est.* Then, in the course of a thorough discussion of the preceding–during which he refers to Boethius by name, calling him *philologus* (*Quod si philologus iste Boetius iterum adderet...*)–he introduces two new ratios: 60/55 ([58+2]/[53+2]) and 50/45 ([53-3]/ [48-3]), thus creating the following series of ,,top-heavy'' fractions in increasing order:

60/55	=	Sesquiundecima proportio
55/50	=	Sesquidecima proportio
50/45	=	Sesquinona proportio

In this series, 58/53 and 53/48 occupy an intermediate position respectively between the first and second ratios and the second and third, thus augmenting the series begun by Boethius. At this point the scholiast pauses to consider why Boethius derives from 55/50 the ratios 58/53 and 53/48 instead of 60/55 and 50/45. The reason he offers is simple enough: Boethius merely divided the difference between the two terms, i.e. 5, into two parts, 3 and 2, using them for his demonstrations. (*Sic solvendum est, quod quantitatem quinarii, quae est differentia praedictorum numerorum, divisit in duas partes, hoc est in tria et duo, et maiorem partem addidit quan-*

---

117   The scholion is the one published by Bragard, *op. cit.*

titati praedictae ut essent maiores numeri et minor proportio et minorem dempsit ex eadem quantitate ut essent minores numeri et maior proportio.)

All these considerations are fairly simple, of course, but they reveal a thorough comprehension of a difficult text, and a certain familiarity with mathematical questions.

On the other hand, neither is there anything transcendental about two scholia by Gerbert d'Aurillac which appear in roughly the same manuscripts, though not included in the *Musica Theorica*. The first of these scholia (*Ad Boetii Musicae Institutionem*, II, 10, pp. 29-30, Bubnov) examines Boethius' statement that *si superparticularis proportio binario multiplicetur, id quod fit, neque superparticulare esse neque multiplex*. Gerbert derives the material for his demonstrations and examples from another part of the musical treatise (IV,2), lifting out whole phrases, which Bubnov has taken the trouble to double-space.[118] The second scholion is more autonomous, but Boethius is still the sole source of the examples. Here Gerbert attempts to demonstrate Boethius' assertion that *ab omni superparticulari si continuam ei superparticularem quis auferat proportionem, quae est scilicet minor, id, quod relinquitur, minus est eius medietate, quae detracta est, proportionis* (p. 254, 4-8). The musical value of this premise is evident: what Boethius is trying to prove is that if we subtract a *proportio sesquitertia*, i.e. a fourth, from a *proportio sesqualtera*, i.e. a fifth, we obtain a *proportio sesquioctava*, i.e. an interval which is less than half of a fourth (the latter interval is in fact composed of two tones and a semitone). Gerbert goes about the demonstration of this premise in the following way. He takes the series 6, 8, 9 where 8 and 9 are respectively the *sesquitertius* and the *sesqualter* of 6. If we now forget about 6, thus eliminating the ratios of *sesqualter* and *sesquitertius*, what remains is a simple ratio of 8 to 9, i.e. a *sesquioctava proportio*. So far, Gerbert has only restated what he read in *DIM* IV, 2 (p. 307, 12-15): *Sesqualterum vero intervallum sit novenarius ad senarium, sesquitertium vero octonarius ad senarium. Novem igitur ad octo sesquioctava proportio est*. Gerbert goes on to demonstrate that *sesquioctava proportio non est medietas minoris proportionis, id est sesquitertiae, quoniam duplicata non efficit eam, sed minor est*. We know that to Boethius, *duplicare proportionem* meant finding a number X where X : B :: B : A. In this case, the problem is to find three numbers such that there is a *sesquioctava proportio* between the first and second, and the second and third, i.e. such that the first is to the second, and the second to the third, as 8 is to 9. Here, too, Gerbert finds the example he needs in Boethius, who gives us the series 64, 72, 81 (64:72=72:81=8:9). Gerbert is thus able to show that the ratio of 81/64 is smaller than a *sesquitertia proportio*, as Boethius says.

Despite the great ease with which these commentators set about unravelling the mathematical complexities of Boethius, it is interesting to note that not one truly critical comment emerges from all their considerations to point a finger at certain errors and approximations whose presence I have had occasion to note in the *DIM*,[119] and not until the 11th century did someone like Hermannus Contractus[120] notice a serious incongruity in that treatise. By then, of course, the work had received scholarly attentions for centuries, while we are mainly concerned here with the period from Bede to Gerbert d'Aurillac.

We have already observed that definitive conclusions on the subject of the genesis of our corpus of scholia and the diffusion and study of the music treatise of Boethius will have to wait for the complete collation of the oldest of those manuscripts which contain glosses and scholia. The absence of Gerbert's scholia from the *Musica Theorica* might seem, at first glance, to justify the hypothesis that the corpus was originally conceived as a unit—in other words,

118   In A and in B.
119   Cf. U. Pizzani, „Studi sulle fonti," pp. 117-118.
120   p. 143 (Gerbert).

that whoever first collected the scholia went about it deliberately, gathering material from a well-defined ambit, if not from a single author. I repeat, however, that the research I have carried out so far does not appear to lead to such a conclusion. On the contrary, it would seem to suggest that the corpus was formed through successive stratifications. But what seems to me to be most important is the fact that at least the beginnings of this process belong to a considerably early age–more than a century before Gerbert d'Aurillac. The proof is that Aurelianus Reomensis, whose *floruit* was in the second half of the 9th century, utilized a text of Boethius which contained a gloss that we now find in the Pseudo-Bede. Let us take a look at the following passage from Aurelian (p. 32, Gerbert): *Iam vero quattuor elementorum diversitates, scilicet hiemis, veris, aestatis, autummi, nisi quaedam harmonia coniungeret, quomodo fieri posset ut in unum corpus materiamque convenirent?* Needless to say, the passage does not make much sense. The *elementa* it refers to ought to be the traditional earth, water, air, and fire, and not the four seasons. This is confirmed by the direct source of this passage, which we find in *DIM* I, 2 (p. 188, 7-10): *Iam vero quattuor elementorum diversitates contrariasque potentias nisi quaedam armonia coniungeret, qui fieri posset ut in unum corpus ac machinam convenirent?* The singular modification introduced by Aurelian seems less inexplicable, however, if we consider that several codices contain a scholion to the following remark made by Boethius just before the interrogative sentence cited above (p. 187, 23): *Et primum ea (sc. musica), quae est mundana, in his maxime perspicienda est, quae in ipso caelo vel compage elementorum vel temporum varietate visuntur.* More precisely, the scholion, which as we said, turns up in the *Musica Theorica* (c. 405,55-57 = c. 911 A, Migne), refers to the words *temporum varietate* and reads as follows: *Quattuor sunt anni tempora* χειμών *hiems,* ἔαρ *ver,* θέρος *aestas* μετόπωρον *autumnus. Hiems comparatur aquae, ver aeri, aestas igni, autumnus terrae.* It is evident that Aurelian's identification of the four seasons of the scholion with the four elements referred to by Boethius influenced his formulation of the rest of the passage in question. But it is just as evident that the text Aurelian was using already contained one of the scholia that were later included in the *Musica Theorica.* Now, to deduce from the antiquity of this scholion that Bede was the author of the corpus is neither easy nor methodologically impeccable. Against the authorship of the Monk of Jarrow still stands the fact that, whereas Bede's interest in music must have been mainly practical and, in all probability, of such a practical nature were the treatises left behind by the Roman choirmaster, the scholia are concerned mainly with theoretical questions (we find, for instance, no scholia on the theory of modes or tropes, discussed at length in Book IV) leaving little place for actual music practice.

The truth is that the scholia are among the most significant expressions of their time of that *musica speculativa* which, owing to its ties with the mathematical disciplines, was kept purposely separate from the rules of music making. Yet the scholia are only one of the many indications, though one of the most important, that the world was at last beginning to wake up to the *De Institutione Musica* of Boethius.

* * * *

It would not be out of order, before we bring this survey to a close, to take a brief look at the more properly musicological production of the 9th and 10th centuries. It is not my intention to examine extensively and *ab ovo* the complex problem of the origin of the ecclesiastical doctrine of eight tones. The doctrine was first explained by Alcuin, if it is true that he was the author of the fragment published by M. Gerbert, but reliable documentary evidence does not appear before the 9th century, when the musical work of Boethius was becoming

131

firmly established. Indeed, the first theorist to give us an extensive discussion of the subject was the same Aurelianus Reomensis whom we have seen to be fully acquainted with the work of Boethius. The fact that Aurelian does not attempt to establish any connections between the ecclesiastical modes and the Boethian constitutes additional proof that the ecclesiastical theory must have been much older, deriving, perhaps, from the Byzantine *oktoechos*. The question is primarily musicological and not really within the bounds of this investigation. But what we can point out is that the absence of the *De Institutione Musica* from the sources of such great teachers of the *quadrivium* as Cassiodorus and Isidor, plus the extreme improbability of its having played any role in the insular and continental cultures of the centuries preceding the 9th, seriously undermines the theory, often put forward in the past, of a Boethian influence acting on the medieval doctrine of ecclesiastical modes through misunderstanding and erroneous interpretations.[121] We should have to suppose either that the cultivators of the musical art kept account of Boethius even as he was being ignored by the most eminent cultural exponents of their time, or that the birth of the eight ecclesiastical tones coincided with the rediscovery of the *De Institutione Musica*. But neither supposition is possible. Suffice it to say that Alcuin (if he it is) does not seem to have heard of the music treatise. If he had, he might have noticed, if nothing more, that Boethius, too, had reduced the old Cassiodorean modes from 15 to 8 (though indeed, both Cassiodorean and Boethian modes were transpositional and not truly modal, like the ecclesiastical). Yet it is just from Cassiodorus that Alcuin obtains his definition of „tone" (Alcuin [?] p. 26, M. Gerbert = Cassiodorus, *Institutiones* II, 5, 7, p. 145, 20-21): *Tonus est totius constitutionis armonicae differentia et quantitas quae in vocis accentu sive tenore consistit.* As for the modal denominations (*protus, deuterus, tritus, tetrarchius*--elsewhere *tetrardus–authenticus, plagius*) their Greek origin is undeniable, but they cannot have been derived from Boethius, who never, even analogically, uses such terms. Yet Alcuin knew Boethius very well, if it is true, as Courcelle (following Brunhölzl)[122] has attempted to show, that the proem of the *Grammatica* of the former was profoundly influenced by the *Consolatio*.

Moreover, Alcuin was not alone in his ignorance of the music treatise. The other great teacher of the Carolingian Renaissance, Hrabanus Maurus, in the music section of the third book of his *De Institutione Clericorum*[123] shows, once again, the influence of Cassiodorus, but no echo of Boethius. Not until the purely and essentially musicological *Musica Disciplina* of Aurelianus Reomensis can we speak of a rediscovery of the *De Institutione Musica*.

Aurelian, too, pays tribute to the age-old authority of Cassiodorus and Isidor: Chapter I, *De Laude Musicae Disciplinae*, is a true mosaic of passages and motifs from both authors,[124] with the addition of biblical references that point up the new religious significance attributed

---

121 See, for a bibliographical orientation, P.L. Kunz, „Die Tonartenlehre des Boethius," *Kirchenmusikalisches Jahrbuch*, 60 (1936), 5.

122 P. Courcelle, „Les sources antiques du prologue d'Alcuin sur les disciplines," *Philologus*, 110 (1966), 293-305.

123 *P.L.* CVII, 401-403.

124 Although the Cassiodorean influence is the more pronounced (consider, for example, what Aurelian says [p. 30] à propos of David: *per hanc artem David egisse, ut scilicet Saulem cantu cytharae a daemone liberaret, quem medicorum ars victa desperabat.*). The source can only be Cassiodorus, who mentions the helplessness of the doctors, whereas Isidor ignores them altogether, though he does report the episode; yet certain particulars could have come only from Isidor, e.g. (Aurelianus, p. 30): *Habet* (i.e. *homo*) ... *quamdam citharam in pectore pulmonis fibris quasi quibusdam distinctam chordis.* The source must be Isidor, *Etymologiae* III, 22,2: *Forma citharae initio similis fuisse traditur pectori humano.* Certainly nothing in Cassiodorus can account for such an illation. It should be noted, moreover, that the rule of harmony over both the cosmos and man's innermost being, described at the end of the proemium, is a concept which already shows a clear Boethian inspiration (cf. *DIM* I,2).

to music by the Middle Ages. But in the second chapter, the exposition of Pythagoras' discovery of the laws of consonance (the anvil episode) no longer stays within the bounds of the brief Cassiodorean narration (p. 142, 13-15), which Aurelian got through the Latin version of the little treatise of Gaudentius, but is modelled into a well-ordered story that is faithful in every detail to Boethius (*DIM* I, 10,11), who is explicitly cited at the end of the chapter: *A Boetio quoque viro eruditissimo et aliis quibusdam praecipue aucta est*. Incidentally, it should be noted that in listing the four intervals studied by Pythagoras (octave, fourth, fifth, tone) Aurelian gives a practical example of each, consisting of an antiphone, or *introit*, composed in each of the four corresponding authentic tones! We shall leave this singular association in the hands of professional musicologists.

Going on to examine, in chapter 3, the tripartite division of music into *mundana, humana* and *instrumentalis*, Aurelian does not shrink from appropriating, almost *en bloc*, the second chapter of Book I of the Boethian treatise. He merely tacks on a passage from the Bible interpreted as concerning the harmony of the spheres (Job 38, 37: *concentum caeli quis dormire facit?*), a brief enlargement on the ill effects of cosmic disharmony caused by *intemperatus solis ardor*, a short phrase identifying man--the seat of *musica humana*--with the *microcosmus* of Isidor,[125] and a reference to the work of Gregory the Great.[126]

Here Aurelian falls into an unusual error: confusing the Boethian *musica humana*, i.e. the inner harmony that governs the functions and physical and mental activities of man, with music as executed materially by men, he introduces, without further ado, the true Cassiodorean categories (*armonica, rhythmica, metrica*, cf. p. 144) as *partes humanae musicae* (chap. 4). The definitions he gives of them coincide with Cassiodorus', but his discussion is much more thorough, and would be worth studying in depth, which I plan to do in a future article.

The fourth chapter ends with a paraphrase of the last part of the first book of the *De Institutione Musica* (p. 225, 3-15). The contents of this book (exclusion of performers and poets from the ranks of the true *musici*, who consist exclusively of pure theoreticians) are completely misunderstood by Aurelian, who takes them to mean that the musical art includes *rhythmica* but not *metrica*! This conception is attributed to Nicomachus, apparently because his name is mentioned by Boethius slightly earlier (p. 222,23).[127]

The next chapter is a bizarre paraphrase of Isidor (*Etymologiae* III, 19-20). In a word, Isidor has made a brief reference to the 15 tones (*Etymologiae* III, 20,7: *Tonus...cuius genera in quindecim partibus musici dividerunt, ex quibus hyperlydius novissimus et acutissimus, hypo-*

125 For the Isidorian conception of *microcosmus* see J. Fontaine, pp. 662 ff.
126 *Ibid.*, p. 663.
127 Aurelian writes (p. 34): *Igitur secundum Nicomachum tertia pars humanae musicae, quae metrica nuncupatur, quoniam non tam speculatione ac ipsius artis ratione, quam naturali instinctu fertur ad carmen; ideo a musica, quamquam ab ea originem trahat, segregandam putat. Rhythmus vero, quia totum in ratione ac speculatione positum est, hoc proprie musicae deputandum arbitratur.* The source of the passage is, without possibility of doubt, Boethius I, 34, p. 225, 3-10: *Secundum vero musicam agentium genus poetarum est, quod non potius speculatione ac ratione, quam naturali quodam instinctu fertur ad carmen. Atque idcirco hoc quoque genus a musica segregandum est. Tertium est quod iudicandi peritiam sumit, ut rythmos cantilenasque totumque carmen possit perpendere. Quod scilicet quoniam totum in ratione ac speculatione positum est, hoc proprie musicae deputabitur.* Aurelian borrows from his model both words and phrases, but shows that he has understood nothing. Boethius, who, before mentioning poets, had spoken of instrumentalists (*citharoedi quique organo ceterisque musicae instrumentis artificium probant*), excluded those two categories from the true *musici*, reserving that title for the theoreticians of song and rhythm alone. Aurelian includes poets among the students of *metrica*, and interprets the expression *ut rhythmos... possit perpendere* as if it referred, *tout court*, to the experts of *rhythmica*. Hence his absurd illation to the effect that *rhythmica*, but not *metrica*, belongs to the musical art!

dorius omnium gravissimus): Aurelian mistakes for the aforementioned 15 tones the successively defined terms of *cantus, arsis, thesis*, and those for the various vocal inflections, which he proceeds to list, counting as he goes (see e.g. Aurelianus, p. 34: *quartus est arsis, id est vocis elevatio, hoc est, initium. Quintus thesis, est enim thesis positio, hoc est, finis* and so on up to the number 15)!

We again find a fusion of Boethius and Cassiodorus in chapter VI where, under a rather comprehensive title, Aurelian discusses the consonances and tones. But now, beside the large segment of the music section of the *Institutiones* of Cassiodorus, transcribed in full (Aurelianus pp. 37-38 = Cassiodorus pp. 146,2-148,15), Aurelian resorts not to the *DIM* but to the *De Institutione Arithmetica* of Boethius, from which he again no more than transcribes a lengthy portion on the doctrine of consonances (Aurelianus, pp. 35-37 = *DIA*, II, 48, pp. 155, 16-158,13).

The last of the Boethian influence is spent, so to speak, on the next chapter (VII), which closely paraphrases the 34th and last chapter from Book I of the music treatise. After a long and porridgy introduction, in which the only echo of Boethius might be termed the fleeting reminder of the doctrine of consonances (p. 41), the remainder of Aurelian's book deals with the eight ecclesiastical modes. As we have already seen, there is not the slightest attempt here to establish a connection between the ecclesiastical theory and that of modes, or tropes, or tones.

We will not attempt to pronounce judgment on the value of Aurelian's contribution to our knowledge of the doctrine of the ecclesiastical modes. Concerning his relationship to Boethius, however, we cannot help observing that every time Aurelian puts down the tool of paraphrase to venture an interpretation, he stumbles into grave and bizarre misunderstandings. Between practice and theory there now lay a large abyss, and to return to a text so complicated and chronologically distant was an undertaking for which the scholars of the 9th century simply were not ready.

This is confirmed by a work that followed Aurelian's opusculum at no great distance–the *De Harmonica Institutione* of Reginald of Prüm, who died in 915. It is no more than a mosaic of passages clipped whole from Boethius, with a sprinkling of contaminations from Martianus Capella, Macrobius, Cassiodorus, the Bible and Aurelianus Reomensis. The fact that there is no effort toward interpretation confers a certain utility upon the treatise, at least so far as to inform us on the contemporary state of the Boethian text, but it also reveals the complete cultural immaturity of Reginald.[128]

Meanwhile, the gradual diffusion of the *De Musica* was nonetheless preparing the terrain for new and fertile developments. Though Remigius of Auxerre, in his commentary on the 9th book of Martianus Capella, merely extracts isolated passages from the *De Institutione Musica* (cf. Remigius p. 329, 15-16, Lutz = *DIM*, p. 365, 9-14; Remigius p. 329,25-26 = *DIM* p. 202,17; Remigius p. 331,7 = *DIM* p. 206,14; Remigius p. 334,13-15 = *DIM* 216,18-20; Remigius p. 338,12 = *DIM* p. 215,17ff.; Remigius 338,18 = *DIM* p. 206,14; Remigius p. 339, 10 = *DIM* p. 346,26; Remigius p. 345,31-346,1 = *DIM* p. 213,8-11; Remigius p. 347,29-30 = *DIM* IV,3) in Hucbald of St. Amand, who died–at the age of ninety–around 930, fifteen years after Reginald, we have a much more conscious and profitable reading of the Boethian treatise. Indeed, though his *dimensio monochordi* derives in its entirety from Boethius (p. 318 ff)–including the obvious inconsistencies in the determination of the numbers corresponding to the chromatic and enharmonic genera–Hucbald by no means just transcribes

128 Cf. W. Brambach, *Die Musiklitteratur des Mittelalters, bis zur Blüte der Reichenauer Sängerschule* (Leipzig, 1883), p. 8.

Boethius. Instead, he reproposes Boethius' thesis, following his own order, and showing a fully mature capacity to orient himself amid the mass of numbers and ratios. The same can be said of the section on consonances and intervals (pp. 107-109, Gerbert) and on the definition of sound in the musical sense (p. 108-109), of the description of the perfect system (pp. 106-116) and of the interpretation of the Greek note-names (p. 117). All this material is taken integrally from Boethius, except for the part concerning the Greek notation, which the author admits having derived from Martianus (cf. p. 117, Gerbert: *Interpretatio autem horum nominum succincte quidem a Boetio attracta, planius autem Martianus exequitur*).

Matters are complicated, however, by Hucbald's attempt to substitute Boethius' notation (which the latter inherited from the Greek tradition) for the neumatic notation, which he regards as unsatisfactory (pp. 117-118). In the first place, Hucbald did not notice the double notation of the Boethian system–vocal and instrumental–which Boethius clearly describes. As a result, Hucbald adopts now one, now the other. For example, for the *trite synemmenon* he uses the sign Θ, which belongs to the vocal notation, while for the *lichanos hypaton* he uses the sign F from the instrumental notation. But often Hucbald makes even greater mistakes, whose origin is presumably to be found in corrupt manuscripts, as in the case of the *parhypate hypaton*, where the Boethian *beta non integram* becomes *beta simplex* in Hucbald.[129] Such errors do not, however, diminish the fact that the following insertion of the ecclesiastical modes into the perfect system (pp. 119-121) is perfectly acceptable from the point of view of expository clarity, especially considering that there is no attempt on Hucbald's part to assimilate the medieval tones with those of antiquity, but only a common collocation in the frame of the double octave.

We have confined ourselves to these few observations on the connections between Boethius and the musicologists of the 9th century with the main intention of illustrating the complexity of the problems that such an examination implies. The difficulties arise principally from the fact that medieval music had by now evolved into forms that no longer corresponded to the next of Boethius. The ecclesiastical tones were really modal scales, founded on the succession of intervals, while the only scheme furnished by Boethius, in an appendix to *De Institutione Musica* IV, 16, refers to the scales of transposition. But if this were all, there would still be no way to explain how there came to be insinuated into the medieval and modern speculations on the ecclesiastical tones the idea of a connection with Boethius. Actually, it was Boethius himself who started all the trouble. For, in addition to the above-mentioned traditional system of scales, Boethius knew another system as well: the Ptolemaic, which not only reduced the tones of Aristoxenus from 13 to 7, but also included the seven tones in the frame of the double octave, by means of the successive displacement of the *mese*, thus altering the melodic succession in such a way as to allow the melody to coincide with that of the corresponding Aristoxenic tone. Such a system, involving scales that varied from too sharp to too flat, depending on whether their position was above or below the doric tone used by Ptolemy as a basis, made it possible for Boethius to see in the central octave between the fifth and twelfth degrees of ascension the seven octave-species he describes in IV, 14. Presumably it is to this very correspondence, noted by Ptolemy himself, between Ptolemaic tones and octave-species, that we must attribute the singular affirmation of Boethius that (IV, 15) *ex diapason igitur consonantiae speciebus existunt, qui appellantur modi, quos eosdem tropos vel tonos nominant*. Only, Boethius doesn't seem to have understood the Ptolemaic doctrine of tones, which is belied by the Boethian scheme, as well as by the following definition of *tropi*, much more in keeping with the traditional scales of transposition: *Sunt autem tropi constitutiones*

---

129   Cf. the observations of A. Auda, *Les modes et les tons de la musique* (Bruxelles, 1931), pp. 76 ff.

in totis vocum ordinibus vel gravitate vel acumine differentes. Thus we cannot speak of a confusion, in Boethius, between tones or tropes on the one hand, and the modes of ancient Greek music on the other, but rather of a confusion between the traditional and the Ptolemaic conceptions of tones or transpositional scales.[130]

It did not elude the theorists of the Middle Ages that the correspondence between tones and octave-species sanctioned by Boethius fitted their own conception of tones, likewise assimilable to the seven octave-species, except for the addition of an eighth mode, homophonous with the first. This eighth mode corresponds to the Hypermixolydian, the eighth mode of Boethius, except that the Hypermixolydian is not homophonous with the first or Hypodorian mode, but belongs to the upper octave. Thus it is not without significance if it is to the *diapason consonantiae species* that those medieval texts which eventually substituted the names of the classical tones found in Boethius for the typically medieval names first used by Alcuin always referred. I allude here to the *De Musica* and the *Alia musica* published by Gerbert respectively under the names of Notker[131] and Hucbald. But, as we have seen, Boethius had become the victim of a serious misunderstanding. On the one hand, under the influence of Ptolemy, he had enumerated the *diapason consonantiae species* and sanctioned, in a way, their assimilation to the *toni;*[132] on the other hand, he had not bothered to fathom the meaning of Ptolemy's assertions, while for the schematization and description of the eight tones (IV, 16-17) he had resorted *sic et simpliciter* to the traditional scales of transposition, which were by no means assimilable to the octave-species. The theorists of the Middle Ages thus found in Boethius no sure guide for their reasoning. They were led to identify the ecclesiastical tones with the classical by the fact that Boethius speaks of a connection between tones and octave-species; but as for their actual denominations, Boethius only supplied them with a list of names. Hence the misunderstandings, the confusions, the inversions that have given scholars of medieval music so much trouble.

From the foregoing, I think it is now possible to extract some basic methodological guidelines for future research in his complex and controversial field:
1) The fact that the ecclesiastical tones might derive from the ancient music of Greece–presumably by way of the Byzantine practice–does not imply any connection, whether direct or indirect, between their formation and the *De Institutione Musica* of Boethius.
2) The eventual assumption of the names of the ancient Greek modes by the ecclesiastical tones does not imply a direct but an indirect connection: we know that already in antiquity the names of the modes had been transferred to the tones, and it is in this second connection that Boethius transmitted those names to the medieval musicology.
3) Boethius' assertion of the equivalence of tones and octave-species gave the musicologists of the Middle Ages what they thought was a license to identify their own tones with the Boethian; but the incongruities between this premise and the actual scheme of tones contained in the *De Institutione Musica* had the effect of disorienting the musicologists and inducing them to try various interpretations, with questionable and often contradictory results.

The theory and practice of music had inevitably collided, since the latter had no longer anything to do with the former as Boethius had left it; but owing to a gross misunderstanding,

---

130   Cf. P.L. Kunz, pp. 14 ff; U. Pizzani, „Studi sulle fonti," pp. 128 ff.
131   For the relationship of Notker to Boethius, see A. Auda, pp. 72 ff.
132   Kunz (p. 15) justly points out that when Boethius says *ex diapason igitur consonantiae speciebus existunt, qui appellantur modi* he is not speaking of identification but of derivation. „*Existere ex* bei Boethius nicht die Bedeutung von *bestehen aus* [as Paul had translated] haben kann. Boethius sagt allgemein *Sie gehen hervor.*" As a matter of fact, however, for the medieval musicologists, whose tones could actually be reduced to *diapason consonantiae speciebus*, the former interpretation was automatic.

every effort was made to bring that theory into conformity with practice. Thus any research on these matters will have to ascertain the reasons for each particular interpretation of the Boethian text.

In sum, anyone researching this question will have to ascertain, on encountering them, the reasons for every single particular interpretation of the Boethian text, without forgetting either the inevitable influence of praxis on theory, or–and here the investigation becomes even subtler–the various modifications undergone by that text through the centuries.

Such work is both delicate and extremely complex, and only the publication of a new critical edition of the *De Institutione Musica* and, above all, of the scholia, not to mention all the other medieval musicological texts (whose publication by the meritorious American Institute of Musicology is now well under way), will enable that work to be exhaustive and definitive.

* * * *

We have seen that the new interest displayed by the 9th century for the musical works of Boethius grew along two coordinates: that of *musica speculativa,* investigating mainly the philosophical and mathematical implications of music, and that of *musica theorica,* inspired by practical music, but seeking at the same time to prescribe the laws governing its execution.[133] These two aspects, while not entirely interdependent, have several points of contact: though the scholia are above all the expression of the speculative tendency and are mainly concerned with the mathematical and philosophical implications of the treatise, they do not fail to give us some tips of a more specifically musicological character, as, for instance, in the long note on intervals and consonances. Conversely, the musicological works of the same period make abundant use, especially in their introductions, of the general ideas on music expressed by Boethius in the proem of his treatise.

Thus we can say that by the 9th century, the career of the music treatise of Boethius was well under way. The later stages of this career, especially in regard to the Boethian concept of music, are discussed in another part of this volume. My own major concern has been to show that in the first centuries of the Middle Ages, at any rate, the diffusion of the *De Institutione Musica* was a very different story from that of the other liberal arts treatises of Boethius. We set out with the observation that the music treatise, though announced and foreseen in the proem of the *De Institutione Arithmetica,* was probably written much later, and without the specific intent of following through with the premises of the arithmetic treatise. This circumstance contributed to the isolation of the music treatise from the other writings of Boethius—a phenomenon which is reflected in the conspicuous absence of that treatise from libraries of such importance as those of Cassiodorus and Isidor of Seville. The hypothesis of a last surviving copy of the work finding shelter in an unidentified Italian library is worthy of every respect, and may be preferred to that indicating the English monastery of Jarrow. It is to Jarrow, however, and the cultural environment of the Venerable Bede that we owe the most promising fruits of our investigation, i.e. the discovery of the scholiastic character of the myterious *Musica Theorica,* and the possibility of surveying the earliest surviving traces of exegetic fervor over the *De Institutione Musica.*

---

133 For the meaning of this distinction, see K.G. Fellerer, ,,Die *musica* in den *artes liberales*'' in *Artes Liberales,* ed. J. Koch (Leiden, 1959), pp. 33-49, especially pp. 38-39.

From the way that treatise was rediscovered after nearly two centuries of utter obscurity, we have drawn occasion and justification for a new approach to the study of Carolingian musicology. This approach would favor the ascertainment of the motives, manner and effects (not always positive) of the introduction of Boethius' work into medieval musicology rather than additional (and probably vain) attempts to identify the lineage of the ecclesiastical tones, seeing that their derivation from Boethius is untenable.

If in the course of our research we have not always been able to arrive at definitive or convincing solutions, perhaps I may count on the reader's indulgence. Nevertheless, I think we may be satisfied with having posed some significant problems and having unearthed new possibilities for research and discussion.

Perugia, Italy

Author's Note:

Since several years now separate the appearance of this article from its presentation in typescript, I wish to beg the reader's indulgence for some now outdated bibliographical references, and to note, further, that some of the opinions expressed herein have been partially modified in my subsequent publications.

U.P.

APPENDIX

SCHOLIA IN BOETHII *DE INSTITUTIONE MUSICA* LIBROS EX [BEDAE PRESBYTERI] *MUSICA THEORICA* QUAE DICITUR DEPROMPTA ET CUM QUATTUOR CODICIBUS COLLATA ET EMENDATA

Conspectus siglorum

H   [Bedae Presbyteri] *Musica theorica* quae dicitur a Iohanne Hervagio primum edita Basileae A.D. 1563 inter opera omnia Venerabilis Bedae (vol. I, cc. 403-414 = P.L. XC, cc. 909-920).

A   Parisinus latinus 7200, saec. IX

B   Parisinus latinus 10275, saec. XI

C   Parisinus latinus 7297, saec. X

M   Ambrosianus Mediolanensis C 128 inf., saec. X/XI

Boethii loci ad quos singula scholia pertinent iuxta textum a Godofredo Friedlein Lipsiae editum A.D. 1867 referuntur.

In marginibus numeri H. siglo distincti ad Hervagii editionem Musicae theoricae, numeri autem M. siglo distincti ad eiusdem textum quem J.P. Migne edidit in vol. XC *Patrologiae Latinae* referuntur.

In critico qui dicitur apparatu varias lectiones minoris momenti vel in orthographia modo discrepantes plerumque omisi. Novam scholiorum editionem locupletiore et lectionum et codicum apparatu instructam nuper curavi (cf. Romanobarbarica 5 [1980], 299-357).

403 H. DE MUSICA ID EST HARMONICA INSTITUTIONE] Notandum quod,[1] cum[2] omnis
909 M. ars in ratione contineatur,[3] musica quoque in ratione numerorum consistit atque versatur. Illud autem quod fit exterius[4] quibusdam instrumentis imitatorium[5] est (cfr. August. *Mus.* I,4,6).

---

1 Notandum est quod *H*, notandum quia *C*; 2 cum *om. H*; 3 continetur *H*; 4 exterius quibusdam]ex tonorum *H*; 5 imitatorium] mutatorium *H*

p. 178,24 Omnium quidem perceptio sensuum] Quinque sunt sensus: ipsorum sensu-
404 H. um duo sunt qui foris extra[1] corpus sentiunt,[2] visus[3] et auditus, et duo sunt qui intra, gustus[4] et tactus. Quintus vero[5] olfactus[6] dubium est utrum intus an foris sentiat. Est autem sensus vinculum corporis et animae.[7]

Schol. om. C; 1 foris extra] iuxta *H*; 2 sentiunt] senciuntur *B*, sumuntur *H*; 3 visus] id est visus *A*; 4 gustus] id est visus *A*, id est gustus *A corr.*; 5 quintus vero] imo vere *H*; 6 id est olfactus *A*; 7 animae et corporis *A*

p. 179,4 quae vero sit ipsorum sensuum, secundum quos agimus, natura eqs.] Quaedam sunt incorporalia et invisibilia, ut anima vel deus[1] quaedam corporalia et visibilia ut sunt corpora, quaedam invisibilia et corporalia ut sensus corporei: corporales[2] sunt quia corpori[3] administrantur et invisibiles[4] quia illud quod dicitur auditus[5] vel visus non potest videri. Unde fit ut cum quinque corporei sensus alia exteriora sentiant, se ipsos non sentiant. Visus enim se ipsum non videt, gustus se ipsum non gustat, quod si faceret

139

numquam ieiunus esset. Sic de ceteris (cfr. Claudian. Mamert. *Stat. an.* I,6). Conside-
randum ergo quia, cum sensus corporis sine labore adhibeamus sensibilibus rebus quae
percipiendae sunt,[6] ab illis non facile potest explicari vel definiri, quae natura ipsorum
quinque sensuum[7] sit vel quae proprietas sensibilium rerum quae[8] percipiuntur. Natura siquidem[9] requiritur sensuum et definitur quod sint corporei[10] et invisibiles, ut est
auditus corporeus et invisibilis, res vero sensibilis, quae[11] percipitur ab auditu, id est
vox, proprietates[12] habet[13] ut intellegatur[14] aer esse commotus et percussus[15] quodam ictu, quae ipsa quoque corporea est et invisibilis.

---

1 ut anima et *H*, ut anima vel deus *A B C M*; 2 corporales] corpola vel *M*, corporalia *H B*; 3 corpore
A C M, corpora *B*; 4 invisibilia *H B*, invisibilis *M*; 5 quod dicitur auditus] ut inanimis *H*; 6 perci-
piendi sunt *B*, percipiuntur *B corr.*; 7 sensuum] sensuum vel corporis *H*, corporum *A*, sensuum
vel corporum *BM*, corporum *C*, sensuum *conieci*; 8 quae *om. H*; 9 si quid *H*; 10 corporei] incor-
porei *BM*; 11 quae] quia *H*; 12 proprietates *H B M*, proprietatem *A C B corr.*; 13 habent *B*, habet
B corr.; 14 intellegatur *om. H*; 15 commodum et percussum *H*

p. 179,9 venientibus ad visum figuris an ad sensibilia radiis emissis] Nam proximiora
facilius visu penetramus[1] quam ea quae[2] sunt remotiora; sed neque clausis oculis aliquid pervidemus corporeum.[3]

Augustinus in libro XI de Sancta trinitate dicit (August. *De Trin.* XI,1,57-115 Mountain): ,,Gignitur ergo ex re visibili visio, sed non ex sola, nisi adsit et videns.[4] Quocirca
ex visibili et vidente gignitur visio, ita sane ut ex vidente sit sensus oculorum et aspi-
cientis atque intuentis[5] intensio. Illa tamen informatio sensus, quae visio dicitur, a solo
informatur[6] corpore quod videtur, id est a re aliqua visibili, qua detracta nulla remanet
forma quae inerat sensui dum adesset illud quod[7] videbatur. Sensus tamen ipse remanet, qui erat et priusquam aliquid sentiretur, velut in aqua vestigium tamdiu est, donec
ipsum corpus quo imprimitur inest. Quo ablato nullum erit, cum remaneat aqua, quae
erat et[8] antequam illam formam corporis caperet. Ideoque non possumus quidem di-
cere quod sensum gignat res visibilis: gignit tamen formam veluti[9] similitudinem suam,
quae fit in sensu cum aliquid videndo sentimus. Sed[10] formam corporis quam videmus
et formam quae ab illa in sensu videntis fit, per eundem sensum non discernimus[11],
quoniam tanta coniunctio est, ut non pateat discernendi locus; sed ratione colligimus
910 M. nequaquam nos potuisse sentire nisi fieret[12] in sensu nostro aliqua similitudo conspec-
ti[13] corporis. Neque enim cum anulus cerae imprimitur, ideo nulla imago facta est,
quia non discernitur nisi cum fuerit separata. Sed quoniam post ceram separatam ma-
net quod factum est, ut videri possit, propterea facile persuadetur quod inerat iam
cerae forma impressa ex anulo et antequam ab illa separaretur. Si autem liquido[14] hu-
405 H. mori adiungeretur anulus, eo detracto nihil imaginis[15] appareret. Nec ideo tamen discer-
nere ratio non deberet fuisse in illo humore antequam detraheretur anuli formam fic-
tam ex anulo, quae distinguenda est ab ea forma, quae in anulo est, unde ista facta est,
quae detracto anulo non erit, quamvis illa in anulo maneat, unde ista facta est. Sic sensus oculorum non ideo non habet imaginem corporis, quod videtur, quamdiu videtur,
quia eo detracto non remanet. Ac per hoc tardioribus ingeniis difficillime persuaderi
potest formari in sensu nostro[16] imaginem rei visibilis, cum eam videmus et eandem
formam esse visionem. Sed[17] qui forte adverterint[18] quod commemorabo, non ita in
hac inquisitione laborabunt, plerumque, cum diuscule attenderimus quaeque luminaria
et deinde clauserimus oculos,[19] quasi versantur in conspectu quidam lucidi colores varie
sese communicantes[20] et minus minusque fulgentes, donec omnino desistant: quas[21]

intellegendum est reliquias[22] esse formae illius quae facta erat in sensu cum corpus lucidum videretur paulatimque et quodammodo gradatim deficiendo variari. Nam et insertarum fenestrarum cancelli, si eos forte intuebamur, saepe in illis apparuere coloribus, ut manifestum sit hanc affectionem sensui nostro[23] ex ea re quae videbatur impressam.[24] Erat ergo etiam cum videremus et illa erat clarior et[25] expressior, sed[26] multum coniuncta cum specie rei eius quae cernebatur ut discerni omnino non posset, et ipsa erat visio. Quin etiam cum lucernae flammula modo quodam divaricatis radiis oculorum quasi geminatur, duae visiones fiunt, cum sit res una quae videtur. Singillatim[27] quippe efficiuntur idem radii de suo quisque oculo emicantes, dum non sinuntur[28] in illud corpus intuendum pariter coniuncteque concurrere, ut unus fiat ex utroque[29] contuitus:[30] et ideo si unum oculum clauserimus, non geminum ignem, sed, sicuti est, unum videbimus.[31] Sinistro igitur clauso[32] illa species videri desinit quae ad dextrum erat vicissimque dextro clauso illa intermoritur quae ad sinistrum erat."

schol., quod om. M. haud integre legitur in A C; 1 visum penetrant *H*; 2 quae *om. B*; 3 *quae sequuntur post* pervidemus corporeum *om. A C M*; 4 videtur *H*; 5 atque intuentis *om. B*; 6 imprimitur *Aug.*; 7 quod *om. B*; 8 et *om. HB*; 9 nedum *H,* velut *Aug.*; 10 sed] si *H*; 11 discernitur *H*; 12 fieret *om. H*; 13 conspectui *H*; 14 a liquido *H*; 15 imaginis] magis *H*; 16 nostro sensu *H*; 17 Sed] Si *H*; 18 adverterint *B et nonnuli Augustini codices,* adverterunt *cett. Aug. codd.,* animadverterint *H*; 19 oculos clauserimus *Aug.*; 20 commutantes *Aug.*; 21 quas] quasi *H*; 22 reliquas *H B*; 23 nostro sensui *Aug.*; 24 impressa *HB*; 25 et] ut *B*; 26 sed] si *H*; 27 sigillatim *H*; 28 finiuntur *H*; 29 utraque *B*; 30 contuitu *H*; 31 videmus *H*; 32 cur autem sinistro clauso *Aug.*

p. 181, 18 recens] adverbialiter

schol. om. C

p. 181,16 Atque hic maxime retinendum est illud, quod si quo modo per parvissimas mutationes eqs.] Nam sicut quando augetur dies vel minuitur non statim sentitur[1] nisi post[2] multos dies, sic etiam[3] musica quando augetur vel[4] minuitur per hemitonia vel 911 M. diesin[5] non continuo percipitur donec illae partes supercrescant.[6]

1 sentitur] praesentatur *H B M*; 2 post] per *H B C*; 3 etiam] etiam nam *M*; 4 vel] et *H*; 5 per diesin *C*; 6 donec....supercrescant *om. M*

p. 185,21 ischiadici doloris tormenta] ischiadici id est coxarum iniuriaticus dolor.

schol. om. M; ischiadici....dolor] coxarum iniuria *A,* coxarum iniuriae *C*

p. 187, 25 compage elementorum] Ut est frigiditas aquae, humiditas aeris, caliditas ignis, siccitas terrae. Nam[1] duo ex his agunt, ignis et aer, duo patiuntur, aqua[2] et terra.

1 Nam *om. C*; 2 ut aqua *A*

p. 187,25 temporum varietate] Quattuor sunt anni tempora:[1] χειμών[2] hiems,[3] ἔαρ[4] ver,[5] θέρος aestas,[6] μετόπωρον[7] autumnus. Hiems comparatur aquae, ver aeri, aestas igni,[8] autumnus terrae.

schol. om. C; 1 sunt anni tempora] autem sunt tempora *H*, anni sunt tempora *B*, animi sunt tempora *M*; 2 χειμών] ΧΙΛΙΟΗ *A*, χιλιον *H*, ΧΙΛΙΟΝ *B M*, ΧΙΜΟΝ *B* corr.; 3 id est hiems *A*; 4 ἔαρ] αἴθαρ *H*, ΛΙεΑΡ *A*, ΑΙΘΑΡ *B M*; 5 id est ver *A*; 6 id est aestas *A*; 7 μετόπωρον]μεζάπορος *H*, ΜΕΤΑΠΟΡΟC *A M*, ΜΕΘΑΠΟΡΟC *B* (*B verbum graecum post latinum* 'autumnus' *ponit)*; 8 ver aeri aestas igni *om. H*

p. 187,27 Etsi ad nostras aures sonus ille non pervenit, quod multis fieri de causis necesse est] Plinius Secundus in libro secundo Naturalis historiae (Plin. *N.H.* II,3,6): „An sit immensus mundus et ideo sensum aurium excedens[1] tantae molis rotatae vertigine adsidua sonitus[2] non quidem facile dixerim, non hercle magis[3] quam circumactorum

406 H.   simul tinnitus siderum suosque volventium orbes an dulcis quidam et incredibili suavitate concentus.[4] Nobis qui intus agimus iuxta diebus noctibusque tacitus labitur."

Dum musica caelestis[5] ex subtilioribus conficitur, sine ulla inconvenientia sonorissima[6] comprehenditur:[7] nam latenter ex superioribus ad inferiora usque ad[8] auditus nostros effunditur, quamvis eam propter consuetudinem non sentimus,[9] sicut sunt illi[10] qui circa καταβαϑμόν[11] habitant, id est descensum Nili. Si autem aliquis in altero mundo nasceretur – si possibile esset ut Sanctus Augustinus affirmat[12] – et[13] in hunc mundum postea venisset, eam sine ullo impedimento audiret eique ultra vires placeret.[14] Musica autem[15] terrestris quamvis[16] nobis placuerit, tamen quia corpulentioribus elementis efficitur, vix sine aliqua incongruentia[17] invenitur. Et hic notandum quod[18] sicut multa anima agit illa ipsa[19] nesciente, ut capilli ungulaeque crescunt, sic etiam multa in auditu ipsius aguntur quae eam propter consuetudinem latent, ut sonitus planetarum et cetera.[20]

Scholion usque ad finem loci Pliniani *om. C*; 1 extendens *H* codd., excedens *Plin.* 2 sonitus *Plin.*, si motus *A B M*, sit motus *H*; 3 non hercle magis] non magis *H B*; 4 concentus *Plin.*, conceptus *A B M H*; 5 caelestis musica *C*; 6 sonorissima *om. B*; 7 comprehenditur] efficitur comprehenditur, efficitur eraso *A*; 8 ad *om. H B*; 9 non sentimus] non consentimus *H, consentimus B ante corr.*; 10 sicut illi *C*, sicut illi sunt *B*; 11 catabathmos *C*; 12 ut Sanctus Augustinus affirmat *om. C*; 13 et] ut *H B*; 14 placeret *H*, placuisset *A B C M*; 15 autem] vero *C*; 16 terrestris quamvis *C*, quamvis terrestris *H A B M*; 17 incongruitate *A C*; 18 Et hoc notandum quod *H*, Et notandum quia *A*; 19 ipsa illa *C*; 20 et cetera *C, om. cett.*

p. 188,28 rationis vivacitatem] Haec[1] est vivacitas rationis[2] ipsa vis rationis animae quae sub silentio in animo latet. Tunc autem[3] miscetur corpori, quando formabiliter[4] per sonos[5] foras egreditur.

---

1 est *om. H B*; 2 rationis] rationem *B*, rationis est *H om. M.*; 3 autem] etiam *C*; 4 formabiliter] mirabiliter *H*; 5 per sonos] personas *B ante corr.*

p. 192,24 speculatio] id est[1] contemplatio regularum[2] ex mente quae graece ϑεώρημα[3] dicitur.

---

1 id est *om. H C M*; 2 regularis *B*; 3 theorema *B C*, ϑεόρεμα *H*, ΘΕΟΡΗΜΑ *A*, ΘΕΟΡΕΜΑ *M*

p. 192,24 Obtinere igitur maiorem ad consonantias potestatem videtur multiplex, consequentem autem superparticularis] Multiplex igitur ideo maiorem potestatem ad consonantias retinet, quia discretae[1] quantitati in augmento crescente similatur. Et cur propterea? Quia arithmetica quae per se est et musica quae consonantiarum demonstratrix est ad discretam quantitatem pertinent, geometria[2] vero et astrologia continuae quantitatis sunt. Cui quia superparticularis in decrescentibus partibus similis est, non eandem quam multiplex ad consonantias vim retinet, sed[3] tamen propter singularitatem partium secundo loco admittitur; superparticularis etiam consonantias tantum, multiplex vero non tam consonantias quam aequisonantias efficit.

Schol. om. A C M; 1 discretae] disertae *H*; 2 geometria] geometrica *B*; 3 sed] si *H*

p. 193,6 gravitas et acumen in quantitate consistunt] Secundum Pythagoricos et Ptolemaeum. Nam[1] secundum Aristoxenum in qualitate.[2]

In A et C schol. non integre legitur folii margine exciso; Nam] natura *H*; 2 equalitate *M*

p. 193,20 Multiplicitas igitur....numeri maxime servat naturam, superparticularitas.... proprietatem servat continuae quantitatis] Omnis enim[1] symphonia multiplex discretae quantitatis proprietatem sequitur[2], non tamen in infinitum,[3] sed per tres tantum[4] gradus, duplum scilicet, triplum et quadruplum. Omnis autem superparticularis symphonia quantitatis continuae naturam servat, non quidem in infinitum, sed tantum[5] per tres gradus, sesquialterum, sesquitertium et[6] sesquioctavum.

C refert hoc scholion, insequenti pospositum in H et B, ad verba ‚multiplex‘ *et* ‚superparticularis‘ *capitis 5 libri I* (p. 192,25-26), *in A idem scriptum est ad initium capitis 6 libri I, in M legitur in margine capitis 4 eiusdem libri I. Ubi primum conscriptum sit non ausim diiudicare*; 1 enim *om. A B M H*; 2 consequitur *B*; 3 ut infinitum *H*; 4 tantum *om. C*; 5 sed tantum *om. M*, sed tamen *C*; 6 et *om. H B M*

p. 193,22 Superparticularitas autem, quoniam in infinitum minorem minuit, proprietatem servat continuae quantitatis] Nam, quamvis in[1] numeris superparticularitas[2] dicatur[3], abusive dicitur cum proprie quicquid per partes partitur continua quantitas intellegatur,[4] quae longitudine, latitudine altitudineque comprehenditur; et ideo[5] super-
912 M. particularitas continuae[6] ascribitur[7] quia[8] per partes partitur.

1 in *om. M*; 2 particularitas *H A C M*; 3 dicitur *B*; 4 intelligitur *A C*; 5 ideo hic *A B C M*; 6 continuae quantitati *A*; continuae quantitatis *C*; 7 scribitur *B C H*; 8 quia] quod *ante corr. B*

p. 194,3 Superpartiens vero iam quodam modo a simplicitate discedit] Duplicat namque superparticulariam[1] proportionem quaecumque sit et per dualem numerum deno-
407 H. minat atque a duali inchoat et in eum redigitur[2] neque pervenit ad unitatem ideoque non[3] servat continuae quantitatis proportionem.[4]

In A schol. non integre legitur folii margine exciso; 1 superparticulariam *A C*, superparticularisam *M*, superparticularis suam *H B : lectionem codicum antiquiorum A et C servavi, coniecerim tamen* superparticularem; 2 reducitur *C M*; 3 non om. *B H*; 4 proprietatem *C*.

p. 194,12 Superpartiens autem....minime musicis consonantiis adhibetur] Transgreditur namque musicae consonantiam ideo[1] quod plures partes excedit et a simplicitate[2] discedit.

schol. om. C, fortasse margine exciso; 1 ideoque *H*; 2 simplici *H*

p. 194,15 Ptolemaeus tamen etiam hanc proportionem inter consonantias ponit ut posterius ostendam] in nono quinti libri capitulo, ut[1] octavo et[2] quarto et tertio

---

1 ut om. *B H M*; 2 et om. *H*

p. 194,15 Ptolemaeus] ipse quoque pythagoricus: hic autem est[1] Ptolemaeus Philadelphus philosophus.

---

schol. om. C, fortasse margine exciso; 1 hic autem est *om. H B M*

p. 194,19 Illud tamen esse cognitum debet quod omnes musicae consonantiae aut in duplici aut in triplici aut in quadrupla aut in sesqualtera aut in sesquitertia proportione consistant] In omnibus his latet epogdous idest sesquioctava proportio ideoque specialiter inter symphonias non connumeratur.[1] Ex ea[2] namque ceterae componuntur. Est enim[3] communis omnium mensura.

---

1 connumerabitur *H*; 2 eo *H B*; 3 Est enim] etenim *M*

p. 194,25 tripla vero diapente ac diapason] Est[1] in vocibus similiter ut[2] tres ad unum tripla, quae continet in se duas consonantias, ut III ad II diapente,[3] ad I diapason.

Schol om. C, fortasse margine exciso; 1 Est *om. A*; 2 similiter *om. A*; 3 diapente id es sesqualtera *A M*

p. 195,12 ad sensum insuaviter uterque transmittitur] quia ille qui[1] nimis est acutus[2] non reflectitur ad gravem ut ei conveniat et ille qui nimis[3] est gravis[4] non vult aliquid erigi.[5]

---

schol. om. M; 1 quia ille qui] ille *H B*; 2 acutus est *H B*; 3 nimis] minus *H*; 4 gravis est *B*; 5 vult aliquid erigi] arigitur ad acutum *A*

p. 195,22 certis regulis sese tenens] quia cognoscit[1] differentias consonantiarum.

---

schol. om. C M; 1 cognovit *B H*

p. 195,26 vario iudicio] id est[1] auditui et non rationi: multa enim varietas est[2] inter sensum et rationem.[3]

---

1 id est om. *H A C*; 2 est *om. A;* 3 multa....rationem *om. C*

p. 195,27 Pythagorici medio quodam feruntur itinere] Medio itinere feruntur[1] quia nec ex toto tribuunt discretionem auribus nex ex toto rationi, sed partim auditui, partim rationi[2], sonum videlicet acutum vel gravem auditui, differentias autem consonantiarum rationi.[3]

---

1 feruntur itinere *A*; 2 rationi partim *A*, partimque rationi *C M*; 3 consonantiarum rationi] consonantiis *C M*

p. 196,7 Nam licet omnium paene artium atque ipsius vitae momenta sensuum occasione producta sint, nullum tamen in his iudicium certum, nulla veri est comprehensio, si arbitrium rationis abscedat] Occasione sensuum[1] producta sunt momenta vel motus artium et vitae.[2] Ea[3] quae discernenda sunt[4] primum sensibus accidunt[5] et per sensus[6] sentiuntur ac postremo[7] ratione discernuntur.

1 Occasione sensuum *C, om. cett.*; 2 producta....vitae *om. A*; 3 quoniam ea *A*; 4 discernenda sunt] discernuntur *A*; 5 et] ac *H*; 6 per sensum *H*; 7 postremum *C*

p. 196,19 Pythagoras] Pythagoras id est[1] non indigens[2] interrogatione vel interrogationis cumulus.[3] Pythos enim interrogatio, agora[4] cumulus: inde[5] agora[6] ecclesia vel synagoga vocatur.

Schol. non legitur in C; 1 id est *om. H*; 2 non indigens *A*; indigens *H B*; 3 cumulo *H*; 4 agoras *H*; 5 agora cumulus inde *om. B*; 6 acora *A*, agara *B*

p. 197,10 sonorum proprietas non in hominum lacertis haerebat, sed mutatos malleos comitabatur] id est[1] quales sonos reddebant primum, tales quoque postquam mutati sunt[2], quia non erat in vi ferientium sonus, sed in magnitudine malleorum.

1 id est om. *H A M*; 2 quales....sunt] similes sonos reddebant post mutationem quoque *A*; quales sonos primum reddebant, tales quoque postquam sunt mutati *C M*, quales sonos reddebant primum, tales quoque postquam mutatae sunt *H*

p. 199,3 συνεχης] ἔχω namque[1] habeo, inde[2] συνέχω[3] continuo.[4]

schol. om. C; 1 namque *om. A M*; 2 inde om. *M*; 3 CIHεχω *B*, ἐνψέχω *H* coεχω *M*; 4 continuo] cohabeo *M*

p. 199,4 διαστηματικη] διάστημα[1] intervallum vel spatium, inde διαστηματική[2] spatiosa vel intervallosa[3]

schol. om. C; 1 ΔΙΑCΤΕΜΑ *A B,* διάκτεμα *H;* 2 inde διαστηματική *om. A,* ΔΙΑCΤΙΜΑΤΙΚΕ *B,* διακτεματική *H*; 3 spatia vel intervalla *H*

p. 200,7 quis modus audiendi sit] Hic nota αἰσϑητήριον[1] id est custodiam omnium sensuum quae primo in corde communiter continetur; inde specialiter ad omnes sensus corporis producitur, ut est luminosum quiddam in oculis[2] quod igneam habet naturam, quiddam[3] mobile, aerium et serenum in auribus quod recipit formas colorabiles vo-

913 M. cum[4] quae[5] fiunt ex superiori[6] elemento igneo id est[7] aere tenuissimo[8], quoddam[9] olfactum in naribus,[10] quod ex inferiori et crassiori aere conficitur; gustus ex aqua, tactus ad terram pertinet.

145

p. 200, 27 prius de tetrachordis disseremus] quia nullum genus musicae invenitur ante illam disciplinam[1] tetrachordorum[2].

---

p. 200,27 quemadmodum auctus nervorum numerus, quo nunc pluralitatis est, usque pervenerit] id est quemadmodum pervenerit nervorum numerus ad pluralitatem in qua nunc[1] est.

---

p. 201,3 *De consonantiis proportionum et tono et semitonio*] Quid sit tonus/Tonus est quando vocula voculam tota sui quantitate superaverit insuper et[1] ipsius superatae
408H. voculae octava[2] parte[3], vel in intensione acuminis vel in remissione gravitatis. Semitonium est quando tonus in duas non aequas sed inaequales partes secatur: alterum[4] semitonium maius[5], alterum[6] semitonium minus[7] dici maluerunt. Diesis est semitonium minus[8] in duas partes divisum[9], quod[10] minus[11] semitonium diesin[12] dixerunt musici. Diatonus melodia[13] dicitur quae et[14] antiquior[15], quamvis subasperior, quando conconantia ex duobus tonis et semitonio vel[16] semitonio et duobus tonis completur. Chromatica est quae et posterior et ad delectationem aurium sua varietate permulcet animos et nimiis minutiis[17] tinnule[18] fertur constatque ex tono et tribus semitoniis vel tribus semitoniis et tono. Enarmonium[19] totam possidet harmoniam[20] et sui dignitate alias praecellit et constat ex duobus diesis et duobus tonis vel[21] duobus tonis[22] et duobus diesis. Consonantia diatessaron est quando vocula intensione sui acuminis voculam in remissione gravitatis totam possidet insuper et[23] tertiam partem superatae voculae. Diapente consonantia est quando vocula voculam tota sui quantitate superat (videlicet[24] superatae vocis) insuper et[25] eius medietate[26] vel in[27] intensione acuminis vel in remissione gravitatis. Diapason non consonantia sed aequisonantia est quotiens vocula[28] sui acumine, si fuerit in intensione, aut sui gravitate, si fuerit in remissione, tota sui quantitate superatae vocis quantitatem[29] bis occupat. Et ut aperte advertas[30] quid sit intensio, quid remissio, quae in omnibus consonantiis videnda est[31], ita noveris quando primam vocem ex ore vel ex chorda[32] vel ex aliqua[33] materia organi emiseris. Fige metam et quicquid super[34] illam primam vocem in altum sui gerit, aut tonum[35], aut diapason, aut diapente, aut diatessaron, noveris illas omnes consonantias in intensione acuminis esse factas. Quicquid vero post[36] illam primam vocem, ubi terminum diximus figendum[37] esse, deorsum remittendum[38] fluxerit, sive tonus, sive diatessaron, sive cetera, scito omnes illas consonantias in remissione gravitatis fieri. Si autem toni sonum[39] vel diatessaron ac reliquarum consonantiarum[40] nosse cupis, talem cape coniecturam. Accipe regulam legneam[41] manibus magistri formatam et, praeparatis[42] tribus articulis vel arculis[43] ex omni parte aeque libratis et cavatis, extende nervum super regulam in duobus capitibus suppositis articulis et non incidendo[44]
914 M. sed metiendo[45] totam chordam in tres partes[46] aequales divide et ubi tertia pars fuerit pone articulum[47] et tange tertiam partem ipsius chordae, tange et alteram partem et

videbis consonantiam[48] diapason. Tertia enim pars bis erit[49] acutior duarum partium et duae partes bis graviores in sono. Ad consonantiam vero diapente divide[50] totum nervum in quinque aequales partes: et[51] ubi tres finitae fuerint partes pone articulum[52] et tange utrasque partes[53] et erit altera pars tota quantitate minoris[54] gravior insuper et eius medietatis, altera vero pars acutior tota quantitate maioris insuper et eius medietatis. Consonantia diatessaron erit si dividas totam chordam in septem partes, et[55] ubi quattuor finitae fuerint partes pone articulum[56] et tange utrasque, partes. Item divide totam chordam in XVII[57] partes: ubi nona[58] pars fuerit[59] pone articulum[60] et tange utrasque partes et invenies minorem partem acutiorem uno tono, maiorem vero graviorem uno tono in tota.

409 H.

---

schol., in C refertur post finem libri V, in A ad capita VIIII et X libri I, in M ad cap. VIIII; 1 et insuper H; 2 octavae B, octavam A C M; 3 partem A C M; 4 alteram A C M; 5 maiorem C M; 6 alteram A C M; 7 minorem C M; 8 minor C; 9 divisus A C; 10 quod B, quem A C M, id est H; 11 minorem C M; 12 diesin et diesin A M: lectionem H B recipere malui Boetium secutus, Mus inst. p. 277,1-4: Philolaus....diesin dicit quam posteri semitonium minus appellavere; 13 Diatonos melodia] melodia A B C H, melotia M, diatonos melodia conieci; 14 et om. A; 15 antiquior] antiquior dixerunt A ante corr. M, antiquiores dixerunt A corr.; 16 vel om. A C M; 17 minuoris A C M; 18 tinnulae A C; 19 Enarmonico A, -a C; 20 enarmonicam M; 21 vel...diesis om. B; 22 tonis om. A; 23 et om. B; 24 videlicet et H; 25 et insuper B; 26 medietatem A B C M; 27 in om. B; 28 vocula voculam H B; 29 quantitatem om. A C; 30 avertas M; 31 videndo est A C, videndo M; 32 vel corde H; 33 vel aliqua H, aut ex aliqua cett.; 34 super] per H; 35 tonus codd.; 36 post] per H; 37 fingendum M; 38 remittendo C M; 39 sonum toni B C M, tonum soni A; 40 consonantium H; 41 lineam M; 42 praepar is M; 43 vel arculis om. A C M; 44 inciendo A B M; 45 in metiendo H; 46 parte C; 47 arculum H B C; 48 consonantia A C M; 49 erit om. H; 50 divide] deinde H; 51 et] id est H; 52 arculum B C; 53 partes om. A C B M; 54 maioris A C; 55 et ubi....partes om. H B; 56 arculum H C; 57 XVII A C M, septem et decem B, septem id est decem H; 58 nonas A; 59 fuerit] finierit A B M; 60 arculum H B C

---

p. 202, 13-15 sesquitertia diatessaron, sesqualtera proportio diapente consonantiam creat, dupla vero diapason efficit symphoniam] quaeritur quare prius posuit diapason, diapente, diatessaron, nunc aliter incipit ordinem[1] ipsarum conconantiarum vertere.[2] Quod sic solvitur: quia in[3] quantum ad proportionalitatem arthmeticae pertinet antecedit dupla sesqualteram, sesqualtera[4] sesquitertiam, sesquitertia[5] postremo ponitur. E contrario vero[6] musicae consonantiae[7] retro speculantur.[8] Nam prima consonantia musicae est[9] sesquitertia id est[10] diatessaron, inde pervenitur ad sequalteram id est[11] diapente, inde ad duplam quae est diapason.[12]

Schol. om. C; 1 et nunc H B M; in ordine H; 2 post vertere add. B: quia ponit diatessaron, diapente, diapason; 3 in om. B; 4 antecedit sesqualtera H M; 5 sesquitertia] quae H; 6 vero om. A; 7 musicae consonantiae] musicae consonantia musicae B, musicae consonantia H M; 8 speculatur H B M; 9 musicae est] est musicae artis H M; 10 hoc est H M; 11 hoc est H M; 12 in B schol., inde ab, id est diatessaron', mire breviatum legitur

p. 205,28 Nicomachus] Nichos victor, machia pugna.[1]

Schol. om. C M; 1 Nichos....pugna] id est victor pugnae A

p. 206,2 Orpheum] orea graece[1] pulchra, phone[2] vox: inde Orpheus pulchra vox dicitur[3] (cfr. Fulgent: Mytol. p. 77,16-17 Heim)

Schol. om. C; 1 graece *om. A*; 2 phone] ΦΟΝΗ *A*, latine fone *B*; 3 inde....dicitur *om. A ubi supra* orpheum *legitur* pulchra vox

p. 215,14 Et sit descriptio eiusmodi eqs.] Similitudo nominum in omnibus, differentia vero in lichanos hypaton[1] chromatice, enarmonios,[2] diatonos.[3] Similiter in lichanos meson et paranete synemmenon et paranete diezeugmenon[4] et paranete hyperboleon. Nam cum sint decem et octo nervi et[5] in diatonico et in chromatico et in enarmonio reliqui similes[6] sunt exceptis quinque: dissimiles ergo de chromatico quinque et de enarmonio quninque sumpti[7] ad decem et octo si adiciuntur qui sunt in diatonico fiunt XXVIII.[8]

Schol. om. A C; 1 hypaten *H*; 2 enaharmonos *H*; 3 diatonicos *H M*; 4 et paranete diezeugmenon *om. H B*; 5 et *om. M*; 6 similiter *H B ante corr.*; 7 sumpta *H B*; 8 XXVIII] 10 et 8 *H*

p. 223,4 Nunc vero quod erat Pythagoricis in more eqs.[1]] S. Ambrosius in expositione Psalmi CXVIII capitulo II ita dicit (Ambr. *Exp. in Psalm.* CXVIII,9,II,5): ,,Puto Pythagoram[2] philosophum, imitatorem prophetarum[3] instituisse sectam ut discipuli sui quinquennio non loquentes tanto silentio loqui discerent''.

Schol. om. A B C M; 1 *cum scholion in omnibus, quos novi, codicibus omnino desit ad hunc Boetii locum coniectura rettuli;* 2 et Pythagoram illum *Ambr.*; 3 prophetarum] prophetum *H*, iuvenis huius prophetici *Ambr.*

p. 231,7 quae quasi axiomata Graeci vocant] Axiomata id est admiratione digna, quae et proloquia[1] dicuntur[2], id est[3] obnoxia[4] veritati vel[5] falsitati.

M amplius scholion praebet in quo eadem fere leguntur; 1 proloquium *A C*; 2 dicuntur om. *A C*; 3 id est] quia *A*; 4 obnoxium *C*, obnoxium est *A*; 5 vel] aut *A*

p. 234,26 Unusquisque multiplex ab unitate scilicet computatus tot superparticulares habitudines praecedit eqs.[1]] A duplo namque sesqualter, a triplo sesquitertius denominantur et reliqui secundum suum ordinem. Sed[2] illa denominatio quantum ad sensum in contrariam partem fit quia cum in primitivis[3] sit[4] in augmentum, in derivativis in deminutione est.[5] In multiplicibus quippe quanto maior est numerus tanto maior fit proportio, in superparticularibus vero crescente numero decrescunt proportiones.

Schol. om. A; 1 *in C et M haec scholion praecedunt*: ,,sive et reliqui tot superparticulares praecedit suae denominationis''; 2 sed] si *H*; 3 *post* primitivis in *M legitur*: ,,in diminutione in diminutivis''; 4 sit] est *C*; 5 est *om. C*

p. 238,31 maioris esse proportionis inter se L et LV quam LIII ad LVIII eqs.] Hic[1] quaeritur quomodo minor proportio est in[2] LIII et LVIII quam in[3] L et LV et quomodo iterum maior[4] proportio est in XLVIII et LIII quam in[5] L et LV. Sic respondendum est,[6] quod si philologus[7] iste Boetius iterum adderet, super LIII,II essent LV et 915 M. ipsum numerum mensuraret quinarius undecies et si adderet super LVIII alia duo essent LX et mensuraret idem numerus illum duodecies et esset sequiundecima proportio id est LV et LX[8] quae est minor sesquidecima[9]. Sed quamvis ad illam proportio-
410 H. nem non pervenit[10] in LIII et LVIII, tamen apparet ex hoc quod minor proportio est

in maioribus numeris, maior[11] in minoribus. Item si demeret III ex XLVIII,[12] essent
XLV et mensuraret illum quinarius novies. Et[13] similiter si tres tolleret de LIII[14]
[iure] remanerent[15] L[16] et[17] mensuraret quinarius illum[18] decies[19] et esset sesquinona[20] proportio quae maior est sesquidecima et est iste numerus[21] L et LV[22] medius
inter maiorem et minorem.[23] Et hic iterum quaeritur quare[24] tres quantitati utriusque
numeri addidit[25] ut maiores efficeret[26] numeros et qua re duos minuit ex eadem
quantitate ut minores[27] faceret.[28] Sic solvendum est quod quantitatem quinarii,
quae[29] est differentia praedictorum numerorum, divisit in duas partes, hoc est in
tria et duo et maiorem partem addidit[30] quantitati praedictae ut essent maiores numeri
et minor proportio et minorem dempsit[31] ex eadem quantitate ut essent minores
numeri et maior proportio.

---

1 Hic om. *H B C M*; 2 in om. *B*; 3 in om. *C*; 4 minor *B*; 5 in om. *H*; 6 est respondendum *A C*; 7
philologus om. *A C*; 8 proportio id est LV et LX] inter LV et LX proportio *A*; 9 est minor sesquidecima *A*, minor est sesquidecima *M*, est minor ex sesquidecima *H B C*; 10 Sed quamvis ad illam proportionem non pervenit] Sed quinarius non pervenit usque ad illam proportionem *A*; 11 et maior
A C M; 12 XLVIII]LXVIII *B ante corr.*; 13 Et: Esset *H*; 14 si tres tolleret de LIII] si tolleret ex LIII
III *A*, si III tolleret de XLIII *M*; 15 iure remanerent *H B*, iure manerent C, remanerent *A M* (iure
manerent *ex* III remanerent *fluxisse videtur*); 16 L]XL *M*; 17 et om. *C M*; 18 quinarius illum *H*,
illum quinarius *A B*, quinarius *C M*; 19 decies] octies *M*; 20 sesquinona] sesquioctava *M*; 21 *post*
numerus *add.* hoc est *A C M*; 22 L et LV *A C M*, XLVIII et LIII *B H*; 23 *post* minorem *in A haec leguntur*: Nam minorem proportionem habet a maiore et maiorem a minore, *in B legitur*: Nam maiorem proportionem habet ad minorem a maiore, *in C denique ob evanidam scripturam dubitanter le-
gimus*: Nam maiorem proportionem habet a maiore et minorem a maiore; 24 quare om. *H*; 25 tres
quantitati utriusque numeri addidit *nos*, tres quantitati utriusque numeri addit *H*, tres addidit quantitati utriusque numeri *A*, tres quantitati numeri addidit utriusque *B C M*; 26 efficiat *H*; 27 minores]
minorem *A*; 28 efficeret *B*; 29 qui *A*; 30 addit *H*; 31 depressit *M*

p. 254,8 Quoniam sesqualtera maior est, sesquitertiam de sesqualtera detrahamus; relinquitur sesquioctava proportio quae duplicata non efficit integram sesquitertiam pro-
portionem] Duodecimus[1] numerus ad VIII sesqualter est, ad VIIII vero sesquitertius.
Sed si duodenarium, qui est ad VIIII sesquitertius, subtraxeris, remanent VIIII ad VIII
in sesquioctava proportione quae exinde non esse media subtracti sesquitertii colligitur, quia si duas continuas sesquioctavas perquisieris, ut in his numeris CXCII CCXVI
CCXLIII, tertius terminus, id est CCXLIII, non poterit esse[2] sesquitertius ad primum,
sed CCLVI, maior videlicet sesquioctavo secundo. Quod si simplex sesquioctavus medietas esset sequitertii, geminatus utique redderet integrum.

Schol. om. *A C M*; 1 Duodenarius *B;* 2 esse om. *H*

p. 254,15 Quodsi sesquiquartum sesquitertio auferas, id, quod relinquitur, medietatem sesquiquarti non efficit.] Vigesimus numerus ad XV sesquitertius est, ad XVI[1]
vero sesquiquartus. Sed si eundem XX numerum qui est ad XVI sesquiquartus dempse-
ris, remanet[2] XVI ad XV in sesquiquinta decima proportione quae non esse medietas
ablati sesquiquarti ex hoc deprehenditur quia, si[3] duas continuas sesquiquintas decimas
habitudines adinveneris, ut in his numeris DCCCC DCCCCLX ĪXXIIII[4], tertius terminus, id est ĪXXIIII[5], non poterit esse sesquiquartus ad primum. Nam si DCCCC partem
quartam[6] sumpseris quae est CCXXV et eisdem[7] adposueris erit numerus ĪCXXV
maior scilicet ĪXXIIII secundo sesquiquinto decimo. Quod si simplex sesquiquinta decima medietas esset sesquiquarti, duplicata sine dubio adintegrasset.[8] Hoc in omnibus

deinceps superparticularibus evenit[9] et si continua minor proportio dematur, quod relinquitur[10] non possit subtractae constare medietas.

Schol. *om. A C M*; 1 XVI] 13 *H*; 2 remanent *H*; 3 quia si] quasi *H*; 4 DCCCC DCCCCLX ĪXXIIII] 909,900.60.10.23 *H*; 5 IXXIIII] vigesimus quartus *H*; 6 quartam partem *H*; 7 eiusdem *H*; 8 ad integra esset *H*; 9 eveniat *B*; 10 delinquitur *B*

p. 254,22 Sit igitur superparticularis proportio diapason consonantia. Auferatur ab ea continua consonantia, id est diapente, relinquitur diatessaron. Bis igitur diatessaron minus est uno diapente et ipsum diatessaron non implet diapente consonantiae medietatem, quod est impossibile.] Duodenarius ad VIII sesqualteram, ad VI vero duplam[1] retinet proportionem, sed si minorem continuam id est[2] sesqualteram subtraxeris remanet[3] VIII ad VI in sesquitertia habitudine quae plus quam medietas dempti sesqualteri ex hoc esse colligitur quia si duas sesquitertias adinvenies, ut in his numeris XVIII XXIIII XXXII, maiores sunt XXVII numero[4] qui est ad XVIII sesqualter.

Schol. om. A C M; 1 duplum *H*; 2 id est] vel *H*; 3 remanent *H*; 4 numero *add. s.v. B*

p. 255,10 Nam in superpartienti vel ceteris mixtis cur poni non possint superius, ut aribitror, explanatum est.] Ubi dictum est multiplices tantum et superparticulares[1] 916 M. notam communem mensuram habere posse in VI capitulo I libri.[2]

Schol. om. A C M; 1 tantum et superparticulares] et superparticulares tantum *B*; 2 in VI capitulo I libri *om. H*

p. 255,25 si duplicem auferamus triplici, quod relinquitur sesqualter est] Nam quater411 H. narius ad binarium duplus est, VI vero ad II triplus; Subtrahe II, ad quem VI triplus est[1] : remanet VI ad IIII in sesqualtera proportione.

Schol. om. A C M; 1 ad quem VI triplus est] qui ad VI subtriplus est *B*

p. 255,30 duae sesqualterae proportiones duplicem vincunt] Duae sesqualterae proportiones sunt VI ad IIII, VIIII[1] ad VI, sed IIII duplus est[2] VIII, minor scilicet VIIII secundo sesqualtero.

Schol. om. *A C M*; 1 VIIII] 8 *H*; 2 est *om. H*

p. 256,10 Rursus statuatur diatessaron quidem in triplici et diapente in quadruplo. Si igitur auferamus triplum a quadruplo, sesquitertius relinquetur.] Nam si unitatem detrahas, ad quam videlicet III triplus, IIII vero quadruplus est, remanet IIII ad III sesquitertius.

Schol. *om. A C M*

p. 256,15 tres sesquitertii uno triplici sunt minores.] Tres sesquitertii sunt XXVII XXXVI XLVIII LXIIII[1] , sed XXVII numeri triplus est LXXXI cui scilicet minores sunt tres sesquitertii.

Schol. om. A C M; 1 LXIIII] 54 *H*

p. 257,1 duo sesquitertii ampliores sunt uno sesqualtero] Duo sesquitertii sunt XVIII XXIIII[1] XXXII, ampliores numero XXVII qui est sesqualter ad XVIII.

Schol. om. A C M; 1 XXIIII] 23 *H*

p. 257,20 Duplex vero proportio ex sesqualtero sesquitertioque componitur] XII ad VIIII sesquitertius est, VIIII vero[1] ad VI sesqualter, sed XII ad VI duplus.[2]

Schol. om. A C M; 1 vero *om. H*; 2 duplex *H*

p. 258,13 Sesquitertium vero si proportioni sesqualterae minuamus, relinquitur sesquioctava proportio.] Si XII, qui ad VIIII[1] sesquitertius, ad VIII sesqualter est, detrahas, remanet VIIII ad VIII in sesquioctava habitudine.

Schol. om. A C M; 1 VIIII] 14 *H*

p. 262,24 $\overline{\text{LXV}}$DXXXVI $\overline{\text{LXII}}$CCVIII $\overline{\text{LVIII}}$XLIII] Differentia $\overline{\text{LVIIII}}$XLVIIII ad $\overline{\text{LXII}}$CCVIII est[1] IIICLVIIII quae ex CCXLIII ter decies multiplicatis excrevit et minus quam minoris ocatvam decimam, plus vero quam nonam decimam[2] obtinet partem.

Schol. om. A C M; 1 est] et *H*; 2 plus vero quam nonam decimam *om. H*

ibid.] Similiter differentia $\overline{\text{LXII}}$CCVIII ad $\overline{\text{LXV}}$DXXXVI est[1] $\overline{\text{III}}$CCCXXVIII quae ex CCLVI ter decies multiplicatis excrevit et $\overline{\text{LXII}}$CCVIII minus quam octavam decimam. plus vero quam nonam decimam obtinet partem.

Schol. om. A C M; 1 est] et *H*

p. 263,9 Praeterea probatuntur autem $\overline{\text{LXV}}$DXXXVI non facere sesquioctavam proportionem, si $\overline{\text{LVIIII}}$XLVIIII unitatibus comparentur] $\overline{\text{LVIIII}}$XLVIIII octava pars est $\overline{\text{VII}}$CCCLXXXI[1] et octava pars unitatis, quae iisdem $\overline{\text{LVIIII}}$XLVIIII addita efficit $\overline{\text{LXVI}}$CCCCXXX et octavam[2], qui superant $\overline{\text{LXV}}$DXXXVI octingentis nonaginta quattuor unitatibus et octava parte unitatis.

Schol. om. A C M; 1 $\overline{\text{VII}}$CCCLXXXI] septem milia trecenti octaginta quattuor *H*; 2 octava *B*

p. 264,3 Si igitur CCXLIII partem recipere octavam possent] Si CCXLIII octava requiritur erit XXX et trium unitatum octavae partes, quae eisdem addita efficit CCLXXIII cum trium unitatum octavis. Sunt ergo in semitonii proportione CCLVI ad CCXLIII[1] quorum differentia XIII minus quam minoris octavam[2] decimam, plus vero quam nonam decimam partem obtinet. Si enim octies decies XIII ducas, efficies CCXXXIIII,[3] qui sunt minores CCXLIII novenario,[4] si novies decies reddes CCXLVII. maiores quam CCXLIII quaternario.[5]

In apotomes vero proportione constant CCLXXIII cum trium unitatum octavis ad CCLVI, quorum differentia, XVII cum trium unitatum[6] octavis, minus quam minoris quartam decimam, plus vero quam quintam decimam obtinet partem, quia si quater et[7] decies XVII ducas erunt CCXXXVIII et si trium unitatum octavas ducas quater et decies efficient V unitates et quadrantem unitatis. Hos CCXXXVIII si iungas[8] fient CCXLIII et quadrans, minores scilicet CCLVI XII unitatibus et tribus quartis partibus unitatis. Si vero quinquies et decies XVII ducas fient CCLV[9], at si trium unitatum octavas per XV numerus[10], reddent integras V unitates et V octavas. Hos iunge CCLV, facies CCLX et quinque octavas qui superant CCLVI quattuor unitatibus et quinque octavis. Igitur si numeris integris haec omnia[11] videre desideras tam suprascriptos terminos quam differentias per octonarium numera et nihil molestum te reperire[12] gaudebis. Duc ergo CCXLIII octies, fient[13] tibi ĪDCCCCXLIIII[14], octies CCLVI ĪĪXLVIII, octies CCLXXIII sunt ĪĪCLXXXIIII, octies tres octavae partes[15] tres integras unitates efficient. Quas iunge ĪĪCLXXXIIII[16]: fient ĪĪCLXXXVII[17] in sesquioctava se continentes habitudine ad ĪDCCCCXLIIII, quorum differentia est CCXLIII, quae ex XXX et trium unitatum octavis, distantia scilicet CCXLIII et CCLXXIII cum trium[18] unitatum octavis sic octies aucta, concrevit: octies XXX sunt CCXL[19], octies trium octavae tres integrae unitates: inde haec differentia CCXLIII summa est. In semitonii vero minoris habitudine[20] constant ĪĪXLVIII ad ĪDCCCCXLIIII quorum differentia est CIIII, ex XIII distantia CCXLIII et CCLVI octuplicata, obtinetque[21] minoris minus quam octavam decimam, plus vero quam nonam decimam, quia octies decies[22] CIIII sunt ĪDCCCLXXII, scilicet ex CCXXXIIII octuplicatis facti, et sunt minores ĪDCCCCXLIII[23] LXXII unitatibus quae ex novenario, quo CCXLIII CCXXXIIII superabant, octies[24] aucto[25] creverunt. Si vero novies decies CIIII augeas habebis ĪDCCCCLXXVI, scilicet ex CCXLVII in octo ductis, qui sunt maiores ĪDCCCCXLIIII his XXXII unitatibus quae ex IIII[26], quo CCXLIII a CCXLVII[27] vincebantur, octies aucto[28] creverunt. At in apotomes[29] proportione consistunt ĪĪCLXXXVII ad ĪĪXLVIII[30] quorum differentia est CXXXVIIII ex XVII et trium unitatum octavis[31] aucta sic:[32] octies XVII sunt CXXXVI, octies octavae trium integrae tres unitates[33] iunctaeque CXXXVI reddunt CXXXVIIII,[34] obtinetque[35] minus quam minoris quartam decimam, plus vero quam quintam decimam, quia si quater[36] decies CXXXVIIII ducas habebis ĪDCCCCXLVI ex CCXLIII et quadrante[37] unitatis sic[38] auctos: octies CCXLIII ĪDCCCCXLIIII quadrans quoque octies auctus[39] duas integras efficit[40] unitates; iunge[41] ĪDCCCCXLIIII,[42] erunt tibi ĪDCCCCXLVI et sunt[43] minores ĪĪXLVIII CII unitatibus quae ex XII et tribus quartis[44] unitatum partibus, qui CCXLIII[45] cum quadrante et CCLVI distabant, sic venerunt. Octies XII LXXXXVI sunt, octies III quartae integrae VI:[46] iunge et tene CII. Quod si quinquies et decies CXXXVIIII facias erunt ĪĪLXXXV ex CCLX et quinque octavis octuplicatis sic: Octies CCLX ĪĪLXXX, octies quinque octavae unitatis partes integras quinque efficiunt: iunge superioribus et habe ĪĪLXXXV[47], qui sunt maiores ĪĪXLVIII his XXXVII monadibus, qui ex quaternario et quinque octavis qui[48] CCLVI vincebant sic pullularunt:[49] octies IIII XXXII, octies quinque octavae integrae quinque sunt: iunge et habe XXXVII.[50]

Schol. om. A C M; 1 CCXLIII] ducentos 44 *H*; 2 octava *H*; 3 CCXXXIIII] 233 *H*; 4 novenario] quaternario *H*; 5 si novies.... quaternario *om. H*; 6 unitatum *om. H*; 7 et *om. H*; 8 si iungas] seiungas *H*; 9 CCLV] 256 *H*; 20 numeres] minores *H*; 11 haec omnia *om. B*; 12 reperire te *B*; 13 fiunt *B*; 14 ĪDCCCCXLIIII] 1943 *H*; 15 partes *supplevi*; 16 ĪĪCLXXXIIII] 2183 *H*; 17 fient ĪĪCLXXXVII *om. H*; 18 cum trium *om. H*; 19 octies XXX sunt CCXL *om. H*; 20 habitudini *B*; 21 obtinet *H*; 22 decies *om. B*; 23 ĪDCCCXLIIII *B*; 24 octies] 8 *H*; 25 aucto] octo *B*; 26 IIII]CIIII *B*; 27 CCXLVII] actis

47 H; 28 aucto] octo B; 29 apotomis B; 30 ad $\overline{II}$XLVIII *om. H*; 31 et trium unitatum octavis] unitati octavis B; 32 sic aucta H; 33 integrae tres unitates] integrae unitatis B; 34 CXXXVI reddunt CXXXVIIII] CXXXVIIII B; 35 obtinet H; 36 si quater] sequatur H; 37 quadrantem H; 38 si H; 39 auctos B; 40 efficit *om. H*; 41 iungo B; 42 $\overline{I}$DCCCCXLIII B; 43 insunt H; 44 quaternis B; 45 CCXLIII] 260 H, CCXL, X *supra versum, B*; 46 octies III quartae integrae VI, octies XII LXXXXVI sunt B; 47 $\overline{II}$LXXXV] 2905 H; 48 qui *om. H*; 49 pullulabunt H; 50 XXXVI B

p. 271,2 Quoniam vero ad XVI numerum XVII numerus comparatus supersesquisextamdecimam obtinet proportionem si eiusdem XVII numeri sextamdecimam requiramus, erit unitas atque unitatis pars sextadecima eqs.] Si quis in integris numeris habitudines pervidere voluerit, oportet ut hac[1] ratione consideret. Si XVI in se ipsos multiplicet fient CCLVI, si vero per XVII[2] fient CCLXXII. Quod si XVII[3] per se ipsos ducat fient CCLXXXVIIII. Erunt igitur duae sesquisextae decimae proportiones CCLVI, CCLXXII, CCLXXXVIIII, quas haud dubio constat sesquioctavum excedere, quia, si CCLVI[4] octava perquiratur quae XXXII unitatibus colligitur eisdemque quorum est octava opponatur, fient CCLXXXVIII qui nimirum ab CCLXXXVIIII unitate superantur. Rursus XVII in se ipsos multiplicet: fient CCLXXXVIIII, si vero eosdem XVII per
413 H. XVIII ducat fient CCCVI. Quod si XVIII per se ipsos colligantur fient[5] CCCXXIIII, quae nimirum duae sesquiseptimae decimae proportiones[6], id est CCLXXXVIIII, CCCVI, CCCXXIIII sesquioctavum non implent, quia si CCLXXXVIIII octava perquiratur, quae XXXVI unitatibus et octava parte unitatis efficitur ac eisdem quorum est
918 M. octava copuletur, erunt CCCXXV et octava, qui superant CCCXXIIII[7] unitate et octava parte unitatis. Quod si haec fortasse octava pars unitatis molesta videbitur, superiores numeri per octonarium multiplicentur et in integris[8] numeris eaedem[9] habitudines reperientur[10]. Multiplicatis igitur[11] CCLVI per VIII sunt[12] $\overline{II}$XLVIII, CCLXXII vero octies ducti $\overline{II}$CLXXVI complent. Similiter CCLXXXVIIII octies facti $\overline{II}$CCCXII reddunt et sunt iterum duae sesquisextae decimae $\overline{II}$XLVIII, $\overline{II}$CLXXVI, $\overline{II}$CCCXII quae constant sesquioctavum superare, quia si $\overline{II}$XLVIII pars eorundem octava id est CCLVI completur fient $\overline{II}$CCCIIII, qui certe superantur a $\overline{II}$CCCXII octo unitatibus. Rursus CCLXXXVIIII per octavum ducti faciunt $\overline{II}$CCCXII,[13] CCC quoque VI octies augmentati faciunt $\overline{II}$CCCCXLVIII.[14] Eodem modo CCCXXIIII octuplicati $\overline{II}$DXCII complebunt[15] et erunt iterum due sesquiseptimae decimae proportiones[16] $\overline{II}$CCCXII, $\overline{II}$CCCCXL VIII, $\overline{II}$DXCII, quae in hoc pervidentur sesquioctavum non implere quia, si $\overline{II}$CCCXII octava ipsorum, id est CCLXXXVIIII, apponatur, fient $\overline{II}$DCI qui pro certo superant $\overline{II}$DXCII VIIII unitatibus. In prioribus ergo numeris unitas differentiam inter sesquioctavum et sesquisextas decimas habitudines fecit, quae eodem numero quo et ipsae summae, quarum differentia fuit augmentata in posterioribus numeris, octo unitatum pluralitate[17] succrevit. Similiter inter sesquioctavum[18] atque sesquiseptimas decimas proportiones unitas et octava pars unitatis distantiam fecit. Unitas ergo per octonarium sicut et illae summae quarum differentia[19] fuit multiplicata in posterioribus ad VIII unitates excrevit, octava vero pars unitatis eodem octonario ducta[20], in integram unitatem profecit. Et ideo in posterioribus numeris[21] inter sesquioctavum et sesquisextas decimas octonarius, inter sesquiseptimas decimas[22] et sesquioctavum novenarius differentia est.

Schol. om. A C M; 1 hac oportet ut B; 2 XVII] 7 et 9 H; 3 XVII] 7 et 9 H; 4 CCLVI] 200 ex 56 H; 6 proportiones *om. H*; 7 CCCXXIIII] 323 $\underline{H}$; 8 integerrimis H; 9 eaedem] decem H; 10 reperiuntur H; 11 igitur] ergo H; 12 sunt] fient B; 13 $\overline{II}$CCCXII] 2362 H; 14 $\overline{II}$CCCCXLVIII] 2648 H; 15 complent H; 16 proportiones *om. H*; 17 pluralitatem H; 18 sesquioctavam B; 19 differentia] distantia B; 20 ducto B; 21 numeris] terminis H; 22 decimus] vero H

p. 274,11 A numero qui est $\overline{\text{CCLXII}}$CXLIIII diatessaron intendo eqs.] $\overline{\text{CCLXII}}$CXLIIII tertia pars[1] est $\overline{\text{LXXXVII}}$CCCLXXXI[2] et $\overline{\text{triens}}$ id est[3] tertia pars unitatis, quae tertia pars[4] addita praedicto numero facit $\overline{\text{CCCXLVIIII}}$DXXV et trientem.

1 tertia pars $\overline{\text{CCLXII}}$CXLIIII *A C M*; 2 $\overline{\text{LXXXVII}}$CCCLXXXI] 80.7381 *H*; 3 triens id est *om. H B*; 4 quae tertia pars eqs. *om. H B*

p. 281,11 Hanc igitur apotomen, si sit commodum, sic sumemus] Si nonam partem netes[1] diezeugmenon vel nonam partem parameses[2] vel nonam utriusque hypate sumpseris, rectissimam utriusque paranete chromatice vel utriusque lichanos chromatice mensuram in monochordo habere poteris, ubi quoque apotomes[3] mensura te nullatenus effugiet. Si commatis quoque mensuram verissimam[4] habere quaesieris, inter lichanon hypaton chromaticam hypolydii modi[5] et parhypaten[6] meson chromaticam hypodorii[7] procul dubio reperies.

Schol. om. A C M; 1 nete *H*; 2 paramese *H B*; 3 apotomos *H*; 4 verissimam *om. B*; 5 hypolumodi *H*; 6 parhypate *H B*; 7 hypodoru *H*

p. 291,13 *Quod semitonium minus maius quidem sit quam XX ad XVIIII, minus vero quam XVIIII S ad XVIII S*] Inter CCXXXIIII[1] et CCXLVII sesquioctava decima proportio est, quia differentia eoram quae est XIII in minori est octies et decies et in maiore novies et decies.[2] Quibus si addideris medietatem differentiae, quae est XIII, id est VI et medium unitatis, fiunt numeri CCXL semis et CCLIII[3] semis, inter quos est proportio sesquioctava decima semis. His adde II et semis, efficies CCXLIII et CCLVI, qui semitonii retinent proportionem, VIIII scilicet unitatibus maiores quam illi qui retinebant sesquioctavam[4] decimam proportionem. Et ideo minoris proportionis sunt quam sesquioctava decima semis. His si addideris IIII fient CCXLVII et CCLX inter quos est[5] sesquinona decima proportio, qua musici semitonii proportio maior est.

414 H.

Schol. om. A C M; 1 CCXXXIIII] 134 *H*; 2 et in maiore novies et decies *om. B*; 3 CCLIII] 233 *H*; 4 sesquioctava *H*; 5 est *om. H*

p. 295,5 minus semitonium minus quidem esse quam IIII commata, minus vero quam III] Differentia qua semitonium minus tria commata superat est $\overline{\text{V}}$CLXV, qua vero a[1] IIII commatibus superatur est $\overline{\text{I}}$DCCCCLXXXVIII quae simul iunctae efficiunt $\overline{\text{VII}}$CLIII[2] in[3] commatis proportione.

919 M.

Schol. om. A C M; 1 a *om. H*; 2 VIICLIII] 7154 *H*; 3 in] id est *H*

p. 296,23 apotome autem maior quidem est quam IIII commata, minor vero quam V] Eadem differentia apotome superat IIII commata qua minus semitonium tria et eadem superatur a quinque commatibus qua semitonium minus a quattuor.

Schol. om. A C M

p. 298,4 tonus minor quidem VIIII esse commatibus, eisdem vero VIII commatibus maior] Differentia qua toni proportio superat VIII commata est $\overline{\mathrm{I}}$DCCCXXV[1], qua vero superatur a VIIII est $\overline{\mathrm{V}}$CCCXXVIII, quae iunctae reddunt comma id est $\overline{\mathrm{VII}}$CLIII.

Schol. om. A C M; $\overline{\mathrm{I}}$DCCCXXV 1925 *H*

p. 307,26 secundum descriptum in arithmetica modum] scilicet ut a sexto octuplo incipiantur inquiri sesquioctavae proportiones 1

Schol. om. A C M
1 portiones *H*

p. 339,9 septima ab eo quod est H ad A] Si H litteram trite synemmenon ascripseris[1] erit ea species quam dicit scilicet mobilibus terminata, cum inter parhypate meson et paramese plus quam diatessaron sit et paramese minime mobilis sit.

Schol. om. A C, M autem in hoc et in insequentibus scholiis omnino deficit cum Boethii textum mutilum exhibeat post cap. 11 libri IV; 1 ascripseris] assumpseris *H*

Ad descriptionem cap. 15 libri IV additam] Descriptio incipit a proslambanomenon hypermixolydii et finitur in nete hyperboleon hypodorii.[1] Sed consideratio vocum diatonici generis, quod in diatessaron tono et tono semitonioque partitur,[2] a nete hyperboleon hypodorii[3] exoritur atque in proslambanomenon hypermixolydii[4] completur. Miroque modo qua habitudine diatonica in longitudine descriptionis singulorum modorum a se nervi differunt, eadem habitudine nervi troporum in ordine a se[5] distinguuntur.

920 M.

Schol. om. A C; 1 hypodoru *H;* 2 pariter *H;* 3 hypodoru *H;* 4 hypermixolidu *H;* 5 a se *om. H*

Ad cap. 9 libri V] Acute hic inspiciendum quod mesen non ideo dicit consonare ad neten diezeugmenon quod ad illam tenet intervallum diapente symphoniae, sed quia per diapason consonantiam hypate meson idem sonat quod nete diezeugmenon. Mese quoque per diapason idem sonat quod nete hyperboleon, nete hyperboleon autem resonat ad neten[1] diezeugmenon diatessaron symphoniam; mese quoque, quae[2] per diapason idem sonat quod nete hyperboleon, ad neten[3] diezeugmenon diatessaron consonat.[4] Idem argumentandum ubi dicit[5] ad graviorem partem paramesen consonare ad hypaten[6] meson. Non enim propter diapente hoc dicit, sed quia per diapason paramese idem sonat quod hypate hypaton. Consonat eadem paramese ad hypaten meson diatessaron sicut hypate hypaton.

Schol. om. A C; 1 nete *H;* 2 quod *H;* 4 consonat *om. B;* 5 dicat *B;* 6 hypate *H B*

p. 367, 23 XLVIII] Quoniam hic primus numerus potest in II et III et IIII dividi, in quae dividit Aristoxenus tonum.

Schol. om. A B C : ad hunc locum coniectura rettuli.

155

p. 369,11 Habetque proportionem secundus ab acutissimo in diatonico genere, id est ĪDCCI, ad secundum ab acutissimo in chromatico genere, id est ĪDCCXCII, eam quam habent CCXLIII ad CCLVI] CCXLIII septies ducti ĪDCCI numerum efficiunt, CCLVI vero septies numerati DCCXCII complent. Similiter XIII, quae est differentia CCLVI et CCXLIII, septuplicata efficit XCI differentiam ĪDCCCXCII et ĪDCCI,[1] et c.[2]

Schol. om. A C; 1 ĪDCCI 1702 *H*; 2 et c. *om. B*

CALVIN M. BOWER

THE ROLE OF BOETHIUS' *DE INSTITUTIONE MUSICA* IN THE SPECULATIVE TRADITION OF WESTERN MUSICAL THOUGHT

An attempt to define the role of Boethius' *De institutione muscia* in the speculative tradition of Western musical thought may appear to be an awesome and even pretentious task, especially in context of a study as brief as the present one. My limitations may seem even more severe in that I will confine my discussion to musical writings before the year 1100. The centuries immediately prior to 1100 saw the birth of that sphere of study which has come to be called musical theory; the nature of the thought which has grown and developed within this sphere was largely shaped during the years between about 500, when Boethius compiled his *De institutione musica*, and the year 1000, when the first full flowering of medieval musical theory was completed in the works of such theorists as Guido of Arezzo and Herman of Reichenau.

If my temporal and spatial boundaries for this study seem small, I would like my consideration of the word „speculative" to seem large. By „speculative tradition" I do not mean what Boethius would term *musica mundana* or even *musica humana*; I mean rather man's verbal reflections and meditations concerning an art so universal yet so difficult to grasp intellectually and articulate verbally. If my study has any basic thesis, it is that Boethius' *De institutione musica* played a highly significant and clearly definable role in shaping the language and concepts with which Western man sought to understand and articulate music. One might begin to prove this thesis by compiling an index of the places in musical theory where Boethius has been quoted or cited, or those relatively few places where he has been both quoted and cited. But such an approach seems too discursive; moreover, it has been basically accomplished in several other studies.[1] The mere quoting of an author does not prove that his thought is crucial in shaping the ideas of the writer quoting, especially during the Middle Ages. My approach will be to examine Boethius' basic position and attitude toward music, both in itself and in comparison with other theorists. Thereafter I will trace the history of Boethius' text and of reflections concerning music in subsequent centuries. Finally, I will show how Boethius' attitude essentially shaped the understanding of and articulation concerning music in the ninth through the eleventh centuries.

In discussing the nature of Boethius' treatise I do so with the understanding that it is basically a translation of Greek sources and not an original work.[2] But for the sake of ease in discourse, as well as the fact that medieval man viewed the work as the creation of Boethius, I shall speak of the basic contents of the work as words and thoughts of Boethius.

In the opening sentences of *De Institutione Musica* Boethius makes the following declaration:

1   W. Brambach, *Die Musiklitteratur des Mittelalters bis zur Blüthe der Reichenauer Sängerschule* (Karlsruhe, 1883). Pietzsch, Gerhard, *Die Klassifikation der Musik von Boetius bis Ugolino von Orvieto* (Halle, 1929).

2   Ubaldo Pizzani, „Studi sulle fonti del „*De Institutione Musica*" die Boezio," *Sacris Erudiri* XVI (1965), 5-160; C.M. Bower, „Boethius and Nicomachus: An Essay Concerning The Sources of *De institutione musica*," *Vivarium* XVI (1978), 1-45.

It follows that, since there are four mathematical disciplines, while others are concerned with investigation of truth, music is associated not only with speculation but with morality as well.[3]

This thesis becomes the foundation of the first chapter of the treatise, and Boethius proceeds to demonstrate that music is such an integral part of man's nature, man could not be without it even if he so wished. One can sense Boethius' discomfort concerning a discipline with such illiberal, such potentially enslaving tendencies. He thus closes the opening chapter of his treatise with the following imperative:

> For this reason the power of the intellect ought to be summoned, so that that which has been implanted in us by nature might be controlled, comprehended by knowledge.[4]

This statement can be viewed as an apology for the remainder of the treatise; for the main thrust of Boethius' thought is toward knowing, grasping, and thus controlling fundamental elements of music. In order for the basic elements to be securely grasped, they must be translated into discrete quantities, quantities which—unlike sound—are immutable;[5] the quantities in turn become the basis for a dialectical system of mathematical proportions. Finally, the proportions are applied to an instrument, the monochord, and only then are they perceived as sounds.[6] Four basic steps sum up the character of the document which is to determine the shape of so much subsequent musical thought: 1) the need to know and control the basic elements of music; 2) the quantification of these elements so they can be known; 3) the building of a quantitative system using arithmetical logic; and 4) the application of the mathematical system to musical sound.

There are other aspects of Boethius' treatise which may be used to trace the influence of his thought through the Middle Ages, such as his musical classification (*musica mundana, humana*, and *instrumentalis*)[7] and his classing of musicians (instrumentalists, poets, and musicologists)[8]; yet these aspects are at least analogous to passages in other treatises,[9] but no other musical document known in the Middle Ages presents a comparable systematic epistemological approach to the fleeting yet seductive realm of musical sound.

Before comparing Boethius' musical treatise with other sources it is important to consider the context in which Boethius approaches the study of music, for this context largely determines the nature of his approach. In the opening passage cited above Boethius introduced music in a context of four mathematical disciplines—arithmetic, music, geometry, and astronomy. In this passage, in the second and third chapters of Book II, and—most importantly—in the Proemium to *De institutione arithmetica*, Boethius discusses the four mathematical disciplines as approaches to abstract truth, truth which, separated from changing materials, is constant and immutable. Boethius considers these four disciplines the training ground of the philosopher; they are propaedeutic to the study of philosophy, and one has no right to call himself a philosopher until he has thoroughly mastered these disciplines.[10] Boethius coins the

3   Boethius *DIM* I.i., Friedlein 179, 20-23, (My translation here and below).
4   Boethius *DIM* I.i., Friedlein 187, 10-12.
5   See Boethius *DIM* I.iii. ff., Friedlein 189 –.
6   See Boethius *DIM* IV.xviii., Friedlein 348-49.
7   Boethius *DIM* I.ii., Friedlein 187-189.
8   Boethius *DIM* I. xxxiv., Friedlein 223-225.
9   See, for example, Plato *Timaeus* 35-36, 32 C, *Laws* 889 B-C, *Symposium* 188A; Cicero *De re publica* vi. 18.18; Macrobius *In Somnium Scipionis* ii. 1.2; Censorinus *De die natali* xii; Pliny ii. 84; Pseudo-Plutarch *De Musica* 1147; Ptolemy *Harmonics* iii. 10-16. 104-111.
10   See Boethius *DIA*, I.i., Friedlein 9, 6-13.

term *quadruvium* in presenting these disciplines; they are the fourfold path „by which the more excellent mind is led away from our procreated senses to the certainties of intellegence."[11] The term *quadrivium* was taken up by scholars in the ninth and tenth centuries and paired with a term of their own coining, *trivium*; these terms then became the organizing principles of the *artes liberales* for the later Middle Ages.

But Boethius was not writing a hand book of the liberal arts; in fact, the terms *artes liberales* do not appear in the works of Boethius. The *artes liberales* were the basic curriculum of the Roman *scoliae publicae*, but in these schools the arts served to train young men in the Roman rhetorical tradition so they could enter public life of law and politics.[12] Boethius, on the other hand, wrote his mathematical works in the tradition of Neo-Platonic literature preparatory to writing philosophy.[13] The mathematical works were expressly Boethius' first works,[14] and after completing these works he did proceed to write philosophy. Boethius' mathematical works were thus never intended to serve as texts in Roman rhetorical schools and they never did.

Whether Boethius ever completed works on all four of the mathematical disciplines remains an open question.[15] Another philosopher in the Neo-Platonic tradition, Augustine, likewise left an unfinished work on music, a work that was also one of his first. But Boethius' works on arithmetic and music are basically one work rather than two; they both treat number, they are both based on related works by Nicomachus, and many passages in the musical treatise refer to passages in the arithmetical treatise. As such they are a record of the young Boethius' preparation for his later works in philosophy.

The Latin treatise which comes closest to Boethius' in character is Augustine's *De Musica*.[16] Augustine's work, like Boethius', is concerned with what one can really know: Augustine is likewise concerned with freeing man's mind of sensual matter and leading him to knowledge of mathematical truths, then hence to spiritual truths. Yet Augustine's *De Musica* does not present a systematic approach to related quantity, but rather discusses at some length the side of music ignored by Boethius, that is, *ars metrica*. Although Augustine's treatise influenced metrics and musical rhythm in the later Middle Ages,[17] it presented neither the fundamentals of musical consonances nor a rigorous mathematical system such as that of Boethius.

A second treatise which must be compared to Boethius' is the final book of Martianus Capella's *De nuptiis Philologiae et Mercurii*.[18] Next to Boethius' work, Martianus' *De musica* is the most complete source of musical facts from antiquity. This work, in a passage similar to the opening of Boethius' treatises, discusses the power and effect of music; it divides music into two areas, harmonics and rhythmics, and presents the basic terminology in each of these areas. Yet Martianus Capella's work clearly represents the Roman rhetorical approach to the

---

11   Boethius *DIA*, I.i., Friedlein 9, 28-10, 1.

12   Concerning character of *scholae publicae* see M.L.W. Laistner, *Thought and Letters in Western Europe*, (Ithaca, 1931), pp. 34-35; Margaret Deanesly, *A History of Early Medieval Europe*, (London, 1956), pp. 222-223.

13   See Leo Schrade, „Das propädeutische Ethos in der Musikanschauung des Boethius," *Zeitschrift für Geschichte der Erziehung und des Unterrichts* XX (1930), 179-215, and „Music in the Philosophy of Boethius," *Musical Quarterly* XXXIII (1947), 188-200.

14   Boethius, *DIA*, Praefatio, Friedlein 5, 22-24: Ita et laboris mei primitias doctissimo iudicio consecrabis et non maiore censebitur auctor merito quam probator.

15   See Courcelle, *Les Lettres Grecques en Occident de Macrobe a Cassiodore* (Paris, 1943), p. 263.

16   S. Augustinus, *De musica, MPL* 32 (Paris, 1877), col. 1081 ff.

17   See W. Waite, *The Rhythm of twelfth-century Polyphony. Its Theory and Practice* (New Haven, 1954).

18   *Martianus Capella*, ed. A. Dick (Leipzig, 1925; Stuttgart, 1969).

liberal arts:[19] his thought is seldom quantitative in any systematic way, and his approach is cursory and encyclopaedic. Compared to Boethius' thoroughly developed musical system Capella's work must be considered a superficial introduction.

Two other late Roman writers known in the Middle Ages touched on music: Censorinus and Macrobius.[20] Their treatment of music must also be considered merely an introduction to certain aspects of the discipline; for although both of these writers are important sources for medieval man's notion of *musica mundana*, their brief passages on music can hardly be termed treatises, and their approach is in no way systematic or thorough.

These treatises then represent the principal Latin sources which, along with Boethius' work, formed medieval man's knowledge of *ars musica.*[21] The path which these treatises took from around the year 500 till around the year 850 is a very difficult one to follow. Nevertheless, these were years which saw the birth of a vital musical practice, and thus we must examine the writings which touch on music during this period and try to reconstruct the role of music in the basic educational system of the period.

Two writers furnished the idea of the liberal arts–and thus of *ars musica*–for most of Europe during these centuries: Cassiodorus and Isidore. The central problem of this paper is not to define the influence of Boethius on Cassiodorus and Isidore nor to determine the extent to which they knew and used the mathematical works of Boethius in compiling their works on the liberal arts.[22] Nevertheless certain general aspects of the relation between Boethius and these writers must be discussed in order to compare their idea of *musica* and the mathematical disciplines with that of Boethius.

Cassiodorus knew Boethius at the court of Theodoric the Ostrogoth, and letters of Cassiodorus to Boethius are extant, one of which refers to translations by Boethius of ancient authors on arithmetic, music, geometry, and astronomy.[23] Cassiodorus never passed up an occasion to praise the Anicii family, the family to which Boethius belonged; he may have even claimed kinship with Boethius and Ennodius.[24] Thus one would naturally expect Cassiodorus to use Boethius' mathematical works as principal sources for his discussions of these disciplines in his *Institutiones*. Yet I hold that it is impossible to establish any direct connection between Cassiodorus' chapters on arithmetic and music and comparable works by Boethius. Cassiodorus mentions Boethius as a translator of Nicomachus in the chapter on arithmetic, but he mentions him along with another translator, Apuleius Madaurensis.[25] Upon close examination of Cassiodorus' text, it seems that Apuleius' translation rather than Boethius' served as the source for this chapter.[26] One must conclude that Cassiodorus did know of Boethius' translation of

19   See William Harris Stahl, *Martianus Capella and the Seven Liberal Arts* (New York and London), 1971, pp. 24-25; also Courcelle, *Les Lettres*, pp. 198-199.
20   Censorini *De die natali liber*, ed. F. Hultsch (Leipzig, 1867), x-xii, pp. 16-24. Macrobius [opera] ed. F. Eyssenhardt (Leipzig, 1868), ii. 1-4, pp. 582-599.
21   Two other Roman sources, which sometimes appear in later medieval musical manuscripts, should be mentioned: Quintillian, *Institutio Oratoria* (ed. M. Winterbottom, Oxford, 1970) i. 10 presents traditional stories of music's power and discusses geometry; Chalcidius, *Commentum in Timaeum Platonis* (ed. J. Wrobel, Leipzig, 1876) iii presents basic proportion and interval theory.
22   Concerning this problem see Courcelle, *Les Lettres,* pp. 313-341, „Histoire d'un brouillon cassiodorien," *Revue des Etudes Anciennes* XLIV (1942), 65-86; Jacques Fontaine, *Isidore de Seville et la culture classique dans L'espagne Wisigòthique* (Paris, 1959), pp. 341-450; Pizzani, essay in this volume. *etc.*
23   Cassiodorus *Variae* i. 45.4. (Ed. Mommsen)
24   See Arnaldo Momigliano, „Cassiodorus and Italian Culture of his Time," *Proceedings of the British Academy* XLI (1955), 207-245, p. 215. Cassiodorus, in *Institutiones* i. 23 (ed. R.A.B. Mynors, Oxford, 1937, p. 62.3), refers to Proba *parens nostra*; Proba was a relative of Boethius and Ennodius.
25   *Institutiones* ii. 4.7 (ed. Mynors p. 140.17-20)
26   Courcelle, *Les Lettres*, pp. 329-30.

Nicomachus on arithmetic, but that Boethius' work did not serve as a source for his discussion of arithmetic. In fact, there is no evidence that the work was among the manuscripts in the library at Vivarium.

Cassiodorus' letter from the early sixth century shows that he was at least aware that Boethius had written something on music, but it does not demonstrate any knowledge of the contents of Boethius' treatise.[27] Courcelle argues that certain glosses in one tradition of *Institutiones* manuscripts are actual glosses by Cassiodorus, and one of his strongest arguments linking this manuscript tradition to Cassiodorus is that Boethius and Dionysius of Hilicarnassus are added to the brief bibliography at the end of the chapter.[28] But again, the mere citation of Boethius does not demonstrate that Cassiodorus had read the work. Cassiodorus' treatment of music reveals, to the contrary, that he had probably *not* read Boethius' *De institutione musica*. Cassiodorus' main source for this discipline seems to have been a translation of Gaudentius by Mutianus[29]; he also seems to have read Latin works on music by Albinus, Censorinus, and Augustine,[30] and these sources may have contributed indirectly to his discussion of music. But Cassiodorus' writing on music is perhaps the most superficial and weakest of any of his chapters on the liberal arts. Although he defines music as that discipline treating related quantity in the introduction to *mathematica*,[31] in the chapter devoted to music he seems to have little comprehension of the quantitative principles of the Pythagoreans. His discussion of the technical aspects of music must have left the student somewhat confused, for when his explanations are not outright errors, his understanding seems to be less than complete.[32] A scholar who was familiar with Boethius' treatise would not have written such a chapter.[33]

Cassiodorus must have possessed Boethius' translation of Euclid's *Elements*, for he urged his disciples to read this treatise to understand the outline of geometry presented in his discussion of the discipline.[34] Whether he actually possessed Boethius' astronomy remains open to question, although Courcelle argues that it was probably Boethius' translation of Ptolemy that Cassiodorus used in compiling his chapter on astronomy.[35]

27 Cassiodorus *Variae* I. 45.4. In this letter Cassiodorus refers to Boethius having translated *Pythagoras* the musician into Latin; such a statement betrays Cassiodorus' lack of knowledge of musical sources as well as of Boethius' treatise. Since this is the only place in which Pythagoras is credited with having written on music, the passage may be taken as a rhetorical reference to works Cassiodorus only knew of second hand.

28 Courcelle, „Histoire d'un brouillon," p. 84. Since Dionysius of Hilicarnassus is unlikely to have been known by any scribe or scholar after Cassiodorus, it is a tenable position to argue that Cassiodorus at least knew of the works by Boethius and Dionysius, and that the glosses in question are by Cassiodorus.

29 *Institutiones* ii.5.1. and 10 (ed. Mynors, pp. 142.16 and 149. 17-18). Courcelle, *Les Lettres*, pp. 330-331.

30 Albinus: ii.5.10 (149. 13-16); Censorinus: ii.5.1 (14, 2-4) and ii.5.10 (149, 24); Augustine: ii. 5.10 (149, 20-24).

31 *Institutiones* ii.3.21 (131-3-5): „musica est disciplina quae de numeris loquitur, qui ad aliquid sunt his qui inveniuntur in sonis."

32 The proportion Cassiodorus assigns to the diapason and diatessaron consonance (ii.5.7, pp. 145-13-15) is a clear mistake: 24:8 is a triple proportion, that of the diapason and diapente. Moreover, his discussion of the „tones" (ii. 5.8, pp. 145-148) shows little understanding.

33 In light of subsequent musical writings, Cassiodorus' most significant contributions are his division of music into three parts–*armonica, rithmica,* and *metrica* (ii. 5.5, pp. 144, 5-11)–and his division of instruments into three classes–*percussionalia, tensibilia,* and *inflatilia* (ii. 5.6, pp. 144, 11-20). He is also the first author, writing in a purely musical context, to draw upon the Judeo-Christian tradition to illustrate the doctrine of ethos, or the affective potential of music (ii. 5.9, pp. 148, 19-24).

34 *Institutiones* ii. 6.3. (152, 12-15).

35 Courcelle, *Les Lettres,* pp. 334-335.

Regardless of the specific content in Cassiodorus' chapters on the mathematical disciplines, and the degree to which he knew or did not know the treatises of Boethius, it is Cassiodorus' general approach to learning that distinguishes him most from his contemporary, Boethius. Cassiodorus was firmly grounded in the tradition of the Roman *scolae publicae*. Thus his training and writing were centered in the Roman rhetorical tradition[36]; none of his works deals with philosophical subjects as such. His treatment of the liberal arts clearly reflects this tradition, for his discussions of grammar, rhetoric, and dialectic are thoroughly developed essays, while his chapters on arithmetic, music, geometry, and astronomy are very general surveys. Cassiodorus acknowledges the Neo-Platonic and Boethian position that these arts lead man up the chain of being to contemplate the divine,[37] but the essays which follow take the form of the *eisagoge* rather than that of the *protreptikos*: they are superficial introductions rather than thoroughly developed systems which really exercise the mind.[38] Cassiodorus' interest in Hellenistic literature, both Christian and Pagan, does make him a unique figure in the Roman rhetorical tradition[39]; nevertheless his presentation of the „secular institutions", · in both manner and content, much more reflect the tradition of Varro and Quintillian than that of Boethius.

As Cassiodorus' and Isidore's lives overlapped, so did their purposes: both were interested in preserving elements of the Roman educational system which could be made relevant to their brothers in Christ. Yet Isidore was almost a lifetime further into the Middle Ages than Cassiodorus, and his treatment of various subjects reflects more the character of the seventh and even eighth centuries than does that of Cassiodorus. Isidore, like Cassiodorus, seems much more oriented toward the arts of grammar, rhetoric, and logic in his *Etymologiae* than he is toward the mathematical disciplines. He devotes an entire book to grammar, one book to rhetoric and logic, while the four mathematical sciences are discussed in one relatively brief book.[40] Isidore's treatment of arithmetic, however, is more extended than that of Cassiodorus. Fontaine has argued that Isidore must have known Boethius' translation of Nicomachus, for Isidore's treatment of the definition of number, of equal and odd numbers, and of the theory of means strongly reflect the translation of Nicomachus by Boethius.[41] Yet enough variants arise between the comparable texts of Isidore and Boethius for some doubt to remain concerning Isidore's direct knowledge of Boethius' *De institutione arithmetica*. When Isidore does quote from another source, he does so quite directly[42]; no such direct quote of Boethius by Isidore occurs. Isidore does cite Apuleius' and Boethius' translations of Nicomachus,[43] but this citation is taken from Cassiodorus, one of Isidore's most important sources for the mathematical disciplines. Isidore develops the notion of arithmetic in a direction far removed from Boethius' idea of a science treating number *per se*. Arithmetic becomes arithmology at the end

36 Momigliano, „Cassiodorus and Italian Culture," p. 214.
37 *Institutiones* ii. 3.22 (131, 17-20): „has dum frequenti meditatione revolvimus, sensum nostrum acuunt limumque ignorantiae detergunt, et ad illam inspectivam contemplationem, si tamen sanitas mentis arrideat, Domino largiente perducunt." Courcelle argues that Ammonius' commentary on Porphyry's *Isagoge* was the source of Cassiodorus' ordering of the four mathematical disciplines and of this essentially Platonic notion (*Les Lettres*, pp. 323-326).
38 See Schrade, „Music in the Philosophy of Boethius," pp. 198-199.
39 Courcelle, *Les Lettres*, pp. 321-323.
40 Isidore *Etymologiae*, ed. W.M. Lindsay (Oxford, 1911). Book I is devoted to Grammar, Book II to Rhetoric and Dialectic, while Book III is given to the mathematical sciences.
41 Fontaine, *Isidore de Seville*, pp. 359-366; Pizzani, essay in this volume.
42 Cf. Isidore's *De Tribus Partibus Musicae* (iii, 18) with Cassiodorus ii. 10.5. This is only one example of many verbatim quotations by Isidore.
43 *Etymologiae* iii.2.

of Isidore's explication of this discipline; following Augustine, he explicates the use of mystical numbers in Biblical contexts. Particular numbers take on mystical significance to the Christian student, and the study of number becomes considerably more medieval than it was in the Roman treatment of Cassiodorus or the neo-Platonic treatment of Boethius.

Isidore's treatment of music follows the same pattern. He is often reliant on Cassiodorus in his presentation, yet his discussion of music is highly original.[44] The definition of music is perhaps most significant, for he transforms the classical definition–*musica est scientia bene modulandi*–into „*Musica est peritia modulationis sono cantuque consistens.* "[45] The emphasis on skill (*peritia*) rather than pure knowledge (*scientia*) and on sound and singing (*sonus cantusque*) rather than abstract measurement (*modulatio*) reflects the changing character in medieval man's approach to this discipline.[46] Isidore exhibits no knowledge of Boethius' musical treatise in his discussion of music. His discussion of the art is such that he would have probably found little of interest in the extended epistemological approach of Boethius.

Cassiodorus' and Isidore's encyclopaedic works may be considered a last glimpse of the Roman *scholia publica* tradition. These treatises represent the final systematic discussion of the liberal arts until the ninth century. As I have shown, the thorough epistemological approach of Boethius to the mathematical disciplines is already lost to these writers. During the sixth, seventh, and eighth centuries, no evidence exists which would prove that Boethius mathematical works were read. The fate of manuscripts containing these works remains unknown until they reappear in the ninth century.

Recent studies have shown that the liberal arts played a rather minor educational role in most of Europe between 500 and 850.[47] It appears that the educational plan of these centuries followed a five-way-path quite different from Boethius' *quadrivium* or Martianus' seven disciplines–a path organized around the fields of study listed in Charlemagne's *Capitular* 72: *psalmi* or liturgy, *notae* or writing, *cantus* or singing, *computus* or calendric studies, and *grammatica* or reading.[48] This plan is essentially that of the Anglo-Saxon schools–particularly Wearmouth and Jarrow–of the seventh and eighth centuries, brought to the continent by Alcuin and others and consequently codified by Charlemagne.[49] The Anglo-Saxon scholars of this period, even Bede, were not acquainted with the mathematical works of Boethius; they based most of their discussions of mathematical matters on Cassiodorus, to a lesser extent on Isidore, and on what they gleaned from Irish monks.[50]

---

44 Concerning the character and originality of Isidore's *musica* see W. Gurlitt, „Zur Bedeutungsgeschichte von ‚musicus' und ‚cantor' bei Isidor von Sevilla," *Abhandlungen der Akademie der Wissenschaften und der Literatur, Geistes- und Sozialwissenschaftliche Klasse*, no. 7 (Mainz, 1950), pp. 543-558; and H. Hüschen, „Der Einfluss Isidors von Sevilla auf die Musikanschauung des Mittelalters," *Miscelanae en Homaje a M. Higino Angles*, Vol. I, pp. 397-407 (Barcelona, 1958-61).

45 For example of classical definition, see Censorinus *De die Natali* x.3. Isidore's definition is found in *Etymologiae* iii. 15.

46 Isidore continued the tradition, introduced by Cassiodorus into such technical eisagoge, of using Biblical examples to illustrate the power of music (iii. 17). He shows, again like Cassiodorus, little familiarity with the Pythagorean quantitative approach to music.

47 Charles W. Jones, „An Early Medieval Liscensing Examination," *Journal of Education Quarterly* III (1963), 19-29; and Joseph Smits van Waesberghe, *Musikerziehung, Lehre und Theorie der Musik im Mittelalter, Musikgeschichte in Bildern*, Band III, Lfg. 3 (Leipzig, 1969), pp. 8-12.

48 See *Admonitio generalis* (789), cap. 72 (*MGH, Leg. Sec.* II, vol. I, pp. 59-60).

49 See Waesberghe, *Musikerziehung*, p. 10. For a vivid description of this curriculum see Bede's account of Theodore and Hadrian and their teaching in *Ecclesiastical History* iv. 2. (*Bede's Ecclesiastical History of the English People*, ed. B. Colgrave and R.A.B. Mynors, Oxford, 1969, pp. 333-335).

50 Charles W. Jones, *Bedae Pseudepigrapha: Scientific Writings Writings Falsely Attributed to Bede* (Ithaca and London, 1939) pp. 49, 51. Bede himself did not know Isidore.

Yet during this period a musical tradition was very much alive in the field of study termed *cantus*. A vast repertoire of chant grew and became more or less standardized and practiced daily as part of the liturgy. This body of music was preserved and handed down from generation to generation basically by memory, for no notation of musical pitch existed. Along with the study and memorizing of melodies developed a verbal tradition concerning music, a tradition which was isolated from the quadrivium tradition and Boethius' mathematical works, but based rather on practical means of describing and organizing the body of chant. Although no real treatise from these centuries is extant, the basic theoretical tradition of the period can be reconstructed by examining the older layers of texts in such treatises as *Musica Enchiriadis*, Aurilian's *Musica Disciplina*, and Regino's *Epistola de harmonica institutione*.[51] All of these treatises are, to some degree, more compilations of pre-existing texts than works of one author. One does not have to probe very deeply into the manuscript tradition of musical theory during the ninth century to discover that extended passages as well as short paragraphs seem to have an existence of their own, and repeatedly appear in treatises assigned to specific authors.[52]

The teaching and learning of Latin grammar was one of the foremost concerns during the early middle ages; thus it is not surprising that, at the most basic level of describing chant, theorists in the *cantus* tradition drew extensively from grammatical vocabulary. The smallest phrase of chant, for example, was called a *comma*, while two commas made up a *colon*, and a series of colons made up a *period*[53]; the rise and fall of a musical phrase was described as *arsis* and *thesis*,[54] and definitions of such terms as *tonus* and *tenor* were taken over literally from gramatical works.[55] Even such terminology as *graves, circumflexus*, and *acutus* were borrowed to describe musical movements and ranges,[56] while the words *barbarismus* or *soloecismus* were used to describe melodic irregularities.[57]

The most basic device for organizing the entire body of chant was the compilation of tonaries, or the classifying of chants according to their tonal and melodic similarities.[58] The chants were organized around four tones, called *protus, deuterus, tritus*, and *tetrardus*, and each of these tones was subdivided into an authentic and a plagal species. Two types of tonaries were compiled, practical tonaries–those used by professional singers to check the tone of any chant–and didactic tonaries–those used to teach students the basic qualities of each tone. It must again be recalled that there was no notation of pitch, only a neumatic notation in the late eighth and ninth centuries serving as a mnemonic device; thus tonaries further

---

51   *Musica Enchiriadis*, in M. Gerbert, *Scriptores Ecclesiastici de Musica* (St. Blasian, 1784), pp. 152-212; concerning origins and authorship of this treatise see Jos. Smits van Waesberghe, „La place exceptionnelle de l'Ars Musica dans le développement des sciences au siècle des Carolingiens," *Revue Grégorienne* XXXI (1952), 81-104, pp. 96-99. *The musica disciplina of Aurelian of Réôme: A Critical Text and Commentary*, ed. Lawrence Gushee (un-published dissertation, Yale University, 1962), Vol. II; *Aureliani Reomensis Musica Disciplina*, ed. L. Gushee, *Corpus Scriptorum de Musica*) (American Institute of Musicology, 1975). Regino of Prüm, *Epistola de harmonica Institutione*, Gerbert, *Scriptores*, I, 230-247.
52   Concerning such textual layering, see C.M. Bower, „Natural and Artificial Music: the Origins and Development of an Aesthetic Concept," *Musica Disciplina* XXV (1971), pp. 18-22; L.A. Gushee, *The* musica disciplina *of Aurelian of Réôme*, Vol. I, pp. 114-183.
53   *Musica Enchiriadis*, Gerbert, *Scriptores*, I, 159b.
54   *Ibid.*
55   L. Gushee, *The* musica disciplina *of Aurelian of Réôme*, vol. I, pp. 189-194.
56   L. Gushee, *The* musica disciplina *of Aurelian of Réôm* vol. I, pp. 216-223; cf. *Johannis Affligemensis De musica cum Tonario* (ed. J. Smits van Waesberghe, Rome, 1950), pp. 61-62, where *graves* and *acutae* mean specific tetrachords.
57   *Musica Enchiriadis*, Gerbert, *Scriptores*, I, 177a.
58   A conprehensive survey and study of tonaries is found in Michel Huglo, *Les Tonaires: Inventaire, Analyse, Comparison* (Paris, 1971).

helped the student or professional singer recall the melodic type and quality of a given chant.

Although certain elementary theory of proportions was known through Cassiodorus and Isidore, the basic approach to musical pitch was *qualitative* rather than *quantitative. Musica Enchiriadis* describes musical pitch in the following terms:

> Each of these four [protus, deuterus, tritus, tetrardus] are dissimilar through the fitting diversity between them in such a way that they differ not only in highness or lowness, but in their very highness and lowness they possess their own natural qualities.[59]

or again:

> Every musical sound has—in both directions—a sound of its own quality at the fifth degree.[60]

Pitch was thus not set or described by quantitative proportion as in Boethius, but by qualitative function. The number of qualities in the cantus tradition was only four, while the quantitatively determined system is built around five tones and two semitones.[61]

But the most distinctive aspect of musical thought during the sixth through the early ninth centuries is its gentle approach to knowing; music is not a field of study in which one grasps firm knowledge. A remark from *Musica Enchiriadis* best introduces this outlook:

> Why only certain pleasant sounds harmonize together, while other sounds, which do not want to come together, disagree unpleasantly, is a very profound and sacred theory, a theory hidden in certain things within the most holy places of nature.[62]

But the broad musical attitude of the period is perhaps best summed up in a version of the Orpheus myth recounted in both *Musica Enchiriadis* and Regino of Prüm's treatise.[63] I paraphrase the myth as follows:

> Aristeus loved the nymph Eurydice, the wife of Orpheus; as she fled from him, she was killed by a serpent. Orpheus means *oreon phone*, that is, *optima vox*, the most skilled at beautiful singing.
>
> Eurydice means *profunda diiudicatio*, that is, profound understanding. Aristeus means *vir bonus*.
>
> If some good man lovingly pursues profound understanding, she is taken away through the serpent as though through divine prudence, lest he be able to possess her;

---

59   *Musica Enchiriadis*, Gerbert, *Scriptores* I, 152a: At singuli horum quatuor sic sunt competenti inter se diversitate dissimiles, ut non solum acumine differant & gravitate, sed in ipso acumine & gravitate proprias naturalitatis suae habeant qualitates.

60   *Musica Enchiriadis*, Gerbert, *Scriptores* I, 154b: Omnis sonus musicus habet in utramque sui partem quinto loco suimet qualitatis sonum.

61   Concerning the conflict between four tones and the diatonic octave, see Regino *Epistola*, Gerbert *Scriptores* I, 232a: „Siquidem toni naturalis musicae sunt quatuor principales. Toni vero artificialis musicae sunt quinque, & duo semitonia. ..."

62   *Musica Enchiriadis*, Gerbert, *Scriptores* I, 171b-172a: Cur namque aliqua tam dulci ad invicem commixtione consentiant, alii vero soni sibi misceri nolentes insuaviter discrepent, profundioris divinaeque est rationis, & in aliquibus inter abditissima naturae latentis.

63   The text of the following paraphrase is from *Musica Enchiriadis*, Gerbert, *Scriptores* I, 172a: Aristeum Eurydicem nympham Orphei coniugem adamasse, quemque dum illa se sequentem fugeret, a serpente extincta sit. Orpheum, cuius nomen Oreophone, id est, optima vox, sonat, in cantore perito seu dulcisono cantu intelligimus, cuius Eurydicen, id est, profundam diiudicationem, si quis vir bonus, quod Aristeus interpretatur, amando sequitur, ne penitus teneri possit, quasi per serpentem divina intercipitur prudentia. Sed dum rursus per Orpheum, id est, per optimum cantilenae sonum, a secretis suis ac si ab

But then she is called again from her secrets and from darkness by Orpheus, that
    is, by the most beautiful sound of song; and, as though in a reflection, she is
    led into the sounds of this life.
But just when she seems to be seen, she is lost.
For among those things which we now know in part and as mysteries,
    this discipline scarcely has reason capable of penetrating in this life.

A comparison of the idea of music expressed in this myth with that presented by Boethius is instructive in defining the role he is to play in subsequent musical speculation. In the Orpheus myth ultimate truths concerning music are hidden from us, they are ungraspable in this life; Boethius, on the other hand, affirms that one holds immutable truths concerning music when he knows related mathematical quantity in the proportions of consonances. In the myth music *qua ratio* and music *qua sonus* are ultimately united, musical sound and musical understanding are man and wife; Boethius, on the other hand, mistrusts the senses and the effects of music, and encourages the student to pursue music only as incorporeal quantity. In the myth, Orpheus is the greatest musician, a man with such ability that he can almost bring the most profound secrets of music into the light of this life; Boethius, on the other hand, argues that the practicing artist is separated from musical science, and thus is not worthy to be named „musician." The real source of conflict between these two views is the extreme epistemological bent of Boethius on the one hand and the gentle mysticism of the Orpheus myth on the other. The one position would hold and control the elements of music, thus it must objectify them through quantity; the other position stands in wonder at the mysteries of music and admits that complete musical knowledge cannot be possessed in this life. In effect, the one attitude reflects the mysticism of the early Middle Ages, while the other reflects the rational tendencies of the later Middle Ages.

In the late eighth and early ninth centuries the liberal arts experienced a vital reintroduction on the European continent as part of the Carolingian Renaissance. The degree to which the liberal arts were actually the curriculum of Charles' palace school and other institutions has been properly questioned, especially in light of his decree concerning the five subjects to be taught in monastic schools.[64] Nevertheless Alcuin referred to the liberal arts in his *Grammatica* as seven gifts of the Holy Spirit and as seven steps to the study of philosophy.[65] Such allegorical descriptions of the arts are consistent with iconographic representations from the same period and poems similarly personifying the arts.[66] Further evidence of the reawakening of interest in the arts is found in Hraban Maurus' *De clericorum institutione*; for Book III of this work contains a reworking of Isidore's treatment of the arts with slight additions.[67] Yet

---

inferis evocatur, imaginarie perducitur usque in auras huius vitae, dumque videri videtur, ammittitur. Scilicet quia inter caetera, quae adhuc ex parte & in aenigmate cernimus, haec etiam disciplina haud ad plenum habet rationem in hac vita penetrabilem. Cf. Regino, *Epistola de harmonica institutione*, Gerbert, *Scriptores* I, 246a.

64   See above note 48. Heinrich Fichtenau, *The Carolingian Empire*, trans. Peter Munz (Oxford, 1957), p. 91.

65   *MPL* vol. 101, col. 853: quae sententia licet ad divinam pertineat sapientiam, quae sibi in utero virginali donum, id est corpus, aedificavit, hanc et septem donis sancti Spiritus confirmavit: vel Ecclesiam, quae est domus Dei, eisdem donis illuminavit; tamen sapientia liberalium litterarum septem columnis confirmatus; nec aliter ad perfectam quemlibet deducit scientiam, nisi his septem columnis vel etiam gradibus exaltetur.

66   M.L.W. Laistner, *Thought and Letters in Western Europe A.D. 500-900* (Ithaca, second edition, 1957), pp. 213-14.

67   *MPL* vol. 107, cols. 353-404.

Alcuin and Hraban Maurus show little knowledge of the arts beyond that presented by Cassiodorus and Isidore; neither shows evidence of having read Boethius' mathematical works.

Alcuin and Hraban Maurus, though important scholars in their century, can hardly be considered philosophers. The context in which Boethius' mathematical works were originally conceived was philosophical; the liberal arts were approaches to abstract truths, and after mastering these truths, one could proceed to philosophy. It is precisely in this context that the mathematical works of Boethius reappear in the ninth century. The earliest quotation of Boethius' mathematical works occurs in the *Grammatica* attributed to Clemens Scotus.[68] In defining wisdom, the opening passage of this work quotes the *Proemium* of Boethius' *De institutione arithmetica:*

> Sapientia est earum rerum, quae sunt propriae quaeque suo nomine essentiae nominatur, cognitio et integra comprehensio.[69]

Philosophy, according to this text, is divided into three genera: physics, ethics, and logic.[70] Physics, in turn, is divided into four principal parts, the four mathematical arts. These four arts are described as the *quadruvium philosophiae* in words taken directly from Boethius.[71] John Scotus Erigena, somewhat later in the ninth century, quotes an even more extended passage from the *Proemium* of Boethius' arithmetical treatise.[72] John also considered the liberal arts to be parts or divisions of physics (*natura*), and he consequently renamed them *artes naturales*.[73] These arts also exemplified the very processes of nature.[74]

Thus as abstract philosophical thinking is reborn, so are the disciplines of the *quadrivium*. Moreover, the arithmetical disciplines are not merely „secular" or „clerical" institutions, but they are rather disciplines leading to clear and unchanging knowledge. They are returned to the philosophical framework wherein, citing Boethius, the more excellent mind is led to the certainties of inteligence.[75]

It is no coincidence that both names citing Boethius contain the term *scottus*; for the revival of the liberal arts and of speculative philosophical thought in the ninth century was largely the result of the work of the *scotti peregrinantes*. They brought to the continent, along with their love of learning and speculative thinking, many books that had been basically unknown for several centuries. Among those books must have been the mathematical works of Boethius, for every early citation of the works in the ninth century can be linked directly or indirectly to Irish scholars. Four ninth century manuscript catalogues contain references to

---

68 Clemens Scotus' *Gramatica* was edited by J. Tolkiehn, *Philologus*, Supplement. Vol. XX, Fasc. III (Leipzig, 1928). The authorship of the work was questioned by Barwick, *Gnomon* VI (1930), 394. The textual tradition of the work has been further explored in *Celtica* III (1955), 211-220 by Bieler and Bischoff. The work is further discussed in Bischoff, „Eine verschollene Einteilung der Wissenschaften," *Archives d'histoire doctrinale et littéraire du moyen âge* XXV (1959), 5-20, where an Irish source of the work dating back as far as 700 is mentioned (p. 14). Though the authorship of this work may be questioned, its Irish origins and composition around 800 seem sure.

69 Clemens, *Grammatica* (ed. Tolkiehn), p. 3; cf. *DIA* Friedlein 9, 8-10.

70 *Ibid.*, p. 6.

71 *Ibid.:* et est hoc illus quadruvium philosophiae, quo, ut Boetius dicit, his viandum quibus excellentior est animus.

72 Book I of John's *de divisione naturae* has appeared in *Scriptores Latini Hiberniae*, Vol. VII: *Iohannis Scotti Eriugenae Periphyseon*, ed. I.P. Sheldon-Williams with the collaboration of Ludwig Bieler (Dublin, 1968); for John's extended quote of *DIA* see Book I, p. 162-164.

73 *De divisio naturae* IV, 8 (*MPL* 122, col. 774); see also *Expositiones super Ierarchiam Caelestem S. Dionysii, MPL* 122, col. 139.

74 *De divisio naturae* V, 4 (*MPL* 122, cols. 868-69).

75 See above note 11.

Boethius' mathematical works: St. Gall, Reichenau, Murbach, and Lorsch.[76] Of these four centers, all but Lorsch can be described as Irish centers. Furthermore, the *Arithmetica Boetii volumen I* is listed in the St. Gall catalogue under the *Libri Scottice scripti.*[77] I would thus speculatively suggest the following history of Boethius' mathematical texts: sometimes during the sixth century a copy of the *De institutione arithmetica* and the *De institutione musica* was taken to Ireland: the remaining copies on the continent, probably all in Italy, were subsequently destroyed during the barbarian invasions. The works were copied and studied in Irish monasteries during the following centuries, where they influenced the mathematical education of the Irish monks.[78] The works were taken to the continent to furnish the libraries of centers such as St. Gall and Reichenau.[79]

Another early ninth-century citation of Boethius' *De institutione arithmetica* occurs in a poem by the Irishman Dungal on the liberal arts. His verse on *arithmetica* contains the following lines:

> Pitagoras huius nam primus dicitur auctor,
> Post quem Nichomacus amplificavit opus.
> Cum quibus et noster celebraris honore, Boeti,
> Pro quo fama tui nominis eva manet.
> Hanc artem, lector, opibus nullius egere
> Noveris, ast aliis hac opus esse scias.
> Haec numeros praestat verbis rationibus atque
> Rebus, et his non est quod queat esse sine.[80]

Dungal could have been drawing the knowledge expressed in these lines from Isidore or even Cassiodorus. But Boethius is here cited as more than a mere translator, and the last lines on the primacy of the study of arithmetic relate more directly to the opening of *De institutione arithmetica* than to Isidore.[81]

One early ninth-century reference to Boethius' *De institutione arithmetica* shows the spread of the work beyond the Irish sphere. In the 830's Servatus Lupus, a young monk from the monastery of Ferrières, traveled to Fulda to study with Hraban Maurus. During these years he made the acquaintance of Einhard, the biographer of Charlemagne; Einhard was in retirement at Seligenstadt, not far from Fulda.[82] Lupus, in 836, wrote to Einhard of his plans to travel to Seligenstadt to return some books he had borrowed and to discuss scholarly

---

76   Max Manitius, *Handschriften antiker Autoren in Mittelalterlichen Bibliothekskatalogen*, ed. Karl Manitius (Leipzig, 1935), p. 275.

77   *Ibid.*; see also Heinrich Brauer, *Die Bücherei von St. Gallen und das althochdeutsche Schrifttum* (Halle, 1926), pp. 15-21.

78   Concerning the Irish knowledge of Boethius' mathematical works see Charles W. Jones, *Bedae Pseudepigrapha: Scientific Writings Falsely Attributed to Bede* (Ithaca and London, 1939), p. 51; and C.W. Jones, *Bedae Opera de Temporibus* (Cambridge, Mass., 1943), p. 111.

79   I am presently studying medieval library catalogues and all extant Boethius mss. to prove or disprove the speculative hypothesis presented in this paragraph.

80   *MGH, Poetae Latini* I, 409.

81   The notes in *MGH, Poetae Latini* I, 409 suggest that this information was taken from Isidore; other passages in the poem seem to depend to a degree on Isidore. Yet it seems to me that this particular passage is related more directly to *DIA*.

82   The letters of Lupus are published in *MGH, Epistolae* VI (ed. Dümmler); for a translation of the letters with notes and an introduction see Graydon W. Regenos, *The Letters of Lupus of Ferrières* (The Hague, 1966).

problems with Einhard.[83] Lupus' trip was delayed, so he wrote to Einhard sending a list of problems he wished to discuss with him.[84] One of the problems concerned Boethius' *arithmetica*; there were passages in the work which Lupus could not understand and he sought Einhard's aid.[85] Evidently Lupus had borrowed this work from Einhard and had taken it to Fulda for study. Einhard had probably learned of the work from Irish scholars such as Clemens Scotus and Dungal while working in the palace school of Charlemagne. Whether the work was read by Hraban Maurus or whether it was copied for Fulda at that time remains unknown.[86]

All of the references cited thus far have been to Boethius' *De institutione arithmetica*, and most of these have referred only to the Proemium of the work. It is difficult to place the earliest references to Boethius' *De institutione musica* in exact chronological order. A ninth-century reference to the musical treatise–probably related to the Irish transmission of the mathematical works–is found in a letter by an anonymous monk or cleric. He writes a very thorough exposition on the music of the spheres, drawing on sources such as Virgil, Servius, and Pliny; such learned and theoretical explication of a musical subject might well be the product of an Irishman. But he did not have a copy of Boethius' *de musica*; he complained about having been away from the text for so long, and he requested that a copy be sent to him.[87] The writer of this letter was probably a monk from an Irish center–such as St. Gall or Reichenau–who was residing in another monastery, and he wrote for a copy of the musical treatise.

The first writer to show a knowledge of both the musical and arithmetical treatises may be Remigius of Auxerre. In his commentary on Martianus Capella he cites not only the quadrivium as the fourfold division of the arts,[88] but he cites the *De institutione arithmetica* in his commentary on Martianus' *arithmetica* and the *De institutione musica* in his commentary on *musica*. These references show that Boethius was the key source for such musical theory as the names of the notes and the tetrachords, Greek notation and modal theory, and the mathematics of the semitone.[89]

The earliest work to quote Boethius' musical treatise at some length is the *Musica disciplina* of Aurelian of Reome. This work, probably compiled around the middle of the ninth century, cites Boethius' musical classification–*musica mundana, musica humana,* and *musica*

---

83   *Epistola* 4: „... ad vos venturus sum et, aliquot apud vos dies facturus, ut et libros vestros vobis restituam et quae indiguero discam fruarque aliquamdiu vestro suavissimo alloquio atque informer mihi gratissimo vestrae gravitatis et honestatis exemplo."

84   *Epistola* 5: „Ceterum profectionis in patriam ac per hoc ad vos tempus eliquantulum producere coactus sum .... Interim haec, quae subjeci, paterna, qua me semper fovetis, pietate considerare dignamini ut ea praevisa facilius mihi expediatis."

85   *Epistola* 5 cites very detailed passages from *DIA*. Any student of *DIA* or *DIM* will appreciate Lupus' reaction to Boethius' comment that finishing certain problems is not difficult for the studious: „In eodem libro, XXXIᵒ capitulo, negat esse *difficile diligentibus*, praeter quas ipse expresserit *partes multiplicis superpartientis secundum* monstratum a se *modum* ceteras repperiri. Quod, si per vos plene quod paulo praemisit superius intellexero, ubi ait: vocabunturque hi..."

86   Hraban never cited the mathematical works and no ms catalogue of the ninth or tenth century exists for Fulda. The earliest check list of Fulda's collection is from the sixteenth century; see Christ, *Die Bibliothek des Klosters Fulda im 16. Jahrhundert* (Leipzig, 1933).

87   *MGH, Epistolae* VI, 197-98: „... ut eodem affectu karitatis, quo id praeceperas, librum Boetii de musica mihi mittas, cuius quidem intelligentia quam longe se a meis sensibus proreptura sit, iam videre videor, nisi mihi tua sacratissima manus annotando porrexerit opem."

88   Remigius of Auxerre, *Commentum in Martianum Capellam*, ed. C.E. Lutz (Leiden, 1962-65), vol. I, p. 150: „Hoc est illud quadruvium sine quo nilli proponitur philosophandum."

89   *Ibid.* vol. II, pp. 334, 339, 346, 347, and others.

instrumentalis[90]; it draws heavily on Boethius' musical mathematics[91]; and, most significantly, it quotes a long passage from the *De institutione musica* which argues that the musician is one who knows, not one who does.[92] Despite the fact that most of Aurelian's treatise is concerned with the practical problems of the *cantus* tradition, the emphasis on *knowing* shows the rise of philosophical thinking in the context of ninth-century musical thought. The source of this philosophical tendency is discovered when *Musica disciplina* divides philosophy into physics, ethics, and logic, and refers to the liberal arts as *disciplinae naturales.*[93] Such a passage links the text to the Irish tradition and explains the presence of Boethius in the treatise.

When Boethius' musical treatise began to be read on the continent, there was already a thriving musical tradition in the older field of study termed *cantus*. This tradition may have known, at least theoretically, the basic mathematical proportions of musical consonances, but it was unfamiliar with an entire musical system built from these consonances and their proportions such as that of Boethius. They had no idea of what it meant that a sesquialter proportion could not be equally divided, and Boethius' extended explication of the semitone left them in wonderment. Regino, after briefly stating that the tone could not be equally divided, using the simplest proof from Boethius, made the following observation:

> If some curious investigator of such profound and perplexing subtlety exists, let
> him read the third book of the oft-cited Boethius' *de institutione harmonica* [*sic*],
> and there he will very likely not only satisfy his curiosity, but will also be able
> to test his genius.[94]

Thus a very pure and „liberal“ discipline–that concerned with related mathematical quantity–came to be mixed with one of the most practical and necessary disciplines, that of daily singing the offices and mass. The confrontation of the „liberal“ with the practical was not limited to music in the Middle Ages, for the discipline of arithmetic–along with astronomy –was mixed with computistical problems, the liberal art of geometry was mixed with the practical problems of surveying, and the abstract principles of astronomy became the practical foundation of such fields as geography and navigation. Yet these other disciplines were able to maintain a degree of detatchment from allied practical skills that music was never able to achieve. The *cantus* tradition, which had existed in the monastic and palace schools since the sixth century, was too strong and firmly rooted to give way completely to the abstract liberal art; the basic elements of the *cantus* tradition, especially the practical description of chants and their classification into tones or modes, were still very valid and important activities in the ninth century, activities which no theory introduced through Boethius could supplant. Moreover, the sheer quantity of melodies sung daily by the person studying music as a liberal discipline forced the student of the pure discipline to bring vocabulary from the practical sphere into the theoretical, and likewise from the theoretical into the practical. Boethius' impact on continental thinking concerning music was therefore not merely the introduction of a pure liberal art. Rather his impact brought about interaction between a strong musical

---

90 Gushee, *The* musica disciplina *of Aurelian*, vol. II, pp. 13-15 (*GS* I, 32-33).
91 *Ibid.*, pp. 21-25 (*GS* I, 35-36).
92 *Ibid.*, pp. 28-29 (*GS* I, 38-39).
93 *Ibid.*, p. 34 (*GS* I, 41).
94 *GS* I, pp. 244-245: „ Si quis vero tantae profundatis asperplexae subtilitatis curiosus investigator existet, legat saepe dicti Boetii tertium librum de harmonica institutione, & ibi fortassis non solum eius curiositati satisfiet, verum etiam suum experiri poterit ingenium.“ This text was probably not written by Regino, but by one who expanded the original brief letter of Regino; this addition dates from the very early tenth century (See Bower, „Artificial and Natural Music,“ pp. 18-22).

tradition and a quantitative approach to truth. Thus the most effective way to define the role of Boethius' treatise in the speculative tradition of Western music is to seek out the way his work affected musical language and understanding as it was assimilated into musical writings during the tenth and eleventh centuries.

Students steeped in *cantus* training must have felt uncomfortable as they began to study Boethius. Music to them was shrouded in mystery—many secrets of the art were hidden in the most secret places of nature. Yet this new treatise told them that they should not trust their sense of hearing, but should rather turn to discrete quantities which hold immutable truth. These quantities were expressed in multiple and superparticular proportions, and the proportions in turn represented musical consonances. Moreover, Boethius used these consonances and proportions to construct an entire musical system, one built around the octave and the diatonic scale of five tones and two semitones. A rationally constructed, self-contained, musical system was totally foreign to continental musical thought before the introduction of Boethius' treatise in the ninth century. The only treatise reflecting the *cantus* tradition which presented a musical system was *Musica enchiriadis*; but the system of this treatise was loosely built around functional considerations of practical music rather than around *a priori* considerations of musical consonances and proportions.[95] Evidence in *Musica enchiriadis* and Regino's *Epistola de harmonica institutione* indicates that, for a time in the ninth and tenth centuries, two musical systems coexisted in musical thought, the one based on qualitative considerations inherited from Byzantium, the other based on quantitative notions taken from Boethius.[96]

Musica enchiriadis most explicitly testifies concerning the introduction of Boethius' text and of the new quantitative approach during the ninth century. Immediately following the passages concerning the mysterious nature of music and the myth of Orpheus, the compiler of this text presents the following:

> Thus, those things which, by the grace of God, we understand concerning this art, let us practice them only in the praises of God. And those things which have been found for us by the more laborious investigation of the ancients, let us receive in jubilation, celebration, and singing. For those things were not known to the sons of men in prior generations, but now have been revealed to his saints. The most eminent author Boethius has laid open many miracles of the musical art, sanctioning all things clearly through the authority of numbers. The following little treatise will, if God nod assent, contain something drawn therefrom.[97]

The treatise of Boethius and his sanctioning through the authority of numbers was new to the generation of musical thought represented in *Musica enchiriadis* and its *Scolia*. The *Scolia* which follows this text does indeed contain something drawn from Boethius, but the quantita-

---

95 Concerning the system of *Musica enchiriadis*, see Philipp Spitta, „Die Musica enchiriadis und ihr Zeitalter," *Vierteljahrsschrift für Musikwissenschaft* V (1889), 443-482; and Michael Markovits, *Das Tonsystem der abendländischen Musik im frühen Mittelalter* (Bern and Stuttgart, 1977), pp. 76-78.

96 Compare Regino's *musica naturalis* with *musica artificialis*, the former consisting of *toni quatuor principales*, the later of *toni quinque et duo semitonia* (Gerbert, *Scriptores* I, ̓232a); note also in *Musica enchiriadis* (Gerbert, *Scriptores* I, 164a) the *mutatio mirabilis* which takes place at the eighth and ninth degrees when shifting from merely singing a melody (*absolute canendo*) to singing in consonances (*in symphonia*).

97 Gerbert, *Scriptores* I, 172a-173b: Igitur quae in hac arte Deo donante sapimus, utamur eis tantum in Dei laudibus, et ea, quae laboriosa veterum indagatione nobis inventa sunt, assumamus in iubilando, celebrando, canendo, quae in prioribus generationibus non sunt agnita filiis hominum, sed nunc revelata sunt sanctis eius. Pandit multa artis miracula praestantissimus auctor Boetius, magisterio numerorum enucleatim cuncta comprobans. Cuius, si Deus annuerit, sequens opusculum aliquod continebit excerptum.

tive thought of Boethius stands in stark contrast to the qualitative approach of *Musica enchiriadis*. The first *scolium* contains nothing of Boethius, but rather centers on problems of melodic alterations or *vitiae* and definition of the modes of ecclesiastical song.[98] The second *scolium* begins with a review of polyphonic practice, but this discussion changes through a rather abrupt transition to a discussion of *musica qua disciplina mathesis*.[99] The end of the second *scolium* and most of the third *scolium* become essentially quantitative, drawing almost exclusively on Boethius; the language and tone remains quantitative until shortly before the end of the third *scolium*, at which point the qualitative language again rather abruptly returns.[100] Like the two musical systems existing side by side, the qualitative and quantitative approaches to musical thought exist side by side in this text; in the generation of *Musica enchiriadis* Boethius' approach had not yet begun to dominate, it was by no means assimilated into musical vocabulary and thought.

By the time Hucbald of St. Amand (d. 930) compiled his *De harmonica institutione*,[101] the quantitative language of Boethius began to dominate musical treatises, and Hucbald and subsequent theorists show increasing dependence on Boethius insofar as musical concepts and vocabulary are concerned. Hucbald seems to have begun the rather fascinating process of trying to make the music of the *cantus* tradition fit into Boethius' system, a tonal system with roots in instrumental music, but constructed rigidly according to the principles of mathematical proportions. It seems to have mattered little to Hucbald and subsequent theorists that there was no necessary correspondence between a music essentially derived from Eastern liturgical practice and a theory derived from Greek mathematics. They did not see that they were trying to make a foot fit into a glove. They were conscious of only two givens: 1) a body of music which was still growing and sung daily, and 2) a new tradition of the *quadrivium* which held that music must be comprehended by the mind and thus controlled. The means for accomplishing the latter end were given in the source which most thoroughly developed the new idea of music, Boethius' *De institutione musica*. At this point we begin to follow the quantification of the *cantus* tradition. The older qualitative and open concepts had to be reduced to closed and discrete truths.

The basic shift in the character of reflection concerning music is seen first of all in the obsession of theorists with musical pitch. This obsession begins with explorations into the two octave system explicated by Boethius in his division of the monochord.[102] Since only certain points on the monochord ruler are legitimate proportions, only certain pitches could be considered valid: thus the number of pitches and intervals available became a closed system. One can safely generalize that treatises concerning the division of the monochord–related either directly or indirectly to Boethius–outnumbered any other type of musical treatise in the tenth and eleventh centuries.[103] Even the most practical of treatises, that attributed to Odo, must

---

98   Gerbert, *Scriptores* I, 173a-184b.

99   Gerbert, *Scriptores* I, 192b: Equidem pertentare licet ... .

100 Gerbert, *Scriptores* I, 209b: Cum sint quatuor tetrachordorum ... .

101 Hucbald's treatise is found in Gerbert, *Scriptores* I, 104-122; cf. Rembert Weakland, „Hucbald as Musician and Theorist," *Musical Quarterly* XLII (1956), 66-84, and Hans Müller, *Hucbalds echte und unechte Schriften über Musik* (Leipzig, 1884).

102 See list of Boethian monochord divisions in Markovits, *Das Tonsystem*, pp. 33-34.

103 See Markovits, *Das Tonsystem*, pp. 29-52; and Sigfrid Wantzloeben, *Das Monochord als Instrument und als System* (Halle, 1911).

begin the discussion of music with a division of the monochord.[104] All of these treatises are in the Boethian quantitative tradition in that they apply *a priori* proportions of the octave, fifth, fourth, and tone to a ruler, and thereby determine the legitimate intervals to be used in music.

In the process of monochord division, again following the example set by Boethius, letters came to be used to mark off segments of string, and these letters in turn become a convenient way of referring to notes with names such as *paranete diezeugmenon*. Since pitch had come to be considered discrete quantity, it could be given a single letter or symbol to represent it, and thus these letters became means of notating pitch. Insofar as the letters were derived from and applied to the two octave system presented in Boethius, only pitches in that system were available to be notated; for other pitches would have no quantitative validity. An examination of practical and theoretical sources using this notation immediately demonstrates the trouble musicians and theorists experienced pouring the old melodies into the new system. Practical sources show endless transpostions of melodies in order to find series of intervals into which they will fit;[105] and the theorists are forced to recommend alteration of the melodies if they cannot be made to fit the discrete system of musical pitch.[106]

There is no better example of tenth- and eleventh-century quantification than the change which took place in the concept of mode. The modes or tones had originally been rather open categories of melodies which sounded alike; they had been means of associating and recalling complete melodies.[107] Early in the tenth century each mode was assigned a note in the two octave scale on which chants belonging to that mode were to end,[108] and then the notion of species of consonances was taken over from Boethius and applied to the modes.[109] Finally, by the time of Herman of Reichenau, the old open categories had become closed concepts, and modes were defined by an octave segment of the two octave system.[110] The older qualitative notion, much too vague to be discrete, thus became a quantitative fact which could be firmly grasped by the mind.

In my description of the quantification of Western musical thought during the tenth and eleventh centuries I do not mean to imply that the Boethian musical system and the notion of mathematical discipline were not altered and diluted by the practice and idea of music inherited from the earlier Middle Ages. Boethius' two octave system had to be stretched a little at either end so certain melodies could fit,[111] and the classical *synemmenon* system had to be incorporated into the pure two octave system so that chromatic alterations necessary in chant could be realized.[112] Moreover, the classical Greek tetrachords became names only, while the

---

104 Text for *Dialogus de musica* in Gerbert, Scriptores I, 252-264, monochord division 252b-253b; concerning *Dialogus* see Michel Huglo, „L'auteur du „Dialogue sur la musique" attribué à Odon," *Revue de Musicologie*, LV (1969), 119-171.

105 See, *e.g.*, transpositions necessary in *modus protus plagus* from D to a (*i.e.*, h) in Montpellier H. 159 (*Paleographie musicale*, vol. 8, Tournai, 1901-05), especially in Graduals and Offertories.

106 See, *e.g.*, *Dialogus* (Gerbert, *Scriptores* I, 256b-257a): Quodsi nulli tono placet, secundum eum tonum emendetur, in quo minus dissonat. Atque hoc observari debet, ut emendatus cantus aut decentius sonet, aut a priori similitudine parum discrepet.

107 Tonaries, the earliest manifestation of modal consciousness, are, among other things, catalogues of melodies which share the same melodic qualities; they further group together melodies which are of one archetype.

108 See, *e.g.*, Hucbald, *De harmonica institutione*, Gerbert, *Scriptores* I, 115.

109 See, *e.g.*, Berno of Reichenau, *Prologus in Tonarium* (Gerbert, *Scriptores* II, 62-79), pp. 70-71.

110 Musica *Hermmanni Contracti* ..., ed. Leonard Ellinwood (Rochester, 1936), pp. 42-56.

111 See *Dialogus*, Gerbert, *Scriptores* I, 253a and Guido, *Micrologus*, cap. ii (*Guidonis aretini Micrologus*, ed. Joseph Smits van Waesberghe, *Corpus Scriptorum de Musica* 4, Rome: The American Institute of Musicology, 1955).

112 See, *e.g.*, in Hucbald, Gerbert, *Scriptores* I, 113a-114a.

functional tetrachords from the *cantus* tradition were applied to the classical system.[113] Ironically, as men came to grasp more and more of the seemingly transient art of music through quantification, they came to see *musica* less and less in the broader Boethian concept of the *quadrivium*. The relative isolation of music from the other arts and its application of liberal principles to practical problems has been described as a key factor in the erosion of the quadrivium during the later Middle Ages.[114]

Yet the most fundamental of Boethius' premises, that music must be known and controlled, had become a firm part of the Western musical tradition. The myth of Orpheus, the most skilled singer who could almost reveal the most profound secrets of an art hidden in darkness, was lost to the literature and consciousness of Western musical thought. The later Middle Ages repeatedly related the musical myth transmitted by Boethius, the myth of Pythagoras, who discovered ultimate truths concerning musical consonance in numbers inscribed on hammers.[115] In the words of a verse attributed to Guido, the instinctive *cantor*, the representative of the *cantus* tradition, is reduced to the level of beast when compared to the *musicus*, the representative of the tradition of knowing:

Musicorum et cantorum, magna est distantia,
Isti dicunt, illi sciunt, quae componit musica.
Nam qui fecit, quod non sapit, diffinitur bestia.[116]

In subsequent centuries, musicians repeatedly turned to quantitative premises and arguments so that they might claim to know, to sanction through the authority of numbers, the procedures which they performed. Boethius' role in Western musical speculation had been determined.

University of North Carolina
Chapel Hill

113 See, *e.g.*, in Berno of Reichenau (Gerbert, *Scriptores* II, 63b), Wilhelmus of Hirsau (*Willehelmi Hirsaugensis Musica*, ed. Denis Harbinson, *Corpus Scriptorum de Musica* 23, American Institute of Musicology, 1975) pp. 16-17, and Herman of Reichenau (ed. Ellinwood), p. 22.

114 See H.M. Klinkenberg, „Der Verfall des Quadriviums im frühen Mittelalter," *Artes liberales von der antiken Bildung zur Wissenschaft des Mittelalters*, ed. J. Koch (*Studien und Texte zur Geistesgeschichte des Mittelalters* 5, Cologne, 1959), pp. 1-32; see especially pp. 20-27.

115 Compare the closing chapter of Guido's *Micrologus* (ed. Smits van Waesberghe, cap. xx), in which Pythagoras' quantification of musical intervals is represented as the dawning of musical science, with the closing of *Musica enchiriadis*, in which the myth of Orpheus is presented. Boethius is the only Latin source presenting the myth of Pythagoras and the hammers.

116 *Musicae Regulae Rhythmicae* (Gerbert, *Scriptores* II, 25-34), p. 25.

JULIA BOLTON HOLLOWAY

THE ASSE TO THE HARPE: BOETHIAN MUSIC IN CHAUCER

>"What! slombrestow as in a litargie?
>Or artow lik an asse to the harpe,
>That hereth sown whan men the strynges plye,
>But in his mynde of that no melodie
>May sinken hym to gladen, for that he
>So dul ys of his bestialite?"

Pandarus, love's preceptor, cries out these words in exasperation at the love-lorn Troilus who has spurned his elegant rhetorical *consolatio*.[1] The words are borrowed from Boethius' Philosophia who had uttered them in a tone of similar exasperation: ,, ,Sentisne, inquit, haec atque animo illabuntur tuo an ὄνος λύρας?' " she says after having sung to him the Metrum 4, ,,Quisquis composito serenus aevo." Chaucer translated this passage: ,, ,Felistow,' quod sche, ,thise thynges, and entren thei aught in thy corage? Artow like an asse to the harpe?' "[2] In the *Troilus and Criseyde*, probably written while Chaucer was translating *Boece* (see ,,Chaucers Wordes unto Adam, His Owne Scriveyn"),[3] Chaucer carried the *asinus ad liram* topos further than did Boethius. He has it jangle even more discordantly in Pandarus' mouth--the advocate of lust--being wrenched out of context by Chaucer's Pandarus from Boethius' Philosophia. Pandarus is the schoolmaster of lust while Philosophia is the schoolmistress of reason. Though one apes the other, yet they are diametrically opposed.

Besides the rhetorical topos of the Ass to the Harp there is also an extensive iconographic use of the harp playing ass. An inlay on the soundbox of a sacred harp from Ur, circa 2600 B.C., shows an ass playing a lyre with other figures.[4] A fresco from Spain, now in the Cloisters Collection, executed about 1220 A.D., has a very similar group of figures in its border, one of whom is the ass, now playing a medieval harp.[5] A capital at Nantes shows the ass with the harp

---

1   *Troilus and Criseyde*, I, 730-5. I use *The Works of Geoffrey Chaucer*, ed. F.N. Robinson (Cambridge, Mass., 1957).

2   *Boece*, I, Prosa 4, 1-3. The Latin text used is *Philosophiae Consolatio*, ed. Karl Büchner (Heidelberg, 1947).

3   Robinson notes, p. 320, that ,,The association of *Boece* and *Troilus* in the *Words to Adam Scriveyn* and the very heavy indebtedness of the *Troilus* to the *Consolation* indicate that Chaucer had the two works in hand at about the same time."

4   The harp is in the possession of the University Museum, Philadelphia. See H.W. Janson, *History of Art* (New York, 1968), p. 66, and André Parrott, *Sumer: The Dawn of Art*, trans. Stuart Gilbert and James Emmons (New York, 1961). Parrott feels the use of the animals adorning the harp reflects incidents sung to that harp. He describes the harp inlay as representing preparations for a banquet, at which an ass will play a lyre, a jackal the sistrum and tambourine, and a bear will dance; also with them are a scorpion man and a gazelle. He notes that the iconography recurs in the satirical papyrus of Turin, in the ostraca from Dei el-Medina, in the fables of Aesop and Phaedrus, and finally in Romanesque capitals.

5   The Metropolitan Museum of Art, the Cloisters Collection, purchase 1931. From the Chapter House of the Monastery of San Pedro de Arlanza, near Hortiguëla, Burgos, Spain.

and again one of the accompanying figures.[6] The crypt of Canterbury Cathedral has a capital repeating these motifs. Chaucer's pilgrims could well have seen it.[7] The iconographical motif thus remained astonishingly intact for nearly four thousand years.

Boethius, in the *Consolation of Philosophy*, makes use of the rhetorical topos, the *asinus ad liram* (I, Prosa 4). Chaucer translates the Boethian text, then uses the topos in the *Troilus and Criseyde* (I. 730-5). But the literary ass does not play the harp. He hears it played by another uncomprehendingly: „That hereth sown whan men the strynges plye, But in his mynde of that no melodie May sinken hym to gladen." This is Chaucer's rendering in *Troilus*. However, Helen Adolf, in a *Speculum* article, considered the inconographical motif of use in analyzing the literary topos.[8] Also, Emile Mâle cites a text where a complaint is lodged against the use of the ass and the lyre of Boethius, „onos lyras Boetii," in the decoration of churches which clearly indicates an awareness during this period of a relationship between the iconographical motif and the rhetorical topos.[9] The motif and topos function in all these instances as irreverent commentary.

The relief upon the Sumerian harp shows the ass playing a harp that is the same as the artifact it ornaments. The Cloisters Collection Wyvern (a chimaera having wings and serpent tail upon a dragon's body) has, for its border, figures which include men with tails who seem to echo the Wyvern in their chimaerical anatomy. Both clusters of figures, from the harp and the fresco, are clearly related to each other despite the passage of time. They are, as it were, an iconographical constellation. Willard Farnham notes the Gothic drollery of the Psalters where the figure of David with his harp is mocked by similar grotesques, apes and asses playing harps, a goat, panpipes and so forth.[10] The capitals and portals of Romanesque and Gothic cathedrals also made use of this irreverent cluster of theriomorphic figures. Neither are the figures uniquely Babylonian or Gothic. They appear as well in Egyptian papyrii where donkeys, lions, crocodiles and apes play musical instruments, the instrument given to the ass being again the lyre.[11]

Though Helen Adolf saw the *asinus ad liram* topos as stretching back into totemic mists where the Babylonian ass was held to be sacred and possibly the inventor of music[12] (certainly medieval manuscript grotesques include the musician whose instrument is the jawbone of an ass, perhaps a vestige of this concept across the bridge of time[13]), C.G. Jung's „On the Psychology of the Trickster-Figure," in *The Archetypes and the Collective Unconscious* discusses apes

6   Emile Mâle, *L'Art religieux du XIIe siècle en France* (Paris, 1924), p. 339, fig. 197. Mâle notes the use of the Ass and the Lyre also at Saint-Sauveur de Nevers, at Saint-Parize-le-Châtel (Nièvre), on the portals of Saint-Aignin de Cosne and of Fleury-la-Montainge (Saône-et-Loire) and Meillers (Allier), at Brionde, and at Saint-Benoit-sur-Loire. He observes: „A la face meridional du vieux clocher de Chartres, on voit encore aujourd'hui la statue de l'âne qui joue de la lyre. Elle invitait à l'application les jeunes clercs qui venaient en foule suivre les leçons des fameux maîtres de Chartres, et, tout à côté, un ange avec son cadran solaire leur mesurait le temps," p. 340.
7   See „From Every Shires Ende: The World of Chaucer's Pilgrims," A Pilgrim Films Production.
8   „The Ass and the Harp," XXIX (1950), 49-57.
9   Mâle, p. 340, because of this thirteenth-century complaint concerning sculpture using Boethius' ass and lyre, considered Boethius the source for the iconography. I observe that the Sumerian harp considerably antedates Boethius.
10 *The Shakespearian Grotesque: Its Genesis and Transformations* (Oxford, 1971), pp. 24-5.
11 Adolf, p. 50. The proverb, incidentally, is extant in a variant form in modern Chinese and is used to convey the same meaning as Philosophia's. It is the „playing a lyre before an ox" (the Sumerian harp has at its base the head of a bull just as it is shown in the plaque) and it may have reached China via the trade routes.
12 P. 51.
13 Emile Mâle, *The Gothic Image* (New York, 1958), p. 61. Also *Hours of Jeanne d'Evreux*, fol. 54.

and asses in the medieval church showing how these were considered diabolical or buffoon figures who aped the sacred.[14] Thus the sense *in bono* of the ass of Sumerian times underwent a reversal. The Pythagoreans held that the ass alone of all animals was not built according to harmony and Dante in explicating Boethius in his own Boethian *Convivio* echoed this concept:

> E però chi dalla ragione si parte, e usa pur la parte sensitiva, non vive uomo, ma vive bestia; siccome dice quello eccelentissimo Boezio: ,Asino vive.'[15]

Chaucer relates the ass to Priapus and his rites in the *Parliament of Fowls* (253-6). This sense of the bestiality of the ass is to be found generally. The 1566 Englishing of Apuleius' *Golden Ass* was prefaced with a delightful imposed allegory by its translator, William Adlington:

> The argument of the book is, how Lucius Apuleius, the author himself, travelled into Thessaly ... where after he has continued a few days, by the mighty force of a violent confection he was changed into a miserable ass, and nothing might reduce him back to his wonted shape but the eating of a rose, which, after the endurance of infinite sorrow, at length he obtained by prayer. Verily under the wrap of this transformation is taxed the life of mortal men, when as we suffer our minds so to be drowned in the sensual lusts of the flesh and the beastly pleasure thereof ... that we lose wholly the use of reason and virtue, which properly should be in a man, and play the parts of brutes and savage beasts .... But as Lucius Apuleius was changed into his human shape by a rose ... so can we never be restored to the right figure of ourselves, except we taste and eat the sweet rose of reason and virtue, which the rather by mediation of prayer we may assuredly attain. Again, may not the meaning of this work be altered and turned in this sort? A man desirous to apply his mind to some excellent art, or given to the study of any of the sciences, at the first appeareth to himself an ass without wit, without knowledge, and not much unlike a brute beast, till such time as by much pain and travail he hath achieved to the perfectness of the same, and tasting the sweet flower and fruit of his studies, doth think himself well brought to the right and very shape of a man. Finally the Metamorphose of Lucius Apuleius may be resembled to youth without discretion, and his reduction to age possessed with wisdom and virtue.[16]

Shakespeare's treatment of Bottom metamorphosed as an unmusical musician ass for whom Titania lusts deals likewise with the ass as symbolizing bestiality and folly.

It is interesting that in the topos of the ass and the lyre music is being parodied where the opposition between Reason and Bestiality is depicted. Chaucer in the *House of Fame* renders the iconography where he describes the mocks who sit beneath the great harpers, Orpheus, Orion, Glascurion and their company:

> ... smale harpers with her gleës
> Sate under hem in dyvers seës,
> And gunne on hem upward to gape,
> And countrefete hem as an ape,
> Or as craft countrefeteth kynde,
>
> (1201-1213)

The true musician, the David, the Orpheus, is in touch with celestial harmonies, the *muscia mundana*. H.W. Janson notes this where a monkey perches atop Orpheus' lyre in mockery and

---

14   Trans. R.F.C. Hull (New York, 1959), pp. 255-272.
15   II. viii. 25.
16   (London, 1935), pp. xvi-xvii.

plays panpipes, and W.C. McDermott has drawn attention to the parody of Orpheus by an ape with a lyre in an Afro-Roman mosaic, these contrasts stressing Orpheus' nobility.[17] The same principle holds with the Sumerian harp and the Burgos fresco. The grotesques ape divine music comically, being too involved with bestiality to hear truly the „hevenyssh melodie" which Troilus is finally to enjoy at his apotheosis, having laid aside lust (V. 1807-1825).

David S. Chamberlain has noted the relationship between Boethius' treatment of music in the *Consolation* and his *De Musica*.[18] In that work Boethius discusses the connection between music and morality in accord with Plato's *Republic* in which music is to be „modesta ac simplex et mascula nec effeminata nec fera nec varia."[19] Boethius then gives an interesting passage, in Doric Greek, concerning the Spartan abhorrence of the music of Timotheus of Milesius who added extra strings to the harp and taught polyphony to the Spartan youth thereby corrupting and softening them. He speaks of Pythagoras and Cicero on the effect of the Phrygian mode upon adolescents. A number of Boethius' statements are concerned with the right guidance of young men. Boethius accounts for the doctrine of the influence of music upon morality (which is Pythagorean) by stating „tota nostrae animae corporisque compago musica coaptione coniuncta sit" (I.i). Earlier he had noted that Plato's world soul was „coniunctam" to music. An excellent discussion of the use of these words in Western literature can be found in Leo Spitzer's *Classical and Christian Ideas of World Harmony*. This ethos still exists in the phrase, „heart strings," which puns in Latin–*cor, chorda*; heart, string.

In Boethius' second chapter music is divided into three parts, the first, *musica mundana*, the second, *musica humana*, the third, *musica instrumentis*. The first, *musica mundana* (Lorenzo's famous speech in *The Merchant of Venice*, V.i. 54-65) is not heard by human ears but is created by the stars in their movements, the *concors discordia* of the warring elements and likewise the harmonious oppositions of the four seasons. The *musica humana* is the harmony between microcosm and macrocosm, body and soul, reason and folly. *Musica instrumentis* is primarily polarized between string and wind instruments: cithara and aulos, which in the Middle Ages become harp and bagpipes.

Later in the *De Musica* Boethius gives the history of the harp. At first it had had four strings, one for each of the elements, which was said to be Mercury's invention and which was the harp Orpheus played. Later the strings were expanded to seven, eight or nine, one for each of the planets and then the spheres so that the harp would accord with the *musica mundana*. The harp of Timotheus of Milesius had eleven strings (I.xx). The concept of the concordance of the chords of the harp with the harmony of the world was punningly seen to relate to the *musica humana* through the heart (*cor*).[20] Chaucer, indeed, translated „animo" as „in thy corage" in the „Asse to the Harpe" passage.

While the *musica instrumentis* is the least noble of the three divisions, being a mere imitation of the *musica mundana*, it in turn ranks its instruments. The harp is noble, wind ins-

---

17 *Apes and Apelore in the Middle Ages and the Renaissance* (London, 1952), p. 108 and Pl. XIIc. *The Ape in Antiquity* (Baltimore, 1938), fig. 489, pp. 288-290. See also Michael Masi, „The Christian Music of Sir Orfeo," *Classical Folia*, 1974 (June), 3-20; Kathi Meyer-Baer, *The Music of the Spheres and the Dance of Death* (Princeton, 1971), pp. 69, 77, 204-8, 222, etc.; John Block Friedman, *Orpheus in the Middle Ages* (Cambridge, Mass., 1970). David in MSS. illuminations is shown with the mocking beasts or with his harp and throne ornamented with bestial forms. See Princeton University Index of Christian Art, David with Harp.

18 „Philosophy of Music in the *Consolatio* of Boethius," *Speculum*, XLV (1970), 80-97. See also Manfred F. Bukofzer „Speculative Thinking in Mediaeval Music," *Speculum*, XVII (1942), 165-180.

19 I use the edition of Godofredus Friedlein (Lipsiae, 1867).

20 Leo Spitzer, *Classical and Christian Ideas of World Harmony: Prolegomena to an Interpretation of the Word „Stimmung,"* ed. Anna Granville Hatcher (Baltimore, 1963), pp. 85-93.

truments are not. The harp represents Reason, wind instruments that Folly which strives to undo the *musica humana*. Two Greek tales underline this concept. Marsyas is flayed because, with his wind instrument, earlier rejected by wise Athena because of the distortions it produced in her face disturbing her *musica humana*, he essays to outdo Apollo's lyre music.[21] And, as the Wife of Bath tells us, King Midas wears ass's ears because in a music contest he voted for Pan's piping over Apollo's harping, for lust over reason, only she twists the tale against herself having the secret that will out entrusted not to the barber but to the wife.[22] Like the Wife who is „somdel deef," so, says Ovid, was Midas dull of ear, „aures stolidas" (174-5) „and that was scathe." We will come to see that this inability to appreciate *musica mundana* is due to defects in ears and hearts, to an imbalance in the *musica humana* towards folly and bestiality. The ass's ears become symbolic of this state. Thus the topos and the iconography of the Ass and the Harp represent a discord in the latter two of the three divisions of *musica mundana, humana* and *instrumentis*.

A further element to the ass's bestiality which counters reason is the Circe story which is recounted in Boethius and which Chaucer translates:

> Than betidith it what, yif thou seest a wyght that be transformed into vices, thow ne mayst nat wene that he be a man. For if he be ardaunt in averyce, and that he be a ravynour by violence of foreyn richesse, thou shalt seyn that he is lik to the wolf; ... and yf he be slow, and astonyd, and lache, he lyveth as an asse; ... and if he be ploungid in fowle and unclene luxuris, he is witholden in the foule delices of the fowle sowe. Than folweth it that he that forleteth bounte and prowesse, he forletith to ben a man; syn he ne may nat passe into the condicion of God, he is torned into a beeste.

(IV. Prosa 3. 101-127)

It is probable that this despised theriomorphosis, encountered not only in Christianity but also in Classic Greece and Rome, is a vestige of earlier cultural totemism, which Lévi-Strauss has taught us to view as but a classificatory system used by most of mankind.[23] It does survive with honor in medieval heraldry and also can be glimpsed in classic and medieval battle similes where heroes fight like lions, tigers, leopards, boars and so forth. It can be glimpsed as well in the mummers' plays and morris dances of England, where some of the dancers wear animal heads (Shakespeare's Bottom is perhaps an aspect of this.)[24] however, the Christian and Classic religions, being anthropomorphic rather than theriomorphic, suppressed this classificatory system to the vices of man, not his virtues. Therefore man's bestiality untunes him. The ass who plays the sacred harp renders it incapable of imitating the *musica mundana* or of restoring the *musica humana* within his hearers. It is *musica instrumentis* at its worse.

Besides the iconography of the *asinus ad liram*, there was also the Aesopic fable of the unmusical musician ass. It, too, finds a place in medieval manuscript illuminations. Professor

---

21   John Hollander, *The Untuning of the Sky* (Princeton, 1961), p. 35. In Sebastian Brant's *The Ship of Fools*, trans. Alexander Barclay (Edinburgh, 1874) are two woodcuts, Vol. I, 256 and Vol. II, 28 in which these themes are crystallized. The Fool chooses the bagpipes over the harp or lute and Marsyas is flayed for choosing the bagpipes over the harp. Both Fool and Marsyas are shown with ass's ears. See also *House of Fame*, III. 1227-1232. Meyer-Baer discusses wind instruments' relation to death and mourning in antiquity accounting for this opprobrium, pp. 219, 289 and passim.

22   *Canterbury Tales*, III. 951-982.

23   *Le Totemisme Aujourd-hui* (Paris, 1962). The principles which Lévi-Strauss discusses in *Mythologiques*, binary distinctions and „zoèmes," are at work in the development of the *asinus ad liram* theme. See *L'Homme Nu* (Paris, 1971), pp. 481-558 and pp. 68-74. Also Victor Turner, *The Ritual Process: Structure and Anti-Structure* (Chicago, 1969), pp. 172-7 & 185-8.

24   Beryl Rowland, *Blind Beasts: Chaucer's Animal World* (Kent, 1971), p. 10.

Robertson notes the marginal use of the unmusical ass whose music offends a lionlike grotesque who is trying in vain to stop up his ears. The illuminations, to which this is but part of the marginalia, concern the rejection of Thamar, where the love-lorn Amnon has followed his pandar's advice (Jonadab) and feigned sickness, asking that Thamar be sent to his bedside. He then throws Thamar upon the bed, dishonors her, and sends her away. The ass and lion provide a mocking yet judgmental commentary upon the text. The action of the *Troilus and Criseyde* echoes this tale in Books II through IV but with the sexes reversed after the first episode.[25]

Juan Ruiz in the *Libro de Buen Amor* retells the fable of the unmusical musician ass and the lion as an analogy to his poem:[26]

> Dueñas, abrid orejas, oíd buena lición,
> entended bien las fablas: guadadvos del varón;
> guardad non vos acaya como con el león
> · al asno sin orejas e sin su coraçón.

Ladies, open your ears, listen to a good lesson, pay careful attention to fables ... be careful that it does not happen to you as with the lion to the ass without ears and without heart.

> El león fue doliente, dolíale la tiesta.
> Quando fue sano d'ella, que la traía enfiesta,
> todos las animalias, un domingo en la siesta,
> venieron ante él todos a fazer buena fiesta.
>
> Estava y el burro, fezieron d'él juglar;
> como estava bien gordo començó a retoçar,
> su atambor tañiendo muy alto a rebuznar:
> al león e a los otros queríalos atronar.
>
> Con las sus caçurrías el león fue sañudo;
> quiso abrirle todo e alcançar non le pudo;
> su atambor tañiendo fuése, más y non estudo.
> Sentiós' por escarnido el león del orejudo.

(892-895)

At the festival held at the recovery of the sick lion the ass has thought himself a fine minstrel, beating his drum (traditionally covered with ass's skin), braying very loudly, and in so doing has enraged the still headachy lion. He flees in fear.

> El león dixo luego que merced le faría;
> mandó que le llamassen, que la fiesta onraría;
> quanto él demandasse tanto le otorgaría;
> la gulhara juglara dixo que l'llamaría.
>
> Fuése la raposilla ado el asno andava
> paciendo en un prado; tan bien lo saludava:
> „Señor," dixo, „confadre, vuestro solaz onrava
> a todos, a agora non valen una hava.
>
> Más valía vuestra albuérbula e vuestro buen solaz,
> vuestro atambor sonante, los sonetes que faz'.
> que todo nuestra fiesta; al león mucho plaz'
> que tornedes al juego en salvo e en paz."

25 *A Preface to Chaucer* (Princeton, 1963), p. 223 and figs. 93-5 from British Museum Egerton MS 3277, fols. 142. 61, 62 verso, 63 verso.
26 Ed. and trans. Raymond S. Willis (Princeton, 1972), pp. 238-241.

Creyó falsos falagos, él escapó peor;
tornóse a la fiesta bailando el cantador;
non sabía la manera el burro del señor:
escota el juglar necio el son del atambor.
  Como el león tenía sus monteros armados,
prendieronlo a don Burro como eran castigados;
al león lo troxieron, abriól' por los costados:
de la su segurança son todos espantados.
                                                    (896-900)

The lion sends off the minstrel vixen to entice the ass back, granting him pardon. The vixen informs the ass that the lion so loved the donkey's cries of jubilation, his drumming, his sweet tunes, that he must return and the show go on. The stupid minstrel does so and is flayed by the lion. (This flaying of the unmusical ass is a variant of that other musical contest, the flaying of Marsyas who, in a woodcut in Sebastian Brant's *Ship of Fools* is shown as the bagpipes player of lust, as is Chaucer's Miller, and with ass's ears, while Apollo plays the lyre of reason.) Later the wolf gobbles up the ass's heart and ears. He tells the lion that the ass was born that way, which suggests the Pythagorean teaching of the ass not being created according (if you will forgive the pun) to the harmony of the *musica humana*, otherwise he could not have fallen for the trickery.

Juan Ruiz concludes as he began:

Assí, señoras dueñas, entended bien el romance:
guar dadvos de amor loco, non vos prenda nin alcance;
abrid vuestras orejas; el coraçón se lance
en amor de Dios limpio, loco amor non le trance.
                                                    (904)

His poem is like the vixen-minstrel's enticement to return to the lion's fiesta wherein great danger lies. Do not be taken in by it. Keep your ears and heart open to the love of God, not to lustful folly (*amor loco*). The beast fable in the *Libro de Buen Amor* functions as Beryl Rowland observes of beast fables in medieval literature generally: „The absurdity of the idea of animals behaving like humans never minimizes the seriousness of the assertion that is being made: in the animal man may see his own characteristics and he can learn."[27] A negative didacticism is at work. Maria Rosa Lida de Malkiel defines the genre of the *Libro* as the *maqāmāt* in which the persona practices the vice the author preaches against, Chaucer's Pardoner's Tale being an example of this literary type. Juan Ruiz, the Archpriest of Hita, counsels against *loco amor*, yet his persona, Don Melón de la Huerta, avidly practices it.[28] However the Archpriest says he uses these escapades of Don Melón „por dar ejemplo, non porque a mí avino."[29] The Archpriest writes ass-like, trickster-savior poetry in order to preach against bestial lust, while appearing to practice it with rather disastrous results: his mistress dies of the poisonous aphrodisiacs his pandaress gives her, he sleeps with revolting mountain girls, his lion/archbishop jails him. The autobiography is fictional yet functions with the paradoxical didacticism we see as a pattern with the topos of the ass as dull and bestial yet teaching, by these binary distinctions, wisdom.

27 *Blind Beasts*, p. 10.
28 María Rosa Lida de Malkiel, „Two Spanish Masterpieces: *The Book of Good Love* and *The Celestina*," *Illinois Studies in Language and Literature*, XLIX (Urbana, 1961), 21-27. Willis and others dislike the term as its Hispano-Hebrew originals were pious and solemn.
29 Willis, p. xlvi.

The figure of the ass is a constant theme in connection with education in Western litera-ture. Nigel Wireker's *Speculum Stultorum*, or, as Chaucer titled it, „Daun Burnel the Asse,“ states that the happy man is he who learns caution from another's folly, being governed by reason: „Est igitur felix aliena pericula cautam / Quem faciunt, formant et ratione regi.“[30] The *Speculum* achieves this in the reader by presenting to him a mock paideia, where an ass learns nothing for all his quest for wisdom. Of its title, the *Speculum Stultorum*, it is said: „It has been given this name in order that foolish men may observe as in a mirror the foolishness of others and may then correct their own folly, and that they may learn to censure in themselves those things which they find reprehensible in others.“ In this vein too we see classic gems carved with the ass as pompous teacher lording it over schoolboys[31] while in later children's literature Pinnocchio will learn wisdom from his folly, being transformed into a donkey and poor Eeyore, like Daun Burnel, suffers the loss of his tail and struggles in vain to become literate. Sebastian Brant's *Ship of Fools* woodcuts show the fools with caps with ass's ears and of them Barclay the translator says: „Asses erys for our folys a lyuray is.“[32] He also, in his introduction to the reader, pleads:

> But ye that shal rede this boke: I you exhorte.
> And you that ar herars therof also I pray
> Where as ye knowe that ye be of this sorte:
> Amende your lyfe and expelle that vyce away.
> Slomber nat in syn. Amende you whyle ye may.
> And yf ye so do and ensue Vertue and grace.
> Within my Ship ye get no rowme ne place.

Brant's *Ship of Fools* is a sermon preached by Wisdom. Erasmus will have his *Encomium Moriae* preached by her opposite number, Stultitia.[33]

The context in which Pandarus uses the Boethian topos in *Troilus and Criseyde* (where it undergoes a transformation from the manner in which Boethius used it; there, by Philosophia advocating Reason, here, by Pandarus advocating its reverse, Lust, much like Erasmus' varia-tion upon Brant) is interesting when seen juxtaposed with the Sumerian harp, the Gothic grotesques, the *Consolation of Philosophy*, the *Golden Ass*, the *Speculum Stultorum*, the *Ship of Fools* and the *Libro del Buen Amor*. Each has a consonance with all the others. The *asinus ad liram* is, in Jung's words, a cultural „shadow,“ a trickster-figure threatening the culture it mocks, profanizing its sanctity, yet for psychic wholeness demanding a voice, thereby becoming its trickster-savior.[34] The discord of the *asinus ad liram* mocks celestial harmony, but that mockery, paradoxically, defines the harmony that would otherwise go unperceived. Perhaps for this reason the Middle Ages cultivated polyphony, creating motets where vernacu-lar profane verses mocked the sacred Latin against Boethius' strictures,[35] and illuminated

---

30 Ll. 3893-4.
31 Princeton University Index of Christian Art. From Cabrol, F. Dict., I[2] (1907), fig. 586.
32 I.181.
33 Walter Kaiser, *Praisers of Folly* (Harvard, 1963), p. 35. William Empson's arguments concerning double plot (*Some Versions of Pastoral*) are applicable here as well as Victor Turner's perception that „The structure of the whole depends on its negative as well as its positive signs,“ p. 201.
34 Pp. 255-272. Till Eulenspiegel (Mirror of Wisdom) is an example. He mocks the learned University by teaching an ass to seem to read.
35 The word, „polyphony,“ occurred in Boethius' account of Timotheus of Milesius. It is of interest that Jan Van Eyck was to paint a portrait of a leading composer of his day giving the portrait the inscription „Timotheus.“ Erwin Panofsky, *Early Netherlandish Painting*, Vol. I, 196-7 and Vol. II, fig. 261, conjec-tures that the portrait is either of Guillaume Dufay or, more probably, of Gilles Binchois.

manuscripts with sacred scenes mocked by *similia Dei*.[36]

Troilus, the Petrarchan lover, is fallen into wanhope. The topos is used to convey this. Curtius when noting the topos of the lute-playing ass in the *Carmina Burana* related it to the *adynata*, the topos of the „World Upsidedown" which Arnaut Daniel made use of to express the havoc wrought in the poet's mind by false love, „amor loco."[37] Thus the topos, by its absurd contraries, expresses the discord wrought in the lover's *musica humana*. Topology is here harnessed to psychology and is used to express a state of madness. Asses belong to the sphere of bagpipes not of harps. „The Ass and the Lyre" is an oxymoron, a zeugma, a paradoxically yoked opposition. It is absurd.

Although Pandarus plies all his sophistic art to heal Troilus' malady (but with the opposite intent than Philosophia) his labor in the long run will be in vain. He is the false physician, while she is the true. Troilus will rebuke him: „ ... thi proverbes may me naught availle. ... Lat be thyne olde ensaumples, [and it is nearly four thousand years old we recall] I the preye' " (I.756-760). But though he insists, „I am nat deef" (753), he is withdrawn from Pandarus, in a „litargie." Philosophia observes Boethius persona to be in a similar state in I, Prosa 2, Boethius being also speechless and unresponsive:

> „he is fallen into a litargie, which that is a commune seknesse to hertes that been desceyved. He hath a litil foryeten hymselve, but certes he schal lightly remembren humself, yif so be that he hath knowen me or now; and that he may so doon, I wil wipe a litil his eien that ben dirked by the cloude of mortel thynges."

In forgetting the precepts of Philosophia, he has fallen into wanhope, „bestialite" and the „cloude of mortel thynges" which corresponds to Lorenzo's „muddy vesture of decay" which „doth grossly" stop up the harmony of immortal music. Troilus, similarly, is unheeding of the harp echoing the music of the spheres and, similarly, is beyond the consolation of philosophy. In short, he is an ass who cannot comprehend harmony. Yet Troilus will–again like Boethius– rise above this „cloude of mortel thynges" and this „muddy vesture of decay." Chaucer is using the Boethian text to adumbrate his characterization of Troilus. What was a comic „ensaumple" at least as old as Ur is in Chaucer's retractatio of Boethius a sophisticated concept endowed with Pythagorean philosophic qualities demonstrating the opposition between Reason and Folly. Thomas Usk in his Boethian *Testament of Love* noted that Chaucer's *Troilus and Criseyde* was a „philosophical" poem and he is correct.[38] However, Chaucer's method is to deliberately pervert Philosophia, then rectify her, in the course of the poem.

Chaucer's use of the topos comments upon a Troilus who hears but does not heed the harp of philosophy. He jangles her harmony. Lillian M.C. Randall mentions one illumination where the ass tramples the harp, exemplifying, she says, the „mere hearer of the Word."[39] That is precisely what Troilus will do to Philosophia's discussion of destiny and free will. (And

---

See *Polyphonies du XIIᵉ siècle, Le Manuscrit H196 de la Faculté de Médecine de Montpellier*, ed. Yvonne Rokseth (Paris, 1936), II, 83-114; and Bukofzer, pp. 173-177.

36 See Janson, and McDermott on fig. 489, pp. 288-290 where the ape apes Orpheus, the ass Christ. Shakespeare plays a similar game where he has Bottom the ass and the rude mechanicals ape the harmony of his *Midsummer Night's Dream*.

37 *European Literature and the Latin Middle Ages*, trans. Willard R. Trask (New York, 1953), p. 95. See *Ancient Misericords in the Priory Church, Great Malvern* (Worcester, n.d.), p. 6.

38 *Chaucerian and Other Pieces*, ed. Walter W. Skeat (Oxford, 1897), p. xxii.

39 „Exempla as a Source of Gothic Marginal Illuminations," *Art Bulletin*, XXXIX (1957), 104. In a similar vein Mâle, *The Gothic Image*, p. 44 and fig. 18, discusses Honorius on the adder: „The adder is the image of the sinner who closes his ears to the words of life" (which relates that image to the „somdel deef" Wife of Bath). The adder shown is similar to the Wyvern and the serpent man of the Burgos fresco and the Sumerian harp, having legs and wings as well as a tail.

so also does Chaucer in robbing Boethius' II, Metrum 8 and perverting it to the celebration of adulterous lust in Book III, 1744-1771, where its original version celebrated *musica mundana* as the harmony of love exemplified by „peples joyned with an holy boond, and knytteth sacrement of mariages of chaste loves.") Troilus wrenches the Boethian text out of harmony just as surely as does the deaf Wife of Bath (associated with Midas' ass's ears) wrench scripture out of context. Yet critics are at odds concerning Troilus and Chaucer's use of Boethius. Some take Troilus' railings on destiny and free will as being Chaucer's own. Others disagree. Discord prevails.[40]

Chaucer twists the matter further. Not only does Troilus not comprehend Pandarus' consolation, being like an ass to the harp, but Pandarus is himself like the iconographical ass playing the harp mocking the celestial music with the bestial, for he has wrenched Boethius' *Consolation of Philosophy* to the uses of lust, not reason, and thus mocks the author of the major music text of the medieval universities by his discord. Pandarus is a grotesque. As lust's preceptor, he is like that ass carved on a gem shown as schoolmaster lording it over boys. This mockery, however, defines the true by its opposition to it. Chaucer has Pandarus cite this principle in the *Troilus and Criseyde* giving the game away: „By his contrairie is every thyng declared" (I.637). This is the principle that underlies the David Psalter illuminations and the Sumerian harp where the mockery comments upon the true while self-consciously appearing within that which it mocks. The commentary of folly is comically didactic.

For a moment recall the Corpus Christi College Cambridge manuscript frontispiece in which Chaucer is seen reading the *Troilus and Criseyde* to Richard II and his court. Recall also the commonplace, which grew out of the concept of the *musica mundana*, of the state as a lute as in Ulysses' famed speech.[41] Consider Chaucer's relationship towards Richard II as that of a Pandarus towards a Troilus. Yet recall also that Chaucer in that illumination is shown as a soberly clad preacher speaking from a pulpit to a gaily bedecked and worldly court. Richard stands in cloth of gold attentively listening. The other figures pay little heed. The poem purports to be a romance, yet, as Thomas Usk pointed out, is „philosophical" in Boethius' manner. Chaucer's game is to seem a Pandarus but not to be such, to seduce his worldly hearers from lust by means of lust's discords. To lead his hearers, especially his king, to the harmony of the *musica mundana* could be crucial to a realm that may well reflect the problems of that Troy from which Richard proudly traces his ancestry. Chaucer may be seeking to tune his kingly *asinus ad liram* to celestial harmonies. He does so through poetry (against which Philosophia railed) and thereby, paradoxically, seduces his hearer to virtue.

An *asinus ad liram* reading of the poem could lead to false conclusions. Troilus and Pandarus and Boethius persona at this point are *asini ad liram*–though Philosophia is not–and are not to be confused with the viewpoint of their authors. This is a common quality of medieval poetry: the poets' personae are presented in a stance of folly, obviously lacking the knowledge and wisdom of their authors. The Jesse tree of such personae, whose progenitor is most likely Boethius, include de Meun, Dante, Juan Ruiz, Chaucer, Erasmus, and More. Their statements are not to be taken at face value but examined critically within the poems' contexts. Physically they may resemble their authors, mentally they do not.[42] Medieval poetry of this type con-

---

40   For an account of the debate on *Troilus and Cryseyde* by Chaucerians see the essay by John P. McCall in *Companion to Chaucer Studies*, ed. Beryl Rowland (Toronto, 1968), pp. 370-384.

41   *Troilus and Cressida*, I. iii. 83-124.

42   On the use of the persona see Leo Spitzer, „Note on the Poetic and the Empirical ‚I' in Medieval Authors," *Traditio*, IV (1946), 414-422. The stance of the author is best exemplified in the Boethius manuscript illuminations garnered by Pierre Courcelle in *La Consolation de Philosophie dans la tradition littéraire* (Paris, 1967). In these and in the illuminations to the *Roman de la Rose* and the *Commedia*,

cerns itself with the reform of the reader, from folly to wisdom, the persona providing a useful scapegoat (a trickster-savior) by means of his naiveté at which the reader can laugh but having done so cannot return himself to that behavior with impunity. Frequently the form is that of the *maqāmāt* in which the persona practices vices the reader and the author know to be wrong, the poem thereby becoming a *speculum stultorum*, and consequently, though paradoxically, of wisdom. Mirrors reverse images.

While Troilus is not Chaucer's persona (though critics confuse his mental debates with Chaucer's own), Pandarus in Chaucer's *Troilus and Criseyde* reverses the relationship of Boethius and Philosophia and is the author's mock persona. Troilus is a member of Richard II's Jesse tree. Chaucer/Pandarus would counsel him. In this Chaucer has altered Boccaccio's poem in which Troilo was the author's persona. In this manner he can adapt the matter to the court of England. But it is necessary for him to do so in the twisted court jester role of Pandarus, rather than of straight Philosophia, or of the youthful Troilus if he is to be heard.

While Troilus, through lust, is temporarily an *asinus ad liram*, Pandarus is a variation on the theme. He appears to ape Philosophia, to play her lyre. But he wrenches her harmonies from the true. In this perhaps he echoes Amis in the *Roman de la Rose* who is introduced following Reason and who there openly tears down her arguments. Chaucer's development conflates Amis with Reason, by having Pandarus „countrefete" Philosophia. Thus Pandarus becomes a „Faus-Semblant" Philosophia, masquerading as that which he is not.[43]

That recalls yet another Aesopic fable concerning the ass who, dressed in a lion's skin, fools fools but not wise men. C.S. Lewis made use of this fable in the *Chronicles of Narnia*. In *The Last Battle* the Apocalypse is wrought through the Ape having the Ass dress as the Lion who is Christ/Aslan. In this instance, C.S. Lewis is using a further variant of the ass theme in medieval thought which is, despite its classic associations with Priapus, its Christ-likeness. The humble ass had conveyed Mary and the Child to Egypt, had borne Christ to Jerusalem, bears on its back the mark of a cross.[44] Kantorowicz cites the messianic prophecies of Isaiah (62:10) and Zachariah (9:9) calling for the use of an ass in the Palm Sunday procession and then its return to its owner. John Crysostom in a sermon analogized this to the Incarnation: *caro remissa est, ratio autem retenta est,*[45] in which context the ass is again flesh versus spirit. Jung discussed the Beauvais celebrations of the *festum asinorum* which, though they began probably as a celebration of Mary's flight into Egypt, degenerated into the mockingly pagan Festival of Fools with theriomorphic elements, the priest and the congregation braying their responses

---

writer and dreamer physically resemble each other but do not occupy the same space. A further aspect is the relationship of the poet to his realm which is similar to that of a prophet. See for example the city Bible illuminations of Jeremiah preaching to Jerusalem showing Jerusalem as their own city which iconographically recurs in the Duomo fresco of Dante reading the *Commedia* to Florence.

43   D.W. Robertson, Jr., *Chaucer's London* (New York, 1968), p. 3, notes Richard of Maidstone's contemporary identification of London as New Troy, the Black Prince of Hector, Richard II, rather unflatteringly, as Troilus.

44   Beryl Rowland, *Animals with Human Faces: A Guide to Animal Symbolism* (Knoxville, 1973), p. 20.

45   Ernest H. Kantorowicz, *The King's Two Bodies: A Study of Mediaeval Political Theology* (Princeton, 1957), p. 85. G.K. Chesterton celebrates the absurd Christ-bearing ass in poetry. Medieval Palm Sunday processions sometimes included wooden figures of Christ astride the ass. The Cloisters Collection and the Detroit Art Museum both possess examples.

at the consecrated altar, foreshadowing Nietzsche's *Thus Spake Zarathustra* in which the disciples, though God is dead, worship God as the Ass. Jung mentions as well the famous mocking crucified ass scratched on a wall in the Palatine.[46]

Pandarus is Chaucer's persona, necessarily incarnated within the text, to set the lustful action afoot. In Boccaccio's text Pandarus is Boccaccio's age; in Chaucer's he is altered to conform with Chaucer's own and so is his physical appearance. He mirrors Chaucer. But he is a mockery of Chaucer, the reverse of Chaucer's intent in writing this poem. Chaucer pretends to be Pandarus, the fleshly and discordant *asinus ad liram*, but concludes with the *musica mundana*, with Pythagorean harmonies: *caro remissa est, ratio autem retenta est*, lust laid aside. The poem thus seduces and pandars the reader, through folly, from folly; Pandarus, thereby, is a trickster-savior. Chaucer in *Troilus and Criseyde* is both Pandarus and Philosophia, both ass and David harping. ,,By his contrairie is every thyng declared,'' he states. The poem has functioned to delineate lust, then its consequence, to involve the reader vicariously in that profane act, then teach its folly. The Boethian proverb, like the iconography of the grotesque upon cathedral and harp and manuscript, functions as a mockingly didactic commentary upon the poem and audience yet is in polyphonic harmony with it. Will Chaucer's reader be an *asinus ad liram* as was Troilus once, or will he come to comprehend Chaucer's deliberate twisting of the Boethian text and its ancient proverb, its ,,olde ensaumple,'' and laugh as Troilus did?

> His lighte goost ful blisfully is went
> Up to the holughnesse of the eighthe spere,
> In convers letyng everich element;
> And ther he saugh, with ful avysement,
> The erratik sterres, herkenyng armonye
> With sownes ful of hevenyssh melodie.
>
> And down from thennes faste he gan avyse
> This litel spot of erthe, that with the se
> Embraced is, and fully gan despise
> This wrecched world, and held al vanite
> To respect of the pleyn felicite
> That is in hevene above, and at the laste,
> Ther he was slayn, his lokyng down he caste.
>
> And in hymself he lough right at the wo
> Of hem that wepten for his deth so faste;
> And dampned al oure werk that foloweth so
> The blynde lust, the which that may nat laste,
> And sholden al oure herte on heven caste.
>   (1808-1825)

Princeton University

---

46   P. 259. See also Félix Clément, ,,L'âne au moyen âge,'' *Annales archéologiques*, XVI (1856), 30-33. The harp, as well as the ass, could allegorize Christ, this being seen by pseudo-Hugh of St. Victor as the cause of David's healing of Saul's madness, *Allegoriae in Vetus Testamentum*, VI. *PL*, 175, 692A. Even this could be mocked. Hieronymus Bosch shows music in hell with, among other figures and instruments, a harp growing out of a lute, figures crucified to both instruments. The music made is obviously discordant and one figure stops up his ears in agony.

The University Museum
Philadelphia

Ur 2600 B.C.
Shell plaque from lyre

Fresco: Wyvern with border
Chapter House of Monastery of San Pedro de Arlanza, Burgos, Spain
XIII century (about 1220 A.D.)
The Metropolitan Museum of Art
The Cloisters Collection, purchase, 1931

MENSO FOLKERTS

THE IMPORTANCE OF THE PSEUDO-BOETHIAN *GEOMETRIA* DURING THE MIDDLE AGES

Compared to the other writings of Boethius on the *Trivium* and *Quadrivium*, his *Geometria* takes a special place. We do not have this work in its original form, but only in two later adaptations: both contain only part of the original but on the other hand they are enlarged through a variety of insertions. Therefore any study of the importance of Boethius' *Geometria* in the Middle Ages should not only try to show the influence of geometrical writings which were transmitted under the name of Boethius, but also should try to understand the origin of such compilations. From these two demands, then, arises the organization of my essay: the first section will be concerned with the scanty evidence known about the authentic *Geometria* as well as with the contents and origins of both extant compilations. In the second part of my essay I will attempt to show the dissemination and impact of both writings during the Middle Ages. For this purpose I will make use of entries of the *Geometria* in medieval library catalogues and of allusions to it in other medieval writings. A broader understanding of the importance of these two writings and of their comprehension in this period can be gained from an analysis of the scholia to one of these compilations which have been neglected up to now. Such a study should make it possible to indicate the value of these treatises in comparison with the other two, authentic, works of the Boethian *quadrivium*–the *Arithmetica* and *Musica*.

I. The authentic Geometria and the origins of the first two basic texts.

1.1 The original translation; earlier fragments of uncertain origin.

Cassiodorus testifies in two places that Boethius had written a geometrical work. In a letter from Theodoric to Boethius, he says that through Boethius' translation, Euclid's work on geometry is now known in the Latin language.[1] Cassiodorus makes a similar reference to Boethius in the *Institutiones*.[2] Therefore there is no doubt that Boethius made a Latin translation of Euclid. To be sure, these testimonies give no information as to whether Boethius translated all of the 13 or 15 books of the *Elements* or only parts of it. But beyond doubt parts of the first five books belonged to that translation as surviving excerpts show (see ahead 1.2 and 1.3). Because of Boethius' approximate date of birth (c. 480) and the date of Cassiodorus' testimony, this translation must have been made in about the year 500. With this, our knowledge concerning the original is exhausted. This original must not have been in use very much after Boethius' time because existing manuscripts and the allusions of other authors are based on the two later compilations of the Boethius *Geometria*, but do not refer to the original work.

---

[1] Cassiodorus, *Variae* I, 45.4: *Translationibus enim tuis Pythagoras inusicus, Ptolemaeus astronomus leguntur Itali. Nicomachus arithmeticus, geometricus Euclides audiuntur Ausonii.*
[2] II, 6.3: *...ex quibus Euclidem translatum Romanae linguae idem vir magnificus Boethius edidit.*

There has been much discussion on the issue of whether two anonymous Latin Euclid fragments from the 5th and 9th centuries respectively have transmitted parts of the original Boethian translation or at least some material originating from the circle around Boethius. The older of these two texts is the famous geometry fragment now extant in the Biblioteca Capitolare of Verona, Ms. XL (38). This manuscript is a palimpsest in which the former text was replaced, in the beginning of the 8th century, by the *Moralia* of Gregory the Great. The original text, now removed, contained portions of Vergil and Livy along with a Latin translation of Euclid from which three double folios are yet decipherable.[3] The extant text contains sections of Euclid's *Elements*: parts of the propositions XI, 24-25; XII, 2-3.8; XIII, 2-3.7, though in the manuscript the books XII and XIII are marked as XIIII and XV. According to M. Geymonat who edited these texts,[4] the writing can be dated to the last years of the 5th century, that is, it is almost contemporary with the original Boethian translation. This fact more than anything else prompted M. Geymonat to conjecture that here we have part of that original translation. This attribution, however, appears to me somewhat risky because the existing manuscript contains only a few fragments--too small to draw solid, safe conclusions about the author. To attribute this translation to Boethius would mean that he prepared it before his 20th birthday.[5]

The second of these two fragments was written at the beginning of the 9th century in a north-east French scriptorium and is now found in the University Library at Munich (Univ. 2⁰ 757). Only two pages are extant, which concern Euclid's propositions I, 37 to 38 and II, 8 to 9. This fragmentary text has been edited by M. Geymonat, as well, based on earlier attempts of M. Curtze and A.A. Björnbo.[6] This text reveals that the translator obviously did not have control of the mathematical contents nor did he master the Latin grammar. Without understanding, the technical mathematical terms are entirely translitterated as Greek expressions having similar letters.[7] Greek letters attached to figures or used to denote the endpoints of segments are taken as number symbols and are accordingly transferred.[8] Already this astounding ignorance forbids us to attribute the text to Boethius. Such a conclusion receives further support from the fact that the only portions which are contained in the Munich fragments as well as in the texts Mc and Md (the last originating without doubt from Boethius),[9] in the Munich text deviate sharply from Mc and Md. Nevertheless Geymonat considers the Munich fragment to be connected with the Boethius translation. He is of the opinion that it goes back to a text of the end of the 5th century which was used as a basis for the true translation. This text was done by a scholar not well versed in the Greek language who came from the circle around Boethius. Perhaps this text descends from an original interlinear translation of a Greek Euclid manuscript.[10] Geymonat's theory is an interesting conjecture on the classification of this Euclid fragment. However, his opinion leaves us with no sure proof. In any case, at the very most the Munich fragment is of interest because of its possible connection with the authentic geometry, but not because of its actual influence in the Middle Ages.

---

3   ff. 331/326, 341/338, 336/343.
4   *Euclidis Latine facti fragmenta Veronensia* (Milano, 1964).
5   In this case, the Verona manuscript would be the autograph or a very early copy of it, if the date (end of the 5th century) is exact.
6   „Nuovi frammenti della geometria ‚boeziana' in un codice del IX secolo?" *Scriptorium*, 21 (1967), 3-16.
7   For example ἥμισυ = *nos quidem sic* (ἡμεῖς), γνώμων = *scito*.
8   For example ΔEZ = *quarto quinto et septimo*.
9   For Mc and Md, see the sections 1.2 and 1.3. In the Munich text there are the enunciations to I, 38 and II, 9 which also exist in Mc/Md.
10 Geymonat (note 6), pp. 7-9.

1.2 The Boethian Geometry in the 8th and 9th century. The origin of Geometria I (in 5 books).

Sure traces of the geometrical work of Boethius can first be found in the 8th and 9th centuries. From this time there are to be discovered excerpts from Euclid in three distinct writings. Parts of these conform with each other and almost certainly go back to Boethius' translation. As B.L. Ullmann has demonstrated convincingly,[11] the fate of Boethius' treatise was closely bound to Corbie, „the gromatic and geometric capital of the medieval world."[12] In the 9th century these three texts were present in that Cloister; in part they were assembled at Corbie in the form in which they came down to us. We are speaking of manuscripts of the *Corpus Agrimensorum* (Mb),[13] a version (the so-called „third" recension) of Cassiodorus' *Institutiones* (Ma)[13] and the Geometria I (*Ars Geometriae*) which has been attributed to Boethius in the manuscripts (Mc).[13]

Roman treatises that dealt with land measurements had, at an early date, already been put into a corpus. In this *Corpus Agrimensorum*, the archetype of which has been dated about 450,[14] geometrical works had a prominent part.[15] Not before the year 550, and probably much later, the gromatic texts in the *Corpus Agrimensorum* were rearranged to serve as geometrical material for the *quadrivium*.[16] This very probably happened at Corbie.[17] From this new recension of the *Corpus Agrimensorum*, two old manuscripts still exist: P (Vat. Palat. Lat. 1564) and G (Codex Guelf. 105 Gud.); both originate from the 9th century. P was probably written in France, very likely at Corbie;[18] G stems from the St. Bertin Cloister in neighboring St. Omer. Both P and G contain, among other things, fragments from Book I of Euclid[19] which, because of their similarity with the Ma and Mc text, may be said to go back to Boethius' translation of Euclid.

Euclidian excerpts from that same Boethian translation were also taken over into the text of the third recension of Cassiodorus' *Institutiones* (Ma) presumably also at Corbie.[20] This recension probably originated in the 8th century–in any case, certainly before Hrabanus Maurus.[21] In Ma, the definitions of Book I and V are present, but the enunciations are missing.[22]

Excerpts from the Boethian Euclid translation form an essential part of a treatise put

11 B.L. Ullman, „Geometry in the Mediaeval Quadrivium," *Studi di bibliografia e di storia in onore di Tammaro de Marinis*, 4 (Verona, 1964), 263-285.

12 Ullman, p. 283.

13 The *sigla* Ma, Mb and Mc for the Euclidian excerpts in this group go back to Bubnov. See N. Bubnov, *Gerberti Opera Mathematica* (Berlin, 1899).

14 G. Thulin, „Die Handschriften des *Corpus Agrimensorum Romanorum,"* *Abhandlungen der Königlichen Preussischen Akademie der Wissenschaften*, Phil.-Hist. Classe (Berlin, 1911).

15 For example, Balbus, *Expositio et ratio omnium formarum*.

16 Ullman, p. 266.

17 Ullman, pp. 273-276.

18 Ullman, p. 274. In contrast to him, Professor B. Bischoff places P in the same scriptorium with the somewhat later agrimensorial manuscript N, Naples VA 13.

19 I def. 1-12.14.13.15-23, post. 1-5, ax. 1.3.2.7, prop. 1-3 with proof. The Mb excerpts are edited by M. Folkerts, „*Boethius*" *Geometria II, ein mathematisches Lehrbuch des Mittelalters* (Wiesbaden, 1970), pp. 173-217.

20 From the Ma manuscripts, Augiensis 106 indicates an origin from northeastern France; Paris, BN Lat. 12963 and 13048 also stem from Corbie. See *Cassiodori Senatoris institutiones*, edited from the manuscripts by R.A.B. Mynors (Oxford, 1937; 1961), introduction, pp. 32-33.

21 Mynors, introduction, p. 39.

22 Extant are: I def. 1-12.14.13.15-23, post. 1-5, ax. 1.3.2.7; II def. 2; V def. 1-8.11.9.10.13.12.14-16.18. 17. The text edited by Mynors was also made use of in the Folkerts edition, pp. 173-217.

together from various sources, presumably in the 8th century, also from Corbie: the so-called Geometria I, consisting of five books. This work, whose Euclidian parts will henceforth be designated as Mc, is, in the manuscripts, overwhelmingly accredited to Boethius and generally carries the title *Ars Geometriae et Arithmeticae*. The task of explaining the origins of Geometria I was essentially completed in the works of N. Bubnov,[23] C. Thulin,[24] and B.L. Ullman;[25] their results have been summarized by Menso Folkerts.[26]

Geometria I incorporates much material from the *Corpus Agrimensorum*; it was not, however, intended for use as a textbook for the student of land surveying, but rather as a mathematical schoolbook in the study of geometry and arithmetic within the *quadrivium*. This work is made up of three writings: arithmetic, gromatic, and geometric. The geometrical part consists of excerpts from Euclid's *Elements*, I-IV (without proofs); it is relatively intact.[27] This geometrical part includes books three and four in the Geometria I, but parts that originally belonged to Book IV ended up in a section marked Book V, and this because of page misplacement. These excerpts, which go back to Boethius' translation, make up the essential value of the collection. The portion on arithmetic takes up the greatest part of book two. It is arbitrarily composed of various portions of Boethius' arithmetic. The gromatic excerpts constitute Book I and part of Book V while the dialogue at the beginning of Book II also depends to some extent on the *Corpus Agrimensorum*. A second longer dialogue is found under the title *Altercatio Duorum Geometricorum de Figuris, Numeris et Mensuris* in the fifth book of Geometria I. Only recently has it been learned that this section does not go back to the original compilor of the collection but is based, instead, on Augustine's *De Quantitate Animae* and his *Soliloquia*.[28]

The Geometria I is a relatively bungling piece of work in which practically every sentence is adapted from some other known work. The compilor's main sources were: Boethius' Euclid translation, from which at least excerpts of Book I-IV were known in the 8th century; Boethius, *De Arithmetica*; a gromatic manuscript of the second class (P, G); some writings of St. Augustine. The compilor also used Isidore's *Etymologies*, Cassiodorus' *Institutiones* and Columella's work on farming.[29] One notes clearly that the compilor did not understand much of what he excerpted, and parts of the text are hopelessly corrupt. One wonders therefore all the more that the Geometria I was considered one of the most famous geometrical works in the Middle Ages up to the dissemination of the Arabic translations, to be compared only with the *Geometria* of Gerbert and its anonymous continuations, with the so-called Geometria II of the Pseudo-Boethius, and with some writings from the *Corpus Agrimensorum*.[30]

23   Bubnov, pp. 161-196.
24   C. Thulin, „Zur Überlieferungsgeschichte des Corpus Agrimensorum. Exzerptenhandschriften und Kompendien," *Göteborgs Kungl. Vetenskaps och Vitterhets-Samhälles Handlingar*, fjärde följden, XIV.1 (Göteborg, 1911).
25   See note 11.
26   M. Folkerts, „Die Altercatio in der Geometrie I des Pseudo-Boethius. Ein Beitrag zur Geometrie im mittelalterlichen Quadrivium," to appear in a volume on medieval „Fachprosa" (Berlin, 1980).
27   Extant are: I def. 1-12.14.13.15-23, post. 1-5, ax. 1.3.2.7; II def. 1.2, prop. 1; III def. 1-6.8-11; IV def. 1.2, prop. 1; III def. 6.8; I prop. 2-4. 6-8. (9). 10-18.21.23.26-28. 31-37.39-41.43.42.44-48; II prop. 1.3-6.9-12.14; III prop. 3.7 beginning. 22 end. 27.30-33; IV prop. 1-4.6.8.12.11; III prop. 7 end. 9.12.10.13. 14.16.18.19.24.22 beginning (all propositions without proof). On these excerpts see Folkerts, pp. 69-82 and the edition pp. 173-214.
28   Folkerts (see note 26).
29   Of this work only two manuscripts are known today which date before 1400; one of these originated in the 9th century at Corbie (now in Leningrad).
30   Especially Balbus as well as Epaphroditus and Vitruvius Rufus.

1.3 The Origin of the Geometria II (in 2 books) by the Pseudo-Boethius.

Besides the Geometria I, there is a second treatise which contains extensive parts of a Euclid translation and which agrees broadly with Mc and therefore must go back to the original Boethian Geometria. This is the so-called Geometria II, in two books, which in manuscript copies is generally attributed to Boethius. Since, in another publication,[31] the sources, origin, and provenience of this treatise have undergone clarification, it should suffice here merely to give a summary. This Geometria is made up of a section on geometry and a section on arithmetic. The geometrical section outweighs the rest; only at the end do both books deal with arithmetic questions, namely, with the arithmetic rules for the abacus. The author of this compilation has used two or three sources: an agrimensorial text from which he possibly took the Euclid excerpts too, and Gerbert's writing about the abacus. The first part of the Geometria II is composed of excerpts from Euclid I-IV (which are designated Md).[32] These excerpts very much resemble both the Geometria I (Mc) and the excerpts transmitted by the agrimensorial writings (Mb): Md has the same interpolations and transpositions as Mc, but since Md contains certain propositions which are absent in Mc, we may presume that the author of the Geometria II used a copy which was more complete than the Pseudo-Boethian Geometria I. Or, alternatively, the author could have used a copy of the Geometria I to which he added propositions lacking in that text but are taken from some source unknown to us and possibly, in accordance with this source, made some changes. There is also the possibility that the author used a manuscript now in Naples (N)[33] or one related to it; this manuscript contains the Geometria I and the demonstrations of Euclid I, 1-3 corresponding to Mb. It belongs to the group X[I] of the agrimensorial manuscripts, on which the other geometrical pieces of the Geometria II are based.[34] The rather unskillfully expressed mathematical rules on the abacus[35] show that for this section the compilor used the version „B" of Gerbert's treatise on the abacus, which did not originate before Gerbert's pontificate (999-1003).[36] This portion of the Geometria II is especially interesting for the history of mathematics since here for the first time a Latin mathematical text exists with early forms of our Indio-Arabic ciphers. Should these early ciphers have originated with Boethius, they would have already been known in the West around the year 500. No wonder then that the mathematical historians found interest in the Geometria II as early as the middle of the 19th century.[37]

Because of the sources used and the nature of the extant manuscripts,[38] the time of the origin of the Geometria II must be limited to the first half of the 11th century. Moreover, the work lends itself to easy localization–the B version of Gerbert's writing on the abacus was later included in the collection of the oldest abacus works, which originated about 995 in Lorraine.[39] Liège at this time was the „Lotharingian Athens" and the center for abacus studies.[40]

---

31 See Folkerts (note 19).
32 Extant are: I def. 1-12.14.13.15-23, post. 1-5, ax. 1.3.2.7; II def. 1.2; III def. 1-6.8-11; IV def. 1.2; I prop. 1-8. (9.) 10-41.43.42. 44-48; II prop. 1.3-6. 9-12.14; III prop. 3.7 beginning. 22.27.30-33; IV prop. 1-4.6.8.12.11 (all propositions without proof); further, I prop. 1-3 with proofs. See the Folkerts edition, pp. 109-135.
33 For this see p.
34 Folkerts, p. 104. Here the author deals chiefly with the calculations of areas.
35 These are at the end of Book I and II of Geometria II.
36 See Folkerts, pp. 83-94.
37 For preparatory works by other scholars, see Folkerts, p. 83.
38 The oldest stem from the middle of the 11th century. See section 2.1.
39 Bubnov, pp. 1-24; 294-296.
40 Heriger, Adelbold, Wazzo, Radulf, and Franco come from Liège. See also Bernelinus, *Liber Abaci* (ed. Bubnov, p. 383, 18-19): *Lotharienses... quos in his cum expertus sum florere.*

The above-mentioned N manuscript, or a closely related manuscript, was also located in Liège in the 11th century. Gerbert used it in 983 at Bobbio and later sent it to Adelbold of Liège.[41] Its author is, therefore, almost of necessity, a Lotharingian. This assumption is strengthened by the fact that the oldest existing manuscripts of this work stem exclusively from what are now Eastern France and Western Germany.[42]

The Geometria II in both theme and presentation fits well into the nature of the work of Lotharingian scholars of the 11th century, of whose work we can delineate a fairly clear picture for ourselves. Aside from the already mentioned writings on computations for the abacus, we are particularly well informed about their geometrical works. First of all, there is the correspondence between Regimbold and Radulph of Liège, of about 1025,[43] which concerned the sum of angles in a triangle. The solution to this problem is found in a somewhat later anonymous text.[44] Another geometrical writing from this setting is a treatise on the squaring of the circle by Franco of Liège written shortly before 1050.[45] As will be clearly demonstrated in section 2.3 below, this treatise is connected with the above mentioned correspondence and with the Geometria II. While the subject matter in the correspondence does not show familiarity with Geometria II, this Pseudo-Boethian treatise does reveal some striking similarities with the writing of Franco. We may, therefore, conclude that the Geometria II originated between 1025 and 1050.

We can now summarize what we know about the fate of Boethius' Euclid translation up to the 11th century. In two different places scholars were engaged, at different times, in this work: in the 8th century at Corbie and in the second quarter of the 11th century in Lorraine. In Corbie in a manuscript M (now lost), there existed at least the fragments of Md as well as the additional enunciations from Book III[46] and the definitions of Book V. Parts of M were then taken over into the third recension of Cassiodorus' *Institutiones* (Ma). A second copy (M_1), which possibly also originated at Corbie–which is now lost–contained at least the definitions and most of the propositions, without proof, from Books I-IV as well as the proofs to I, prop. 1-3. From this source M_1 came the Euclidian excerpts in the later recension of the *Agrimensores* collection (Mb) and a text (M_2) with the mistakes, glosses, and transpositions which are typical for the Geometria I (Mc). Both these (Mb and Mc) were put together at Corbie. Then in the 11th century an unknown Lotharingian scholar took from the original M_2 or from Mc most of the excerpts from Euclid I-IV and combined them as part of the Geometria II (Md). Indeed, he was trying to improve his original source, though with little success.

---

41   See Folkerts, p. 35.

42   See section 2.1.

43   Edited with commentary by P. Tannery and M. Clerval, „Une correspondance d'écolâtres du XIe siècle," *Notices et extraits des manuscrits de la Bibliothèque Nationale*, 36, no. 2 (Paris, 1901), 487-543; reprinted in P. Tannery, *Mémoires scientifiques*, 5 (Toulouse, Paris, 1922), 229-303.

44   This text was edited and classified, scientifically and historically, by J.E. Hofmann, according to manuscript 190 of Kues, ff. 1v-3r, „Zum Winkelstreit der rheinischen Scholastiker in der ersten Hälfte des 11. Jahrhunderts," *Abhandlungen der Preussischen Akademie der Wissenschaften*, math.-naturwiss. Klasse (1942), no. 8.

45   Edited by A.J.E.M. Smeur, „De verhandeling over de cirkelkwadratuur van Franco van Luik van omstreeks 1050," *Mededelingen van de Koninklijke Vlaamse Academie voor Wetenschappen, Letteren en Schone Kunsten van Belgïe*, 30.11 (Brussels, 1968). A new edition of this treatise with an English commentary by A.J.E.M. Smeur and M. Folkerts has appeared in *Archives internationales d'histoire des sciences*, 26 (1976), 59-105.225-253.

46   See note 27.

Boethius

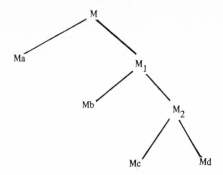

2. The dissemination and importance of both Geometries.

2.1 The preserved and reconstructable manuscripts.

The existing manuscripts give us the first information about the dissemination of both geometries in the Middle Ages. Today there are still about 25 codices extant of each of the two writings. This is a small number when compared with the Arithmetic or Music of which more than a hundred manuscripts are at hand, yet it is significantly more than of some other important texts of late antiquity and the Middle Ages. This already shows that both Geometries were not of little importance in the Middle Ages. When one classifies the existing manuscripts according to their place of origin and time, it allows one to come to a conclusion as to when and where the manuscripts of both were especially read and copied. Fortunately today there is considerable clarity about the dating and placing of the important manuscripts, so that some secure conclusions can be made.

The so called „Geometria I" evidently blossomed rather soon after its birth, whereas it was hardly copied at all in the late Middle Ages: of the 26 existing manuscripts, 17 stem from the 9th-11th century and of those 10 were probably written before the year 1000. Three of the oldest manuscripts originated in Corbie, the home of Geometria I (Paris, BN lat. 13020, 13955, 14080). These manuscripts were written there in the 2nd or 3rd quarter of the 9th century, not around the year 1000, as it was earlier thought.[47] A codex of the 10th century found today in Prague (Universitní Knihovna, lat. 1717 = IX. C. 6) is related to these manuscripts. I know nothing of the origin of this manuscript. At Reichenau the geometrical text in the Munich codex CLM 560 was written during the 9th century.[48] This manuscript is closely

---

[47]   The early date has been proved by B. Bischoff in „Hadoard und die Klassikerhandschriften aus Corbie," *Mittelalterliche Studien*, Band 1 (Stuttgart, 1966), p. 60.

[48]   B. Bischoff, *Die südostdeutschen Schreibschulen und Bibliotheken in der Karolingerzeit*, Teil 1 (Wiesbaden, 2nd edition, 1960), p. 262, note 3.

related to a now lost codex, which was mentioned in the Reichenau catalogue of the year 822.[49] One of the oldest manuscripts is the famous codex Naples V A 13 from the beginning of the 10th century. This manuscript was possibly used by Gerbert in 983 at Bobbio and he sent it, or a copy of it, to Liège around 997.[50] The corrections in this manuscript were made by Gerbert or one of his students. Yet a second manuscript could have been associated with Gerbert: the codex Bamberg, Ms. class. 55. This manuscript, also originating from the beginning of the 10th century, perhaps came through Johannes Scottus (+ about 875) and Gerbert shortly after 1000 to the newly founded library of the Bamberg cathedral.[51] Further codices from the 10th century are Cambridge, Trinity College 939 (originally at Canterbury) and the Einsiedeln manuscripts 298 and 358. Both of the last two manuscripts, which were probably written towards the end of the century in Reims or Trier, were most probably conveyed with St. Wolfgang from Trier to Einsiedeln.

Seven·manuscripts stem from the 11th century: the only precisely dated copy of Geometria I (Berne 87) was written in June of 1004 by a clergyman Constantius in Luxeuil. Bishop Werinharius (1002-1027) bestowed this codex to the Church of St. Mary in Strasbourg. A second manuscript from Berne (Ms. lat. 299) probably originated from some French source. Codex 830 from the Stiftsbibliothek in St. Gall, which was written there in the 1st half of the 11th century, shows handwritten notes of Ekkehart IV (+ about 1060). Likewise in the first half of the 11th century, not from the 13th century,[52] the manuscript Vienna 2269 originated in France and this contains a *Bibliotheca Septem Artium*. In England, perhaps at Canterbury, the Oxford manuscript Douce 125 was written and about the same time another copy originated in South Germany (Vienna 55). Vat. Barb. lat. 92 is more recent (Western Germany, about 1100).

From the following two centuries only six manuscripts of Geometria I are known. The oldest of them is Chartres 498. This codex, along with Chartres 497, makes up the *Heptateuchon* by Thierry of Chartres, an encyclopedia of the seven liberal arts which originated in the 2nd quarter of the 12th century.[53] There are two remaining manuscripts of the 12th century. One of these, the agrimensorial manuscript London, BM Add. 47679, is compiled from several sources.[54] The second, Vat. Ottob. Lat. 1862, is from the 2nd half of the 12th century and from eastern France. From the 13th century stem Munich, CLM 4024a (from France); Rostock, Ms. phil. 18; Florence, Laur. Plut. 29.19. The last manuscript was copied around 1250, perhaps from a Corbie codex, for Richard de Fournival from Amiens. It was brought to the Sorbonne in 1271 by Gerard de Abbeville.[55]

Only three manuscripts which are more recent are known, all in a humanistic hand of the 15th century: Breslau, Rehdig. 55 (copied from the Rostock manuscript); New York, Columbia University, Plimpton 164 (copied from Naples V A 14); Cesena, Plut. sin. XXVI.1 (written about 1450-1465 for the Malatesta Library).

The existing manuscripts testify therefore that in the 9th to 11th centuries the Geometria I was well circulated, most notably in the area of eastern France–western Germany. This probably relates to the presumed place of origin, Corbie. The work appears also relatively early

---

49   For this, see chapter 2.2 (p. 198).
50   Bubnov, *Gerberti Opera*, pp. 398.475. Thulin, „Zur Überlieferungsgeschichte", p. 5 f.
51   L. Traube, „Paläographische Forschungen," 4. Teil, *Abhandlungen der Königlich Bayerischen Akademie der Wissenschaften*, III. Klasse, 24 (1904), 10.
52   Bischoff, *Mittelalterliche Studien*, Band 2 (Stuttgart, 1967), p. 81, n. 26.
53   See chapter 2.3 (p. 201).
54   For this, see M. Folkerts, *Rheinisches Museum für Philologie*, NF 112 (1969), 53-70.
55   Ullman, „Geometry in the Medieval Quadrivium," pp. 279-282.

isolated in southern Germany, northern Italy, and England. Then from the 12th century the number of manuscripts diminished regularly, until the 15th century when a few humanists discovered and copied this writing anew.

The dissemination of the Geometria II is in many ways similar to that of the Geometria I. The existing manuscripts indicate that like the older Geometria I this treatise was also copied frequently very soon after its origin while in the subsequent centuries the manuscripts were less widely circulated.[56] Of the 23 extant manuscripts (eight of which contain only extracts of this work), 13 stem from the 11th or 12th century: the oldest codex (Erlangen 379) was probably written in southern Germany around 1050 – only a little later than the original. Closely related to this manuscript is the somewhat more recent incomplete codex Berlin, Ms. lat. oct. 162 (beginning of the 12th century) from the Benedictine monastery of St. Eucharius-Matthias in Trier. Likewise from the middle of the 11th century stems a London manuscript, BM Harley 3595. This codex is of west German origin. Towards the end of the 11th century in eastern France, perhaps in Reims, a manuscript was written which is presently found in Paris (BN lat. 7377C). Just a little more recent is Vat. Barb. lat. 92 (around 1100, from western Germany or Belgium).[57] From the 12th century come the following manuscripts: Chartres 498[58]; Munich, CLM 13021 (from Prüfening near Regensburg, after 1165); Vat. Lat. 3123 (western Germany or eastern France); Vat. Ottob. Lat. 1862 (eastern France);[59] Paris, BN lat. 7185 (end of the century, Normandy or England). Only parts of the treatise are found in Brussels, Bibliothèque Royale, Ms. Lat. 4499-4503 (beginning of the 12th century; this manuscript contains, among other things, mathematical texts of the agrimensores and writings from the Gerbert circle); Vat. Reg. lat. 1071 (France); London, BM Add. 47679.[60]

To the 13th century belong the following four manuscripts: Munich, CLM 23511 (southern Germany: Tegernsee?); London, BM Arundel 339 (Southern Germany: Kastl near Regensburg?); and the already mentioned Geometria I codices Munich, CLM 4024a (France) and Rostock, Ms. phil. 18, both of which contain only a small portion of Geometria II. The remaining six manuscripts are humanistic copies from the 15th century: London, BM Lansdowne 842 B (Italy, from the papal curia?); Cesena, Bibl. Malatestiana, Plut. sin. XXVI.1 (Cesena 1450-1465);[61] New York, Columbia University Library, Ms Plimpton 250 (copied from Vat. Lat. 3123, around 1500, Italy); Groningen 103 (monastery Thabor/West Friesland, about 1500) and the two incomplete manuscripts Breslau, Rehdigeranus 55 (Italy),[62] and Berne 87 (the beginning of the 16th century).[63]

Even more clearly than with the Geometria I, the extant manuscripts indicate that the Geometria II in the two centuries after its origin (1050-1250) was copied relatively often, then, however, it fell into oblivion. This treatise was also rediscovered first in the Renaissance by Italian humanists. All the older manuscripts (with the exception of Paris 7185) stem, in accordance to the character of the script, from western France or south and west Germany,

---

56 Only conjectural times and places of origin will be named below. A closer account on the contents of these manuscripts, their characteristics, and early ownership can be found in Folkerts, „Boethius" Geometrie II, pp. 3-33.

57 This manuscript also contains the Geometria I.

58 For this manuscript, which also contains the Geometria I, see pp. 194 and 201.

59 This manuscript also contains the Geometria I.

60 For this manuscript, which also contains the Geometria I, see p. 194.

61 Also contains the Geometria I.

62 Also contains the Geometria I.

63 Only the first lines of the Geometria II are added in this later hand. The greater part of the codex was written in the year 1004 at Luxeuil. See p.

respectively. This supports the likelihood[64] that the author of this treatise might have been a Lotharingian. This fact furthermore means that the Geometria II was well known in the Latin-speaking centers in Medieval Europe but was barely copied in the peripheral regions (England, Spain, Italy).

If one explores and compares the texts of the extant manuscripts, then one is able to see *a posteriori* the existence of manuscripts no longer surviving: common defects which are found in different manuscripts simultaneously demonstrate that these codices go back to a manuscript which today is lost. In this way one can find out the interdependence of these manuscripts and clarify it with a stemma. For the two geometries, the following stemmata are presented (taking the necessary precautions):[65]

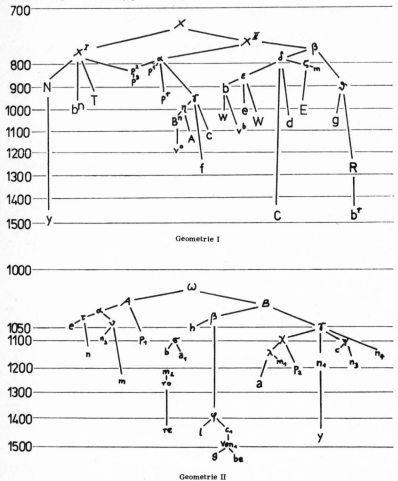

Geometrie I

Geometrie II

64 See chapter 1.3 (p. 192).
65 The stemma of the Geometria I results from the researches of Folkerts, „Die Altercatio,“ and the stemma of Geometria II from Folkerts, *Geometrie II*, pp. 51-61.

In these stemmata the lost codices are designated with Greek or cursively written letters, the extant manuscripts are designated with Latin characters. We know that there were at least twice as many manuscripts as are now extant.[66] Moreover, one sees how often the two Geometries were copied in the two centuries after their composition. So, for example, the autograph of Geometry II was written after 1000,[67] and the oldest extant manuscript (e = Erlangen 379) stems from about 1050. Between the autograph ω and e there are posited no less than three lost manuscripts, whose existence can be discovered from common flaws (A, a, τ). The four codices A, a, τ, e must have been written in a space of less than 50 years from each other. Geometria I has a similar situation: here there are as examples between the old manuscript b (Bamberg, Ms. class. 55) or m (CLM 560) and the autograph X four intermediate levels reconstructable (ϵ/ζ, δ, β, X^{II}).

2.2 The two Geometries in medieval manuscript catalogues.

The number of existing manuscripts points out that the two Geometries of Boethius were not so rarely read from the 11th to 15th centuries, but were significantly less well known than the other extant writings of Boethius on the *Quadrivium*. Further indications have shown that both writings were copied in a relatively limited geographic region (Germany, eastern France, England) and that from about 1250 until the beginning of the 15th century no copy was made.

This will all be confirmed through the citations in medieval catalogues. In this we are able to draw only tentative conclusions, because on the one hand merely parts of the medieval library catalogues are published and evaluated in a scholarly way; on the other hand, the accounts in these catalogues are often so generalized that the writings are not clearly identifiable.[68]

At least 64 libraries contained the Boethius arithmetic, 52 his music, and many of them contained two or more manuscripts of these works.[69] In contrast, only 18 places mention the Geometry of Boethius. Four mentionings are drawn from surely identifiable manuscripts: Prague, University, 1370 = Prague, Lat. 1717; St. Gall, 1461 = Stiftsbibliothek 830; Canterbury, St. Augustine, at the end of the 15th century = Cambridge, Trinity College 939; Paris, Sorbonne, 1338, no. 49[70] = Florence, Laur. XXIX, 19.[71]

With some of the other mentionings, the probability is great that some already known manuscripts are designated: in three Corbie manuscript catalogues from the 10th and 12th centuries[72] geometries of Boethius are cited, and these may be identified with the existing Paris manuscripts 13020, 13955, and 14080. At Corbie four manuscripts of the Geometry

---

66   The total number of manuscripts must have been higher. The representation in the stemma is very much a simplification. It is practically impossible that in the Geometria I there were four direct manuscript copies from reconstructed codex a (p^2, p^1, p^r, γ): one must presume that a much greater number of other manuscripts came between.

67   Chapter 1.3 (p. 192).

68   The following account is based mainly on G. Becker, *Catalogi bibliothecarum antiqui* (Bonn, 1885); P. Lehmann and others, *Mittelalterliche Bibliothekskataloge Deutschlands und der Schweiz* (Munich, 1918 ff.); M. Manitius, *Handschriften antiker Autoren in mittelalterlichen Bibliothekskatalogen* (Leipzig, 1935). A more detailed discussion is found in Folkerts, *Geometrie II*, pp. 33-39.

69   Manitius, *Handschriften antiker Autoren*, pp. 275-300.

70   L. Delisle, *Le cabinet des manuscrits*, III (Paris, 1881), p. 68.

71   This manuscript is identical with number 44 in the catalogue of Richard de Fournival, about 1250; see Ullman, „Geometry in the Medieval Quadrivium," p. 281. To Fournival's books cf. R.H. Rouse, in *Revue d'Histoire des Textes* 3 (1973) 253 ff.

72   Becker, nos. 55, 79, 136.

were present around 1200.[73] Related to one of these manuscripts was very possibly a codex entitled *Boetius de geometria et astronomia* which was found in the 12th century in St. Bertin,[74] because between Corbie and the neighboring St. Bertin there existed close contacts. Gerbert saw in 983, at Bobbio, *VIII volumina Boetii de astrologia praeclarissima quoque figurarum geometriae, aliaque non minus admiranda.*[75] Bubnov,[76] Thulin,[77] and Ullman[78] have demonstrated that this manuscript is identical with Naples V A 15 or with its predecessor. Gerbert sent this manuscript or a copy of it around 997 to Adelbold of Liège.[79] Perhaps a manuscript which was found at Liège[80] in the 11th century[81] is identical with the one sent from Gerbert to Adelbold.[82]

We will now cite those libraries in which a copy of the Geometry was found during the Middle Ages but is now lost. Already by 821-822 there was at Reichenau a codex which among other things contained the Geometria I.[83] A second manuscript, enlarged by other texts, which is closely related to this codex is mentioned by the Reichenau monk Reginbert in his book inventory, about 840.[84] The Reichenau manuscript(s) are related to the Munich CLM 560 codex mentioned above,[85] and probably also to a codex which was present at Murbach in the 9th century and was designated as *Geometrica Liber I* in that library's catalogue.[86] Murbach was founded by Reichenau. Between these two monasteries there was a lively exchange of books: two thirds of the Reichenau books also appear in the Murbach catalogue, written about 840. A further foundation from Reichenau was the Benedictine house of Pfävers. Here also there is a library catalogue (which was written in 1155) where a *Liber Geometriae* is mentioned and which is probably ascribed to Boethius.[87] Because between Pfävers and Reichenau on the one hand, as well as St. Gall on the other, there was a lively exchange of books, it is possible that the Pfävers manuscript is related to the Reichenau codex from the 9th century or the Geometria I manuscript of St. Gall.[88] At Fulda there were in the 16th century three manuscripts entitled *Geometria Boetii.*[89] At least one of these was a codex of Geometria I, as the incipit of the Fulda catalogue shows.[90] The remaining citations are too vague to permit any certain conclusions which geometry is meant. In some of these citations it is even doubtful whether one is dealing with the writings of Boethius: for example, Weihenstephan (11th

---

73   *Ibid.*, no. 136, mss. 272, 274, 275, 281.
74   *Ibid.*, no. 77, ms. 61.
75   Bubnov, p. 99f.
76   *Ibid.*, p. 475.
77   Thulin, p. 5 f.
78   Ullman, p. 278.
79   Bubnov, p. 398.
80   It is not altogether sure that this catalogue draws on St. Laurent in Liège. See H. Silvestre, *Le Chronicon S. Laurentii Leodiensis* (Louvain, 1952), p. 40.
81   Becker, no. 60, ms. 24: *geometrica Boetii.* The library catalogue which is transmitted in Brussels 9668 was newly edited by J. Gessler (Tongres, 1927).
82   Ullman, p. 278, note 4.
83   Bubnov points this out persuasively on p. 181.
84   On this see Ullman, p. 277 f.
85   See p. 194.
86   W. Milde, *Der Murbacher Bibliothekskatalog des 9. Jahrhunderts* (Euphorion, Beiheft, 1967).
87   Lehmann, Band 1, p. 486, 11-14.
88   On this see p. 194.
89   No. IX 2, 14; X 2, 32 and X 4, 26 of catalogue F which includes the entire Fulda collection. See K. Christ, „Die Bibliothek des Klosters Fulda im 16. Jahrhundert," *Zentralblatt für das Bibliothekswesen,* Beiheft 64 (Leipzig, 1933).
90   V, no. 503; see Christ, p. 159.

century),[91] Toul (before 1084),[92] Durham (12th century)[93] and an unknown Italian or French library (13th century).[94]

The medieval library catalogues allow us to conjecture that Reichenau also played an important role in the dissemination of the Geometria I in the 9th-10th centuries. The influence that Fulda had in this early period is uncertain, because a Geometria of Boethius is only mentioned in relatively recent Fulda catalogues. We have seen that the accounts of the medieval catalogues are very generally stated so that one can only seldom know whether one is dealing with a codex of the Geometria I or II. None of these citations can lead to a certain conclusion that the codex was Geometria II: some of the citations must have been the Geometria I.

2.3 Citations by other authors.

To be able to answer the question to what extent the Boethian writings on Geometry were known and used in the Middle Ages, it would be helpful to know not only of references to these manuscripts in medieval catalogues, but also to have all references to these texts, whether in the form of direct quotation or as citations of the name of the author or of the title of the writings. That type of all-inclusive list of citations is presently not possible for many reasons, especially since only parts of the medieval texts are edited. Therefore a much more modest goal should be worked for: because the two geometries do contain much concrete mathematical materials, these writings must have been interesting particularly for the authors of medieval textbooks. I have examined the most important mathematical writings of the Latin Middle Ages in the hope of finding traces which would indicate that the writer was familiar with one of the two geometries.

According to the findings of the previous sections, it should be no surprise that in the mathematical writings up to the 12th century some knowledge of the Geometries is apparent. The name of the author was seldom mentioned, yet similarities in the Latin texts testify that one of the two geometries was known.

As one of the seven *artes liberales*, geometry was studied from late antiquity as part of the medieval framework of studies. It seems, however, as if geometry lapsed behind the other disciplines of the quadrivium—no wonder, from the scanty materials which the scholars up to the 12th century had at their disposal! In addition to the general geometrical concepts from the *encyclopaediae* of Cassiodorus, Martianus Capella and Isidore of Seville, it seems that the mathematicians of this time took their geometrical knowledge primarily from the writings of the *Corpus Agrimensorum*, from the two Geometries attributed to Boethius, and from the Geometry of Gerbert with expansions by some unknown author. Among these writings there is a complex interdependence in which the Geometries of Boethius are interwoven.

The anonymous geometry, which is connected with the Geometry of Gerbert (the *Geometria incerti auctoris*, hereafter shortened als *GIA*) passed for a long time as a part of Gerbert's geometry. It was Bubnov who made the first critical edition of this writing[95] and he was able to show convincingly that this work originated before Gerbert: The GIA is based on Arabic writings on the astrolabe. However, it was also present in the agrimensorial manuscript

---

91   Becker, no. 73, mss. 40.41; it is uncertain whether this refers to Boethius.
92   Becker, no. 68, ms. 251: *musica Boetii cum Euclide de geometria vol. I.* Because this catalogue was put together before the Arabic-Latin Euclid translations, it must concern itself with a manuscript of the Boethian tradition.
93   Becker, no. 117, ms. 186; it is uncertain whether this refers to Boethius.
94   No. 65: *Geometria Boecii et Hugonis.* See Manitius, p. 291.
95   Bubnov, pp. 310-365.

which Gerbert used in 983. The GIA therefore did not originate before the 9th or after the 10th century. The author of the GIA also utilized the Geometria I of Boethius, which he excerpted without mentioning either the work or its author.[96]

The most important geometrical work which was at the disposal of the West before the time of the translations from the Arabic was the *Geometria* of Gerbert which did not originate before 983.[97] The phraseology in this work often brings to mind the Geometria I, especially the Euclidian section. So it is very possible already, by reason of its contents, that Gerbert made use of the Geometria I in writing his geometry. This conjecture becomes more certain when one considers that Gerbert was acquainted with an agrimensorial manuscript at Bobbio which also contained the Geometria I.[98] Furthermore, Gerbert often cites the name of Boethius, though never in connection with geometry;[99] perhaps he perceived that the Geometria I was not genuine.

The two Geometries of Boethius, particularly the Geometria I, contain much gromatic material. So it is not surprising that the Geometria I was very quickly taken up by the monks (at the latest in the 9th century) who—obviously for the study of geometry within the quadrivium and less for surveyor–work[100]– would put together new geometrical and gromatic works from the transmitted texts. At least two of this type of compendia exist: a *Geometrica ars anonymi* (designated as Y by Thulin),[101] and a *Geometria Gisemundi* (designated as Z by Thulin).[102]

The *Geometrica ars*, divided into 34 chapters, contains few gromatic texts in the strict sense of the word. First of all, we find geometrical excerpts. The author presents the explanation given by Cassiodorus on geometry,[103] filled out and enlarged by excerpts from Censorinus, Balbus and the Geometria I of Pseudo-Boethius. Moreover, the Geometria I was particularly drawn upon and partly excerpted word for word.[104] The text is contained in five manuscripts: the oldest and best is CLM 13084, ff. 48v-69v, from the 10th century (Regensburg); from this was copied Munich, CLM 6406 (11th century, Freising) and CLM 14836 (11th century). A manuscript related to CLM 13084 is Vienna 51 (12th century). The fifth manuscript, Sélestat 1153bis (10th century, Worms)[105] is likewise akin to CLM 13084. It appears as if this version originated east of the Rhine and later it was particularly well known in that area.

The *Geometria Gisemundi* is a gromatic-geometric compendium of Spanish origin which is found in two manuscripts (Barcelona, Ripoll 106, ff. 76-89, 10th century; Paris, BN lat. 8812, about 900). The main source for the compilor who, according to his own account made use of more than one manuscript, was the Geometria I of Boethius from which he excerpted

---

96   Bubnov, p. 336, note 24; p. 400, 471.
97   The critical edition is by Bubnov, pp. 46-97. Hofmann (see note 44), p. 4.9.11, conjectures that the Geometry in its present form does not stem from Gerbert but rather is a version from the early 11th century.
98   See p. 198.
99   Gerbert cites Boethius' arithmetic and his commentary on Aristotle's *Categories*. That Gerbert also knew the Geometria I Bubnov has shown (p. 48, n. 3 with corrigenda on p. 556; p. 51, n. 1 with corrigenda on p. 556f.; p. 181, n. 3; p. 397f.).
100 Ullman, pp. 263-269, has shown convincingly that in the Middle Ages gromatical texts were used for the instruction of geometry but not to educate surveyors.
101 Analyzed by Thulin, pp. 44-54.
102 Analyzed by Thulin, pp. 55-68.
103 Chapter 6 from the *De Artibus ac Disciplinis Liberalium Artium*.
104 The contents are given by Thulin, pp. 44-48.
105 A. Giry, „Notes sur un ms. de la Bibliothèque de Schlestadt," *Revue de Philologie* (1879).

nearly all that concerned itself with land surveying.[106] He also used a gromatic manuscript, from the so called „Mischklasse."[107] The *Geometria Gisemundi* contains nothing of the arithmetic and geometric extracts which are present in books 2-4 of the Geometria I and nothing from the first dialogue. The excerpted Boethian text is also not a continuous work, but rather is broken down into about 30 chapters which are rarely in the same order as in the Pseudo-Boethius, and often they are separated by other excerpts. This Spanish handbook, which must have originated not later than in the 9th century, shows in any case that at this early time the Geometria I was also known in northern Spain (Ripoll).

Traces of the Geometria I also appear occasionally in the 12th century in the works of other authors. Thierry of Chartres, an important scholar of the 12th century, composed, probably before 1141, a book entitled *Heptateuchon*[108] or the *Bibliotheca septem artium liberalium*.[109] In this work Thierry presents not only a solid grounding for the encyclopedia of learning, but also arranged the learning which had evolved before his time into a self-contained unity and put it into order. In his *Heptateuchon* Thierry took up those writings which he valued most for the study of the *artes liberales*. For the quadrivium there were cited, naturally, Boethius' works on arithmetic and music. These geometrical writings are given: Adelard's Euclid translation (version II); the gromatical excerpts from Boethius' Geometria I, Book 5; other gromatical texts, among these the writings of Epaphroditus and Vitruvius Rufus and the *Liber Podismi*; excerpts from Gerbert's geometry; the Pseudo-Boethian Geometria II; Gerland's writing on the abacus.[110] These works can surely be taken as representative of the geometrical teachings in the early and high Middle Ages. Noticeably Thierry took into consideration both Geometries of Boethius. Yet he did not take all of the Geometria I–rather, typically, merely the *altercatio* of Book 5.[111] The excerpts from Boethius' Arithmetic and the *Elementa* of Euclid which are present in the Geometria I are notably missing. Both works were unnecessary since Thierry copied them in another part of his manuscript. Through what channel did Thierry know the writings of Boethius? Ullman has conjectured[112] that it took place through Fulbert who in the century before Thierry had been a teacher at Chartres and was probably a student of Gerbert. It is likely that Fulbert read the Corbie manuscript (Paris 13955) at Chartres which also contains the Geometria I.[113]

---

106 Contents by Thulin, pp. 55-58.
107 Thulin, pp. 58-61.
108 The name is openly based on the Pentateuch. In medieval catalogues manuscripts and commentaries on the Bible sometimes are entitled *Eptateuchus* or *Eptaticus*.
109 Chartres, Ms. 497-498. The manuscripts were burned in W W II but there has survived a microfilm. The text of the prologue to the *Heptateuchon* is published by E. Jeauneau, „Le Prologus in Eptatheucon de Thierry de Chartres," *Mediaeval Studies*, 16 (1954), 171-175 (reprinted in: *Lectio Philosophorum, Recherches sur l'Ecole de Chartres*, Amsterdam 1973, pp. 87-91). From the extensive literature on Thierry and the school of Chartres one may cite: A. Clerval, *L'enseignement des arts libéraux à Chartres et à Paris dans la première moitié du XIIe siècle d'après l'Heptateuchon de Thierry de Chartres* (Paris, 1889); A. Clerval, *Les écoles de Chartres au moyen âge* (Paris, 1895); Charles Haskins, *Studies in the History of Mediaeval Science* (Cambridge, 1924), especially p. 91; G. Paré, A. Brunet, and P. Tremblay, *La renaissance du XIIe siècle: Les écoles et l'enseignement* (Paris, Ottawa, 1933), pp. 94 ff.; R. Klibansky, „The School of Chartres," *Twelfth-century Europe and the Foundations of Modern Society*, ed. M. Clagett, Gaines Post, and R. Reynolds (Madison, 1961), pp. 3-14.
110 According to the order of texts in the manuscript, the Gerland writing belongs to Geometry. It was a wide-spread notion in the Middle Ages that the reckoning on the abacus is part of geometry.
111 Thulin's assumption (p. 18) that the end of the work is in the part of the manuscript now lost is wrong.
112 Ullman, p. 278.
113 A conjecture by B. Bischoff. Ullman's doubt concerning the connection between Gerbert and Thierry (see note 11, p. 279) seems now to be without reasons: a close analysis of the Geometria I text in Thier-

As we have seen, the Geometria I of Boethius was linked at least with Chartres by the 12th century in the established writings on the *quadrivium*. It may have been used in other places as well: there is a list of textbooks for the seven liberal arts probably made by Alexander Neckam at the end of the 12th century while he was teaching in Paris.[114] Neckam stated: *Institutis arsmetice informandus arismeticam Boecii et Euclidis legat*. It seems that this reference draws from the Goemetria I of the Pseudo-Boethius.[115]

So much for the citations of the Geometria I. The Geometria II originated, as we have seen, in the 11th century in Lorraine and was in the following hundred years spread mainly throughout western Germany and eastern France. This geometry must be seen as related to the works of a group of Liège mathematicians whose influence extended beyond Lorraine in the first half of the 11th century. These scholars wrote works on the abacus and also geometrical treatises. The most important of these texts–aside from the Geometria II– is a lengthy correspondence between the Cologne scholastic Regimbold and Radulph of Liège about the year 1025 and the treatise of Franco of Liège on the squaring of the circle (shortly before 1050). It is not surprising that in both cases there are connections to the Geometries of Boethius.

In the 11th century in geometry beside skimpy accounts in the *Corpus Agrimensorum* and in the encyclopedic writings of the Romans, only faulty excerpts from the first books of Euclid (without the proofs) were known. What was needed, above all, was a clarification on geometrical principles. In the course of the correspondence between Regimbold and Radulph,[116] the question comes up about what is an inner and an outer angle. In spite of various statements, no conclusive definition is found. Only a little later will the question concerning the sum of angles in a triangle be resolved experimentally, as it is known according to an anonymous text at Kues.[117] In the correspondence of these Rhineland scholars, there are no signs that they knew the Geometria II; probably this writing originated after 1125.[118] In two places, indeed, are Euclidian passages cited, both of which show that Regimbold knew the Geometria I of Pseudo-Boethius. The two statements of Regimbold read thus:[119]

I.16[120]   *Omnium triangulorum exterior angulus utrisque interioribus et ex adverso constitutis angulis maior existit.*

I.32[121]   *Omnium triangulorum et exterior angulus duobus angulis interius et ex adverso constitutis est aequalis, interiores tres anguli duobus rectis angulis sunt aequales.*

If one neglects insignificant changes, both phraseologies correspond with the Euclidian text which was carried over into the Geometria I and II. A small item, moreover, emerges to esta-

---

ry's manuscript Chartres 498 indicates that this codex (like Paris 13955) belongs to the subclass X[II], but that Thierry used another codex which, as Gerbert's manuscript, belonged to class X[I]. Using this manuscript, Thierry expertly corrected essential mistakes of his X[II] source. It is noteworthy that in the manuscript Berne 299 (on this see p. 194) there exist many corrections which correspond with the corrected text of Thierry's manuscript.

114   Charles H. Haskins, *Harvard Studies in Classical Philology*, 20 (1909), 75.
115   The citation of Euclid is not surprising in this connection because in the rubrics of the Geometria I Euclid's name occurs often.
116   Edited by Tannery and Clerval (see n. 43). Below, the page numbers will be cited from the *Mémoires Scientifiques*.
117   Edited by Hofmann (see. n. 44).
118   Tannery rightly remarks on p. 248 that at least for the metrological questions both correspondents would have drawn on the Geometria II if it had been known to them.
119   Regimbold cites here the name of Boethius but not his work: *testimonio ipsius Boetii ita scribentis* (Tannery, p. 280).
120   Tannery, p. 281.
121   *Ibid.*

blish that Regimbold used a manuscript copy of Geometria I that belongs to class X^{II}: only in this group of manuscripts does one find in I.32 the word *et* after *triangulorum*. In the manuscript group X^I and in the Geometria II the *et* does not occur. It is improbable that Regimbold inserted this word by himself. Probably Regimbold here followed the Geometria I manuscript Paris 13955.[122]

Also, a very striking resemblance exists between the Geometria II and the possibly somewhat more recent writing on the squaring of the circle which Franco of Liège wrote shortly before 1050.[123] The similar rhetorical style in both works is obvious, particularly in the prefaces of Franco's six books. The reckoning of the circle in Franco[124] recalls the formulae and substituted values in the corresponding place of the Geometria II.[125] In addition, the mention of *porticus, miliaria, stadia*, and *fluvii* in Franco find their correspondences in the Pseudo-Boethius.[126] The praise of Pythagoras and of Patricius Symmachus in relation with Boethius[127] could draw upon the arithmetic,[128] but also is in common with the Geometria II.[129] Many striking formulations in Franco bear such a strong resemblance to places in the Geometria II that one simply must consider it an influence.[130]

The Geometria II is the oldest extant writing known in the west in which an abacus of the Gerbert school and the Indic-Arabic figures (including the zero) are presented. For this reason the work is of special interest for the historians of science and it is conceivable that those authors who in the 11th and 12th century wrote discussions on reckoning with the abacus drew upon the Geometria II of the Pseudo-Boethius. The most important masters of the abacus whose works we know are: Odo,[131] Gerbert (+ 1003),[132] Abbo of Fleury (+ 1004),[133] Heriger of Lobbes (+ 1007),[134] Bernelinus (possibly a student of Gerbert),[135] Hermannus Contractus (1013-1054),[136] Turchillus (England, before 1117),[137] Gerland of Besançon (1st

---

122 This codex draws on class X^{II}; Fulbert (+ 1028) may have used it at Chartres (see p. 201). Regimbold cites in another letter of his correspondence (Tannery, p. 288) a discussion which he had at Chartres with Fulbert on the angles of a triangle. Therefore it is not improbable that Regimbold knew of the Boethius manuscript through Fulbert.

123 See note 45. The Franco text will be cited below in the edition by M. Folkerts and A.J.E.M. Smeur, ,,A Treatise on the Squaring of the Circle by Franco of Liège of about 1050," Part I, *Archives internationales d'histoire des sciences*, 26 (1976), 59-105.

124 *Ibid.*, p. 70, lines 111-116.

125 Folkerts, *Geometrie II*, p. 166, lines 885-888.

126 Franco, p. 71, l. 144f. = Boethius, p. 147, l. 560 f.

127 Franco, p. 78, l. 30-34.

128 In Friedlein's edition, p. 3, 1.1 11. 13; p. 7, 1.21-26.

129 See Folkerts, *Geometrie II*, p. 113, l.2; p. 138, lines 439-441; p. 139, l. 447-453; p. 169, l. 927-930.

130 E.g., *geometricae disciplinae peritissimi* (Franco, p. 76, 1. 148f.) = Pseudo-Boethius, p. 150, l. 607; *dubitationis obscuritate ... exempli luce* (Franco, p. 87, 1. 83f.) = Pseudo-Boethius, p. 132, l. 324f.; *Pythagorica subtilitas* (Franco, p. 90, l. 10) = Pseudo-Boethius, p. 139, l.447 f.; *Patricius* (= Symmachus) (Franco, p. 90, l. 21) = Pseudo-Boethius, p. 113, l. 2.

131 It is questionable whether he is to be identified with Odo of Cluny (878-942); he could be better placed early in the 12th century. His *Regulae super abacum* are edited by M. Gerbert, *Scriptores Ecclesiastici de Musica*, I (Sankt Blasien, 1784), pp. 296-302 and later by Migne, *P.L.*, 133, col. 807-814.

132 His work on the abacus has been critically edited by Bubnov, pp. 6-22.

133 Edited by Bubnov, pp. 197-204.

134 Edited by Bubnov, pp. 205-225.

135 His *Liber abaci* has been edited by A. Olleris, *Oeuvres de Gerbert* (Clermont-Ferrand, Paris, 1867), pp. 357-400.

136 Edited by Treutlein in *Bullettino Boncompagni*, 10 (1877), 643-647.

137 Edited by E. Narducci in *Bullettino Boncompagni*, 15 (1882), 111-162. See also Haskins (note 109), pp. 327-335.

half of the 12th century),[138] Adelard of Bath (1st half of the 12th century),[139] Radulph of Laon (+ 1131).[140] In addition there are some commentaries on Gerbert's writing about the abacus[141] and anonymous writings, mostly from the 12th century.[142] In their works, many of these authors make comments about Gerbert as the inventor or the disseminator of the abacus.[143] At times Herman of Reichenau is also cited.[144] In addition, one often finds Pythagoras mentioned.[145] Boethius' name is cited only by Adelard, but only in connection with his arithmetic[146] and music[147]. In general, these authors make use of the works of Gerbert or of his students but not of the abacus portion of the Geometria II. On the other hand, a singular item emerges from the Geometria II: in this treatise it is stated for the first time that the abacus was invented by Pythagoras, and for that reason it was called the *mensa Pythagorea*.[148] One also finds this statement in Adelard[149] and Odo who, very clumsily in this connection, mentions the „translation activity" of Boethius.[150] The amazing similarity in the phraseology between the Geometria II and Adelard apparently indicates that Adelard knew of this work.[151] It is uncertain if Odo also knew of it.[152] Among all the other masters of the abacus there is no sure sign that they had read the Geometria II.[153]

2.4 The two Geometries and the Euclid translations from the Arabic.

As we have seen in chapter I,[154] the Geometria I as well as the Geometria II contain extensive excerpts from the *Elements* of Euclid, Book 1-4 (without proofs). The transmitted

138 Edited by Treutlein in *Bull. Bonc.* 10 (1877), 595-607.
139 Edited by B. Boncompagni in *Bull. Bonc.* 14 (1881), 91-134.
140 Edited by A. Nagl in *Zeitschrift für Mathematik und Physik*, Supplement, 34 (1889), 85-133.
141 Edited by Bubnov, pp. 245-284.
142 Edited by Treutlein in *Bull. Bonc.* 10 (1877), 607-629, 630-639, 639f.; Bubnov, pp. 225-244 (from the 10th century) and pp. 291-293.
143 For example, see Bernelinus (note 135), p. 357; Radulph (n. 140), pp. 100, 102, 103; Adelard (n. 139), pp. 91, 99, 100.
144 For example, see Radulph (n. 140), p. 100.
145 See notes 148, 149, 150.
146 Adelard (n. 139), pp. 108, 111.
147 Adelard, p. 111.
148 Folkerts, *Geometrie II*, p. 139, lines 447-453: *Pytagorici vero, ne in multiplicationibus et partitionibus et in podismis aliquando fallerentur, ut in omnibus erant ingeniosissimi et subtilissimi, descripserunt sibi quandam formulam, quam ob honorem sui praeceptoris mensam Pytagoream nominabant, quia hoc, quod depinxerant, magistro praemonstrante cognoverant--a posterioribus appellabatur abacus--ut, quod alta mente conceperant, melius, si quasi videndo ostenderent, in notitiam omnium transfundere possent, eamque subterius habita sat mira descriptione formabant.* On the origin of this legend, see Folkerts, *Ibid.*, p. 89.
149 Adelard (n. 139), p. 91, lines 7-10: *Pythagorici hoc opus* (i.e. *abacum) composuerunt, ut ea, quae magistro suo Pythagora docente audierant, oculis subiecta retinerent et firmius custodirent. Quod ipsi quidem mensam Pythagoream ob magistri sui reverentiam vocaverunt; sed posteri tamen abacum dixerunt.*
150 Odo (n. 131), p. 296: *Haec ars non a modernis, sed ab antiquis inventa, ideo a multis negligitur, quia numerorum perplexione valde implicatur, ut maiorum relatione didicimus. Huius artis inventorem Pythagoram habemus. ... Hanc* (i.e. *artem) antiquitus graece conscriptam a Boethio credimus in Latinum translatam.* Also in Radulph (n. 140), p. 90, the *mensa philosophorum* could have meant the *mensa Pythagorica*. On the identification of the abacus with the *mensa Pythagorica* see Bubnov, p. 157, note 17.
151 The other parts of Adelard's writing on the abacus yield no further arguments which support this assumption. Adelard mentions such names as Pythagoras (see n. 149), Boethius (note 146, 147) and Gerbert (n. 143) and then only Guichardus (p. 100), and a certain H. (p. 91).
152 It is very likely that Odo knew the assertions in the Geometria II only indirectly.
153 In a commentary on Gerbert's *Regulae* which originated about 1000, a passage was cited word by word from the Geometria I of Pseudo-Boethius: Bubnov, p. 250, note 6.
154 Pages pp. 187-188.

text is corrupt and often obscured. Scholars in western Europe drew their knowledge of Euclid up to the 12th century almost exclusively from these two works.

The situation advanced haphazardly in the 12th century when in the process of translations from the Arabic, the masterwork of Euclid was also translated into Latin more than once. Intensive studies of historians of science in the last decades have gone far to shed light on the various versions and treatises; even though the manuscript material is still not completely elucidated and especially have not all the Arabic sources for each translation been yet identified.[155] For my research the following condensed formulation may be made: one of the earliest translations from Arabic, the so called Version II by Adelard of Bath (originating about 1120) was disseminated rapidly already in the 12th century and supplanted the other Arabic to Latin translations of Euclid. Of Adelard II there exist over 50 manuscripts. More widespread in the Middle Ages was only the treatise which Johannes Campanus of Novara composed before 1260. His work, which is extant in more than 100 manuscripts, relies essentially on the Adelard II text. Both the Adelard II and the Campanus could be considered as *the* Euclid texts of the high and late Middle Ages, so that the Adelard II text especially in the 12th and 13th century, and the Campanus text in the 14th and 15th centuries became particularly important.

The question as to how Adelard produced his Euclid translation (or translations) cannot yet be conclusively answered despite the work of Clagett, Murdoch, and Busard.[156] Inasmuch as Adelard probably knew the Geometria II of Boethius,[157] the possibility cannot be excluded that he also took the Euclidian excerpts from this treatise for his translation; but this is not altogether clear.

With the Euclid translation of Adelard there was presented for the first time since late antiquity a complete Euclidian text in the Latin language which, in contrast to the previous texts of the Boethian tradition, also contained the proofs and encorporated hardly any translation or transmission errors. One would expect that these preferences for the Adelard text would have led to the disappearance of the insufficient Boethius tradition within a short time. But this does not seem to have been the case; rather, in the 12th century, some scholars attempted in various places to put the Euclidian excerpts in the Geometria I and II of the Pseudo-Boethius and the text of Adelard together into a new work and fit these with each other. To the modern observor it seems amazing that despite the widely read and good translation of Adelard, scholars held fast to the Boethian text full of flaws. The explanation for this could be found in the name „Boethius" which throughout the entire Middle Ages was highly honored. In the material to follow I would like to discuss this combination of Boethius and Adelard. Because this has been studied in another place with more detailed research,[158] it should suffice to bring together the results here and present some new supporting material.[159]

---

155 Good information is given by F. Sezgin, *Geschichte des arabischen Schrifttums, Band 5. Mathematik* (Leiden, 1974), pp. 83-120. The basic work on the Arabic-Latin Euclid translations is Marshall Clagett, „The Medieval Latin Translations from the Arabic of the Elements of Euclid, with Special Emphasis on the Versions of Adelard of Bath," *Isis*, 44 (1953), 16-42. See as well J.E. Murdoch, „The Medieval Character of the Medieval Euclid: Salient Aspects of the Translations of the Elements by Adelard of Bath and Campanus of Novara," *XIIe Congrès International d'Histoire des Sciences, Colloques (= Revue de Synthese*, vol. 89, 1968), pp. 67-94. H.L.L. Busard is preparing critical editions of all the significant Arabic-Latin Euclid translations.

156 See note 155.

157 See p. 201.

158 M. Folkerts, „Anonyme lateinische Euklidbearbeitungen aus dem 12. Jahrhundert," *Österreichische Akademie der Wissenschaften, Math.-nat. Klasse, Denkschriften*, 116. Band , 1. Abhandlung (Vienna, 1971).

159 Since the above work, I have found two further manuscripts: Leiden, Voss. lat. qu. 92, and San Juan Capistrano, Honeyman Ms. 50 (see below).

At two places in western Europe scholars undertook in the 12th century, independently from each other, an attempt to combine the Boethius work and Adelard's Euclidian translation. From one of these mélanges there is only a single manuscript now known (Luneburg, Ratsbibliothek, Ms. misc. D 4⁰ 48, ff. 13r-17v). This manuscript, which was written in northern Germany about 1200 and which an otherwise unknown *magister Helmoldus* presented to the Michaelis monastery in Hildesheim, contains most of the definitions, postulates, axioms, and propositions of the first four books of Euclid which also exist in the Geometria II. The author of the Luneburg manuscript used a codex of the Adelard translation and one of the Geometria II in such a manner that he preferred in his text of the definitions and postulates the Boethian formulation; the axioms and propositions, for the most part, follow Adelard's phraseology. The compilor carefully put his text together from the two sources; often he improved the defective text of the Boethian tradition. In many places the author writes his own text which deviates from both Boethius and Adelard, but is clearly intelligible and meaningful. The contaminated versions of the theorems and definitions are mathematically sound and unobjectionable. They indicate that the author had a great mathematical ability for his time. This means that the Luneburg excerpts are an advance over the very corrupt portions of the Euclidian excerpts in the Geometria II of the Pseudo-Boethius.[160]

Of the second compilation there are extant the following six manuscripts all of which come from the 12th century:

M_1 = Munich, CLM 13021, ff. 164r-186v[161]
M_2 = Munich, CLM 23511, ff. 1r-27r[162]
O = Oxford, Digby 98, ff. 78r-85v[163]
P = Paris, BN lat. 10257, ff. 1-88 (from Chartres)
V = Leiden, Voss. lat. qu. 92, ff. 2rv.1rv[164]
H = formerly San Juan Capistrano, Honeyman Ms. 50[165].

On the one hand, these six manuscripts show similarities; on the other, they represent distinctly different levels of treatment: the noteworthy but awkward text of the axioms indicates that all the known manuscripts were taken from a common source X. This source X used manuscripts of the Adelard and Boethius tradition such that it drew upon the Boethian text and completed it with the Adelard text. It appears that the author of X had a Boethius text of Geometria I and another one of the Geometria II at his disposal, but preferred the Geometria II. The Adelard text first is used to any great extent in book 3 where not all the propositions are found in the Boethius text. The manuscripts O and V are „cleanly" copied from source X. The mistakes in O are mainly the fault of the copyist. The author of the version O has drawn on no other manuscript. The short fragment in V[166] departs greatly from the text of manu-

---

160 A more complete account of the manuscript and the working method of the compiler may be seen in Folkerts, „Lateinische Euklidbearbeitungen," pp. 12-19. The Euclidian text has been reproduced in facsimile, *Ein neuer Text des Euclides Latinus*, ed. M. Folkerts (Hildesheim, 1970).
161 See p. 195.
162 See p. 195. M_2 contains only Books 4-15.
163 This ends with Euclid III, def. 4.
164 A fragment. This includes III, 34-36; IV, 14-16. See note 166.
165 Ms. 24 in C.U. Faye, W.H. Bond, *Supplement to the Census of Medieval and Renaissance Manuscripts in the United States and Canada* (New York, 1962), p. 22. Mr. Honeyman has very kindly sent me photographs of his manuscript. In the meantime, it has been sold by Sotheby Parke Bernet & Co., London (see *The Honeyman Collection of Scientific Books and Manuscripts*, Part III, lot 1086).
166 There is on f.2, r-v: the end from III, 34 Heiberg (= 33 Adelard) according to Adelard II (only the words *-onem abscindere*); an addition as in the Pseudo-Boethian Geometria II after Euclid III, 7 (see Folkerts, *Geometrie II*, p. 130, lines 279f.: *Similes ... trigone sint*); III, 35 Heiberg (= 34 Adelard) according to

scripts M_1M_2HP; V shows similarities with the Boethius tradition more clearly than the remaining codices.[167] This particular classification combines V with O so that both manuscripts possibly represent the same version.[168]

The mélange X was not only copied literally (OV) but was again adapted by another compilor (Y). Y has in many places altered the X text with the help of an Adelard codex and through conjecture. Y may be reconstructed from the texts contained in M (= M_1M_2) and P. Both texts are not straight copies but rather editorial modifications from text Y: the author of M hardly made changes of his own, but used an Adelard text, from which he took some propositions and inserted them in the corresponding place in the Boethian text. On the other hand P tried to adapt the Adelard text to the Greek-Latin tradition. For this purpose the writer designated the various irrationalities in Book 10 with expressions which are transcriptions of Greek *termini*.[169] Therefore, OV is closest to Boethius and M to the Adelard text. P takes a middle place. The manuscript H is a direct copy of the corrected text in the manuscript P.[170]

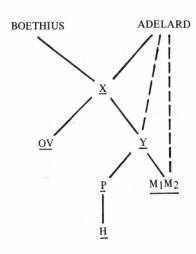

Adelard II; III, 7 beginning and addition as in the Geometria II (Folkerts, *Geometrie II*, p. 129, lines 272-279: *Si intra circulum ... perhibeatur*); III, 36 Heiberg (= 35 Adelard) according to Adelard II (broken off at the end of the page). On f.1, r-v: IV, 14-16 Heiberg (= 14-19 Adelard) according to Adelard II; an addition as in the Geometria II, after Euclid IV, 11 (Folkerts, *Geometrie II*, p. 132, lines 319-321: *Nam que ... terminum facientes); subscriptio: Euclidis philosophi liber quartus explicit. Incipit quintus viginti sex theoremata continens. et XVI^{cim} elementa.*

167 In V there are parts of the Boethius addition after Euclid III, 7 and IV, 11 (see note 166). P also contains a section of the addition after III, 7. M_1 and M_2 have nothing of the two additions.

168 The text in O breaks off before V begins.

169 For example, *diamese* for ἐκ δύο μέσων, *apotomese* for μέσης ἀποτομή, *dionimum* for ἐκ δύο ὀνομάτων, *longisimetrum* for σύμμετρον ᾗ μήκει, *longiretum* for εὐθεῖα ῥητή. These Greek terms had already appeared in Martianus Capella.

170 H shows all the errors of the corrected manuscript P and even particular mistakes of its own. The following fact especially speaks for a direct copying: because of the page ending, P left out the conclusion of proposition I, 47 so that instead of *lateribus continetur*, there is only *la*. H has correctly added *lateribus* but not the necessary *continetur*.

Through a careful consideration of the seven manuscripts mentioned above we have taken a look at the transformation which the 12th century mathematics went through as a result of the Euclid translations from the Arabic. We saw to what extent the Greek-Latin and the Arabic-Latin tradition within a few decades emerged and became fruitfully interwoven. We could trace the existence of two mutually independent collections of the *Euclides Latinus* (MOVP and Luneburg), the first of which had further revisions within a few years. Various attempts to revise the Euclid text are reflected in the various levels of the original mélange. The scholars took the trouble, with the help of codices by Adelard (Y, M) or through sources which were similar to the Greek (P), to improve their text. This three-fold symphysis of the original Boethian text with the help of Adelard's treatise is similar to the many redactions to which Adelard's translation was submitted in the course of the 12th and 13th century; the most important at that time was the Campanus version which likewise stands in the Adelard tradition.

2.5 The Geometries in the Renaissance.

After the two Geometries had long fallen into oblivion in the 13th and 14th centuries, the interest of the humanists turned to the Geometry I and II, which they doubtlessly interpreted as the authentic writings of Boethius. In the libraries of eight scholars from the 15th and 16th centuries there is found with certainty a copy of the Geometria II: Conrad Peutinger, Willibald Pirckheimer, Frans Nans, Jean Nicot, Pierre Pithou, Jacques-Auguste de Thou, Jacob Rehdiger and Marquard Freher. In addition to some of these humanists the following also possessed manuscripts of the Geometria I: Jacques Bongars, Hans Jakob Fugger, Hermann and Hartmann Schedel, Pieter Schrijver. Among the existing manuscripts of both Geometries there are still seven humanistic codices; these originate, for the most part, from Italy.[171] One of these manuscripts (Cesena, Plut. sin. XXVI.1), which originated in Cesena after 1450, is the text upon which the *editio princeps* is based.[172]

The first printing of the two Geometries was published in 1492 by Johannes and Gregorius de Gregoriis in Venice.[173] It is part of the first printed collection of Boethius' works; it contains the Geometria II in its entirety but the Geometria I with only the first two books.[174] It is not clear who edited these geometries.[175] The edition of the Geometria II stands out because of its numerous good conjectures. Often the editor corrected accumulated errors of his text and without the help of other codices, reconstructed thè original text. The editor's conjectures show his abilities: aside from a few cases where he changed the text unnecessarily, often in places where the other manuscripts made a faulty transmission, he arrived at a logical text. For the Euclidian section he seems to have used a Greek Euclid text. In some places he even corrected the author of the Geometria II whose text was very faulty. Nevertheless, it is the editio Veneta that regardless of its inadequacies was the best text available until 1867.

All of the subsequent editions are derived from this *editio princeps*, as the new printing of Venice, 1499,[176] the edition contained in the Boethius collection by Heinrich Loriti (Gla-

---

171 See pp. 192, 194, and 195.
172 See Folkerts, *Geometrie II*, p. 56.
173 *Gesamtkatalog der Wiegendrucke*, no. 4511.
174 Presumably the rest has not been printed, because the Euclid excerpts, which make up the greatest part of books 3-5, are also present in the Geometria II.
175 In the printed edition there is a letter from the Venetian Nicolaus Judecus to Donatus Civalellus as preface. It does not inform us who was the editor of the Geometries.
176 *Gesamtkatalog der Wiegendrucke*, no. 4512.

reanus) (Basil, 1546), and its reprinting (1570) as well as the excerpts which were published by Henri Estienne and Simon de Colines (Paris, 1500 and after).[177]

2.6 Conclusion.

The role played by the two geometries attributed to Boethius in the Middle Ages can only be understood in the context of the evolution of mathematics. Because geometry had acquired a stable position in the *quadrivium* and no better geometrical text had come from antiquity, even these inadequate compilations survived. But more than that, because of the famous name „Boethius" and the fact that these texts contained otherwise inaccessible information (the Euclidian excerpts) both writings underwent, up until the 12th century, a certain blossoming and wide circulation as is evidenced by the number of manuscripts and the citations by other writers. Scholars also strove for an understanding of the more obscure parts; for this purpose there grew up scholia which are found in a few manuscripts of the Geometria II.[178] The significance of both geometries diminished as the fixed scheme of the *artes liberales* gradually became more flexible and new ideas in the medieval learning forced their way in.[179] The diminishing importance of the Geometries became particularly obvious after the 11th century as learned texts were continually translated from the Arabic. Computations on the abacus were gradually replaced by the Indic-Arabic methods; many new geometrical writings, also, were available in Latin translation. Especially, scholars now had the opportunity to use a complete and reliable Euclid text. Under these circumstances there was hardly any place left for the obsolete and faulty geometries of the Pseudo-Boethius. In the 12th century a few scholars tried to preserve the Euclidian part by combining it with the Latin Arabic tradition, but this was only a transitory phase. After the 13th century the Geometries fell into oblivion until they appeared again in the Humanistic context.

Universität Oldenburg, Germany

---

177 In addition to Sacrobosco's *De Sphaera* there are printed only the Euclid excerpts, taken from the Geometria II. Further information about these and other editions may be seen in Folkerts, *Geometrie II*, pp. 41-49.

178 These will be evaluated in another place.

179 For this one may consult the collection *Artes Liberales: Von der antiken Bildung zur Wissenschaft des Mittelalters*, ed. J. Koch (Leiden, Köln, 1959) and especially the essays by H.M. Klinkenberg, „Der Verfall des Quadriviums im frühen Mittelalter," and O. Pedersen, „Du quadrivium à la physique."

PIERRE COURCELLE

BOETHIUS, LADY PHILOSOPHY, AND THE
REPRESENTATIONS OF THE MUSES

In the pictorial representations of Boethius and the muses, it is possible to perceive a blending of the muses with the allegorical representations of the liberal arts during the late Middle Ages. In order to demonstrate this development, I would like to group together those pictures which illustrate the first book of the *Consolation of Philosophy*; these generally are directly related to the text and seem to form a complete set of representations. In such illustrations, the muses appear at the bedside of Boethius in the company of Lady Philosophy. They are elegant women, usually without specific attributes; they vary in number (2,3,4,7,9) and are ordinarily standing side by side, at the foot of the bed. Some painters have desired to evoke Philosophy dismissing the poetical muses in a somewhat animated scene, but most of them have preferred to depict the philosophical muses at the service of their mistress, and they have represented them then in the manner of figures from the *quadrivium*. These figures from the liberal arts may be seen in a separate tradition of illustrations dating from the second quarter of the 9th century, such as that at the beginning of the Boethian *De Arithmetica* in an admirable Tours manuscript[1] (fig. 1).

Boethius and the muses sometimes constitute the only illustration of a manuscript of the *Consolation* and usually this picture forms a prologue or an epilogue to the scenes where Boethius and Philosophy are discoursing alone with each other. In a Munich manuscript, Lat. 15, 825, f. 1[v], dating from the early 11th century and originally from St. Peter's of Salzbourg,[2] there is united in a single scene an activity which the *Consolation* describes as occurring in succession: Philosophy appears, she discourses with the indisposed Boethius, the muses flee. This design offers us one of the most ancient examples of illustrations for the first book of Boethius' work (fig. 2). In it, the artist orders his numerous personages at the heart of an imposing and decorative architecture. At the left and at the right, two towers, one pierced by a high door, enclose the ramparts of a citadel. The lower scene is also bound by turrets at the corners and by a wall at the top, detailed stone by stone: this is the cell of Boethius. In the center of the upper portion is the detached symbolic figure of Lady Philosophy. She appears above the prison, extends her arms, presents an open book with her right hand and in her left waves a scepter terminating in a cruciform floret. A rigid ladder with nine degrees is designed evenly on the folds of her garment, from the hem of the robe to the shoulders. The bottom

This essay has been adapted from Professor Courcelle's book *La Consolation de Philosophie dans la tradition littéraire* (Paris, 1967), pp. 90-99, and translated by Susanne Strom. The author has kindly approved minor changes made for the English version.

1   Bamberg, Staatliche Bibliothek, class. 5 (HJ, IV, 12), f. 9v. This manuscript was written at Tours for Charles the Bald about the year 845. Cf. W. Kohler, *Die karolingischen Miniaturen*, Berlin, I (1930), 255, 401; II (1933), 65, Pl. 90. *Werdendes Abendland*, no. 304; V.H. Elbern, *Das erste Jahrtausend*, Tafelband, 2nd ed. (Düsseldorf, 1962), pl. 257; Boethius, *De Arithmetica*, ed. G. Friedlein (Leipzig, 1867), pp. 5ff.

2   G. Swarzenski, *Die Salzburger Malerei* (Leipzig, 1931), p. 94, n. 1.

rung is inscribed with a Π and the top with a Θ. Below, Boethius is seen seated on a bed, long haired and bearded; he is meditating, his head leaning on his left hand, and with his right hand he is holding a stylus directed toward an open book with blank pages.[3] Philosophy, seated at the foot of the bed, seems to be making an exposition, as the gesture of her hands indicates. The dismissed poetic muses are leaving by the door, faces strangely deprived of expression.[4] Visible above them is the sketch of a head which seems to have no significance.

If this illustration is compared with the first miniatures representing Boethius as prisoner, which I have published elsewhere, a striking resemblance may be seen between this manuscript originating in Salzbourg and the feudal architectural structures of a Vienna manuscript.[5] But if the style of personages is examined, the design is seen to be closer to the miniatures of Maihingen and of Sélestat.[6] One may see here the same manner of narrowly enclosing figures within the architectural boundaries, the way of placing the ladder on the front of Lady Philosophy without its being an adornment of her garment. The scepter is rigid and large, as in the illustration of the manuscript at Paris, BN, lat. 6401, from the 11th century.[7] Like the artist of the Sélestat manuscript, the Munich illustrator is removed from the antique style, but he does represent twisted columns; the folds of draperies have become geometric, the gestures stiff, the background without relief. The muses are no longer undressed as on the manuscripts of Vienna and of Sélestat.

With the manuscript of Besancon 434, f. 294v (S. XIV) one discovers a more animated manner of presenting this scene. Boethius and Philosophy have not changed so much since the *Grandes Invasions germanique* (fig. 3), although the philosophy of Besancon wears a crown. The muses represented here are now the philosophical muses, that is to say, the liberal arts. The known representations of the arts of the quadrivium date from the 9th century, as I have mentioned, in connection with a text of Boethius' *De Arithmetica*. Here, on the other hand, we are dealing with the muses of the trivium, as in plate 40a of the *Grandes Invasions*; crowded close together at the foot of the bed, with their sovereign, they seem to reproach Boethius for his lethargy.

Let me now survey briefly a series of later illustrations that we may examine the varieties in representations of the muses. These will then be seen to emerge gradually as the representatives of the liberal arts. The initial C (for *Carmina*) of Book I from the *Consolation,* as found in the manuscript of Vienna 198, f. 1, of Lombard origin and from the early 15 century, contains an attractive scene representing Boethius, Philosophy, and four poetic muses. The miniature is, unfortunately, very damaged.[8] A London manuscript, BM Royal 20 a XIX, is originally from France and dates about 1420. On ff. 4 and 29 (fig. 4-5) it contains two somewhat similar drawings in pen. In the first illustration, the crowned Philosophy extends her hands and dismisses two poetic muses who are leaving with crestfallen expressions. In the second illustration Philosophy holds a sceptor in her left hand and repeats her gesture of dismissing the muses with her right hand.

The first miniature of the manuscript of Rouen, 3045, f.3v, similar to the above illustra-

3   Cf. Boethius, *Consolation*, I, pr. i: Haec dum mecum tacitus ipse reputarem querimoniamque lacrimabilem stili officio signarum.... ed L. Bieler (Turnholt, 1957).

4   *Ibid.* I, pr. i. Sed abite potius, Sirens usque in exitium dulces, meisque eum Musis curandum sanandumque relinquite.

5   P. Courcelle, *Histoire littéraire des grandes invasions germanique,* 3rd ed. (Paris, 1964), pl. 37b.

6   *Ibid.*, pl. 38-39.

7   *Ibid.*, pl. 40a.

8   H.J. Hermann, *Die Handschriften und Inkunabeln der italienischen Renaissance*, I (Leipzig, 1930), 2-3; pl. I.

tion, depicts the philosophical muses as four in number (fig. 6). Boethius is extended on a sort of mattress on the ground. Philosophy is coming forward, books in her right hand, a scepter in her left, a crown on her head. The artist of this miniature possesses a rather singular style and he immobilizes the diverse gestures of these personages so well that the ensemble takes on the aspect of a pantomime played in various costumes in front of a tapestry background. The stairs, the doorways, accentuate the effect of a theatre. At the right is found a view of the countryside which harmonizes large boulders, shrubs, and a starry sky in a very poetic vision.

The artist of the illustration in the Paris manuscript BN Fr. 1100, f. 3, has handled this familiar scene according to a planned decorative purpose (fig. 7). Visible on the left are Boethius, overwhelmed with sorrow, and Philosophy, who holds out her arms towards him to console him. Music, Rhetoric, and Poetry, arranged from left to right, play respectively the harp, trumpet, and cithara. Despite the initial position of this miniature in the manuscript and the presence of Poetica, it appears that the scene does not represent the poetic muses whom philosophy is going to dismiss. It corresponds rather to the passage of Book II where Philosophy declares: „Adsit igitur rhetoricae suadela dulcedinis...cumque hac Musica laris nostri vernacula nunc leviores nunc graviores modos succinat."[9] It is most probable that the artist has blended or confused the two scenes.

The muses at Boethius' bedside appear on the title page of the French manuscript in the Pierpont Morgan Library, Ms 222, f. 1 (fig. 8). The scene on the right shows the interior of Boethius' chamber. He is seated on the edge of his bed; behind him we find two female figures. Philosophy advances majestically to the foreground, holding book and sceptor. In an unusual style, the Θ and Π, separated by rungs, form a horizontal adornment across her robe, from which a man with a death-like expression behind her has surreptitiously torn a piece.[10] One can admire this illustrator who has grouped in a single harmonious miniature the scene of a dedication to a king and the account in imagery of the first pages of the *Consolation*. The sensitive treatment of the personages and of the marginal border are evidence of great artistic skill.

On f. 4, this artist takes the same scene in order to give it the aspect of a frontispiece for Book I, and he completes it as for a photographic enlargement (fig. 9). Boethius, hands joined, humbly receives Philosophy who is followed by the same personages as before; but he is now escorted by two other notable persons with long robes and harsh features. These are three philosophers, for each holds in his hand a piece of the beautiful robe of Philosophy that they have just torn. Four poetic muses, very elegant and liberally décolleté, are grouped at the right; a charming countryside, at the left, enlarges and gives airiness to the scene.

The same scene is precisely repeated in BN Fr. 1098, f. 2ᵛ (fig. 10). Reproduced here are not only the allegorical details–rents in the robe, pieces of fabric in the hands of the philosophers–but also the minor elements of decor: the circular picture above the bed, the fringe on the curtain, the disheveled hair of the muses. The artist is content to furnish Philosophy with a hennin surmounted by a monumental cornet and to allow to slide to the bottom of her robe the band with the Π and the Θ.

A very different composition on the same theme is found again at the beginning of Book

9   *Consolatio* II, pr. i.
10 *Consolatio* I, pr. iii. Cuius hereditatem cum deinceps Epicurem vulgus ac stoicum ceterique pro sua quisque parte raptum ire molirentur meque reclamantem renintentemque velut in partem praedae traherent, vestem quam meis texueram manibus disciderunt abreptisque ab ea panniculis totam me sibi cessisse credentes abiere.... Quodsi nec Anaxagorae fugam nec Socratis venenum nec Zenonis tormenta, quoniam sunt peregrina, novisti, at Canios, at Senecas, at Soranos, quorum nec pervetustusta nec incelebris memoria est, scire potuisti.

III. Here the illustrator is no longer inspired directly by the opening of the *Consolation*. Philosophy presents the liberal arts, in the form of feminine figures, to Boethius who raises his left hand as a sign of welcome or of admiration. The trivium appears in front.

In the Pierpont Morgan manuscript, f. 39, Grammar, a figure extended by her flowing robes, veiled and light colored, holds an open book; behind her, Rhetoric writes on the leaf of a book; Dialectic displays a scroll on which is seen: „Ergo, ergo." The figures of the quadrivium, neatly grouped, comprise the remainder of the liberal arts. Music is recognized by the score that she holds in front of her; Geometry carries a level with a plumb line; Astronomy points to the sky with her right index finger and leans with her left hand on an astrolabe; Arithmetic, standing in the rear, holds a scroll full of numbers. All the attributes are minutely designed, but the symbolic aspect of the scene does not prevent the miniaturist from composing his group in a refined manner through costumes, varied postures, and lively facial expressions. The chateau-fort which completes the composition at the left, the country-side of water, of verdure, and of sky which is extended behind the terrace, are all highly evocative. The poetry and the calm of the twilight are suitable to the serenity of the allegory.

The personages and the symbols of the previous examples are again found on the miniature of the BN Fr. 1098, f. 40^v (fig. 11). The painter however has unfortunately divided the scene in two by a column. He specifies the exact moment of the scene, since Boethius is saying to Philosophy: „O Souverain confort" (*Consolation*, III, pr. i). Grammar and Rhetoric are easily recognized, but they have reversed their positions and their attributes. Dialectic is separated from them, wears a veil, and pronounces „Ergo, ergo," instead of carrying a scroll with these words. She now takes her place at the head of the figures of the quadrivium. The latter are faithfully copied, even to their realistic profiles which are contrasted with the ideal beauty of Philosophy and with the long and sad countenance of Grammar. However, a carpenter's square has replaced the plumb line of Geometry. The crescent moon is also recognizable, but the countryside on the whole remains very inferior to its model.

A total lack of experience characterizes the illustrator of the manuscript of Paris, BN Fr. 1099, f. 9. Two muses with long hair and with rustic profile are firmly stationed at the foot of Boethius' bed. Philosophy is characterized by her robe with enormous rents; the symbolic letters, however, are completely deformed. Two other Paris manuscripts, BN Lat. 9323. f. 1 and Fr. 1949, f. 4^v, each contain the image of Boethius lying in bed, visited by the muses and Philosophy. In the miniature of the first manuscript which is superior and more carefully executed, Philosophy advances to the foreground, furnished with all her attributes. The P and the T of the ladder of degrees form on her robe two decorative rings joined by links. Two muses--undoubtedly the poetic muses–are leaving at her approach, passing through the door without haste and directing their steps towards the lovely garden bordering an apse of a church which forms the right side of the tableau. Two other muses, who remain at Boethius' bedside, are doubtlessly the philosophical muses who replace them.

Two other manuscripts, BM Harley 4335 and BN Lat. 6643 also show a great similarity in this scene (fig. 12-13). One sees in both an unusual number of women, gathered closely together in an arc at the right side of the picture. In each, the bed on which Boethius lies is enhanced by placing it in front of a drapery background. But the principal personage, Philosophy, changes her aspect. In the older, from the Harley manuscript, Philosophy is a long and slender figure of light color, standing upright next to the books placed flat on the bed. She has neither scepter nor crown and seems to be an unreal apparition at which the sleeping Boethius does not look. In the Paris manuscript, the painter has carefully indicated the rents in the robe, the brocade which is studded with a quantity of Π and Θ's. Philosophy carries a long scepter with both hands and a high crown encircles her forehead. Her behavior, nevertheless, suggests a woman of flesh and bone, as do her seven followers who represent the liberal arts. The

214

painter was probably inspired by the London manuscript for his composition, but his erudite spirit and his mode of painting have not preserved the poetic qualities of his model.

German illustrations of the *Consolation* seem more rare than the French. The Berlin manuscript, Codices Electorales (Rose, N° 1025), Lat. fol. 25, preserved today at the Library of Tübingen, dates from 1485 and contains five large miniatures, each at the beginning of one of the five books of the *Consolation*, which accompanies the commentary of the Pseudo-Thomas Aquinas. The artist represents a very austere interior, which is the same in all five miniatures, with grilled windows and rustic furniture. Boethius, bearded and wearing a hat, is vested each time with the same cloak and fur collar. The gestures, the poses, the expressions, the costumes of the diverse personages are marked with stiffness. All the fantasy of the pictures resides in the interminable scrolls, which, with baroque sinuousness, are unrolled to the margins of which they form the border. Each scene is explicated thus by a long extract from the text of the *Consolation*, and it is not possible to be more precise about the moment being depicted.

The first of these miniatures is found on f. 86ᵛ (fig. 14). Here Philosophy appears in a mandorla in the upper right corner, embellished with all her allegorical attributes. An inscription is laid out in the manner of a ladder mounting from P to T, the length of her robe; the rungs are the various liberal arts. They appear to read:

gra	[mmatica]	loquitur
dia	[lectica]	vera docet
rhe	[torica]	verba ministrat
mu	[sica]	canit
ari	[thmetica]	numerat
ge	[ometria]	ponderat
ast	[ronomia]	colit astra

Philosophy reappears in the lower left corner, seated this time on the foot of Boethius' bed, pictured as an elegant woman of strict bearing, with a bare forehead that emerges from a hairnet on which is set a slender crown. She does not seem to address the muses lined up opposite her, on the other side of a round table. The scroll, however, indicates the purport of her discourse: ,,Quis, inquit, has sciencias meretriculas ad hunc egrum permisit accedere, que dolores eius non modo foverent [n]ullis remediis, verum dulcibus insuper alerent veniens? Abit pocius, Syrenes usque in exicium dulces meisque eum Musis curandum relinquit" (I, pr. i). Each of the three muses discourses similarly. The first says: ,,Hic quondam celo libero aperto suetus ire ethereos ire meatus cernebat rosei lumina solis" (I, met. ii). The second declares, her hand on her heart, ,,Intempestivi funduntur vertice cani et tremit effeto corpore laxa cutis" (I, met. i). The third explains, ,,Mors hominum felix que se nec dulcibus annis inserit et mestis sepe vocata venit" (I, met. i). But they do not hesitate to obey the injunction of Philosophy, and one sees them again, soon after, in the process of leaving through the door at the right.

A miniaturist of the Ghent- Bruges school has preferred to an often seen old allegory, his own version of an animated and realistic scene. On f. 1 of ms 10,474 at the Bibliothèque Royale of Brussels, Philosophy is seen brandishing her book and her scepter with an angry gesture. The poetic muses, four in all, flee backwards with forceful gestures and two of them join their hands as if asking for mercy. Philosophy wears her crown, her cape is silvered with ermine. From her belt hangs the scale of degrees, represented as a chain terminating at the two ends by the letters P and T, but the P has been mistakenly painted at the top, the T at the bottom. The face of Boethius under his night cap is piteous.

Among the later miniatures we shall consider are some painted on a full page preserved from two incunnabula printed by the illustrious Antoine Vérard for Charles VIII. These incunnabula contain the translation in prose and in verse of the commentary of Regnier de Saint-

215

Trond, under the title: „Grant Boece de Consolacion nouuellement imprimé à Paris" in 1494. They are kept at Paris, one at the BN, Réserve 488, the other at the Musée du Petit Palais, Dutuit Collection, No 114.[11] The two artists have utilized the same texts for the scrolls and reproduce the same inconographic motifs, without, however, copying them in a servile manner. While these rich paintings, in quarto format, in which gold glitters on the costumes, do not constitute an artistic progress–one may say their psychological content is deceptive–they are yet notable for a new and striking inconographic motif. In the center of each tableau, Boethius, seated on his bed, his full face visible, is chained to a column which forms the center of the decor. In the example from the Bibliothèque Nationale, the grilled windows add to the melancholy sadness of the setting.

On f. 1, Philosophy, with neither scepter nor book, presses the hand of the philosopher. In the illustration from the BN, a muse places her left hand on the arm of Boethius as if attempting to capture his attention. In the example from the Pétit Palais, the three muses are gesticulating and have the faces of shrews rather than of seductresses. The scroll of Philosophy proclaims: „Quis has sciencias meretriculas ad hunc egrum permisit accedere?"[12] Yet her face remains very inexpressive. Behind Philosophy, three friends of Boethius regard him with compassion while he is saying to them: „Quid me felicem tociens iactasis, amici?" (I, met. i). Gold glitters on the garments and on the wainscottings, but the figures are flat and have among them no other bond than their gestures.

A work printed in Strasbourg in 1501 illustrates the *Consolation* from beginning to end. In the anecdotal style of the Rhenish engravers of the period, but lively and picturesquely, it evokes Philosophy at the bedside of Boethius at the beginning of Book I. The latter is stretched out fully dressed on his bed, and his face leaning against an immense square pillow reflects his desolation. Philosophy, who advances toward him, veil blowing in the breeze, carries a long scepter in her left hand. Her skirt is ornamented by transverse rays which from a distance suggest a ladder of degrees; one sees at the bottom and the top a gigantic P and T. Philosophy has just dismissed the poetic muses who are departing with ill-natured expressions. Thus at the dawn of the 16th century one finds again all the elements of the illustrations of the 11th century.

In contrast to this long series, one may single out some exceptional illustrations. One such is the illumination of a manuscript from Montpellier, École de Médecine 43, f. 2, from the early 14th century, which is not dependent on the iconographic tradition. Boethius is half reclining at the right in that painting, under the sky. Philosophy has the same appearance as in the other paintings of the same manuscript (fig. 15), but she is turning around and with her left forefinger is pointing out to Boethius two personages who follow her. These have caps, long hair and enveloping mantles, and carry books in the crooks of their right arms. The illustrator is here inspired by the passage from Book I relating to the philosopher-martyrs; one should, perhaps, also recognize Socrates with his pointed beard as one of the personages. We have previously seen the philosophers who tear Lady Philosophy's robe, but there, on the contrary, one feels that she has full confidence in them and proposes them as guides.

An analogous but more comical illustration is offered us by the painter of the Cambridge manuscript, Trinity College 12, who has desired to represent on the same page (f. 6, recto and verso) all the consequences of Boethius' discourse on Philosophy: the sects which have torn her tunic, the torments inflicted on Socrates, on Zeno of Elium, and on the philosopher victims of Nero. On the recto at the top of the right column are seen „Epigurus" and „Stoicus"

11   E. Rahir, *La collection Dutuit, livres et manuscrits* (Paris, 1899), pp. 52-53.
12   *Consolation* I, pr. i.

tearing at the „tunica philosophie." Below is seen the „carcer Socratis." As the French translator puts it:

> Le duc d'Athenes le fist prendre
> et le fist en prison mourir.

The illustration shows us the „dux Atheniensis," armed with a club, in the process of successively beating the disciples of Socrates who come to beg for the liberation of their master; the tree calls to mind, perhaps, the famous plantain of the Phedre. Another illustration represents „Zenon" in a chemise, his hands bound, on whom fall the blows of the executioners' bludgeons. On the verso is „Nero" seated on a throne; his scepter in hand, he has decapitated by a „tortor" four „Consules Romani" with blindfolded eyes. A head has already rolled on the ground. In the manuscript of Toulouse, no. 822, from the 15th century, another painter shows us Nero who from the height of a tower watches Rome burn.[13]

> A Rome le feu mettre fait
> et en un haut lieu se retrait,
> dont a grant ioie regardoit
> le feu qui la cité ardoit.

The most curious image in the Cambridge manuscript is from the column at the right where, following the text of Boethius, one sees Reason recalling her troops into her citadel, here named „turris refugii."[14] At each stage of this tower a contemplative visage appears at the window. Guards armed with lances are on watch at the upper crenellations. At the foot of the tower the enemies, that is to say the men sunken in material things, are in the process of feasting, armed with all the false goods that they have plundered.

As the various plates which we have just studied should show, Book I, especially the first pages, is of incomparable importance from the iconographic point of view. The personage of Philosophy is the image repeated with most satisfaction by the illustrators of the *Consolation*, not only at the beginning of Book I, but often at the beginning of each other book. From the 12th to the 16th centuries, Philosophy adorns the frontispiece of the manuscript and one can follow from plate to plate the plastic evolution of her figure. Rarely is she represented alone, and then only in the manuscripts before the beginning of the 14th century. Ordinarily she is seen at the bedside of Boethius, but occasionally among other personages. If the manuscript contains a single illustration, it is habitually Philosophy close by Boethius who forms its subject; if each book has its own frontispiece, one rediscovers in the five images the same personage that has been established from the beginning. The artists of the Romanesque period put the accent on the unreal, abstract, and allegorical character of the apparition. Also for a long time several painters felt themselves constrained by respecting the text, in which Boethius describes Philosophy with a large number of precise attributes, and these resulted in considerable monotony: scepter, books, ladder, torn robe, etc. Further, certain painters preferred another symbolic element: Philosophy nourishing Boethius with her milk (as in Rouen, ms 3045, f.4v). It is true that, later, certain liberties were taken with the text. Occasionally a crown or halo was imposed on Philosophy to accentuate her majesty. Most often—in the 15th

---

13 *Consolation* II, met. vi.
14 *Consolation* I, pr. iii. (with reference to evil men): Quorum quidem tametsi est numerosus exercitus, spernendus tamen est, quoniam nullo duce regitur, sed errore tantum temere ac passim lymphante raptatur. Qui si quando contra nos aciem stuens valentior incubuerit, nostra quidem dux copias suas in arcem contrahit, illi vero circa diripiendas inutiles sarcinulas occupantur. At nos desuper irridemus vilissima rerum quaeque rapientes securi totius furiosi tumultus eoque vallo muniti quo grassantis stultitiae aspirare fas non sit. Cf. Gregory the Great, *Moralia in Job*, VII, 14, 17. *P.L.* LXXV, 775A: „In internae rationis arce."

century–all the symbols are suppressed in order to lend to Philosophy the calm air of a consoler (e.g. BN Reserve, 488, f 1) or even the appealing look of a woman of fashion (BN Fr. 1100, f. 41ᵛ).

As for Boethius, the artists accorded to him, following the text, the habit or the sensitivity of hearing belonging to the arithmetician or the musician, the majestic authority of the theologian, the reflective air of the philosopher, or the melancholy of one condemned to death. Boethius as a philosopher, who is best suited to the beginning of the *Consolation*, almost invariably wears a costume of the „doctor." In the 14th and 15th centuries, the artist seemed pleased to display about him the equipment of the intellectual struggler, truly, even an entire library. More rarely, an attempt is made to reconstruct, in the form of historical scenes, the vicissitudes of his life. In an unusual style, there appears eventually, in the 15th century, a countryside. The spirit of the artist frequently expresses itself only in the harmony between the figure of the philosopher and the initial C which encircles him.

The full scene that suggests the beginning of the *Consolation* includes the muses as well. But the text leaves to the artists the choice between the poetic muses or the philosophical muses. In the first case, young persons with the charms of courtesans have been painted, provided, if needed, with musical instruments. In the second case the muses correspond to the liberal arts in the form of seven very dignified women, recognizable by their attributes. The most venturesome arists have delighted in representing Philosophy full of action, driving the courtesans away from Boethius' bedside (fig. 4).

Among so many illustrations, many seem negligible or mediocre; many others are successes as plastic art, but remain cold. Some of them, among the most ancient, are beyond comparison; on the manuscript of Vienna 51, for example, the intellectual Boethius who is retired within himself appears in all his grandeur. The manuscripts of Brussels and of Madrid depict in a poignant fashion, through the figure of Boethius, the regret of happiness lost. All show some aspect of the complex traditions found in the iconographic realizations associated with the *Consolation of Philosophy*. In this tradition, as we have seen, there is an intrusion of liberal arts representations. That in turn reflects a blend in the history of Boethian ideas during the Middle Ages, particularly as they are associated with the texts of the *Consolation* itself.

Collège de France, Paris

ILLUSTRATIONS

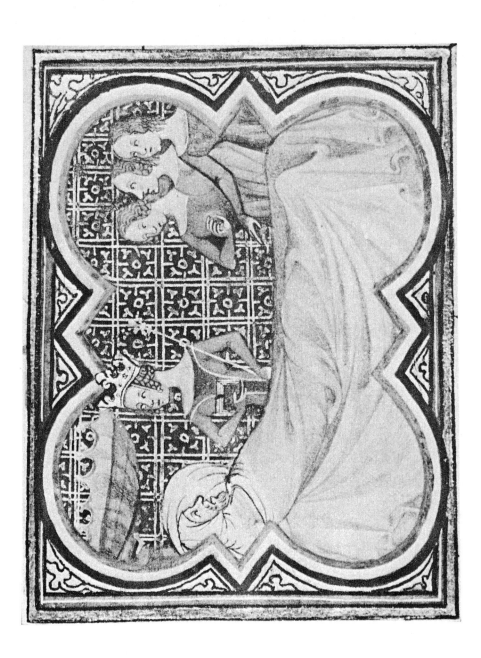

A ouez le comencement

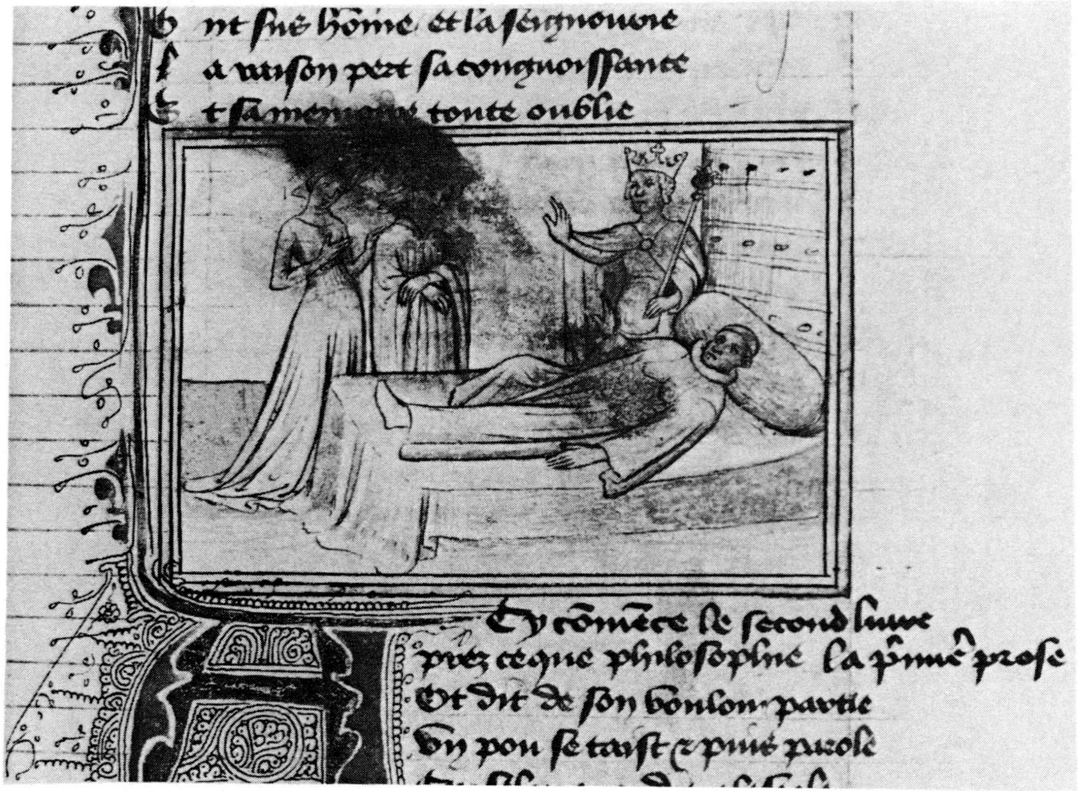

Cy commence le proleme ou prologue du liure de boece
de consolacion. Le quel maistre Iehan de meun tras-
lata de latin en francois. Si comme il se contient
cy aprez en auant et semonn au roy phelippe
le quint.

A tres noble maieste tresnoble prince par
la grace de dieu roy de france phelippe
le quint. Ie Iehan de meun qui iadiz
ou romant de la rose puis que ialou
sie ot mis en prison les amans ensei-
gnay la maniere du chastel prendre

Cy commence le prologue sur le suite de livre de consolacion translate de latin en francois avec la glose de maistre Iehan de meun

Ta roynl maieste noble prince par la
grace de dieu roy de france plusieurs le ont
Ie iehan de mehun ont iadiz ou iounne
de la rose puis que ialousie et mis enprison
son bel acueil entasciauai la maniere d'ich
ꝑciel prendre et de la rose acueillu. et traufla
lay de latin en francois le liure de la vegere de la cheualerie. et le
liure des mevueilles d'yllande. et la vie et les epistre maistre pi
eur abaisart et selonc sa femme. et le liure claux de esperitue
le amistie. entroy ouce Boece de consolacion que lay trauslate
de latin en francois. ia soit ce que tu entendes bien latin: mac
tourtouoye est moult plus legier a entendre le francois que le
latin. Et voir et que ru me diz lequel dye te rien acoumante
ment. que ie veusse plautement la sentente de lauctour sans
noy enfuir les puoles du latin. ie lay fait a mon gre pou on
fromme ta deboumaurte se me coumanda. ꝺꝺ Or pzie ie a
rous ceulx qui ce liure verront. se il leur semble en aucuns lieur
que ie me soie noy esloigne des puoles de lauctour ou que ie
ap mis aucuneffois plus de puoles que lauctour ny met ou
aucuneffois moins: que il le me pardoueut. Car se ie te cause

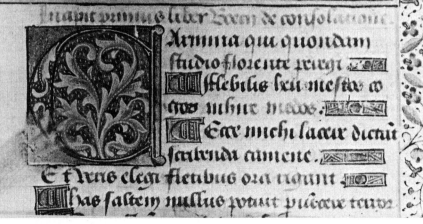

Inapit primus liber Xxn de conſolacione

Armnta qui quondam
studio florente piriqi.
Flebilis heu meſtos co
gor inhire mados.
Ecce michi lacerr dictat
ſcribenda camene.
Et veris elegi fletibus ora rigant.
Has ſaltem nullus potuit piecere terror

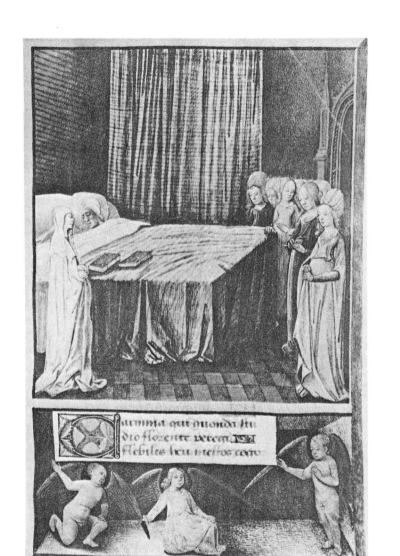

Donc mait ma clartei rendue
Et repris force ma weue
Si com les nues p mol vent
Vont les estoiles esmouent
Soloil ne estoile ne luit
Mais samble en terre quil soit nuit
Se la bise est de sa taniere.
Les trouble nues chasse arriere
Iliours reuient et li soulaus
Esbahist de son rai les taus.

¶ Haec aliue nebulis. ¶ Dont en teil giu
te la nue de tristece si dept et choisi le ciel et
pri cuer de recognoistre ma fisiaane. Et
que io bien fichie mes ieulz en luy le re
cognui ma nozrice en cui maison ie auoie
couersei des menstance seit philosophie et
li dis. O maistresse de toutes vtus coment
ais tu laissiez les sieges souerains por venir
en desert de nre estil. Est ce por estre blamee
auec moy q tu soies acusee fauremet dest
corpable ¶ En mot te alup. ¶ Coment
dit elle te lairoie q es mes nozris ne ne soi
porteroie auec toi la charge q tu portes
p raison de moi. Nauoie pt ainsi en ton tra
uail. Certes il nestoit pas raison que phi
losophie na copagnast la vie del inocent
Toute uoie te dour mon blame ainsi co se
chose nouelle fust auenue por ieusse er
tour ¶ Enuie eus pnui ¶ Cuides tu que
ores a pmes sapience soit poeue des ma
uais. Ne scois tu q on temps ancien auant
q nre platons fust nez. nous eumes mais
escris contre la psuption de folie. Et en so
temps ses maistres socrates resut mort a
tort en ma psence ¶ Cui hereditate co dei
Ie au heritage li eppcurent et autres
plusours cuiderent piendre et moi recla
mant et contradisant traiuerei a force et

ropirent mai robe q iauoie cosue de mes
mains. et chacius en porta sa piece et me
cuiderent auoir toute entiere. Et por ce
q auoiet aucunes de nos escptures. Il
sol cuiderent quil fuissent des nos. si les p
surent uisca la mort. Et se tu ne sceis la sute
te varagoras ne leuenimement de socrates
ne les tormes de zenom. car cest chose trop
vielle. amons pues tu sauoir les malz
ql soffrirent. Caynons. Soctates et sozain
car ce nest pas chose trop ansienne et
lor renomee est mlt comune. Les queilz
nulle autre cause nes mist a destruction
fors ce q estoiet enformer de nos bones
mours et estoiet trop dessamblas as ma
uais ¶ Ita q nichil e qd ¶ Por ce ne te
dois tu pais miueillier se nous somes tu
boleis p la tempeste as mauais. Et com
bien que il soient grt copaignie il sont
a despriser. car il nont nul bon goune
ment. mais to esgarei uout pelle melle
or.sa. or la. Et se il auient q il facet batel
le contre nos et soient plus fort nre guierres
ce retrait on donion. Et cil si occupent a
reculler. j. por de teil hernez. et nos nos mo
cons deals. de ce q il prenent ce q ries ne
valt. Et nos somes tour asseur enclos
de teil pallis en la cruautei de folie ne
puet ataindre ¶ Quis qd copolito

Qui poroir son aier ordeneir
Et fortune soz piez meneir.
Que lun et lautre regardaist
Tout droit q son vis ne clinast
Cil ne douteroit la tempeste
De mier ne de nulle autre moleste
De feu ne de fudre esprise
Qui les tours abat et debrise
Chaitis p coi doute tyrans
Qui son sens force forcenans
Qui ne crient riens ne desire
Aus tyrans art de sarme lure
Mais cui cui couoitise a bat
Ou paour il nait poin destat
Son escu por enchaunei
Est pfeu souent atraiers